THE ACTS OF THE APOSTLES

THE ACTS OF THE APOSTLES

by

Ellen M. Knox

YESTERDAY'S CLASSICS

ITHACA, NEW YORK

Cover and arrangement © 2021 Yesterday's Classics, LLC.

This edition, first published in 2021 by Yesterday's Classics, an imprint of Yesterday's Classics, LLC, is an unabridged republication of the text originally published by Macmillan and Co., Limited, 1908. For the complete listing of the books that are published by Yesterday's Classics, please visit www.yesterdaysclassics.com. Yesterday's Classics is the publishing arm of Gateway to the Classics which presents the complete text of hundreds of classic books for children at www.gatewaytotheclassics.com.

ISBN: 978-1-63334-132-6

Yesterday's Classics, LLC
PO Box 339
Ithaca, NY 14851

PREFACE

The Acts of the Apostles are so rich in variety and interest that they are more frequently studied in schools than any other book of the Bible. Students turn to a historian who is picturesque, accurate, statesmanlike in appreciating vital issues, and clear-sighted enough to keep a just balance between the movement in which he himself is an actor and the other world-movements of his age. And yet, strangely enough, it is in this very wealth and variety that the danger of the study of the Acts lies, for men are tempted to linger, as it were, so long upon the outskirts of the citadel, or beneath its walls, that they fail to find the presence chamber of the King within.

The following lessons are drawn up with a view of leading teachers and pupils, whilst availing themselves of every modern research and accessory, to study the Acts as a whole instead of dwelling upon its exterior and incidental parts. If the student would find the secret of the greatest of all movements he must pass beyond the glamour of the knighthood of St. Peter and St. Paul, the civic problem of a Corinth and an Ephesus, the adventure of a stoning at Lystra and a shipwreck, to the spiritual power which awakened that knighthood, inspired the character of its leaders and taught the world what Christian love, joy and endurance might be.

In the second place, the lessons strive to show how the men who lived and walked with Jesus understood and applied the first principles of His teaching and acts to the religious and social problems of their day, to the institution of ordinances such as Baptism, the Lord's Supper and the regulation of Church discipline and organization. It is from a right understanding of the power which transformed the first century that the student gains an insight into the power that is transforming the present century, and learns how to grapple with the problems of his own day and generation.

And lastly, the lessons seek to show how these same leaders translated the teaching of Jesus, whether given in parable, paradox or precept, into the spirituality and earnest obedience of their own personal life, a spirituality which found its natural outcome in the active missionary labour of a St. Peter and a St. Paul abroad, and the no less active though quieter service of a Lydia and a Dorcas at home.

The book is intended primarily for the use of the teacher, but secondarily for the use of the pupil also, and has been divided into sections so that facts can be the more easily underlined and paragraphs studied. It has been found that the use of a text book in Scripture teaching lightens the work of note taking, insures accuracy and prepares the way for the elucidation of the chapter taken in connection with it.

PREFACE

In conclusion, it is only necessary to acknowledge the constant indebtedness of the Author to writers such as Ramsay, Knowling, Rackham, Shaw, Harnack, Conybeare and Howson, the Hastings' Bible, the Expositor's Bible, and very many others whose works are now held to be the classics on this subject and who lead the way not only for the preacher and theological student but also for the more preparatory work of the teacher and scholar.

ELLEN M. KNOX

HAVERGAL COLLEGE,
October 19th, 1908

CONTENTS

I. Introductory: The Book and Its Author.......................1

II. The Ascension 13

III. The Falling of the Lot of Matthias....................... 22

IV. The Day of Pentecost........... 28

V. St. Peter's Sermon 39

VI. The Apostles' Doctrine and Fellowship 48

VII. A Miracle and Its Outcome..... 53

VIII. The First Conflict between the Church and the Sanhedrin 63

IX. The Interdict and Its Outcome . 73

X. The Generosity of Barnabas 81

XI. Ananias and Sapphira........... 89

XII. The Gift of Healing 97

XIII. The Responsibility of Leadership 106

CONTENTS

XIV. The Appointment of Divers Orders.................. 116

XV. The Character of Stephen..... 125

XVI. The Apology of Stephen....... 133

XVII. The Death of St. Stephen...... 144

XVIII. The Gospel in Samaria......... 154

XIX. The Baptism in the Wilderness. 165

XX. Saul and the Church.......... 175

XXI. Saul's Conversion............ 183

XXII. "Rise, Stand upon Thy Feet".... 189

XXIII. The Dayspring of the Gentiles. 200

XXIII. The Dayspring of the Gentiles (continued).............. 207

XXIV. The Call of the Gentile World........................ 213

XXV. The Pentecost of the Gentiles. 223

XXVI. The Church at Antioch........ 234

XXVII. The Third Persecution of the Church 245

XXVIII. St. Paul's First Missionary Journey 259

XXIX. The Gospel in Galatia......... 273

CONTENTS

XXX. The Gospel of St. Paul to the Heathen 282

XXXI. The Council of Jerusalem and the Churches of the Gentiles . 294

XXXII. The Council of Jerusalem...... 306

XXXIII. The Severance of Friendship... 320

XXXIV. The Passing into Macedonia ... 332

XXXV. The Churches of Thessalonica and Berea 348

XXXVI. At Athens Alone 362

XXXVII. The Bridge of the Sea......... 379

XXXVIII. The Further History of the Church of Corinth 391

XXXIX. Diana of the Ephesians 403

XL. Paul and Demetrius 417

XLI. The Statesmanship of St. Paul .. 430

XLII. The Turning towards Jerusalem 442

XLIII. The Appeal to the Multitude .. 455

XLIV. The Last Appeal to the Sanhedrin.................... 470

XLV. The Investigation before the Roman Governor, Felix........ 484

CONTENTS

XLVI. THE LAST OF THE KINGS......... 498

XLVII. THE SHIPWRECK................ 507

XLVIII. ROME....................... 520

XLIX. LATER EPISTLES OF ST. PAUL 534

L. THE LAST IMPRISONMENT OF
   ST. PAUL 545

CHAPTER I

INTRODUCTORY: THE BOOK AND ITS AUTHOR

The Acts of the Apostles, or "The Gospel of the Holy Ghost," is a record of the chief historical facts concerning the Church which took place between the years *Anno Domini* 30 and 60.

As the four Gospels tell of the incarnation, life, death, and resurrection of the Son of God; so the Gospel of the Holy Ghost tells of the effect of that life, death, and resurrection as it was brought to bear upon the hearts and lives of men.

The Old Testament had told of the settling down of a dark cloud of sin between the world and God, and of the gradual illumination of that cloud as pierced by light from Heaven or lit up by the teaching of the Prophets. The New Testament tells of the enlightening and dispelling of the cloud by the rising of the Sun of Righteousness with healing in His wings.

THE ACTS OF THE APOSTLES

The Distinction between the Gospels and the Acts

In the Gospels we see the brightness of the visible manifestation of Christ; in the Acts of the Apostles the continued manifestation of Christ, not by His visible presence but by the presence of the Holy Ghost. Throughout the succeeding ages the light of the Holy Spirit has continued, but its progress is not recorded in Holy Writ. We learn of it from human records, or by tracing the work of God's servants in the world around us.

The Gospels concern us more intimately and are more helpful to us than the Acts of the Apostles, in so far as they tell the history of the coming of the living Christ into the world, of His marvellous personality, His words, His acts; they are the record of the manifestation of the Son of God in human flesh. They stand first among all records because they contain the revelation of a personal Saviour, the coming of a mighty power into the world, a power which would change the whole face of human history. But whilst the Gospels stand first as a revelation of God in man, the Acts of the Apostles stand next as a revelation of the same God in man, as also of the way of approach to the invisible Christ. It is true that in some respects the way of approach always has been and always will be the same, whether trodden by the men who saw Christ, as Peter and John, or by the men who had not seen Him, as Moses. It was ever the same path of penitence, faith, and love, the only difference being that those who drew near before Christ came, or after He was ascended into the heavens, drew near by faith rather than by sight. It is the revelation of this drawing near by faith through the power of the Holy Spirit which makes the history of the years which immediately succeeded the death of Christ of transcendent importance to us. The Acts of the Apostles, inasmuch as they tell how the great facts of His life, death, and resurrection were translated so that they became a living reality to the men who had not personally seen or known Him, touch us also very closely.

They tell us also how the first preaching of the Gospel influenced and changed the every-day life and character of the early disciples, so that from them we learn how it should influence and change our lives also.

The Acts of the Apostles are of first importance in the world of history, theology, and biography. In history because they tell the story of a decisive crisis in the world, of a time when a great intellectual, spiritual, and moral change began to make itself felt, and they tell this story in a masterly way, from the point of view of a contemporary, one who was himself an actor in the scene.

In theology they are equally important, for they give the effect of the first preaching of the risen Christ upon the Jewish and Gentile world. In biography they stand second only to the Gospels, for they give a lifelike sketch of two of the greatest heroes of the Christian faith, men who followed Christ so closely that they marked out, as it were, a path of life for the generations of Christians who came after them.

THE ACTS OF THE APOSTLES

The Leadership of St. Peter and St. Paul

The Acts of the Apostles might be called the Acts of St. Peter and St. Paul, or the Acts of the Holy Spirit as shown through St. Peter and St. Paul. St. Peter was a man of ready perception, so ready that he opened as with a key the door of everlasting truth, and cried out, "Thou art the Christ, the Son of the living God." It was Peter also who first entered the empty tomb of Jesus, and, perceiving somewhat of the import of what he saw, "departed wondering within himself at that which had come to pass." It was Peter who was the first to interpret the meaning of the descent of the Holy Ghost. Peter, again, who opened the door to the Gentiles as he spoke the pregnant words, "I perceive that God is no respecter of persons." The work which Peter began was carried out by Paul, for Paul was a statesman as well as a man of keen spiritual instinct, and he was the first to apprehend the marvellous power of Christianity and the change which it would bring into the world. It was Paul who conceived, and who not only conceived but also carried into effect, the laying of the foundations of the Spiritual Kingdom of Righteousness, Paul who knew that that Kingdom contained within itself elements of power and of greatness which would make it mightier and more far-reaching than the Empire of Rome under which he lived, and which was the world-empire of his day.

The Author of the Acts—St. Luke

All tradition unites in ascribing the authorship of the Acts to St. Luke, although his name is never expressly mentioned as the writer. This testimony is confirmed by the study of the book itself, for the author of the Acts is clearly the same man as the writer of the Gospel of St. Luke. He has the same literary style; he opens his epistle as he opens his Gospel with a preface, and addresses it to the same man, "the most excellent Theophilus," a convert evidently of high rank among the disciples. He is also a co-worker with, and a lover of St. Paul. He is an eye-witness, for he has been present at many of the scenes which he narrates, and he describes them with an accuracy and a detail which distinguish them from other parts of his writing; as for instance in the closing chapters of the book. These are full of personal touches which could only have been given by one who had himself taken part in what he describes, and contrast in this respect with the earlier chapters, which are comparatively vague and wanting in little touches of detail, the record of what the author has heard and learned rather than of what he himself has seen. Then again, the latter chapters are distinguished by the pronoun "we," and St. Luke tells of the time when he was with St. Paul, when they were together at Troas and Philippi, when they journeyed from Miletus to Jerusalem and from Jerusalem to Rome. These chapters are so vivid that the reader is carried away by them, and becomes for the time himself a living actor in the scene, an eye-witness of all that passes. He is one of the assembly, he hears Paul speak, sees him beckon with his hand, stands beside him on the ship, hears the clank of the iron in the prison at Rome, and watches keenly the effect of his teaching on those who believe the things which are spoken and those who believe them not.

His Nationality and Method

The writer probably is a Gentile, and one who sympathizes with and understands the importance of the revelation of which he is speaking, not only to the Jew but also to the Gentile. This tone runs through the Gospel of St. Luke as well as that of the Acts, for in each book the purpose of the writer is practically the same. He wishes to set forth a clear account of a matter which he holds to be of the first importance, and "to set to" his seal to what is true. He is a witness to that which he most surely believes, and which will be as surely believed by those who read his writings, because they, too, know the facts as to what has been passing around them and will recognize the truth of which he writes. His first desire is to tell of Christ and of the spread of Christianity, but in doing so he desires especially to emphasize the attitude of Christ towards the Gentiles and the attitude of the early Church generally towards the Gentile world. Thus he writes from a wide point of view, from the standpoint of one who sees beyond his day, and as seeing beyond his day welcomes not only the revelation of the Godhead to those who had already received light, but also to the Gentiles who were lying in the shadow of death. Thus in the Gospel we see how vividly he narrates the healing of the Gentile widow, the Gentile leper; how carefully he notes that repentance and remission of sins are to be preached among all nations.

In like manner in the Acts of the Apostles he eagerly welcomes the progress of the Gospel as it passes from the Church at Jerusalem to the Church at Galatia and at Rome. He views with as keen an interest the movement of the Church towards the Gentiles and the response of the Gentiles towards Christianity as he had watched the movement of Christ towards the individual Gentile and the reply of the individual Gentile to Christ.

Thus underlying the apparently abrupt transitions of the narrative is a real order and movement. St. Luke is giving in a few master-strokes the effect of the first facts about the foundation of the Church upon the countries of Syria, Asia Minor, and Europe, the first appeal of the Gospel to varying nationalities and types of thought, and he gives together with the appeal the particular response which it evoked, whether that response came from the philosophers of Athens, or the theologians of Jerusalem, or the barbarians of the island of Melita.

His Relation to St. Paul

In the third place we can see from the narrative that St. Luke was the chosen companion of St. Paul, and a co-worker with him in the Gentile world. He writes with the pen of a man of action, one who knows that whereof he speaks. The whole narrative is the work of a man who is spending himself as fully upon the future of Christianity, upon the manifestation of Christ to the Gentiles, as St. Paul himself, and who loves Paul with an intensity beyond all other loves, not only for himself, but still more because of the future of the cause which he represents. From the brief notices it seems that it was St. Luke who stood beside St. Paul and protected him throughout the darkest days of persecution. It was he who watched over the life of the great Apostle with the affectionate reverence of a disciple as well as with the tender care of a physician, and whose writing is the passionate outcome of his soul. He has caught from St. Paul a fire and enthusiasm for Christianity equal only to that of St. Paul himself, so that in the last extremity when the call comes to St. Paul to witness by a martyr's death to the truth which he proclaimed, St. Luke for the sake of Christianity does not deem that sacrifice to have been in vain.

His History

Very little is known as to St. Luke himself. He was probably a Gentile, and, according to tradition, came from Antioch in Syria. He uses Greek idioms in his writings, and has a Grecian accent. His name is only mentioned three times in Scripture:—

"Luke, the beloved physician" (Colossians iv. 4).

"Luke, my fellow labourer" (Philemon 24).

THE BOOK AND ITS AUTHOR

"Only Luke is with me" (2 Timothy iv. 11).

Three sentences only, three master-strokes only, but strokes which delineate the outlines of a great character; a man whose personal charm attracted all around him; one whose faithfulness endured when that of all others had fallen away; one who by the power of the Holy Spirit laboured side by side and endured with the greatest, the most inexhaustible, the most self-sacrificing hero the world has ever seen.

His Characteristics

There are many little touches in the Gospel of St. Luke and in the Acts of the Apostles which show the writer to be a physician as well as a scholar. St. Luke gives an accurate account of every miracle of healing performed either by Christ or by His disciples; and as he gives them he shows he has a physician's compassion for and understanding of suffering as well as a physician's consideration for all who are weak— for women, children, and slaves. Thus he shows his sympathy for women and his consideration of them by the way in which he speaks of them and by the position which he gives them in the Church. He is careful to narrate any service which they have been able to render to the Church, whether it comes from the hand of a maidservant like Rhoda or from a woman of standing like Lydia at Philippi.

Tradition says that St. Luke was a poet and a painter, and in some of the churches in Italy there are pictures shown which are said to have been painted by him. But no authority can be given for this statement; it is a mere tradition. On the other hand, it is quite possible that St. Luke was a painter and a poet; for although his style is abrupt and rugged, yet there are many touches in his writings which show that he had a keen sense of beauty, that he saw every scene with an artist's eye, and that he illuminated what he saw with a poet's thought.

St. Luke, in addition to his compassion and sympathy, was also full of faith and of the spirit of prayer. Throughout his writings we find that he realized the power of prayer, and rejoiced in the expression of the faith which manifests itself in prayer. The whole trend of his spirit is towards love and unity. He exposes self-seeking and covetousness, and shows how it destroys the spirit of unity and love which he is striving to spread upon the earth. It is little wonder, therefore, that Christians of all ages have especially prized the Gospel of St. Luke and the Acts of the Apostles—for they are aglow with a fire of faith and love.

The Title of the Book

This book is always called the Acts of the Apostles, although it might be divided into two parts: Acts i.-xii., the life and works of St. Peter; Acts xiii.-xxviii., the life and works of St. Paul. It passes from the one to the other, as the first and second books of Samuel pass from the story of Samuel to that of David and of Solomon.

Why Did Jesus Begin to Do, and Yet at the Same Time Say "It is Finished"?

Christ had said upon the Cross, "It is finished." It is true that His life-work and His atonement for sin were finished, but the effect of His life-work and atonement were not finished. They were only begun, and would be continued in the Acts of the Apostles and in the acts of His servants in succeeding generations, because they contained within themselves an inexhaustible store of light and truth. There was more light and truth in the concise suggestions which were found in the personal acts and deeds of the living Christ during three years than can be found in the personal acts and deeds of the lives of all other men of all other ages.

The whole life of the Church is a continuation of the life of Christ, because Christ acts through the characters, the words, and the acts of His servants. Hence in whatever service man renders to God, his cry ought to be "not unto us, O Lord, not unto us, but unto Thy name give the praise," because it is the Spirit of Christ Who is working in him to will and to do of His pleasure. All work that is done in the power of Christ and for His sake, whether it be the release of a fellow-man from the leprosy of body or from the leprosy of soul, is a continuation of the vitality and of the very life of Jesus, because the hand which breaks the chain of suffering or of sin which is dragging down a fellow-man derives its power from Christ Himself. Christ in the person of His servant continues to take part in the conflict which He began, and which He will continue until the strongholds of sin and of Satan have been for ever thrown down and cast away.

CHAPTER II

ACTS I. 1-11

THE ASCENSION

The Forty Days

The first verses of chapter i. are written in the form of a preface and give the summary of the intercourse which took place between Christ and His disciples during the last forty days. As Elijah had passed from school to school of the sons of the prophets to prepare them for his coming departure, so Christ spent the last 40 days in instructing and preparing the Apostles for the task which was about to be committed to them. Christ knew the need for such preparation, for he understood the weakness and the heaviness of their nature. He had literally borne their griefs and carried their sorrows. He knew also the gravity of the work about to be committed to them. The task which lay before them was the regeneration of the world. Who and what were they to undertake it?

THE ACTS OF THE APOSTLES

The Preparation of the Disciples—
I. The Royal Commands

Christ prepared the disciples in three ways. In the first place He gave commandments as to the nature and order of the spiritual kingdom which they were about to found on earth. He their King would be absent from that kingdom, but they were to witness for Him and to carry out His commands.

When Christ was upon the earth the disciples had been slow of heart to receive and understand His teaching. Would they be able to receive the commands which He was now giving them? The conditions were changed. The disciples who had formerly been slow of heart to understand His teaching had been given power through the gift of the Holy Ghost. After His Resurrection Christ had breathed upon them and had said: "Receive ye the Holy Ghost." They had been made partakers, in a measure, of His Spirit, the Spirit of Wisdom and understanding, the Spirit of Knowledge and of the fear of God. He spake unto them through the Holy Ghost, and through the power of that Holy Ghost they could apprehend the nature of His commands, and could execute His bidding.

Furthermore, He gave them commandment as to their immediate work. They were not to depart from Jerusalem, but were to "wait for the promise of the Father." The natural impulse of the disciples would have been to leave the place which had rejected and crucified their Master, and which was ready to persecute them also. Why should they not witness to Christ's Resurrection in cities which had not as yet heard and which might be ready to receive their testimony? But it was in Jerusalem that they were to proclaim the fact of the Resurrection—the place where the witness of that fact could be corroborated by over 500 brethren who had seen Jesus at once. If the fact of the Resurrection were accepted in Jerusalem, where there was abundant power of proof or disproof, it would be accepted by every other kingdom and nation also. Moreover, they were to wait in Jerusalem and to expect the promise of the Father. They might in their zeal have thought that the King's message required haste and been eager to go forth and to bear witness immediately, whilst all men were still speaking of the Crucified and Risen Jesus. But Christ taught them then, and through them teaches us, that all witness is in vain unless it is accompanied by the power of the Holy Ghost, and that the first requisite is to wait for the inspiration and power of that Spirit. "They that wait upon the Lord shall renew their strength."

II. The Proof of the Resurrection

The second preparation was the distinct proof of His Resurrection. Paul spoke truly when he said: "Touching the resurrection of the dead, I am called in question"; for that was to him, as it has been to all disciples, the turning-point of their faith. With the Resurrection of Jesus Christ, it has been truly said, stands or falls the Divinity of Christ; and with the Divinity of Christ stands or falls the Christian faith and hope. The disciples must wait until they knew even more certainly that Christ was risen, for to this they must witness before their enemies, who would assail them to the utmost of their power, and therefore Christ, in order to strengthen their faith, appeared to them at intervals for forty days. He showed them His hands and His feet, that He was body and not Spirit only. "A Spirit hath not flesh and bones as ye see Me have." In the second place He showed them that His body partook in larger measure of the spiritual than of the fleshy nature; for He came and went at will, He was circumscribed neither by the laws of time nor of space. This power was used in order to prepare the disciples for His ultimate withdrawal, the suddenness of His appearance and disappearance giving them a consciousness of His spiritual nearness at all times, and preparing them to walk by faith and not by sight. Lastly, the Resurrection as it became more vivid to their spiritual even than to their bodily vision—as, for instance, when "He opened their understanding so that they might understand the Scriptures"—gave them an absolute certainty of His bodily, mental, and spiritual identity—a certainty which could never pass away.

III. *The Promise of the Holy Ghost*

In the third place He prepared them for the baptism of the Holy Ghost. They had been baptized with the baptism of repentance; that is to say, they had been cleansed from past sin by an act the outward and visible sign of which was water; but now they were to receive the indwelling gift of the Holy Spirit, that Spirit of which a foretaste had already been given them, a baptism far exceeding that of John.

The Response of the Disciples

At first sight the attitude of the disciples is disappointing. They were gathered together with Christ for the last time, and it may be that their hearts were heavy with a dim consciousness that God would take away their Master from their head this day. What last request had they to make to Him? What last protestation of faith and of love? They asked that which lay upon their hearts, the great question which they had often asked before, "Lord, wilt Thou at this time restore again the kingdom to Israel?" As we hear them speak their words seem so sad, so far away from what they might have been. They had followed Jesus from the first with this hope and expectation, and this thought had been foremost with them, although He had striven to raise their thoughts from the temporal Messiahship to the spiritual kingdom. But does this question really show that they were no further, in anticipation and in understanding, than they had been at first? Was this heritage of longing which they had received from generations of their forefathers, who had waited for the coming of the Messiah and for the establishment of an earthly kingdom of surpassing glory and majesty, still their predominating and only thought? It may have been so, but as we think the matter over we find that there may have been a deeper meaning to their question.

Why need their King be parted from them? Would he not, even at this eleventh hour, return and reign among them? Could he not again restore the kingdom to Israel? Could he not again turn the hearts of all men to Him, their true and only King? Their question was, after all, practically the same as that which John the Baptist had asked in his prison, as that which we and all who love the Lord Jesus Christ from age to age have asked, and are still asking, either with our lips or dumbly within our hearts—why need the long time of suspense, of doubt, of difficulty, of pain and weariness, of sin and distress still continue? Why need the work of Christ be carried on by such feeble agency and in the midst of so many difficulties? Why will not, why cannot, our Master return and restore again the kingdom to Himself?

The Reply Which Jesus Makes

Jesus answers them and at the same time answers us also. He takes the whole responsibility of the matter into His own hands. He quiets at once the restlessness and the longing. The question of the sin and of the weariness of the world concerns them only in so far as they can feel for it and relieve it. The Father Who has created all, Whose love yearns over all, has the times and the power and the seasons in His own hand. He will bring them forth in His own time, and with them His own peace. Meanwhile He calls upon His followers, whether they are Apostles or whether they are disciples of succeeding generations, in the first place to wait for the promise of the Holy Ghost; and, in the second place, to witness first in their own homes and then unto the uttermost parts of the earth.

Jesus promises there will be times and seasons of special refreshment; that is to say, of outpouring of His Holy Spirit. They will come from God at the time known only to Him and in the manner He has chosen. They will be veiled from human eyes. The disciples are to go forward on their way—a clear commission in their hands and an absolute knowledge of the truth which they are witnessing, a truth about to be assailed by the whole force of infidelity. They are to be at rest even as they press forward; for the future, with all its perplexities and apparent impossibilities, is in their Master's hand.

The Great Cloud of Witnesses

Thus Jesus bade them go forth "to the uttermost parts of the earth." These are His last words. As He stood on the Mount Olivet and looked once more at the world which He was about to leave, we wonder whether the future once again unrolled itself before His eyes; whether He saw passing before Him, as it were in a long, continuous train, His witnesses, His servants, who from age to age and from generation to generation would go forth to minister in His name, until they passed even to the uttermost ends of the earth. Did all the kingdoms of the world and the glory of them thus a second time pass before his eyes, but did He see them lighted up with the coming glory, His kingdom instead of the kingdom of Satan? As He gazed did the shadows flee away before his eyes—was death swallowed up in victory?

Truth and Light: The Characteristics of the Kingdom of Christ

The inflowing light which is gradually covering the earth is the second great witness of the Resurrection, just as the Divine character, as shown in the life of Christ, is the first and greatest witness of it. If the disciples had spread a lie, if the Resurrection itself had been a lie, then the outcome of untruth must have been untruth. The witness of a lie must have overspread every country into which it came with a cloud of darkness and with a desolation of separation from God. "By their fruits ye shall know them." Whereas we know that wherever Christ's heralds have proclaimed that He is God and that He is risen from the dead, a river of the water of life has flowed forth and carried with it the healing of the nations.

The Ascension

His command given, a command which is in itself both a promise and a prophecy, Christ was parted from His disciples. He was lifted up before their eyes, and a cloud received Him out of their sight. The revelation of His glory was seen but for a moment and then passed

THE ASCENSION

away in mystery and in cloud, and Christ became an unseen but still surrounding presence.

The disciples stood gazing wistfully towards heaven in the vain hope that as He had at other times departed and come again so He would once more appear before their eyes. Their agonized gaze must have been akin to that with which we watch the angel of death take away from us the desire of our eyes. The great question was whether when they knew that He had gone they would, like the sons of the Prophets, go hither and thither to seek Him in the hope that in some mountain or valley He might even yet appear, or sink into hopelessness, feeling paralyzed at the thought that they were left alone to witness in a city and in a world which had rejected Him.

Whilst they were gazing two messengers stood beside them—two angels sent from heaven to witness to them just as they were about to be sent to witness to the world. These angels had no new message which they could give; they did but reiterate the command and the promise of a sure return. They warned the disciples against letting their attitude be one of wonder or of longing, or of attempting to pierce into mysteries mercifully veiled from them. They bade them turn away their eyes and concentrate their thought and energy upon the allotted work. Their Master would one day return and would take account of His servants. He would come as mysteriously and as suddenly as He had gone, and the assurance of this return would be their stay and hope, the secret of their endurance.

CHAPTER III

ACTS I. 13 TO END

THE FALLING OF THE LOT OF MATTHIAS

The Gathering in the Upper Room

Christ was gone "through the veils of time and space," "passed into the Holiest Place," and the disciples had returned filled with awe and wonder to carry the tidings of their Master's departure to the company assembled together in the upper room awaiting them.

This upper room, according to tradition, was in the house of Mark, and had been for a long time set apart for the use of Jesus and His disciples. It was here that the Passover was said to have been eaten, and here also not long after that the Holy Ghost would be given at Pentecost.

Amongst those who were gathered together were the eleven disciples and Mary, the mother of Jesus, and the brethren of Jesus also. This is the last time that Mary is mentioned in Scripture. She had been blessed among women, but the greatest part of her life-work was now over, and we see her for the last time united in prayer and supplication among those who had seen the risen Christ and been witnesses of His resurrection. We see also the brethren of Jesus, the men who had so long doubted His divinity, who had dared to think and to say that He was beside Himself, but who now knew that He was risen from the dead, for He had appeared to James as well as to other of the disciples, and by their presence showed that they were prepared to witness to His power and resurrection.

The Action of Peter

But however many might be gathered together He, to whom each eye had turned, each heart had been uplifted, was no longer in the midst of them. Whither should they go, to whom should they turn for guidance and for aid? It was not the sense of emptiness alone, it was the sense of responsibility also, a responsibility greater than could be borne, intermingling with an even greater sense of loss, and which, if it had not been resisted, might have paralyzed thought and action. But Peter, who from the time of his first call seems to have taken the lead among the disciples, saw that not only the place of his Master but that of the traitor was empty also, and nerving himself he took the first step towards completing the band of disciples, and thus preparing for the coming responsibility. Standing up, therefore, he rehearsed the fate which had befallen Judas, and as the leader, but not as the ruler over the disciples, called upon them to appoint another in his place. We notice the change which had passed over the disciples and the way in which they had grown in spiritual understanding even during the few hours which had elapsed since they were with Jesus and had put that last question to Him. We see a spirit of union, of prayer and of supplication, far away from their former attitude, and very far away from the hopelessness which had taken possession of them when they were scattered hither and thither after Jesus had been crucified and for the first time parted from them.

Judas: His Character and His Weakness

Peter tells the story of Judas. His words are few in number, but terrible in signification. Judas had been numbered with the disciples. He had been called to and had taken part in the ministry of Christ, though what the motives were which attracted him to Jesus we cannot tell. Judas seems to have been naturally the ablest of all the disciples, and in some respects the most far-seeing amongst them. He may have recognized the beauty and the power of the character of Christ and have anticipated that He would speedily be recognized and acknowledged as the Messiah of His people. If so, he probably expected that the disciple who now carried the money-bag would obtain the post of greatest power and influence under the new King—might possibly even be the Chancellor of His kingdom. But however great his ambition, so much the greater was the tragedy of his fall. Christ had warned him of his besetting sin of avarice, but Judas had despised His words. He deliberately chose the evil and left the good. When at last startled by the realization of his crime, when too late he recognized that Jesus was the Son of God, he came to the Temple and threw down the money as though the very touch of it was hateful to him; but he received scant comfort from those who had been the partners in his sin. "What is that to us? See thou to that." Deserted of man, and, as he believed, deserted of God, he seems to have clung to what was left, to have gathered up the pieces of money and to have bought with them a field, the reward of his iniquity. This field which Judas bought stands as one of the terrible monuments in Scripture of the things for which men have been content to sell their souls. Eve's apple, Esau's mess of pottage, Achan's wedge of gold, the young ruler's riches, Judas's field—all alike the price of a soul. "What shall it profit a man if he gain the whole world and lose his own soul?"

Judas: His Reward and His End

Judas received as little comfort from the reward of his iniquity as iniquity ever gives. In a passionate fit of remorse he threw himself over a precipice in the field purchased by the priests with the money returned to them (and thus rhetorically said to be purchased by himself) and died there. It is recorded that he went down "to his own place." Some have thought that this place signified Gehenna; some the place which he deserved, or the one which he had chosen; but whichever it might be, it was not the place to which Jesus had called him and to which, if he had been faithful to his Master, he might have been chosen.

As we read the story we cannot help wondering whether, if he had turned even at the last hour, as Peter turned, his most awful sin might have been pardoned; whether Jesus would have had mercy upon him? But Judas did not turn. He probably believed that it was too late, and that there was nothing left for him to do but to destroy himself and to meet his fate.

The spot where he died was shunned by all, and was called Aceldama ("the field of blood")—a field marked out not only by his own blood, but, in a sense, by his Master's also. In his despair when he realized that Jesus was God, and that the wrath of God must surely fall upon him for his awful betrayal of the Son of God, we find even Judas numbered amongst those who despite themselves have witnessed to the Godhead of Christ.

Matthias Chosen

In the prayer of Peter, when the choice between Joseph and Matthias was about to be made, we see how clearly the disciples realized that Jesus was still spiritually present among them. They spoke to Him as they would have spoken had He been standing in their midst. Peter seems to realize that Jesus lived, loved, understood, just as much at that moment as when He went in and out amongst them. He whose eye had read the thoughts and intents of men when He was upon earth would read the hearts of the two men standing before Him and would choose one so that he might be numbered among the disciples and rise to the high hope and calling which had been set before Judas. The lot was cast and fell upon Matthias. This is the last time that the use of the lot is recorded in Scripture. Some have thought that Peter was too impulsive, and should not without clear guidance have sought to fill the vacant place. They believe that it was Paul who was called of God to complete the number of the disciples, and that Peter should have waited God's time, just as the Israelites should have waited for David.

We cannot tell how this may be. There is no record left of Matthias or of his work further than this one mention; but that does not necessarily mean that he was not a chosen servant of God. There are many of God's saints of whose work no record remains save the influence which they have exercised upon their day and generation, and through that generation upon succeeding generations. The life and work of Matthias may one day be found where we would each wish that our life-work might be found also; that is to say, in the Book of Remembrance before God and in the great sum-total of influence for good in the world.

CHAPTER IV

ACTS II. 1-13

THE DAY OF PENTECOST

The Feast of the Passover was the most important of the three great Jewish feasts at which all the males in Israel were commanded to appear before God. The Feast of Pentecost was the second great feast of the old dispensation, and at the period with which we are dealing it was, according to a census taken in the time of Nero, more generally attended by the Jewish people than even the Passover Feast itself. The Jews assembled together not only from Jerusalem and from the surrounding districts, but also from the outlying provinces of the Empire. Two causes contributed to the popularity of this feast. In the first place it was more convenient for those who laboured on the land to come to Jerusalem when their work was completed, and they could rejoice in the consciousness of an ingathered harvest; in the second place Pentecost (the Feast of Weeks), being seven weeks later than the Feast of the Passover, the season of navigation was further advanced and it was easier for the Jews from the west to come by sea to Jerusalem.

THE DAY OF PENTECOST

The Feast of Pentecost

At the commencement of the harvest, the second day of the Passover, a sheaf of ripe corn was always cut from the field and brought to the temple and waved in it as the first fruit of the coming ingathering. This wave-sheaf was not accompanied by any sin-offering because it prefigured Christ the first-fruit of the Resurrection, for whom no sin offering could be made, because He was without sin.

On the day of Pentecost (Gk. *Pente*) seven weeks later, when the harvest was completed, two wave-loaves, prepared from the best wheat of the country and baked in the temple itself, were offered, accompanied by a sin-offering of seven lambs, one young bullock and two rams. This feast was an expression of national gratitude, a joyful acknowledgment of the completed harvest; but it prefigured also the final ingathering of souls redeemed by the blood of Christ and by the outpouring of His spirit. The sin-offering was for all, for all alike had sinned and come short of the glory of God.

Besides the thanksgiving for the harvest of wheat and the looking forward to the final harvest of souls there was a commemoration also of the redemption of the children of Israel from the land of Judaea, so that there was a threefold meaning in the Feast of the Pemtecost.

Pentecost and Sinai

According to Jewish tradition the Feast of Pentecost was the time not only of the feast of ingathering but also for the remembrance of the giving of the law upon Mount Sinai. That law had been accompanied by earthquake and fire as well as by the whirlwind, and the law then given, although Divine and instinct with power and purity, was written only upon stone; whereas the new law, which was to come, like the still small voice to Elijah, after the earthquake and the lightning, was to be written on the table of the heart. The giving of this second law brought no destruction with it. It was itself life, and as life it entered into and controlled the outcome of the heart, finding expression not only in the thoughts and words, but also in the whole life of the recipient. It is not probable that the disciples understood, until long after, the full bearing of either of these aspects of the Day of Pentecost. It was comparatively easy to see the connection between the ingathering of the harvest of wheat and the ingathering of the harvest of souls, but the connection between "the rushing mighty wind" of Pentecost and "the thunderings and lightnings" of Mount Sinai was not so clearly manifest until they saw how the old dispensation was fulfilled in the new, and the laws given upon Mount Sinai were illuminated by the light and teaching of the Holy Spirit.

THE DAY OF PENTECOST

The Waiting Disciples

During the preceding day bands of pilgrims from all quarters had gathered in Jerusalem. They came up with joy and gladness, for this was the one great festival in which public peace and thank-offerings were offered for the whole nation. The city at this time was in the full beauty of early summer, and as the pilgrims approached the end of their journey and looked towards the glistening towers of the Temple a glow of joy and of religious patriotism must have arisen in every heart on the Day of Pentecost. The disciples had probably joined in the early service of the Temple, but had now withdrawn, and were waiting in the upper room in prayer and supplication. Christ, the first-fruits of the Resurrection, had, like the Passover sheaf, been given back to them, and they were waiting in the hope that God would hear their prayer and would grant, together with the ingathering of the harvest of wheat, the gift of the Holy Spirit, the longed-for ingathering of the harvest of souls also.

The Descent of the Spirit

Their prayer was heard; whilst the service was still in progress, most probably during the time of the offering of the wave-lambs and the wave-bread, the sound of a rushing mighty wind was heard all over Jerusalem which centred and circled around the house where the disciples were gathered together.

Whilst the disciples were listening in awe-struck wonder the room in which they were sitting was suddenly illuminated by a glowing sheet of fire. This fiery cloud or sheet was cloven, and seemed to be like tongues of fire which separated the one from the other and alighted upon the heads of the disciples.

> "The fires that rushed on Sinai down
> In sudden torrents dread,
> Now gently light, a glorious crown,
> On every sainted head."

"OUT OF THE FULNESS OF THE HEART THE MOUTH SPEAKETH."

These cloven tongues were typical of the new breath or Spirit which had descended from God and which, being cloven or distributed, were about to enter into the hearts of the disciples and to become part of their very life, even of themselves. In the beginning God the Creator had breathed into man a first breath of life; in the fulness of time God the Redeemer had renewed life by conquering death; and now in these latter days God the Sanctifier had breathed upon the world a newer and yet fuller life. This life was symbolized by glowing tongues of fire, a sign of the power which was about to be given, for the tongue, being set on fire of the Spirit, would glow with enthusiasm and life, and be used of God to kindle a like fire and enthusiasm in the hearts of others also.

As fire purifies and destroys evil, so the Spirit of God would purify and cleanse the hearts of men; and as fire is the symbol of life and of energy, so the Holy Spirit would fill the hearts of the disciples with a zeal and God-given energy which would enable them for their work.

The First Results

The new life which descended upon the disciples took entire possession of them. They were carried away by the Spirit, and as in old time "holy men of old spake as they were moved by the Holy Ghost," so the disciples in like manner on this Day of Pentecost spake as they were moved, and one after another proclaimed the glad tidings not only in their own tongue but even in tongues which they did not before understand, so that each man heard in his own vernacular the wonderful words of life.

The Gathering of the Multitude

It is generally thought that as soon as the disciples had received the gift of the Holy Spirit they went up to the Temple to return thanks to God, and that either in Solomon's porch or in the great gathering place outside the Temple the scene which is recorded in the amphitheatre took place. An old writer says that it seemed as if a rushing mighty wind like a great bell from heaven had summoned men from every part of Jerusalem to come together and know what this thing may be. It was a strange and representative crowd that was gathered together. For hundreds of years the

Jews had been dispersed into almost every part of the Roman Empire, and among the number of those who had been carried away or who went away of their own free will were many who in their heart had remained true to the Jewish faith, truer even than the dwellers in Jerusalem themselves. A great number of these men came up from time to time to the annual feasts from the most distant parts of the Empire. They were the Jews of the Dispersion, a dispersion rightly regarded as a punishment for sin, but by the mercy of God turned into a blessing not only to the Jews themselves but also to the Gentiles; for just as these Jews by coming into contact with other men and other thoughts were more ready than the Jews of Jerusalem for the newer and wider conception of the relationship between God and man, so too the Gentiles amongst whom they settled were brought into contact with the teaching of the Synagogue and thus prepared for the coming of the Gospel.

The Scene in Solomon's Porch

The whole crowd was filled with amazement. They saw before them a band of people, for the most part rude and unlettered, united in an outcry of joy and thanksgiving to God. Everyone who listened, to his amazement, heard in his own language words of joy and thanksgiving, even though he could not fully understand what this joy and thanksgiving meant. He knew by the dress and bearing of the men that they were Galileans, but how could Galileans speak in foreign

THE DAY OF PENTECOST

tongues and utter words which could be understood without an interpreter? When we remember from what a wide area this multitude was gathered together we cannot wonder at their astonishment. They came from the East, West, North, and South. From the East, where dwelt the Parthians, Medes, and Elamites—that is to say, a remnant of the Jews which had been carried away into Babylon, as well as a remnant of the ten tribes; from the West, the strangers of Rome; from the North, descendants of the company which Antiochus the Great had exported into Galatia and Phrygia, and who had now become a powerful and wealthy people; from the nearer West, men of the great Colony of Cyprus; and from the South, especially from Egypt and Alexandria, men of learning and position.

The first effect of the gift of tongues was one of pure amazement and astonishment upon all who had heard it. This gift of tongues stands, as it were, mid-way in the history of the world between the dispersion of tongues in Babel and the gathering together in one of the great multitudes which is prophesied in the Book of Revelation. The effect of Babel was the confusion, after which it was named, and the scattering apart of men from one another upon earth; the effect of Pentecost was amazement. It was different also in its consequences; it was followed, not by a scattering of the nations as at Babel, but by a gathering together, a union of peace and love, foreshadowing the perfect union of the hereafter when the servants of God will unite in one common song of praise to "Him Who sitteth upon the throne and unto the Lamb."

The men who listened were divided then, as now, into two great classes. There are always those who mock and who are ready to ascribe anything which they do not understand to sin, and there are those who seek to find out the truth of the phenomena which they witness and who ask what these things mean.

The Meaning of the Gift of Pentecost

We find in the Old Testament that the gift of the Spirit seems sometimes to have been an abiding presence within a man: sometimes a power which descended for a time and was, as it were, without the man—that is to say, the Spirit rested upon and endued the man with strength, but if he were not obedient to the will of God would too soon pass away. Thus the Spirit fell upon Samson and gave him an arm of strength; upon Balaam and enabled him to see visions of God; upon Saul, and, despite his natural incapacity for religion, nerved him to carry out the will of God. But the gift of Pentecost seems to have been given in fuller and more abiding measure and to have been an indwelling such as we find in the case of Moses and other of the Old Testament saints of God. We see that it was lasting and enduring, that it became the very life of the men who received it; that they were changed in character, were ennobled, strengthened. It is true they were still men of like passions with ourselves, they had still the natural qualifications and limitations of their characters. They were liable to frailty and even to sin; but they were changed men, and their lives showed that they had been taught of God.

How Far Was the Gift of Tongues Permanent?

It is not clear how far the gift of tongues, which was the peculiar manifestation of the Spirit upon the Day of Pentecost, remained permanently with the disciples. We find that St. Paul says that he had the power to speak with more tongues than any of his fellow disciples, and we conclude that this power was given to him as to the other early converts. We find, too, that at Lystra he seems to have spoken without difficulty in the tongue of the people. Ramsay says that although Greek was generally understood by the Jews of the Dispersion, there is no question but that St. Paul must have spoken to the common people wherever he went in their own tongue. The question is one, therefore, which cannot be answered. It is probable that, like the gift of healing, the gift of tongues rested in large measure upon the disciples in order to fit them for the exceedingly difficult work which they were called upon to do.

The Effect of the Spirit upon the Character of the Disciple

Whether the peculiar aptitude of speech passed away or not there is no question that the other great manifestation, the change of character, remained permanently with the disciples. The spirit of their teaching was changed, and the men who received the Holy Ghost from that time forward began to speak with the courage of their Master. The tongue which in its natural state is, as St. James says, "set on fire of hell" and "full of deadly poison" became, when set on fire of heaven, full of grace and truth, and being full of grace and truth the Christian's greatest weapon in his warfare against sin. The Christian has been told to put up his sword into its sheath, but he has been commissioned to speak words of wisdom, love, and consolation—words which are mighty even to the pulling down of the strongholds of sin.

CHAPTER V

ACTS II. 14-40

ST. PETER'S SERMON

Whilst all men were lost in amazement at the wonders of the Day of Pentecost, the disciples themselves probably echoed in their hearts somewhat of the cry which they heard around them, "What meaneth this?"—when Peter, who was ever the first to apprehend the things of God, unlocked, as it were, the door which barred the way to their understanding, and lifting up his voice interpreted the matter, and spoke words which marked one of the great turning-points in his own spiritual life. Otherwise how would he, who had joined with the disciples in asking Christ but ten days before whether He would not restore again the kingdom to Israel, have suddenly, as it were, recognized the spiritual nature of the kingdom of righteousness? How otherwise would he have seen the whole purpose of the life, death, and resurrection of Christ lie open before him? How have shown so great a change of character as well as understanding? Until now Peter had been so easily swayed by the multitude, so ready to take the impressions of all around him; but he now stands up, and in the very town and in the face of the multitude who had cried "Crucify Him! crucify Him!" dares single-handed and alone to arraign them as the murderers of his Master, and to charge them with the murder of the Son of God.

The Sermon of St. Peter

He begins with words of quiet calm and conviction. He forces them to withdraw the charge that they have made by bidding them remember how impossible it was that such a thing could be. They knew themselves that the Jews, especially on the Day of Pentecost, when engaged at one of the most solemn festivals of the year, could not and would not be drunken at the third hour of the day. Then with a swift turn, as they become conscious of their injustice, he gives them the true explanation, speaking not in his own words but in the words and by the authority of the Scriptures themselves.

The Prophecy of Joel

Peter points out that the events which have just taken place are but the fulfilment of prophecy, and quotes the words of the prophet Joel. The whole multitude is suddenly hushed. What may this thing be? Is this outpouring of the Spirit indeed a fulfilment of prophecy, a drawing near of God to them? Joel had been writing about the judgment of locusts which, at his intercession, had been removed from the land, and he had turned the thoughts of the people away from judgment to the future mercy and promises of God. He had given one of the broad outline visions which are so frequently met with in the Old Testament, and in which we seem to stand upon some mountain top and see unrolled before our eyes, in the light of a glorious sunset, a great and mysterious landscape—a landscape in which the sea and mountains, clouds, and glory, are in the far distance blurred and mingled into one glorious whole.

This is the prophecy which Peter quotes, and as he speaks the people stand amazed; the first part of the verse has unquestionably just come true—the sons and daughters have prophesied and God has poured out of His Spirit upon all flesh. The question which each man is asking is, Will the rest of the words come true also? Are signs and wonders about to show themselves in the heaven above and in the earth beneath? Will the sun be turned into fire and the moon into blood? Is the great and notable day of the Lord at hand? If so, what does this wonderful word of promise mean? Is it true that whosoever shall call upon the Name of the Lord shall be saved? Whilst they are thus silent with amazement, with apprehension, and with wonder, he makes another swift turn and brings their thoughts back from the future and in upon themselves.

The Miracles of Jesus and the Miracle of Pentecost

The miracle that has just taken place is in its nature akin to those miracles of love and wonder which Jesus,

Whom they had known and seen, and Whom they had just crucified, had been working in their midst. They see now that the miracles of Jesus are the miracles of the Son of God, Whom they have taken and by wicked hands have crucified and slain. They stand powerless and undone. They cannot undo their deed; nor can they prevent the end of the world, which is coming and in which they must answer for their deed. Then when the sky is dark with thunder and with clouds Peter gives a ray of hope. It is true that they cannot frustrate the purpose of God any more than by their crucifixion of Jesus they were able to frustrate His mercy and His purpose towards them. He has burst the bonds of death, He has ascended into heaven. He is there, and His ascension is proved in the same way that the gift of Pentecost has been proved. His death and ascension have been foretold as surely in their very Scriptures as the passage which he has just narrated.

The Prophecy of David

Peter then applies the words of David as swiftly and as suddenly as he had applied those of Joel. David foresaw that Christ would burst the bonds of death; He could not be holden of it. "His soul was not left in hell, neither His flesh did see corruption." David spoke of Christ and of no one else; for if he had spoken of himself his tomb, still containing his body, would have contradicted his words; whereas the tomb of Christ, with the stone rolled away and empty, is a witness of the Resurrection. They have the testimony of the empty tomb and the testimony of their own senses also. They know two things; they know that the risen Jesus has been seen by very many of their own number, and they know that He must have ascended because He has poured out this gift of tongues of which they see the effects before their very eyes. Then he gives a sudden personal application such as he had given at the close of the quotation from Joel. David, like Joel, bids them beware that Jesus is about to make His foes His footstool. Who are His foes? Let all the house of Israel know assuredly that the Jesus Whom they have crucified is that Jesus Who is sitting on the right hand of God, Who as Lord and Christ is waiting until they, His foes, are brought beneath His feet.

The Call to Repentance

We see the vast multitude shaken physically by what they have seen, and spiritually by what they have heard; they stand convicted. They are pricked to the heart and beside themselves with fear. Each man is brought before the judgment-seat of his own conscience and he cries, "Men and brethren, what shall we do?" Like Christian when he rushed from the City of Destruction, he is filled with one thought and one thought only—the way of escape. The Holy Spirit has been moving upon the audience, and has accompanied with power the words of Peter.

The Ingathering

We can almost see the vast multitude as Peter passes up and down amongst them. They are cut to the heart at the thought that they have crucified the Lord of Glory, and Peter sees their anguish and exhorts them with many words to save themselves from this untoward generation. As he speaks great numbers gladly receive his word and are baptized, and the same day there are added to the Lord three thousand souls.

The Preaching of Christ and of St. Peter

As we consider the effect produced by this sermon of St. Peter upon the multitude we cannot help wondering, when Jesus was preaching upon earth, why a like conviction of sin and a like understanding of the nature of sin and of the true position of the soul before God did not take possession of the multitude of that time also. The answer is found in the words of Christ Himself. "It is expedient for you that I go away." When Christ was upon earth He deliberately let His words fall only where He would. He called unto Himself whom He would, and at times He turned away and left the multitude just when they seemed as though they were about to believe and to understand His words. But now all is changed; He has burst the gates of hell and of death, and has ascended up to heaven. He has opened the gate of life and outpoured the gift of life upon men.

It is through this new life that Peter is speaking and convicting his hearers so that they have turned to God and repented of their sin.

The Message of St. Peter

Peter, like John the Baptist and like the prophets of old, calls on all to repent; but he follows the call with a promise fuller than they were able to give. He bids men not only repent, but also be baptized in the Name of Christ and receive from Him the remission of sins. He tells them that the chain which holds them down may be broken, that they may receive the gift of the Holy Spirit, that they may arise and walk. For them the dark cloud of guilt and of death may be for ever rolled away. They may, if they will, belong not to the number of those who must bend beneath the footstool of God's throne, but to the number who will receive the word of welcome and will stand at the right hand of their Master for ever. Peter foretells even more than this, for he is carried further still by the inspiration of the Holy Spirit and prophesies that the promise is not only to those who hear him but also to their children and to all that are afar off "even to as many as our God shall call."

Did Peter realize the full significance of his words? Probably not, for it was not until after he had fallen into a trance and seen the heavens opened that he realized that the promise was indeed to all that were afar off, and that God was no respecter of persons, but that Jew and Gentile alike would hear and respond to His call. At dawn on the Day of Pentecost there were one hundred and twenty men and women who were the avowed followers of Christ, but when the day closed other three thousand souls had been added to the Church. All this had come to pass through the outpouring of the gift of the Holy Spirit; but it had come to pass in part also, under God, through the instrumentality of St. Peter. How had Peter been prepared to do so great a work? How was he able on the impulse of the moment to interpret the signs of the times and by the light of the Scriptures to point the great multitude to Christ? The Spirit in which we meet a great crisis is not the outcome of that crisis itself. It is the outcome of daily events, of daily smaller crises that have occurred in our lives, and which, according as we have met them, have made us what we are when the decisive moment comes. Peter spoke, no doubt, under the direct inspiration of the Holy Ghost, but he spoke also under the influence of the teaching of our Lord and out of his three years' intercourse with Him. Jesus had, day by day, taught His disciples out of the Scriptures and interpreted their meaning. Thus Peter was able to call to mind the Scriptures and to understand the signification which might otherwise have been veiled from him.

Encouragement to Workers

There is encouragement in this for all who labour in God's vineyard, for all who strive to teach the Scriptures to children or to those who seem to understand so little and to be far away in heart from Him. "My word shall not return unto Me void." The words learned, precept upon precept and line upon line, may seem like the seed sown upon the stony ground; but when that ground is broken up and watered by the dew of heaven, the seed will spring up and bring forth fruit, some thirty-fold, some sixty-fold, some an hundred-fold.

CHAPTER VI

ACTS II. 41 TO III. 3

THE APOSTLES' DOCTRINE AND FELLOWSHIP

Let There Be Light

Three thousand souls had been added to the Church, three thousand men and women, touched by the Spirit of God, had been convicted of sin and had repented and turned to Christ, but, although called to follow Christ, they as yet knew little about Him, understood little of the meaning of the change which had passed over them. If they had been left to themselves they might have wandered back to their old homes, some, perhaps, to far distant provinces of the Roman Empire, and drifted away into error and indifference, and the glorious dawn of Christianity been overshadowed by clouds and darkness. But the apostles who had themselves been taught and led of Christ were now prepared, under the guidance of the Holy Spirit, to lead and teach others also, and we read that the converts "continued steadfastly in the apostles' doctrine and fellowship, and in breaking of bread and in prayers." We can almost see the apostles and the one hundred and twenty men and women who had been praying together in the upper room passing up and down among the converts, and we can hear them tell in glowing words the story of their Master Jesus; we can hear them reveal that which formerly they did not themselves understand, which had been hidden because of the hardness of their hearts, but was now manifest through the power of the Holy Spirit. They could tell as none other of His marvellous personality, His compassion, and long-suffering. They had witnessed His miracles of healing and of love; they had been in the garden of Gethsemane; had stood at the foot of the Cross; had seen His empty tomb; had heard Him say, "It is I, be not afraid"; they had been told by the angels that He Who had been taken from them would come again in like manner as they had seen Him go into heaven. What would we have not given to have been among the number of the converts, to have heard the story from the lips of the apostles also.

The Fellowship of the Disciples

The words of the disciples were exemplified by their lives. If we turn from an account of the Court of Rome at this period—from the record of the lives of the Roman citizens and nobles, with their selfishness, bloodthirstiness, and pride—to the fellowship of the disciples, to the love and unity amongst them, we see how marked the contrast was between them and the men of their day and generation. The life of holiness and communion with God, of peace and goodwill towards one another, must have attracted the multitude and helped them to understand the recital of the words and deeds of Jesus, and to keep them true to the faith which they confessed; but for this there would have been a great temptation, after the first impression of Peter's speech had passed away, to go back to the old life and to leave a faith which demanded everything from them.

They knew that Christ had not where to lay His head, that persecution and death had for ever dogged His steps, and that He Himself had foretold that the shadow of the Cross which had fallen upon Him would fall upon them also, and that shadow had already fallen. The temper of the multitude was as hostile towards them as it had been towards Jesus, how could they face that multitude, how bear the persecution and death which lay before them? If they looked towards earth they would only be drawn back again, but if they looked towards Heaven the thought of pain and persecution would be swallowed up in victory. We seem to feel a breath of Heaven passing over earth in a time of marvellous teaching, communion and fellowship, when all the followers of Jesus were joined in the love feast, partook of the memorials of their Master's death, and saw the deeds which the apostles were enabled to work through the power of the Holy Spirit.

The Unity in Prayer

This foretaste of Heaven upon earth gave a simplicity of faith and a realization of the immanence of Christ, which has been an inspiration to all succeeding generations. They turned to Christ as readily for guidance and help as for pardon for their sins; "Lord, show whether of these two thou hast chosen," "Lord, behold their threatenings," "Lord Jesus, receive my spirit."

They realized the immediate presence of their Master and turned to Him not only for pardon, but also for guidance and help. The new converts were taught by the disciples to pray, they were brought by them into the same beauty of holiness, they came into the presence chamber of the Master Himself, they learnt from the disciples the secret of prayer—a secret which enabled Stephen to see Jesus in place of his persecutors and to say: "Lord Jesus, receive my spirit."

The Community of Goods

A further teaching of the true character of love was given in the manner in which they "had all things common." From what we find in the following chapter of the Acts it seems as though this community of goods was not so much what we understand by Socialism as an idealization of the thought of stewardship. Jesus had throughout His life emphasized this sense of stewardship, not only by His words, but also by His teaching and actions. He gave to every man according as he had need, He fed the multitude, He healed the sick, Himself He had not where to lay His head. This was the attitude which the Christians were learning to show towards their worldly possessions. They were stewards over them as well as over the mysteries of Christ. They knew that they had to follow their Master's example and to give account to Him for all He had entrusted to their hands.

When we come to think how many men and women were thus suddenly withdrawn from their former surroundings and occupied for the most part in learning the Christian faith, we can see that a great sacrifice of money and goods was necessary on the part of the wealthier converts, a selling of possessions and goods and a parting of them to all men as every man had need, if those who were poor were to have opportunity for learning the Gospel also. This was possibly not as strange to them as it might be to the Christian of to-day, for they lived in an atmosphere of immediate anticipation of the return of Christ, and in that anticipation gathered together "daily with one accord in the Temple, and breaking bread from house to house, did eat their meat with gladness and singleness of heart, praising God, and having favour with all the people." By thus following in the footsteps of Christ they attracted others to the faith, "and the Lord added to the Church daily such as should be saved."

CHAPTER VII

ACTS III. TO IV. 3

A MIRACLE AND ITS OUTCOME

The Attitude of the Sanhedrin towards the Disciples

For several months the Jews made little or no movement of hostility against the new converts, but waited to see from the life and doctrine of the disciples and their followers whether or no they would dissociate themselves from the Temple and from taking part in its rites or ceremonies. It seemed quite possible that they would be willing to obey the Sanhedrin and unite in the service of the Temple; they had only to cast over that which had been revolutionary to the teaching of their Master and to conform to the existing constitution of the Jewish religion in order to escape the penalty, persecution and death. In the Sanhedrin itself the Sadducees were the representatives of what may be called the materialistic side of the nation,—the men who tolerated religion, who viewed the spiritual life from a materialistic point of view, denying the supernatural and affirming the freedom of the will, whilst they despised the tradition of the elders. They believed in God and the Law, but they laughed to scorn the thought of angels, spirit, or the resurrection. They have been followed in every age by those who, if they do not deny the Resurrection in words, yet deny it in their life and deeds, and show that the present, that which they can see, and from which they derive present benefit, is all that they seek for. But besides the Sadducees there were also in the Sanhedrin a large number of Pharisees also. The Pharisees were outwardly far more religious and earnest than the Sadducees, and understood far better than the Sadducees the supreme reality of the unseen as held by the apostles. They too claimed that religion should be first, but by their life they showed that it was a religion of outward form and ceremony, conformed to dictates of their own ideas and superstitions rather than to the commands of God.

Both these bodies of men must have watched the Christians with anxiety, and waited until they took some step by which they declared their views and indicated their future line of policy. Their Master having been killed, it remained to be seen whether they would be faithful to His teaching or not. If, on the one hand, they still taught that God was a Spirit, and to be worshipped in spirit and in truth, what would become of the observances, of the tithes and offerings by which the Pharisees maintained their power? If, on the other, as a public body, they proclaimed the Resurrection, what would become of the doctrine of the Sadducees? The disciples must have been equally aware of the difficult position in which they stood, and that the time was coming when they must declare themselves.

The Scene of the Miracle

Peter and John went up together to the Temple about the hour of prayer, being the ninth hour, that is to say, about three in the afternoon. We cannot help wondering, in passing, why men who had such exquisite Christian fellowship, such prayer, such communion of soul and spirit, should have gone up to the Temple to worship when that worship was so overlaid with rites and ceremonies, with superstitions and ordinances of man's advising, that the power of its spirituality had almost died away. But whether they realized it or not the disciples themselves were in far truer harmony with the service of the Temple than the Pharisees and Sadducees who had obscured its light and teaching, for they saw fulfilled in Christ the meaning of the rites and ceremonies ordained by Moses. They were the exponents, not of a new religion, but of a fuller revelation which would interpret the types and ceremonies about to vanish and pass away.

As the disciples approached the Temple a beautiful sight opened out before their view. The Temple of Herod was very much larger than that of Solomon. At the northwestern corner stood the tower of Antonia, which commanded all the buildings of the Temple, and was in the hands of the Roman garrison, who, from the ancient castle of Hezekiah and Nehemiah, overlooked not only the Temple, but also the whole city, and by a subterranean passage had power of instant approach even into the Temple itself in case of tumult or insurrection.

The Temple at this time occupied an area of about 1000 feet—that is to say, it was about double the length of St. Paul's Cathedral and had a width as great as the length. St. Paul's Cathedral is 520½ feet long. The Temple was 1000 feet square. The Temple itself consisted of several inclosures, one within the other. There was a large outer wall having nine great gates of entrance; within these there was a second and higher wall enclosing a long and oblong space. This oblong space contained in turn three courts—the Court of the Women, the Court of Israel, and the Court of the Priests; the Court of the Priests contained again within itself another and a still higher building which was divided into parts—the house of God and the most Holy Place.

As the disciples entered the court they were met by a little company who were carrying a lame man to his accustomed place beside the Beautiful Gate of the Temple. He was probably brought in at the Royal Porch, and carried past the large inclosure surrounded by pillars until he came to the long colonnade or cloister which was called Solomon's Porch. In this Jesus had been accustomed to walk and to teach His disciples. The Beautiful Gate was the chief gate by which entrance was made from the outer court into the Court of the Women. Day after day the lame man had lain beside this wonderful gate. It was made of dazzling Corinthian brass, was richly ornamented, and was the regular gathering-place of a crowd of beggars who waited beside it in the hope of alms.

The way in which the poor of all ages and countries have gathered around the gates of temples and churches, instead of at the doors of theatres or places of amusement, has witnessed to the way in which they know that the heart which has been opened by approach to God will overflow in kindness to man.

The Subject of the Miracle

As the lame man was carried in he probably muttered an appeal for alms to everyone who passed, to Peter and to John as to others before them, and he seems to have made this customary appeal without even looking upon them. But Peter, either because he was moved with compassion, or because through the Holy Spirit he knew that the man had faith to be healed, bade him look upon him. The man's attention was caught and he looked, although he had no thought of anything save an alms wherewith to relieve his need. Then Peter said: "Silver and gold have I none; but what I have, that give I thee. In the Name of Jesus of Nazareth, rise up and walk."

The words were full of significance, as showing in what the true wealth as well as the poverty of the disciples and of their followers has consisted and ever will consist. The servants of Jesus as a rule have little earthly wealth that they can give, but they can speak in the name of Jesus and in the power of His Resurrection, and they can give, like their Master, personal consideration, sympathy and succour; in a word, they can help to restore vitality to body and soul. Peter took him by the right hand and lifted him up, and immediately his feet and ankle bones received strength. What Peter did then, God's servants have in a measure done in succeeding ages; they have lifted not only individuals, but nations also from sin and suffering, have restored them to comparative purity, health, and strength.

The lame man had lain from day to day at the gate of the Temple. He had seen Christ pass in and out on His errands of mercy. He had seen many of His great works; he had even seen those who had been healed by Him come up to the Temple to return thanks, and he had listened to His words of teaching. But though so near he had seemed somehow to lie outside it all, and to be beyond the reach of help. All he looked forward to was the occasional alms of those who went into the Temple, which, whilst they availed to keep body and soul together, were of little account compared with life and health. But when Peter lifted him up he passed, as it were, from death to life; he burst forth into joy and thanksgiving; he entered into the Temple leaping and praising God.

The Character and the Importance of the Miracle

As Peter stepped forward to touch the lame man he not only made open declaration of his faith but also crossed the boundary line of departure and began the new evangelistic work of the world. Henceforth the

Church of Christ would seek and save that which was lost, would draw near to the poor, to the distressed in body, soul and spirit, and would point them, as Peter pointed the lame man, to the God of consolation, would bid them in the name of Jesus arise and walk.

It seems strange that a movement of goodwill and benevolence should have brought the Church into conflict with the State, but we have to remember that Christ for a like movement was arraigned also, his accusation in reality being that he had gone about doing good and healing all that were oppressed.

The Effect of the Miracle

The miracle took place in the full view of the crowds gathered in the outer court of the Temple; and as the man returned from the Inner Temple in an ecstasy of joy, clinging to those who had healed him, they all gathered together into Solomon's Porch and marvelled at the change. Those who had seen the miracles of Christ must have recognized a like power in this miracle also, and wondered whether Peter and John, who were known to be His followers, had indeed a like control over life and death. As Peter saw this movement of wonder, he saw also a chance of witnessing for Jesus, but together with the chance a personal temptation also. How far would he ascribe the glory to God, how far to himself? When performing the miracle he had spoken only in the Name of Jesus; he had bidden the lame man—by the personality, by the Divinity, of Christ—to arise and walk. But now that the great deed of healing was done, and all men's eyes were on him, what position would he take? The answer is given in his words. As Joseph said, "It is not in me; God shall give Pharaoh an answer of peace," so Peter said, "Why look ye so earnestly on us, as though by our own power or holiness we have made this man to walk?" "The faith which is by Him hath given him this perfect soundness in the presence of you all." The men who do great acts for Christ are those who have lost themselves for the sake of the kingdom of God, who have given up everything which threatened to cloud or hinder the power of their King as manifested in them.

The Defence of the Miracle

Peter's words are few and emphatic. Jesus, the Prince of Life, had been in their midst. God had set before them in His person the great choice between life and death; between Jesus and Barabbas. They had desired the murderer; they had killed Jesus.

Then just as a realization of their madness as well as of their sin passes over the crowd, Peter, in the words of an old writer, has the multitude in his net, and like a skilful fisherman he draws it in. They are filled with remorse. What can they do? He opens to them a door of hope. It is true they have killed the Prince of Life, but He could not be holden by death. Though no longer visible among them, His power is still there, and they can see His work. Will they disavow the deed done in ignorance and by the hands of their rulers? Will they repent, and will they await the outpouring of new life which Jesus from the right hand of God is willing to bestow upon them? They must make their decision now. If they will not hear, if they will not receive this Prince of Life whom Moses had foretold, then destruction and death must fall upon them, as upon every soul which refuses to hear His words. This offer marks a great climax in their history. It has been foretold by Samuel and by the prophets which followed after him. They, the children of the Covenant, have this last offer made to them. God has raised up His Son Jesus, and sent Him to bless them in turning every one of them, if they will, from their iniquities.

The Answer to the Miracle

At first it must have seemed as though this marvellous appeal had been made in vain; for immediately a tremendous uproar arose, and all the rulers of the Temple, the priests, the captain of the Temple, and the Sadducees, came down upon the disciples and arrested them. These men had heard all; but they would not be convinced by the forcible representation of the truth which Peter had made, any more than the Jews would be convinced of the Godhead of Jesus by the raising of Lazarus from the dead. If they admitted the truth of Peter's words, their power, their wealth and their ascendancy were gone for ever; they would have to own that they were the murderers of the Son of God, that they had killed the Prince of Life; they would have to stand and cry for pardon, stripped of everything they possessed. One resource alone was left to them.

They could attack the apostles and stop their power of speech if they could not refute their words. Therefore, they laid hands upon them, and put them in hold until the next day, for it was now eventide. But the apostle's words had not been spoken in vain, for a great number had heard and believed; the number of men altogether now being about five thousand.

CHAPTER VIII

ACTS IV. 5-14

THE FIRST CONFLICT BETWEEN THE CHURCH AND THE SANHEDRIN

At the close of the third chapter we had seen the whole multitude in the Temple listening to the words of Peter. They could not deny that the lame man had been healed. They could not deny that Jesus had done like deeds of healing, and that they had crucified Him. Each man, so far as he had rejected Christ and His apostles, was face to face with his own lot and part in the matter; each man had either, by persisting in his iniquity, to number himself among the murderers who refused to hear the prophet and were in danger of destruction, or to repent and to turn from his iniquity. But among those who listened there was a small band of men so preoccupied with their own personal privileges and position that what was said as to the future and as to the spiritual was to them of comparatively little moment.

The Captain of the Temple

These men were the priests, the captain of the Temple, and the Sadducees. The name "captain of the Temple" occurs several times in the Acts, and it is well to understand clearly the distinction between him and the chief captain. The captain, or "ruler of the mountain of the house," as he was sometimes called, was the official chosen by the Jews to maintain guard over the Temple and to preserve its sanctity. The various entrances to the Temple were guarded in three places by priests and in twenty-one by Levites. Jealous watch was kept that neither women nor Gentiles went beyond the bounds prescribed to them. A confirmation of the strictness of this law can be found in an inscription on a stone which was recently discovered and is now in the museum of the Sultan at Constantinople. This stone, which at one time formed part of the Temple, contained an inscription in Greek forbidding Gentiles, under penalty of death, to enter into the sacred precincts. This edict shows that the Hebrews had still the right of life and death over any man who dared to infringe the sanctity of the Temple, and the captain of the guard was held to be responsible for maintaining the sanctity of its precincts and guarding jealously its rights. He was the man to whom Judas went when he sought to betray Jesus. His office and duty were quite distinct from those of the chief captain, who commanded the Roman garrison in the Tower of Antonia, and who took cognizance of any disturbance in the Temple which might threaten the peace of the town, and who therefore at a later period rescued Paul.

The priests and the Sadducees combined with the captain of the Temple against the disciples. They were as deeply concerned as he was in maintaining the ascendancy of the present administration and in opposing any teaching which threatened that ascendancy. Thus, for instance, even in the time of our Lord they had said that they could not let Him alone, for if they did "all men would believe on Him, and the Romans would come and take away both their place and nation."

The Arrest of the Disciples

The sacrifice in the Temple must by this time have been ended, as well as the hour long past for closing the gates, that is to say, four o'clock in the afternoon, so that the authorities were within their rights when they dispersed the crowd which had gathered in Solomon's Porch. They were not, however, so well within their rights when they laid hands on the disciples and imprisoned them in one of the chambers surrounding the Temple. They were determined that the new teaching should not spread any further among the people. But though they could arrest the disciples, they could not stop the effect of their words, and the "number of the men came to be about five thousand" who had "heard the word and believed."

The Trial before the Sanhedrin

The Sanhedrin were accustomed to assemble in a large room or basilica called the Gazith or stone chamber. The Sanhedrin consisted of seventy-one members, of whom twenty-three formed a quorum. It was composed, according to its ancient constitution, of rulers, elders and scribes, the elders being notable heads of families, and the scribes the teachers of the people. On the present occasion there were the two high priests, Annas, who had been appointed by the Jews but deposed by the Romans, and who was still in the eyes of the Jews the lawful high priest, and Caiaphas, who had been appointed high priest after the deposition of Annas.

There seems to have been a full assembly, especially of the kindred of the high priest, who of set purpose had been gathered together. They waited till morning and were, therefore, a more legal assembly than that which had been hastily gathered together but a few weeks or months before to question Jesus as they were now about to question His disciples.

For the second time a Galilean stood before the highest legal assembly of his nation, and for the second time in his person and in that of the High Priest the witness of the kingdom of God was given and rejected; behind the Galilean was the eternal truth of God; behind the High Priest the whole nation of Israel. Caiaphas and Annas, the two High Priests, were present as representatives of the intelligence, will, and heart of the nation; and as at the first trial scene they had rejected the Gospel of Jesus and refused to render their allegiance to Him as King, so now at the second trial they rejected the Gospel of the Holy Ghost and refused Jesus once again in the presence of His servants. After this, a third opportunity would be given to them in the witness of Stephen. If they refused his appeal, the disciples would turn to the Gentiles. This chapter, therefore, marks one of the great crises in the history of the Church and of the Jewish nation. It was one of the three times when, as Peter denied his Master, so the High Priest and rulers denied Him also; but whereas Peter repented and was pardoned, hundreds of years have elapsed, and may even yet elapse, before the Jews will in like manner return to Jesus and seek for pardon.

We can almost see the scene before our eyes—the representatives of the learning and power of Israel, gathered together and seated in a wide semicircle commanding a full view of the prisoners, men well trained in Jewish law, but who could not take a calm or judicial view of the case on account of their bitter animosity and anxiety; at a respectful distance on benches the learners of the law, if, as usual, they were present to watch the proceedings; and the disciples standing in their midst, men unaccustomed to schools of learning, but by their quiet dignity recalling Him Who but a short time before had stood in the same place, charged with the same offence.

The Question Put

The rulers opened the trial with the customary words, and asked by what power or by what name the disciples had done this deed.

According to the law of Moses (Deuteronomy xiii. 1 to 6), the Sanhedrin had power of life and death over a dreamer of dreams or a worker of miracles, if these miracles were wrought to turn men from Jehovah to other gods. The Sanhedrin were well aware of this fact when they asked the disciples in whose name the deed had been done, and hoped thus to entrap them. This helps us to understand the stress which is always laid upon the question of "the Name" throughout Old Testament history.

Moses, when he was called to free the children of Israel, asked by what name God would be known to them. The prophet Isaiah, when he was giving a marvellous prophecy of Jesus, could give it no better than through a name—"Wonderful, Counsellor, the Mighty God, the Everlasting Father, the Prince of Peace." The name included the whole personality, the character, the Divine origin of Him Who was called by it. It was in the Name of Jesus that the lame man walked. It was in that Name, and none other, that Peter was proclaiming salvation among men whereby they might be saved.

The Answer Given

The reply of Peter shows the change which had come upon him through the working of the Holy Spirit. We see some of his former characteristics—his quick insight, his appreciation of the inner meaning and of the bearing of all that is passing around him; but we see more also. He who had formerly been so impulsive is now wise and considerate in all that he says; he who had been so quickly daunted is calm and unmoved before what represented to him the most terrible tribunal in the world. It had been one thing, in the midst of a vast assembly, just after the marvellous gift of Pentecost, or again, just after the healing of the lame man, when all were in sympathy with the miracle, to witness boldly for Jesus; it was another thing, after a night spent in prison, for the man who had prevaricated at the word of a maid-servant, to confront with boldness more than seventy learned, cynical, and bitterly antagonistic men; and not merely to confront them, but to dare to accuse them of a deliberate murder, and that murder the crucifixion of the Son of God.

Jesus had forewarned His disciples that they would be brought before governors and kings for his Name's sake; but He had promised at the same time that it should be given them in that hour what they should speak, and that it would be the Spirit of their Father which should speak in them, and this promise He was now about to fulfil in Peter.

THE ACTS OF THE APOSTLES

The Argument of the Speech

Peter, despite the injustice of his imprisonment, speaks without bitterness or reproach. He addresses the Sanhedrin as the "rulers of the Temple and elders of Israel," and gives them the title of their full official dignity and standing. He then openly declares that the miracle has been done in the Name of Jesus, and that Jesus is the Divinely appointed Messiah and the power of God.

He then at once deals with the question of the Name, and declares that the miracle has been done in the Name of Jesus, and that this Jesus is not an alien God; He is the Divinely appointed Messiah whom they have crucified, but who has been raised from the dead and who is the living power of God. He then proceeds to read the title of their condemnation by placing before them, as it were, on the one side, the good deed which God has wrought by him; on the other, the evil which they have committed. He then, in clear-cut words from the text of the lame man and of the Scriptures, makes an offer of full and free salvation in the Name of Jesus. He points from the lame man, standing whole and upright in their midst, to Jesus, by Whose power he has been healed, but Whom they in their madness have crucified. He points, as David did, from the stone rejected by the builders which alone could have united the great foundation walls of the Temple to Jesus, Who can, and will, unite the wall of Jew and Gentile into one, and then boldly proclaims that the Name which they have rejected is the one power of God unto salvation. "There is none other Name," personality, or Divinity "under Heaven given among men whereby they must be saved."

The Effect of the Speech

If the multitude had been astonished at the appeal which Peter had made on the preceding day, the Sanhedrin were even more astonished at his present words. They marvelled at the boldness of Peter and John. How could men in peril of their lives dare to turn upon their judges and accuse them not only of being the murderers of their Messiah, but also of having destroyed Him Who would have been the life and joy of the nation? Further, how was it that they who were unlearned—that is to say, who had never been taught in the Rabbinical schools—were able thus to quote the Scriptures and to reveal thoughts contained in them which were hidden from the greatest scribe in the assembly? How was it they who were ignorant (Greek "idiots")—that is to say, private individuals having no official connection with the Temple—were thus able to discern and to speak of the things of God? "They took knowledge of them that they had been with Jesus." This does not mean that they had not from the first recognized Peter and John, and known who and what they were. They must have done so, for John was well known to the High Priest and was one of his kinsmen. What it does mean is that they took knowledge of them that they had walked with Jesus and learned of Him, that He had taught them to look upon the law from the same spiritual point of view from which He had interpreted it Himself, that He had inspired them to look upon their fellow-men with the same feelings of compassion and mercy with which He had gone about amongst them doing good. They took knowledge also that the same spirit of courage and of quiet dignity rested upon them in measure which in its fulness had rested upon Christ. They felt the power of God in their midst. We do not wonder that they were speechless. Like the soldiers who were sent to arrest Jesus, but "who went backward and fell to the ground," they could do nothing but hold their peace, and by their very silence they condemned themselves.

CHAPTER IX

ACTS IV. 15 TO 31

THE INTERDICT AND ITS OUTCOME

The Effect of St. Peter's Address upon the Sadducees

Bidding the disciples go aside out of their presence, the Sanhedrin held a council of war as to what could be done to silence Peter. They knew, none better, that if a report of this miracle were spread abroad men would realize that Jesus had risen from the dead and that His Spirit and power were once more working in their midst. The Sadducees were even more vitally affected than the Pharisees, for they had rejected the doctrine of the resurrection and interpreted the Old Testament in a manner highly satisfactory to themselves. They admitted the high ideals which were contained in the law, as they would at times acquiesce in the high ideals put before them by Jesus; but, whilst admitting and admiring them, they did not strenuously strive after them, nor require others to do so either. Their acquiescence in some of the teaching of the Old Testament was sufficient to dull their consciences and to quiet any uneasy feeling either as to the present or the hereafter; but it left them free to follow that for which they yearned—the pursuit of pleasure and of earthly advantage. Like the lotus-eaters, they only wanted to be left alone. But Peter's speech, like a trumpet-call, aroused them from their sleep, and, whether they would or no, must inevitably arouse others also. It was dangerous, therefore, to take active measures against the disciples, for men had seen the miracle and knew that God had witnessed to their words. All that they could do was to endeavour that it might spread no further; and, therefore, summoning the disciples into their presence, they commanded them not to speak at all nor to teach in the Name of Jesus.

This injunction was really of more moment than at first sight it appears to be; it was no mere threat which the disciples could disregard if they were brave enough to do so. From this time forward, if they dared to preach or to teach in the Name of Jesus, they put themselves in peril of the law. If they gathered together for prayer, for preaching, or for the instruction of the new converts, it would henceforth be contrary to the will of the Sanhedrin, and would be opposed by them. But it meant to the disciples even more than this. The followers of Jesus and the members of the new Church were members also of the whole Jewish Church. They attended the Temple and they worshipped in it. There had been no shock as yet to the religious beliefs and traditions which they had inherited from their fathers, and we know in the case of the Jews how very strong those beliefs and traditions were. It was not till Stephen and Paul conceived the true bearing and far-reaching character of the teaching of Jesus that men learnt that the old types and ceremonies had been fulfilled in Jesus and were ready to vanish away. At the present moment all they knew was that their teaching was declared to be illegal and that they must choose between the authority of the Sanhedrin and that of Jesus. The whole matter came so suddenly upon Peter and John that it was little wonder if they could not see at a glance the other and the greater side of the question. It was true that a separation must thenceforward exist between them and the adherents of the Temple, but it was in reality the Sanhedrin, which by its own act was separating itself from all that constituted the essence of the teaching of the Temple, and not the disciples, who were being separated. The disciples would carry with them the true spirit of the Old Testament. They would take with them the great lessons as to God and man which it had taught, whilst they left the outside forms, the rites and the ceremonies, the empty husks, as it were, to the Temple and to its worshippers.

The Reply of the Apostles

What answer would Peter and John make? The same which the servants of God ever have made and must make whenever the command of man comes into conflict with the express will of God. Whether the Sanhedrin chose to think that their commands ought to transcend the command of God or not (and here the disciples touched the live issue, not only between themselves and the Sanhedrin, but between all true religion and false), there was only one thing which they could do. They had been anointed with the Holy Ghost; they had received the cloven tongue distributed and set on fire: they could not but use that God-given power, they could not but speak the things which they had heard and seen.

The Action of the Church

As Peter and John spoke, the ring of fearlessness in their words and absolute loyalty to an Unseen Presence recalled only too vividly to the rulers the tone and Spirit of Jesus, and convinced them of the hopelessness of their task, even if they had refused to be swayed by the presence of the man who had been healed standing in the midst, and the shouts and acclamations which reached them from the multitude outside. They decided to threaten the disciples still further and let them go, thus yielding for the moment to the temporal danger, although resisting the greater spiritual danger which overhung them. They refused to realize that they were adding to their first rejection of the life of Jesus a further rejection of the witness of His death and resurrection, and were thus placing the Jewish nation and the new faith in direct opposition to one another.

Peter and John hastened back to their own company and reported all that the chief priests and elders had done. The tidings which they carried were of great import. On the one hand they had to tell the converts that they had been rejected by the Jewish Church, that they were forbidden to preach and to teach, and open to the attack of the law: on the other hand, they had to tell of the power of God which had shielded them from the hands of their oppressors. There was not one of the company gathered together but must have realized the peril of his position, and the character of the response made in the face of that peril is all the more striking in consequence. With one consent, with one common voice, they cried aloud to Him Who was their refuge and strength, and made their appeal to Him.

The Prayer of the Church

This prayer has been called a song of thanksgiving; but it might also be called a song of assurance, for there is not a word of doubt or of fear in it; on the contrary, it is an outpouring of faith and thanksgiving. How wonderful this seems when we remember that but a few months ago there was only one man of all the company of Jesus who had perceived His Divinity and by a sudden flash of inspiration had acknowledged it! Now the whole body of believers is carried away by an absolute assurance of that Divinity. The first breath of persecution has fanned the fire of the Church into one glowing flame of enthusiasm and faith. "Lord, Thou art God; which hast made heaven and earth and the sea, and all that in them is." They are in no wise terrified by their adversaries. In the light of Scripture they see that what has passed is nothing but the fulfilment of prophecy; they see more clearly than before that the conflict between Jesus and those who crucified Him was a conflict between the powers of good and of evil. The representatives of the Jews and of the Gentiles of the whole world had stood up, had gathered themselves together, and had triumphed over Jesus, although as they did so they did not know that they had but fulfilled the long-foretold and predetermined counsel of God. They recognize that the power which is working against them is the power which opposed Jesus; that the conflict is still the conflict between the host of evil, under the command of the prince of this world, and the armies of the living God. They know that the ultimate victory is assured, despite the darkness of the coming persecution, for it is in the hands of God and is working out His predetermined counsel, and therefore they pray that He will look upon them so that in the light of His countenance they may prevail. They pray also that they may continue to witness, that they may speak the word with boldness, and that whilst they are speaking the visible presence of God may be manifest to them and to all around them, and that miracles akin to that of the healing of the lame man may accompany and confirm their words.

Whilst we marvel at the faith and courage of the disciples, we cannot help wondering why, since they had been told that whatsoever they asked in prayer, believing, they would receive, they did not pray that this cup of persecution might pass away from them altogether. The answer is that the disciples had learnt from Christ to look beyond themselves to the great hereafter, to seek the working out of the kingdom of God and its righteousness rather than their own personal salvation either from peril or from pain. They were content, as it were, to leave the pattern in the hand of the Great Master Weaver, asking only that they might do His will.

The Answer from On High

Their prayer was granted almost as soon as it was uttered. "The place was shaken where they were assembled together" by an earthquake, similar to that which had accompanied the giving of the law upon Mount Sinai, and the still small voice which spoke to Elijah, but which had not accompanied the outpouring of the Spirit at Pentecost. In this hour of trial, as a further proof of the presence of God amongst His servants, the earth, as it were, trembled at the more immediate presence of God, and the Holy Spirit fell in great abundance upon all who were gathered together, so that they were enabled to speak the word of God with boldness. The second Pentecost, like the first, was the outpouring of the spirit of love, self-sacrifice, and zeal. All that believed "were of one heart and of one soul, neither said any that ought of the things which he possessed was his own; but they had all things in common." How could Jerusalem prevail against the witness of lives so full of power and self-sacrifice, against men filled with such a realization of the majesty of the kingdom of God and its righteousness? What can the world of to-day do in the face of men filled with the Holy Ghost? How does Christianity prevail? How has it ever prevailed? "Not by might, nor by power, but by My Spirit, saith the Lord."

CHAPTER X

ACTS IV. 32 TO END

THE GENEROSITY OF BARNABAS

The Question of Socialism

The Sanhedrin had cast out the disciples and laid an interdict upon them, but God heard their prayer and bestowed His Holy Spirit in more abundant measure upon them. The rulers had attempted in vain to stop the witness of their words, but they could not stop the witness of their lives. The common danger, the common expectation of the return of their Master, united them in a bond of self-sacrifice and love. There was a foretaste of the Millennium, a beauty of holiness which afforded an ideal not only to all who came in contact with them but to the men of succeeding ages also. From time to time men have asked themselves whether such a spirit ought not once again to prevail, whether such an ideal should not be binding upon the Church of to-day, and, if so, whether Socialism does not embody this ideal and show forth in special manner the will and the mind of Christ.

These questions are hard to answer, and yet they are among the most living problems of to-day. The Puritan Movement emphasized the individual responsibility of the soul and the independence of thought and judgment, and this sense of individuality was still further emphasized by the Evangelical Movement of the last century. This Movement was very powerful, but it was succeeded by others which changed the trend of thought and action into an opposite direction. Men began to hesitate about undertaking individual responsibility, and sought rather union with corporate bodies and organizations, a movement which is still working and has not as yet reached its ultimate development. Whether that development will find its final outcome in Socialism or no, and how far, if so, such an outcome is its right and best development, is one of the great questions of to-day.

As we read this fourth chapter of Acts we wonder how far it bears upon this point, how far the power of living in unity which was shown by the early Christians was, like the gift of tongues, a special grace to meet a special need, or an example to be followed by later generations of the Church in actual form and deed.

How Far Is the Example of the Early Church Beneficial or Binding upon the Christians of To-day?

The more carefully we examine the passage, the more we see that the special need of the disciples at this time was twofold: (1) Power to speak and to give a reason of the faith that was in them; (2) a spirit of self-sacrifice which would let their light so shine before men that they would see their good works and glorify their Father which was in heaven. These two needs were met by the gift of tongues, and the gift of a love so great that it led to a community of goods and provided means not only for those who needed instruction but also for those who were to a certain extent outlawed by the State. It was the result of a drawing together of men, united by a common danger and by the hourly expectation of the return of their Lord. As such it was an ideal possible in a comparatively small community, but impossible to the world at large—a temporary measure which met a temporary need, but was afterwards abandoned by the disciples, and was not recommended by them in any of their letters to the Church.

The Later Attitude of the Disciples towards Their Goods

We find that the community of goods was not practised after the persecution of Stephen and the dispersion of the Church. As the number of converts grew, it opened the door to difficulties like that of Ananias and Sapphira; and in its later outcome did not foster a healthy independence and desire for work. Probably it was difficult and irksome to those who had been withdrawn from daily labour to take it up again. There is a strain of intense laziness as well as of selfishness in every one of us, and the mixed multitude who ever follow and hamper a great movement would probably take advantage of the opportunity to indulge in emotionalism rather than in work. Thus we find that the Church at Jerusalem became poor, and had to be supported by other Christian Churches, who sent alms to them once and again according as they had need—a condition which seems strange to us, since the Church at Jerusalem embraced men of wealth and standing, like Joseph and Nicodemus. St. Paul, therefore, does not speak of a community of goods, but he does bid the Romans distribute to the necessity of the saints, and be given to hospitality. He extols among the Corinthians the bestowal of goods to feed the poor as one of the great Christian graces; he bids the Ephesians labour, so that they may have to give to him that needeth.

The summary of the whole matter seems to be that after the outpouring of the second Pentecost there is a glimpse of the hereafter rather than an example for to-day. For the present moment, as faithful stewards, we may not cast off the responsibility of the right disposition of our earthly goods, despite our desire to smooth away the inequalities of life and to give felicity to all. Our duty is to place our souls in the right relationship towards God, so that we may learn from Him the true disposition not only of our lives, but also of all that He has entrusted to us, so that we may one day give account with joy, and render in its fulness that which He has entrusted to us.

THE GENEROSITY OF BARNABAS

"A Good Man and Full of the Holy Ghost"

After the second Pentecost believers were added to the Church, multitudes both of men and women, and all alike were distinguished by the same spirit of love and generosity. They were also distinguished by the goodwill which they had to one another and by their spirit of generosity to the Church. Two names are mentioned as having been especially remarkable—Joses surnamed Barnabas, and Ananias. Joses—or, as he is more generally called, Barnabas—seems to have been a man of marked personality, character, and position. He was a Levite, of the country of Cyprus, and had probably acquired great wealth; for the land of Cyprus was very valuable at this time, not only on account of the fruit which was grown there, but also because of the copper mines which were found in great abundance.

Tradition says that he was a man of striking appearance, and this is probably true; for we find that when he and Paul came to Lystra, Paul, on account of his oratorical power, was named Mercurius, and Barnabas, probably because of his personal appearance, Jupiter. "He was a good man, and full of the Holy Ghost," or, as the Collect for St. Barnabas's Day says, "endued with singular gifts of the Holy Ghost." He exerted great influence over the Church, partly by his power, partly by the charm of his personal character. He was "the son of Consolation or Exhortation," the one to whom all turned, for, like his Master, he had compassion upon all, and gave of his strength and sympathy to as many as had need.

They Shall Have No Inheritance

The coming of Barnabas and the surrender of his possessions to the Church was specially recorded by St. Luke, partly because of the interest naturally attached to a man of his character and influence, partly because of the contrast which his action afforded to that of Ananias. Some have thought that Barnabas had no right either to possess land or to dispose of it, because the Levites (see Numbers xviii. 20-23) were to have no part or inheritance among the Children of Israel; but we find from Jeremiah xxxii. that this law had for a long time been disregarded by the Levites, and further, there is no record that Barnabas either possessed or sold land in Israel. He was of the country of Cyprus, and it is more than probable that the land he sold was the property which he had acquired during his sojourn in the island of Cyprus.

The Influence of the Hellenists upon the Church

The gift was remarkable because it showed how generously the Jews who came from the distant colonies were disposed towards the Christians at Jerusalem. The whole question of the Hellenists (that is to say, Jews of

THE GENEROSITY OF BARNABAS

the Dispersion who spoke the Greek language), and of the part which they played in the history of the early Church, is of especial interest. There seems to have been a large body of these men amongst the Christians at Jerusalem, some of whom had received Jewish training and were learned in the Law. Thus, according to tradition, Barnabas and Saul had both been brought up at the feet of Gamaliel. These men added to this early training a width of thought and experience which they had gained from travel and from their contact with the Greeks, so that they rapidly became leaders in the Church. Barnabas, Stephen, and Philip were all Hellenists, and played a very important part, not only in the spread of the Gospel, but in the conception of the true ideal of Christianity.

They had travelled farther than the Jews of Jerusalem; they had met, and had had to deal with men of all characters and classes. They understood Greek thought, literature, and learning, and, from their broader outlook, were better able, under the inspiration of the Holy Spirit, to distinguish the things which were temporal and the things which were eternal in the Jewish religion; that is to say, between the doctrines which were essential to the spirit of the new Christianity and those forms and ceremonies which were essentially Jewish and therefore of the day.

The character of Barnabas is shown even in this first mention of him by his manner of giving. His heart had been touched by the common need and by the common danger, and he placed all his wealth at the feet of the Apostles, thus showing that he gave it in trust to them and signifying his entire allegiance and submission to them.

CHAPTER XI

ACTS V. 1-11

ANANIAS AND SAPPHIRA

The Character of Ananias

A great and good man almost invariably calls forth a mean and shallow imitator. A strong and magnanimous Barnabas is almost invariably followed by a covetous and hypocritical Ananias. The two men stand side by side upon the painter's canvas, and the beauty of the character of the one accentuates the deformity of the character of the other. There are other contrasts brought before us at the same time—the joyful harmony of the Church as it greets the surrender of Barnabas, and the sorrow and death caused by the entrance into the Church of the first public sin. In still further contrast we can see the working of the Spirit of God in Barnabas and that of the Spirit of Mammon in Ananias. Sin like a withering blast passes across the glory of a summer day and destroys the peace and beauty of a second Eden. The very thought and presence of sin at such a time seems as uncalled for as that of Adam and Eve in the Garden of Eden, or Achan after the overthrow of Jericho; it is committed in the sight of God at the moment when His hand is pouring out rich treasures of His love.

The story is only too easily understood. "The root thereof is in ourselves"; its counterpart is in every Church and in all ages. Ananias could see the magnanimity of the action of Barnabas and the enthusiasm of joy which it elicited. He had apparently been attracted by the spirit of Christianity and wished to partake of the benefits of the kingdom of righteousness; but he was also keenly alive to his own personal gain. He wished to stand well with the Church and to do as others were doing—the publicity of the gift compensating for the sacrifice—an element too apt to enter at any time into religious work. Stimulated possibly by the example of Barnabas, he sold his land; but when once the money was in his hand, neither he nor his wife could bear the thought of parting with it, although at the same time they were determined to gain the love and approbation of the Church. He was under no compulsion to sell the land, nor to give the whole price when it was sold; but he was under compulsion to seek credit only for that which he deserved. His fault lay in his avarice and hypocrisy.

The Sin of Ananias

The disciples seem to have been assembled together at their daily gathering for prayer and meditation when Ananias entered, and, standing forth as Barnabas had done a few days before, laid the price of the land which he had sold at the apostles' feet. It was probably the custom for all who took part in this community of goods to surrender everything they possessed as a token of love and consecration to the service of God. It was at this moment, when a general murmur of good-will and thankfulness to God might have arisen from the assembly, that Peter spoke, and each word as he uttered it fell like a blow upon the man before him. Ananias had come in flushed with the hope and desire of applause, but his attitude quickly changed from expectant self-satisfaction to terror at the detection of his sin. The words of Peter are clear and straightforward. Satan has entered into the heart of Ananias, as he entered into the garden of Eden and into the heart of Judas, and Ananias has suffered him to be there and has yielded to his temptation; he has striven to deceive God Himself. There is no excuse for his sin; he was under no compulsion from outside, no temptation save from his own evil passions, and those passions had carried him farther than even he was aware of. He had opened his heart, and Satan had filled it. He had lied not unto man but unto God.

Men are apt nowadays to mock at the thought of Satan and make light of his personality and power, and they forget that that very mockery and affectation of indifference by casting them off their guard exposes them all the more to his malice and power.

The Death of Ananias—

The effect upon Ananias was instantaneous. He knew that Peter had spoken through the power of the Holy Ghost, that he had read his heart as Christ had read the hearts of all who stood before Him. Each word spoken revealed to Ananias his conduct in its true character. He saw that he had gone red-handed, as it were, into the very presence of God and striven with a lie to deceive even God Himself. Stricken down by the power of God, or overcome by the shock at the discovery of his sin, he fell down and gave up the ghost, whilst the multitude around watched and waited in awe-struck silence. It was the first judgment that had fallen upon the Christians. God had shielded them from the rulers and from their enemies without; but He had not shielded them from this blow, because it was the outcome of sin within. In silence Ananias fell and died, and in silence men waited whilst the young men arose, wound up the body, and carried it out—a first and sad funeral procession, and one very full of warning to the Church.

—and of Sapphira

Three hours had passed, and during this time no one seems to have left the assembly, but waited in prayer and supplication, not knowing the extent of the sin or how far the example might have spread. At last Sapphira

ANANIAS AND SAPPHIRA

came into the midst, and as she came she looked with wonder and astonishment around her. She had been privy to the deception which her husband had practised, and she had probably passed the time of his absence in eager anticipation of his return and in anxiety to hear of the success of his mission, and of the estimation in which from that time forward they would be held by the Church. At the last, when Ananias did not return, and she could wait no longer, she came; but found instead of the joyful reception which she anticipated the eyes of all turned upon her, and the money still lying at the feet of Peter. In answer to her mute inquiry Peter spoke, and in mercy, in order to give her an opportunity of escape, asked her a direct question, one which admitted of no circumlocution in its answer: "Tell me whether ye sold the land for so much?" At the fatal words: "Yea, for so much," the judgment of God fell. No question of sex could avert the blow. If women were to be admitted to the full fellowship and communion of the Church they must take their full share of responsibility, and must conform in all respects to its high spiritual standard. It was not Peter who had slain her husband, neither was it his lip that gave the sentence against her; he did but proclaim her doom and prophesied that she, like her husband, had sinned against the spiritual life of the Church and, therefore, must atone for her sin by the loss of physical life also.

Ananias and Sapphira had both enrolled themselves as servants of God, and, according to the ideal afterwards put forward by the disciples, were united together for mutual society, help, and comfort—Ananias to love his wife as Christ loved the Church, guiding her and protecting her from sin; Sapphira to love her husband and, if he were unbelieving, so to walk that he might be won by the conversation of his wife. What a constrast does this Christian ideal form to the fact contained in the words "his wife also being privy to it"!

The Acted Lie

Why should an acted lie have been punished so severely? Why did it involve the penalty of instantaneous death? We must remember there is no difference between a spoken and an acted lie; both alike spring from the same root, and the very fact that the half lie or the acted lie hopes to deceive, and at the same time to evade the responsibility and punishment of deceit, makes it almost more hateful than the open lie, which knows and dares to take the temporal and spiritual punishment which is its own.

The second question that arises is why Sapphira was as guilty as her husband, and deserved as hard a judgment. Was it not her business to support her husband and to stand by him? And even if she had wished to do so she could not have told the truth without running the risk of condemning him. This question touches the problem which causes so much perplexity and difficulty in all families, schools, and communities. A boy who speaks the truth, and by doing so exposes his comrade, is very apt to think that he has acted meanly, and to be shunned by his companions as a coward and a traitor, and yet in all probability he is very far from being either the one or the other. Thus Joseph had to bear the hatred of his brethren because he was faithful to his duty when he was placed in authority over them. We have to remember there are certain great primal laws which must take precedence of other obligations, and which must be obeyed, no matter what difficulty ensues from doing so. Truth is the first of these great primal laws. If we belong to the God of truth, if we are ourselves children of truth, then truth must be the distinguishing characteristic not only of our speech but also of our actions, and no desire to shield a companion or to screen his fault can interfere with this first duty. Furthermore, we have to remember that we must do whatever will be for the ultimate good not only of those immediately around us, but also of the society in which we live. A deception successfully carried out cannot be for the ultimate good of anyone who is party to it, nor for the good of the whole community. Therefore Sapphira, however painful her position, had to make her choice, had to obey the law of her God rather than the law of her husband. Had she been faithful in the first instance, had she refused to be privy to the deceit, the second and more terrible position would never have come; had she then made straight paths for her feet she had not been turned out of the way.

The Need of Discipline

A third question arises as to why the sin of Ananias and Sapphira was so severely dealt with. To understand this we have to remember that great opportunity brings great responsibility. The Spirit of God had been shed in very full measure upon the Church, opening the hearts of men to love and truth, and inclining them in more than ordinary measure to deeds of love and self-sacrifice. Therefore a transgression, a sin against the power of the Holy Ghost, was a very heinous offence. In the second place, there was the question of the discipline of the whole Church. Just as the sin of Achan was punished in a very signal manner, in order that the Israelites, who were about to take possession of the land of Canaan, might be warned of the necessity of their absolute obedience to Him Who was their Leader and their God, so the Church had to be warned that the God in Whose service they were rejoicing was a God not only of love, but also of holiness and of judgment.

In Old Testament times the thought of God as a God of judgment Who required truth in the inward parts had been very present before the Children of Israel; after the coming of Jesus, and after His death and Resurrection, the thought of God as a God of love was the more present. Hence the necessity that the one should not be lost sight of in the other, that even the thought of the holiness of God should not be forgotten in the overpowering sense of His love, and that men should remember that much was required of them, even truth in their inward parts.

CHAPTER XII

ACTS V. 12-32

THE GIFT OF HEALING

"The Blessing of the Lord, It Maketh Rich"

In Old Testament times whenever sin was put away it was followed by a time of refreshment and a renewal of the sense of the Divine Presence; and the same is true in New Testament history.

Some first shadows had fallen upon the disciples when they had been forbidden to speak in the Name of Jesus and judgment had fallen from God upon two of the members, but the passing of these shadows left a sunshine and joy more visible than before, more marvellous communion and self-sacrifice, greater gifts of healing, and even the very presence of the Lord in the person of His angel rescuing them from prison.

The Gift of Healing

The apostles refused to obey the interdict which had been laid upon them, but went up to the Temple and stood in Solomon's porch. The Spirit of God rested upon them more manifestly than before—so manifestly that they seemed to be separated even from the rest of the disciples. A holy awe surrounded them; no man durst join himself to them; so that, far from being under a cloud either in their own eyes or in those of the populace, we read that "the people magnified them." Men strove eagerly to approach them, or, if that were impossible, at the least to place themselves where the shadow of Peter passing by might overshadow some of them.

This marvellous power of healing which was displayed by Peter and the apostles has been, like the question of Socialism, much discussed of late years. Men ask whether this gift of healing, like the gift of tongues, was a peculiar manifestation of the Holy Spirit, which was given for a time in order to attest the truth of the words spoken, or whether it was a grace which still accompanies, or might accompany, the presence of the Holy Spirit in the heart of the believer. They ask, further, if the latter case be true, why we have not to-day the same gifts of the Holy Spirit among us; why we do not seek a fuller communion with God, a more lively faith so that once again the power of speaking with divers tongues and the power of healing might be ours also.

The Gift and the Early Church

In order to answer this question it is well to see clearly how the gift of healing was granted not only in the Old, but also in the New Testament, and from this

THE GIFT OF HEALING

gain light upon the position of to-day. We know that in old time men of God spake as they were moved by the Holy Ghost, and that they did deeds of power also according as they were moved by the same Spirit. When Jesus was upon earth He passed up and down among men who were all alike suffering from the curse of sin and of death, that curse being manifested both in their bodies and in their souls, and that as He drew near to them He drew near with the fulness of God, for "in Him dwelt all the fulness of the Godhead bodily." When His perfect nature came into contact with their imperfect nature He dispelled the curse of sickness either of body or of soul according as He willed.

What Jesus did Himself, He commanded His disciples to do also (St. Luke x. 9). He sent them forth to heal the sick, and, as they healed, to say, "The Kingdom of God is come nigh unto you." When His presence was about to be withdrawn, He continued to lay the same charge upon them— "Go ye into all the world and preach the Gospel to every creature"—also He promised that those who believed in Him should have power to lay hands on the sick and they should recover (Mark xvi. 18). This promise was fulfilled, and the gift of the Holy Spirit was accompanied by marvellous gifts of healing. After the Pentecost the disciples continued the same work of healing through the power of the Godhead—that is to say, through the gift of the Holy Spirit which was still manifested in them. They found that they could help the sick not only by the touch of their hand, but that they could transmit their power of healing through inanimate means also (Acts xix. 12).

Thus they had a power of transmission which had been denied even to an Elisha (2 Kings iv. 29 and 32). Further, St. James in writing his Epistle bade the elders of the Church "pray over the sick and anoint him with oil" in the Name of the Lord and promised "that the prayer of faith" should save him and the Lord would raise him up.

The Question of Faith-Healing

Without entering into what might be called the superstitious approach to this question which is found in the Roman Catholic Church, or to the deification of the human intellect and will-power which is found among the Christian Scientists, we must stop to consider the question of faith-healing as it is generally found amongst us, because it is one of the vital questions of to-day. There are Christians who hold that Christ bore the curse of the body as well as the curse of the soul upon the Cross, and that therefore the faith which avails for the healing of the soul should avail for the healing of the body also. They say further that the example of Christ and of the early Church, together with the injunction of St. James, confirms this belief, and that when we take all this evidence into consideration we are face to face with the fact that it is our unbelief, and our unbelief alone, which holds back this gift of healing from us to-day.

THE GIFT OF HEALING

The Practice of the Early Church in Regard to Faith-Healing

On the other hand, we find that the gift of healing did not necessarily accompany a full measure of the Holy Ghost; but that it was rather a gift which was bestowed when and as God willed. Thus St. Paul says: Are all workers of miracles? Have all the gift of healing? Do all speak with tongues? Do all interpret? Implying apparently that these miraculous manifestations were occasionally given, and that believers received sometimes the one and sometimes the other. In the second place, we find that the disciples used the gift not as men wish to use it to-day, purely in order to aid the sufferer, but rather as a sign to those who did not as yet know God, and in order definitely to attest His presence and manifest His power. Had the apostles, because of their faith, been able to remove sickness and death from one another as they willed, then the curse given in Eden would have been removed, and man would according to his faith have had power to reverse the general ordering of providence. We notice that greater power in respect of healing was given to St. Paul and to St. Peter than to any of the other disciples. If these two men had been moved by love only or by pity, why did not St. Paul heal Epaphroditus?—for there was no question that he longed for his recovery (Philippians ii. 27). Why did he leave Trophimus at Miletus sick? (2 Timothy iv. 20.) Why did he not cure Timothy of his weakness? Why did not God hear his prayer and remove the thorn in his own flesh?

The Absence of Reference in the Letters of St. Paul

It is a remarkable fact that, except in the general Epistle of St. James, none of the letters to the early Church give any recommendation or advice upon this subject. St. Paul did not counsel the men to whom he was writing to seek faith from God so that they might speak with tongues and heal, although he referred to gifts of healing when writing to the Corinthians. Even when he wrote his last letter to Timothy—a letter filled with yearning desire that he might have power to witness effectually when Paul was no longer with him—nothing was said by him upon this particular point.

Is This Gift Still Present in the Church?

We cannot say what the ordering of God is in the world, or whether this gift or any gift of God is withdrawn from us or not. We hear of miraculous answers to prayer on every side. We see in the darkest places of the earth—as for instance, in the case of missionaries such as Pastor Hsi in China—that God still accompanies His word with signs. We know that the Lord's arm is not shortened, that the prayer of faith is heard, and that we are justified in pouring out our hearts before Him, in believing that He is touched to-day with a feeling of our infirmities, just as when He was upon earth; but since the law of general effort prevails in the spiritual world as well as in the temporal world, and since it is in obedience to that law that the Christian finds his safest ground, he approaches God by means of appointed channels as well as by faith; he finds Him in prayer and in the study of His Word. In like manner, in obedience to the same law of appointed means and of effort, he does all the work which God gives him to do. Thus, for instance, if that work should be the learning of languages or the healing of the sick he does it in dependence upon God, he accompanies his work by prayer, and he leaves all that he does in the hand of his Master for His blessing to rest upon it according to His will. At the same time he has confidence that he may pour out his heart before Him, that he may wrestle in prayer, like Jacob at Penuel, and seek for a full abundance of blessing.

The Action of the Sadducees

It was at the time of the most marvellous manifestation of the gift of healing that the Sadducees were aroused to active measures against the disciples. They saw that it was impossible that such a state of things could continue. Either the religion of Jesus must conquer throughout Jerusalem or it must be conquered, and therefore they arose filled with indignation, and laid their hands upon the Apostles and put them in the common prison. It was comparatively easy to arrest them; it was not so easy to determine how to deal with them after they were arrested. They sent messengers to arrest them in the morning, before the multitude was gathered together in the Temple, and put them in prison until they could summon them before the judgment seat, and then silence them, if possible, for ever.

The Angel of the Lord

But while "the kings of the earth set themselves, and the rulers take counsel together, He that dwelleth in heaven shall laugh them to scorn, the Lord shall have them in derision" (Psalms ii. 2, 4). Suddenly, in the darkness of the night, a light shone in the prison. The angel of the Lord opened the doors and bade them go and stand in the Temple and there speak "all the words of this life." They might take back not one word of the truth which they had been proclaiming, those words which had been a stumbling-block to the Sadducees, but life to the multitude. With mingled awe and joy the disciples left the suddenly-illuminated prison and went forth into the early-morning light, rejoicing that their royal commission had been given back into their hands again and by a royal messenger from the King Himself. How gladly they went to the Temple! How fervently they witnessed to the words of life!

The Overshadowing of the Hosts of God

Throughout the Old and New Testament we find mention again and again of the presence of the unseen hosts of heaven and of the protection afforded to the children of men. Thus the angel of the Lord appeared in visible form to servants of God such as Abraham, Jacob, Moses, and Joshua; the hosts of the Lord appeared to the servants of Elisha, and proclaimed to the shepherds the news of Christ's birth; so in the New Testament the angel of the Lord appeared to Zacharias, Philip, and Peter. If Satan entered into the heart of an Ananias and a Sapphira, the angel of the Lord opened the door for a Peter, and filled his heart with joy and gladness. But as we think over this question of the angel host we ask why their presence was not still oftener manifested, why it did not more consciously intervene on behalf of God's servants? Why, for instance, if God's ministering angels surrounded his servants at all times, did they not deliver them from pain and death? Why did not the angel of the Lord rescue the apostles before they were beaten? This question touches the whole problem of pain and suffering, and cannot be fully entered into here; it is sufficient for the present purpose to remember that God's servants, wherever they are and whatever they are doing, whether they are angels or men, must seek first and seek last whatever will tend to the Kingdom of God and its righteousness, and cannot hinder or change the general ordering of the Providence of God. If it is the will of God that the prison door shall be opened, Peter is freed; but if the persecution of the apostles will lead to the furtherance of His Kingdom, then the angel of the Lord will support those who suffer, although He will not interfere to hinder those who are persecuting them. In the midst of their suffering, they know that "in all their affliction He is afflicted, and that the angel of His presence saves them."

CHAPTER XIII

ACTS V. 32 TO END

THE RESPONSIBILITY OF LEADERSHIP

The Gathering of the Council and the Senate

When the morning came an assembly of the Council and of the Senate of the children of Israel was called, and met not in all probability in the Temple or its precincts, but in the meeting-place in the town. The rulers probably thought it safer to hold their court at a distance from the Temple, lest the multitude which would be gathered together there in anxiety awaiting the disciples should descend upon the Senate and attempt to rescue them. We can almost see the Sanhedrin as they gathered together—men of weight, learning, and standing in Israel, but bearing in their faces the mark of deep-set prejudice and of a fanaticism which would lead them to die sooner than relinquish either their own tenure of office or the creed upon which in their estimation not only that tenure, but even the very existence of the nation, seemed to depend. In anxious suspense

THE RESPONSIBILITY OF LEADERSHIP

and muttered consultation they awaited the return of the officers who had been sent to fetch the apostles from prison. What was their astonishment when they heard that the prison doors had been found shut with all safety, and the keepers standing without, but no man within! The rulers immediately recognized the presence of supernatural power; for instead of sending for the keepers of the prison and questioning them, as Herod did in a similar position, it is said "they doubted what this may mean," they questioned "whereunto this would grow." To this consciousness that they were engaged in a struggle with a power beyond their own was added also the desire to keep everything quiet in the town. In the height of their perplexity and astonishment a messenger came hastily into their presence and brought the astounding news that the men whom they had put in prison were standing in the Temple and teaching the people. Who could daunt or intimidate men so utterly devoid of fear? It was certain that no threat or power of the Sanhedrin, nothing short of death, would prevail against them.

The Arrest of the Apostles

The Sanhedrin determined hastily to arrest them again at all costs, and the captain and his officers were despatched to fetch them, but without violence, for it would have been very dangerous at the time to create a public riot in Jerusalem. Such a riot would have brought about not only the intervention of the multitude, but also that of the Roman Government; and if the Roman

Government were to intervene, and, swayed by the general temper of the multitude, were to give protection to the disciples instead of punishing them, all chance of repressing the new faith would be gone for ever.

We are tempted to wonder why Peter and the apostles a second time so quietly obeyed the captain of the Temple and the officers; but the lesson which Jesus had given Peter in the Garden of Gethsemane, when he bade him put up his sword in its sheath, must have been still present with him, for they made no resistance, but followed the officers into the midst of the Council. As they came in their accusers must have looked upon them with mingled fear and hatred. It was a strange scene. On one side, in sullen doggedness and despair, the representatives of what ought to have been the highest intellectual and religious aristocracy in Israel, on the other side the two Galileans, calm and unmoved, conscious of the presence of their Master and of little else around them.

The Exhortation of the High Priest

The High Priest charged them, in the first place, with disobedience; in the second place, with the spreading of their doctrines throughout Jerusalem; in the third place, and here the real charge appears, with bringing the blood of Jesus upon the men who had crucified Him. It is this third accusation which shows how thoroughly the Sanhedrin realized the position of affairs. They knew that they had conspired together to kill the Son of God. They knew that they had said,

"Come, let us kill Him and the inheritance will be ours." They knew that they had cried out in their passion, "His blood be upon us and upon our children." It was the consciousness of these words which ever since they uttered them had day by day and month by month been writing themselves in ever clearer letters upon the wall against them, until at last they had become, as it were, the title of an accusation above them, a title written only too truly upon themselves, and, what was worse, by themselves also.

Peter Defines the Limits between Civil and Religious Authority

Peter, in his reply, does not discuss the question of the judgment which was impending over the rulers; that was a matter between themselves and God. What he does answer is the part which concerns himself and the disciples. A plain issue stands before them, and they are brought face to face with it. They have to make their choice; to obey God or man. Peter's words ring out with no uncertain sound, words which have passed down from Christian to Christian, as the watchword of each succeeding generation. The Prince of this world is ever at enmity with the Prince of life. The servants of God have day by day and year by year to make their choice, to obey either the one or the other. The conflict may not take the form of open persecution, of torture, or of martyrdom, but it will certainly take the form of worldly loss and shame; and as such it will enter into the daily life of every servant of God. The

Waldenses in the valleys of the Vaudois, the Huguenots in France, the Reformers in England, each man in his daily business, among his friends, in his family, makes his decision, obeys his Master or obeys men. Peter first states this greatest axiom, and from this axiom puts clearly before the Sanhedrin the deed they have done and the consequences of their deed, shows them that the Jesus Whom they slew has been by the power of God exalted to be a Prince and Saviour, and bids them know that it is through this very Man's forgiveness alone that they can find remission of guilt.

When Peter speaks thus the Sanhedrin are beside themselves with fear. They are stung to the quick by the consciousness of their sin and of their folly. They are self-condemned, and in their rage and despair nothing is impossible to them; they would incur the indignation of the multitude and the fury of the Romans, they would slay the apostles if only they could silence them for ever. Better death, better the suppression of their nation, than this terror for ever hanging over their heads and menacing them.

The Counsel of Gamaliel

But whilst they are in the midst of this madness and despair, Gamaliel, one of their leaders, a man of high reputation, arises, and with infinite skill and infinite knowledge of the men to whom he is speaking, subdues their passions and quiets them with words, irresistible because full of reasoning and truth.

THE RESPONSIBILITY OF LEADERSHIP

Gamaliel is generally held to be a grandson of Hillel, a famous Rabbi in Israel and a leader of the more liberal section of the Pharisees. His father, Simeon, may have been the Simeon who waited for our Lord in the Temple. There are many traditions still extant about him. He seems to have been a very learned man, one of the first of the seven Jewish doctors who were called "Rabbi" or master. It is said that he gave precepts enjoining courteous relations between the Jews and the heathen around them; also laws protecting wives against unprincipled husbands, and widows against unscrupulous children. There was a tradition that he later became a Christian, but this cannot be proved. One thing we do know is that Paul learned the Jewish law at his feet; and we wonder how it was that one so wise, so statesmanlike, and so moderate should have inspired his disciple with such a fiery enthusiasm and relentless passion. At the present moment Gamaliel dealt very wisely with the rulers of the people. He bade them for their own sake take heed to themselves as to what they were doing.

This must have struck home and calmed the audience at once, for they knew only too well the dangerous ground upon which they were treading. In the second place, he gives them hope, for he cites the instances of Theudas and Judas, both of whom claimed to be the Messiahs of their people; both of whom, like Jesus, had had disciples, but having been found to be impostors, perished and "as many as obeyed them had been scattered and came to naught." If this was the case with

Judas and Theudas, why should it not be the same with Jesus also and the Apostles? Arguing from this point, he bids them refrain from these men and let them alone, "For if this counsel or this work be of men it will come to naught; but if it be of God ye cannot overthrow it, lest haply ye be found even to fight against God." His words took effect; but they could not altogether restrain the bitter hatred and animosity of the assembly. The rulers called the apostles before them, and, ignoring altogether the temper of the men with whom they had to deal, determined to try force, but force of a nature which would not bring them into direct conflict with the multitude or the Roman Government. They ordered them to be beaten, and commanded them that they should not speak in the Name of Jesus, and let them go.

The effect of the persecution and prohibition was exactly what might have been expected. Those who had seen their Master suffer before their eyes, those who realized that His presence was still immediately around them, would only rejoice in so far as they were partakers of His suffering. The sons of Zebedee had been promised by Christ that they might drink of the cup which He drank of, and be baptised with the baptism which He had been baptised with. Peter had denied his Master, but now he was permitted to witness for Him. Therefore he and they rejoiced, and "daily in the Temple and in every house they ceased not to teach and to preach Jesus Christ."

THE RESPONSIBILITY OF LEADERSHIP

The Leaders of a Nation

Gamaliel and Erasmus are typical examples of men whose caution and intellect are stronger than their power of action, who are constitutionally timid, who give wise counsel, but choose the middle course for themselves and for others; and yet despite his caution there is something majestic in the character as well as in the words of Gamaliel. He stands, together with Nicodemus and Joseph of Arimathaea, as an outstanding leader of the highest type among the Pharisees, and it is from this highest type of Pharisee, rather than Sadducee, that the noblest men of Israel are found, just as it is from the men who have the capacity for religion, who understand the things of God as well as the things of man, who think, as it were, the thoughts of God after Him, who place religion first, that the highest leaders of a nation are found to-day. It is rarely from the Sadducee, from the tolerant, easy-going, wide-minded philosopher, the man with a capacity for self, that the heroes of a race are found.

The Value of the Counsel of Gamaliel

At first sight Gamaliel seems almost to be inspired by the Spirit of God and to give a counsel in unison with that Spirit, for what could be wiser, what more well pleasing in the sight of God than to leave the whole matter in the hand of God Himself; for, if the counsel were of God, it would most assuredly be established, and in the meantime the passionate action of the Sanhedrin was arrested, the disciples were rescued, and could return to their work. But when we look more closely we see that a nobler course lay open before Gamaliel, and one which, if he had been true to his highest instincts, he would have followed. Gamaliel must have known that these men represented a leader of a wholly different type either from a Theudas or from a Judas. If he had not seen Jesus Christ Himself, he had seen and heard enough from the disciples to convince him that what they said might very probably be true, that Jesus might indeed be the Messiah, in fact he admits as much by his words. His duty therefore, as one more highly learned in the Law than any of the other Jewish Rabbis, as the man with the greatest reputation for wisdom and moderation, was to inquire into the truth for himself and to counsel the Sanhedrin to inquire also, and to find out whether this were indeed the very Christ. If he had ascertained whether the matter was from God or from man he might, instead of merely restraining others from fighting against God, have fought for Him, and, as the representative of the most learned school in Jerusalem, have led the highest intellects of Jerusalem towards the truth. The curse of God was called down upon the children of Meroz in the song of Jael because, like Gamaliel, they let matters work themselves out for themselves. "They came not to the help of the Lord against the mighty." What is true of Gamaliel is true of each one of us. We are called upon to be infinitely more than spectators in life's battle, whether we are great or small, whether we have much intellect or little; we are called upon to inquire and find out the truth, to arise and play our part according to the God-given might within us.

CHAPTER XIV

ACTS VI

THE APPOINTMENT OF DIVERS ORDERS

The Political Condition of Jerusalem

The events which are recorded in this chapter probably took place about four years after the death of Christ. The rulers of the Jews had threatened the apostles and beaten them, but despite the ever-increasing number of their followers, no further steps were taken against them, although they were known to be in the Temple and witnessing as earnestly for Christ as before. This respite cannot be accounted for by a change of attitude on the part of the rulers, but may have been due to the disturbed political condition of Jerusalem itself. Pontius Pilate had been Governor of the Jews for ten years, but had become very obnoxious to them. According to Josephus, he had taken the Temple tax, which was exacted not only from every Jew in Jerusalem but also from the Jews throughout the provinces, and had used it to build an aqueduct; and as this tax amounted to a very considerable sum it materially affected the income of the Temple. He had also excited the religious hatred of the Jews by ordering images of the Emperor to be set up in different parts of the city, and had openly encouraged the worship of the Emperor, which later spread throughout the Roman Provinces. Finally, according to Josephus, he had attacked and slain some religious adventurers as they were making their way to the Temple of Gerizim, and had slain many of them. A complaint had in consequence been made against him, and he had been summoned to Rome to answer for his misdeeds. The hostility between the Sanhedrin and Pilate explains the absence of further action against the disciples; it explains also why, the measures of Pilate being obnoxious to every Jew alike, the disciples were for the moment united with the rulers in their distrust of and enmity against Pilate.

Dissension in the Church

It was during this time of peace between the Christians and the Jews that the Christians—who were now a large body, numbering many Grecians or Greek-speaking Jews among their adherents—found themselves threatened with internal dissensions likely to be more serious than the troubles without. The Christians—partly from their Jewish upbringing, which taught them the duty of caring for the poor and aged, partly from the example of Jesus—were particularly solicitous in ministering to all around them. But, besides the donations to the poor, there was also the ministration of the daily Agape, or love feast, which was partaken of by all the adherents of the Church, now numbering over 5000; and, in addition, there was the distribution of relief to the widows dependent upon them. It was in respect to this latter ministration that there had been difficulty. Complaint was made—and apparently rightly, if we may judge from the action which the apostles subsequently took in the matter— that injustice had been shown to the widows of the Greeks. This injustice probably had its origin in the long-standing jealousy between the Jews and the Grecians, dating back even to the time of the Maccabees. The line of distinction in thought and language which had arisen between the Jews, who had been born and brought up in foreign countries and used the Septuagint version of the Old Testament, and the Hebrews, who spoke Aramaic, used the old Hebrew Scriptures, and were strict in their observance of the Law, could never be effaced. But, apart from this distinction, other troubles might easily have arisen. We know only too well how readily grievances and murmurings arise wherever philanthropic work is carried on; and the point which interests us is to see the way in which the disciples dealt with it. Their first impulse naturally was to solve the whole difficulty by placing the administration of the money in the hands of Peter and John. The personal weight of their character, added to the dignity of their office would inspire trust, and so enable them to satisfy everybody. Moses in days of old had taken upon himself the settlement of all the grievances and disputes which arose among the Israelites in the Wilderness. He knew

THE APPOINTMENT OF DIVERS ORDERS

that his judgment had greater weight than that of any of the elders of Israel, and how essential it was at the outset that the foundations of Israelitish law should be laid upon a sure basis. Therefore from morning till evening he sat and judged the people, till Jethro intervened, and pointed out that it was far more essential for him and for the nation that he should train up others to this part of the work. It was unwise to wear himself away—he who was called to "be for the people to Godward."

It is well to bear in mind the way in which this question arose in the New Testament as well as in the Old Testament; for it is a distinctly practical one, and touches upon the religious life of to-day. Thoughtless men call upon the clergy to undertake this duty and that. They wish them to minister to the temporal and social as well as to the spiritual needs of their people; and they urge exactly the same plea as that which was put forward in the case of Moses and the Apostles—that they can do the work better than anyone else because they add the weight of their office to that of their personal character. How did the Apostles answer the call and deal with the matter?

A Clear Definition of the Work of the Apostles

In the first place, the twelve apostles, lest there should be anything arbitrary about the proceedings, called the multitude of the disciples together and entered into conference with them. In the second place, they explained carefully the position of affairs; they drew a clear definition between the work of those who minister the Word of God and those who minister about earthly things, a definition which holds as true to-day as in the early Church. Those who are engaged in the ministry of the Word cannot afford any more than the apostles to take as active a part in the affairs of ordinary life as other men. They must be freed as far as possible from the turmoil of earth if they are to be attuned to the harmony of Heaven. The first duty of a minister is unquestionably the ministry of the Word, and for that right ministry he must give himself continually to prayer. He is called upon to distinguish between what may be called his great primal duties—that is to say, those which he took upon himself when he promised to lay "aside the study of the world and flesh" and "to be diligent in prayers and in the reading of the Holy Scriptures"—and those which are only temporary and secondary. Among these temporal duties are those of ministering to the intellectual, moral, and social life of those around him; and he should respond to these only in subordination to his greatest work and in proportion to the time and strength which can be given from that work.

The Character and Office of the Diaconate

Peter bade the multitude choose seven men "to serve tables"—that is, to distribute provisions and to undertake the practical work of the organization. They were not called, as far as we know, by any particular title, but have been known to all subsequent ages of the Church by the name which denotes their office in the

THE APPOINTMENT OF DIVERS ORDERS

Church, by the Greek verb *diaconein* ("to serve"). These seven men correspond to the seventy elders who were appointed to assist Moses in ruling over Israel, and the qualifications which were required for their office were practically the same as those which Jethro bade Moses look for in the men who were to judge Israel—"able men, such as feared God, men of truth, hating covetousness"; "full of the Holy Ghost," the guidance of God being as necessary in the every-day matters of life as in the ministry of the Word; "men of wisdom," of cool, clear, quiet sense, corresponding to the "able" of Jethro. These deacons were apparently not to minister themselves, but to take charge of the business of distribution. When we consider the community of goods which probably still prevailed among the Christians and the large number of disciples we can see to what an important and difficult work they were called.

The Choice of Deacons

All the seven men who were chosen have Greek names. In all probability they were Greeks, and were selected to represent the Hellenist interest. The Church had evidently determined that, whatever injustice there had been in the past, there should be none in the future.

Stephen and Philip stand out among them as men of great intellectual as well as spiritual power. There is no record of the life or work of the other five deacons, although Irenaeus says that Nicolas the proselyte (that is to say, a Jew by adoption, but not by race) was the founder of the sect of the Nicolaitanes (Revelation ii. 6); but we have no Scriptural authority for this. If it were so, it would be strange that, as a Judas was found among the twelve apostles, so a leader of the Nicolaitanes may have been among the deacons. The very thought is full of practical teaching. We wonder how often a Judas or a Nicolas is found among our own communities of workers also, and we see the hopelessness as well as the wrongfulness of seceding from a Church because of the character of a leader or leaders in it. It is useless to complain that while some are in earnest, others are hypocrites and self-seekers; useless to try to found a separate community, one free from error and from men of mixed motives—a Church, in short, in which there shall be no tares among the wheat. We forget Christ's teaching upon this point. He has told us that the tares have grown, and ever will grow, do what we will, among the wheat until the time of harvest. We forget that it is better to have patience, and in that patience to possess our souls.

The Ordination of the Seven Deacons

The seven men having been chosen by the multitude, were brought to the apostles for ordination—that is to say, for the laying-on of hands and for prayer. From earliest times the laying-on of hands has symbolized the passing of some power or virtue, the transference of some quality of good or evil from the layer-on of hands to the recipient. Thus the high priest, as representative of the nation, laid his hands upon the scapegoat

(Numbers xxviii. 18-23) in order that by doing so he might symbolize the transference of the guilt of the nation to a living creature, one who had had neither part nor lot in the matter, and who carried it thence into the wastes of the wilderness. In New Testament times the laying-on of hands was a sign of blessing, a transference of good and not of evil. Thus Christ laid His hands upon the little children and blessed them. He touched those who were sick with divers diseases and healed them. Thus, too, Ananias laid his hands upon Saul. Together with the imposition of hands there has been usually also the bestowal of a special grace or power. "Then laid they their hands on them, and they received the Holy Ghost" (Acts viii. 17). "From the eyes of Saul there fell as it had been scales." In the present instance, after the laying-on of hands Stephen arose full of faith and power, and did great wonders and miracles among the people.

The Effect of the Healing of the Dissension

The work of God can be hindered as effectually by dissension as by sin, and therefore we are not surprised to find that the effect of the healing of the dissension was followed, like the putting away of sin, by a great increase in the number of the converts. Among the new converts we learn for the first time that a great company of priests were obedient to the faith. It seems strange that any of the priests could have joined the new Church, especially when that Church was lying under the interdict of the Sanhedrin; but we have to remember that there was a strong line of demarcation between the rulers who represented the upper class of priest and the lower class of priests probably here spoken of, and that disputes constantly arose between them because the higher priests infringed the rights of those below them. These priests were a poor and neglected class of men, and they must have hailed with joy the advent of a new sect which, if it became, as seemed likely, the predominating sect in Jerusalem, would extend a hand of equal fellowship and communion to all who belonged to them, whether they were high or low. We notice also that the number of adherents multiplied in Jerusalem, but apparently in Jerusalem only. So far the command of Christ to witness even to the uttermost ends of the earth was still in abeyance. The disciples had carried out the first command to tarry in Jerusalem, but, as we see from the account of the conversion of Cornelius, they had not understood the meaning of the second, nor had they obeyed it. The time had now come for the Dispersion; and the path, which so far had been hidden from the eyes of the disciples, would be opened for them by their enemies, who would point out through persecution and martyrdom that path, which they either had not found out or had not dared to follow for themselves.

CHAPTER XV

ACTS VI

THE CHARACTER OF STEPHEN

Stephen seems, from the first time that he is mentioned, to have been a leader not only among the seven deacons, but also among all the disciples. He was probably a man of standing and position, for he addresses the Sanhedrin as "brethren and fathers." He is generally thought to have been a Hellenist—that is to say, a Greek-speaking Jew—or one of the Roman freed men, and his speech is said to savour of Alexandrian culture. There is no question that he had outstanding ability as an orator, and was distinguished for his power of organization. He must have had immense sway over the early Christians, as also over the Greek-speaking Jews, who had become an exceedingly powerful body in the Church, as powerful in numbers as in force of character and intellect. Men such as Stephen and Paul had travelled and come in contact with the learning of Alexandria, and had a breadth of thought entirely beyond their fellows. Bearing this in mind, we can understand how it was that Stephen and Paul were the first to conceive what may be called the statesmanship of the Church—that is to say, the bearing of its relationship not only towards the Jews but towards the world at large. In his speech Stephen showed that he had grasped the transitory character of the Mosaic dispensation, and he forced his hearers for the moment to grasp it also; but they fiercely resented his suggestion, and rose in anger against him.

The Early Death of Stephen

As we consider the character and the intellectual and spiritual capacity of Stephen we wonder why a man who was apparently so invaluable to the Church should have been so early taken from it. The period during which he stood forth as a leader and as an orator was short, scarcely two years in duration, and he left behind him no one capable of succeeding him. Why was he cut off in his days? This is a question almost as old as the Christian Church itself. Men have been brought face to face with it again and again, and in the midst of their perplexity and bereavement have asked why those who seemed invaluable to the work of God were taken away, but they have found no answer. It is only now and again, just as in the present instance, when we stand, as it were, afar off and see the overruling power of God, that we learn something of what that purpose is. We see the martyr Stephen die, and as he dies we see the reason of his death, and we learn to trust the wise purpose of the Hand which beckoned him away as It summons one of our own number, one whom we ourselves lean upon and who seems indispensable to the work of God at large.

We who stand afar off know now that the death of St. Stephen was the birth-throe of St. Paul. We see that a convulsion as mighty as this was needed in order to shake the deep-rooted convictions of St. Paul and to prepare the way for the heavenly vision.

The Ministry of Stephen

The work of St. Stephen seems to have been of many kinds. In the first place, as leader among the seven, he effectually quelled the murmuring and discontent of the multitude, by organizing the ministration to the poor in a wise and business-like manner; in the second place, he did great wonders and miracles among the people, being filled with the Holy Ghost; and in the third place he witnessed from synagogue to synagogue in Jerusalem with a power which his adversaries were unable to gainsay. Tradition says that there were 480 synagogues in Jerusalem at this time, and that these various synagogues were especially acceptable to the Jews of the Dispersion, who gathered in them according to their nationality for interchange of thought and of worship. St. Stephen, being a Hellenist, would naturally go to the synagogues which were set apart for the use of the Hellenistic Jews—that is to say, to the men of the same type of thought, even if they were not exactly of the same nationality, as himself. The people with whom he was accustomed to argue were the Libertines, the Cyrenians, and the Alexandrians, as well as those of Cilicia and of Asia.

"Certain of the Synagogue ... Disputing with Stephen"

It is interesting to pass in thought with Stephen from synagogue to synagogue and to see the various nationalities and types of men whom he would meet in them. In the synagogue of the Libertines, for instance, he would meet the descendants of the Jews who had been taken captive by Pompey, but who had been liberated and who, being now all freed men, had returned in great numbers to Jerusalem. In the synagogue of Cyrene he would come in contact with some of the most influential Jews of the Dispersion, for Cyrene was the capital of a small province in North Africa which had offered such peculiar privileges and rights of freedom to the Jews who settled in it that it had become the Greek centre and the representative city of the Hellenist Jews. It would have a peculiar interest for us also because of Simon the Cyrenian, who had been compelled by the Roman soldiers to carry the Cross, and who, if he were still living and in Jerusalem, would unquestionably worship there also. If he were not there probably his two sons, Alexander and Rufus, would from time to time be present, for we know from St. Mark that they were men of outstanding character and influence in the early Church.

Passing from the synagogue of the Cyrenians to that of the Alexandrians, we come to the most lettered class among the Grecian Jews, the men who were especially prepared for the reception of the new thought, for it was in Alexandria that the Scriptures had been translated into Greek, and the Alexandrians were accustomed to think of religion as presented to them in the Greek tongue. They came also from what was then the centre of literary and philosophical thought, and were accustomed to look at questions in all their bearings and from a wide standpoint of view. These Alexandrians were also in all probability men of wealth and standing, as well as of education, for Alexandria was at this time the great centre of the corn trade with Italy, and this trade had passed almost entirely into the hands of the Jewish merchants.

But the synagogue of Cilicia, could we have gone thither, would have been of far greater interest to us than any of the other synagogues. It was the gathering-place of Cilicia and of the men of Tarsus, and it was here that Saul would worship when he was in Jerusalem; it was here also that, if he heard Stephen speak, he would probably take part in the arguments against him.

We cannot help stopping for a moment to try and picture the scene, if it were so. We see Stephen full of the Holy Ghost and of wisdom, conscious of the truth which is his very life, with all the force of his commanding intellect and knowledge and with all the charm of his personal character, and Saul with an even surpassing keenness of intellect, a more fiery zeal, and wider conception of the vast issues at stake, which were already more to him than life itself. But all the learning of Saul, of the Alexandrians, and of the other members of the synagogue, was powerless when opposed to the wisdom and to the spirit of Stephen. He seems, through the Holy Spirit, to have been surrounded by an atmosphere of holiness and truth of the same character as that which surrounded his Master, and these men could no more resist the wisdom of Stephen than the rulers could ask Jesus any further questions.

The Accusation of Stephen

How was it that the whole multitude of the Sanhedrin and of the people were unanimous in their hatred of Stephen, whilst they were divided amongst themselves as to the treatment of Peter and John, so divided that they could not take any really serious measures against them?

We must remember that in addition to the interregnum in the Governorship the accusation this time was far more cleverly laid than it had been in the case of Peter and John, as also that the attack which Stephen was making upon the Mosaic Law was far more wide-reaching and dangerous. The Pharisees had looked on with comparative coolness whilst the Sadducees were defeated on the question of the Resurrection, but they were vitally affected when an attack was made upon the Law of Moses, and only too ready to join in the outcry against Stephen. The emissaries of the elders and the Scribes came upon him and caught him, possibly when he was arguing in one of the synagogues, and brought him before the Council.

THE CHARACTER OF STEPHEN

St. Stephen before the Council

It is strange to think how nearly alike the accusation as well as the circumstances of the trial of Stephen were to that of his Master. Stephen was standing where Jesus had stood, probably in the presence of many who had been members of the Council ten years before, and who had changed only in so far that they were harder and bitterer in their antagonism than ever. His accusation was practically identical with that of his Master, for blasphemy according to the Jews was a wilful sin against God, and Stephen had said that Jesus would destroy the Temple and change the customs which Moses had delivered. Stephen knew from the first that he was powerless in their hands, his accusation was too dangerous; it contained too many elements of truth, and therefore, like all half truths, was the more impossible to withstand. Moreover, he could turn to no one for sympathy or support. It is true that the Sanhedrin had legally no power over life or death, and that from the time of the second Hyrcanus and his sons it had as a body been gradually losing its power; but despite that loss of power Stephen stood in imminent danger, for he could hear the multitude raging without like hungry wolves, ready and waiting only till the decree of the Sanhedrin might point in the direction of tumultuous and irregular murder.

"His Face As It Had Been the Face of an Angel"

But Stephen seems to have given no heed either to himself or his own personal danger. One thought only possessed his mind. He could witness for his Master; he could, through the power of the Holy Spirit, make one more mighty effort to convince the Jews; he could attempt to meet them on their own grounds, and by clear and intellectual reasoning open their minds to the truth; he could strive to change their attitude from one of blind hostility to one of conviction or inquiry. If they were convinced, why might not the whole Jewish nation be gradually convinced also? The whole matter lay so clearly and evidently before him. He had studied the Old Testament Scriptures as carefully as any of the rulers; he had seen the whole bearing of the sequence of events of Jewish history; he understood what the gradual unfolding of the Law meant. He was speaking to the ablest men of Israel. Why could not their eyes be opened? Why could they not see Jesus as the Messiah? And as they saw the truth, why could they not join the vast body of Christians in Jerusalem, and Jerusalem become in very deed the city of the great King? That Stephen had forgotten his own danger is evident from his face as well as from his words, so evident that even his enemies were aware of it. "They saw his face as it had been the face of an angel." Stephen's face was lit not so much by a glory of the Shekinah, as in the case of Moses or the disciples upon the Mount of Transfiguration, as by the Spirit of his Master within, a spirit and a beauty akin to that which lights up the face of many an aged saint of God.

CHAPTER XVI

ACTS VII. 1-53

THE APOLOGY OF STEPHEN

*A Further Breach
between the Church and the Sanhedrin*

In the presence of the Sanhedrin the disciples had put forward as a first axiom of their faith the declaration that they "ought to obey God rather than men," and the rulers knew that the disciples neither could, nor would, swerve from this position. They knew that as Jesus had refused to fall down and worship the Prince of this world, so the disciples would not only refuse, but die sooner than obey a command of the Sanhedrin which they knew to be contrary to the command of God. This made an irreconcilable breach between the disciples and the rulers, and the breach was further increased when Stephen, as the leader of the Hellenistic Jews, saw how far-reaching the character of the spiritual teaching of Jesus was, saw that if this teaching were carried out in its fulness the materialistic side of the Jewish religion, together with the centralization of faith in the visible Temple, must pass away. It was the statement of this second position, together with the consciousness that Stephen, like Peter and the apostles, was prepared to die in the defence of the truth he had apprehended, that had roused beyond all bounds the indignation of the Sanhedrin and of the multitude also.

The Wisdom and the Spirit of Stephen

Stephen had been appointed leader in the administration of that most difficult part of Church organization—the management of its finance and charity. He had executed this work so efficiently that there is no further mention of dispute or difficulty, and he is a leader in thought as well as work. He was one of those rare men who, being ahead of their age, catch, as it were from afar, the echo of a coming dispensation, and translate the thoughts and will of God to men. The disciples had been slow of heart whilst Jesus had been with them, and they were slow of heart still—not in devotion and unflinching obedience, but in interpreting the command which Christ had given them as to the evangelization of the world. They had not as yet gone beyond Jerusalem. Stephen was the first who, under the guidance of the Holy Spirit, broke loose from the trammels of form and locality and demonstrated the spiritual nature of the worship of God. For this far-seeing conception his training as a Hellenist Jew had probably prepared him. We can see from the nationality of the synagogues which he disputed in, and from the tone of his address to the Sanhedrin, that he was in sympathy with the Greeks and Greek thought; indeed, some writers have said that his speech shows traces of Alexandrian learning also.

The Charge Preferred against Stephen

The charge which was brought against Stephen was that he had threatened the institutions of the Law and of Moses, even going so far as to touch the supremacy of the Temple itself. This charge was false in so far as it declared his words to be blasphemous and destructive, for, on the contrary, they were divinely inspired and constructive of the new and spiritual Temple of God; it was, however, true in so far as it threatened the existing order, the religious rites, and the Temple in Jerusalem, and was in accord with and justified by the general tenor of his teaching. His words had been winged with wisdom and with truth, and enforced by his personality, by the living conviction of his whole being, in a way that was irresistible to his hearers. The keen-witted Hellenists, truer even to the Jewish customs than the Jews themselves, saw clearly what the outcome of his teaching must be—more clearly even than the Sanhedrin itself.

The Eagerness of the Hellenist Jews

It is strange that this first wide conception of Christianity, as well as this clear-sighted recognition of the danger of its precepts, should have emanated not from the apostles and Jews of Jerusalem, but from the Grecians—from men standing, as it were, outside, rather than from those who were within and were the natural defenders of the faith. These men saw that the whole existing order of Jewish theology was at stake, and determined to silence Stephen by force if they could not silence him by words. "Therefore they stirred up the people, the elders, and the Scribes, and came upon him and caught him, and brought him to the Council."

The Scene before the Council

Stephen was most probably arrested either when speaking in one of the synagogues or when ministering to the poor; and, having been caught by the angry populace, was borne down into the Gazith, or stone chamber close to the Temple, where the Sanhedrin were accustomed to assemble. For a moment the air of judicial quiet and authority within the assembly must have come upon him like a welcome deliverance from the shouts and violence of the populace without, but Stephen knew only too well that he had passed from peril of death into the very jaws of death; for if the wider-minded Hellenists could not be brought to see the truth of the new religion, what chance was there that the Jews and elders, weighted down as they were with the inherited prejudices of centuries, and having not only their wealth but also their authority at stake, would see it either?

The Judgment Seat of Man and the Judgment Seat of God

But one chance remained. Stephen cared little if the trial which brought death to him might through that very death bring life to his hearers also, and with this hope in view he laid down his life with the words which he spoke more truly and more voluntarily than at the moment when he fell asleep without the city. As he made his decision, as he gave his life to his Master his spirit gained such an ascendency that his face seemed to catch the reflection of his Master's, and all who gazed upon him were filled with awe and wonder. The elders saw a strange scene, one man helpless and alone, at the mercy of his judges within, and of the raging multitude without; but as we look upon it we see a stranger sight still, we see Stephen standing before his judges but we see also those very judges standing before the judgment seat of God. They are being given a last appeal, a last chance in order that they may save themselves and save their nation also.

The Appeal of the Gospel of Jesus and the Appeal of the Gospel of the Holy Spirit

The Jewish nation and the rulers had had the witness of Jesus. He had stood where Stephen was now standing, and, although he had made no apology for His life and deeds, He had witnessed that He was the

Son of God, and they had rejected His witness. Stephen was about to make an apology for his life and teaching; but he was also at the same time, through the power of the Holy Spirit, to witness that Jesus was the Son of God. When the Sanhedrin had had the full witness of the life and teaching of Jesus brought before them, they had rejected Jesus and condemned Him; now they were to have the full weight of the life, death, and *Resurrection* of Jesus brought before them—brought before them with all the moving influence of the Holy Spirit, and they were about to reject this influence also. From henceforward their branch would be broken off, and the Gentile world—"the wild olive tree"—"graffed, contrary to Nature," in their place.

The Indictment against Stephen and the Response Made to It

The indictment falls under two heads—blasphemy against (1) the holy place and (2) the Law. The trial begins, according to custom, with the question which corresponds to the "Guilty or not guilty?" of our English law. "Are these things so?" At first sight Stephen's speech seems disappointing, a recital of well-known facts, a ministering to the national pride, a playing upon time and opportunity. We wonder whither it is leading, why it has no direct testimony to Jesus; we wonder again it is so circumstantial, so detailed that it wanders on until it comes to a sudden break, a passionate declaration, and the great opportunity has passed away for ever. But when, instead of merely reading the speech, we become one of his adversaries, listen with the subtle ear of a Jewish Rabbi, and follow the Oriental line of argument, we find where the delicacy as well as the power of the argument lies. We see how marvellously the style of reasoning is suited to the hearers, and we no longer wonder how and why the climax comes. We hear only too well the sullen growl of murmuring rise till it bursts into an angry roar; we see the rulers cut to the heart; we understand why the rulers turn upon Stephen like the men in the synagogue had turned before them, and why, with an angry rush, they silence in death the truth they cannot silence in life.

The Line of Argument

Stephen, standing before the Sanhedrin, has to deal partly with himself and partly with his hearers—that is to say, he has to rebut the charge made against him, and having rebutted it to arraign his hearers upon a like offence. He strives but little for himself; what he does strive for is to open the eyes of the Sanhedrin, to turn them so that instead of being bigoted adherents of a corrupt faith they may become searchers and inquirers after truth. This is why he adopts an indirect line of argument, and, under the form of a laudatory address, of an outline sketch, extols the great events, the deeds and heroes of early Jewish history, and leads his hearers back to the dayspring, to the first dawn of God's appearance to the Jewish nation, in order that from the light of that first appearance they may gain an insight into His later dealings also. This is why he deals so tenderly, one might almost say so graciously, with them. He steps down, as it were, into their own arena; he speaks as a Jew to a Jew; he shows that in these respects he is one at heart with them; his words are filled with a gracious loyalty to the Jewish nation, to their past history, and to the great heroes who have made that history; and yet as he passes along he illuminates the whole path of that history and the lives of those heroes with a new light, with a full and living interpretation. He touches point after point with a delicate but unerring hand. He mixes sentiments and facts which are acceptable and irrefutable with deductions which are unacceptable, fatal, and irrefutable also. He leads the Sanhedrin, as it were, irresistibly and imperceptibly along their own path, and they gladly follow him, until they find themselves in the new path into which God is beckoning them, but into which they are determined not to go.

The Response to the Indictment

There are several lines in the argument, but the two main lines which stand out most clearly are those which are contained in the indictment itself, and which are summed up in the sudden application or summary. (1) In the first place Stephen proves that God was worshipped by their forefathers, not only in Canaan, but in the land of Chaldaea, in Egypt, in the wilderness, in countries other than Jerusalem and in places other than the Temple. He shows that the times when God specially manifested Himself to their forefathers and accepted their worship had been in the days before there was a Temple and in countries far away from Jerusalem. He points out that Abraham called upon God in whatever country he came, and that in that country God answered him. He shows that God drew near to Moses in the Wilderness, and by the burning bush told him to "put off his shoes from off his feet," for even that far-away spot in the desert "was holy ground." He shows, too, that the Tabernacle was as divinely ordered and constructed as the Temple, even though it was intended to move from place to place, in a land which was then in the possession of the Gentiles. It was true that Solomon had built Him a house, but it was also true that as he dedicated that house he said: "The Most High dwelleth not in temples made with hands"; and that not only Solomon, but Isaiah also, the greatest of the prophets, had said: "Heaven is My throne and the earth My footstool. What house will ye build Me, or what is the place of My rest?"

The Second Line of Argument

The second line, which may be called the supreme line of the argument, is peculiarly powerful. Stephen has been charged with blasphemy against the law and against Moses. He takes that law, and in the words of the law or in the words which are the epitome of the law, condemns the rulers of the very crime with which they have charged him, thus showing that he is in perfect sympathy with the law of God, whereas that it is they themselves who, when placed at the bar of that law, are condemned by it. He does this gradually step by step; he shows then that as there has been a unity in the graciousness of God's dealing towards them, so there has been unity in the stiff-neckedness and rebelliousness of their dealing with Him, and that according as God has revealed Himself to them in a progressive revelation, so they have, true to their character, shown a steady and systematic resistance to every line of that progress. God has sent deliverer after deliverer, and they have rejected them. The patriarchs sold Joseph into Egypt; the Israelites in their hour of need accepted Joseph, but at his first appearance resisted Moses. They now profess to accept Moses, but they refuse Jesus. Did they know that in refusing Jesus they were refusing Moses also? Moses had told them to look forward to the coming of a new and Greater Prophet; he had told them that the authority of that Prophet was to supersede his own authority; but they had said to Jesus, as their forefathers to Moses, "Who made thee a ruler and a judge?" and, true to their own character, had refused deliverance at His hand. Stephen is bringing the new and greater Prophet a second time before them; Jesus is appearing in his words as Moses appeared in the land of Egypt. Will they take Him; will they accept His deliverance? This is why Stephen's speech leads up to the question of deliverance; why he tells the story of the two deliverers, Joseph and Moses; why he brings out step by step the points in which they resemble and foreshadow Christ. It is all done in order that Jesus may be the more evidently presented before them, so that if they reject Him it will be not in His own character alone but in the character of the long foreshadowing of Scripture.

The Application of the Argument

We see how slowly but surely Stephen has been leading up to the point where his argument can be applied to his audience; but as he turns to make his cutting indictment of the rulers it is well to pause and see not only how his speech bears upon the history of to-day, but also how it shows that the inspired words of the Old Testament are illuminated by the life, death, and resurrection of Christ. As we read his speech the Spirit of God seems to move over the pages of the Old Testament and to bring into relief the compassion of the Great Deliverer —the universality, spirituality, and the holiness of God—the stiff-neckedness and rebellion of man. And furthermore we see that it is not the rulers alone who are condemned by his words, it is we—as a nation and as individuals—who are condemned also. How often have we been content to be subject to the bands of those sins which by our frailty we have committed, instead of seeking to be loosed from them? How often have we wandered towards the far country unmindful of our great deliverer, unmindful of the spirituality and the holiness of God? May not the day of our visitation draw near also only to pass away for ever?

CHAPTER XVII

ACTS VII. 54 TO END

THE DEATH OF ST. STEPHEN

"A New Prophet" and "Him Shall Ye Hear"

Stephen had been charged with blasphemy of the holy place and of the law. In reply he had shown that the worship of God was not localized in any one place—not even in the Temple—"for He dwelleth not in temples made with hands," but is to be worshipped wherever His presence is manifested to man. Stephen had shown his reverence for the law by saying that he and his fellow-Christians were prepared to obey the law and the Prophet whom Moses had foretold to Israel. In reply to the charge that Jesus would destroy the Temple and change its rites, Stephen had shown that Jesus came not to destroy but to fulfil. If the Temple were no longer to be the centre of Jewish life and power, then in its place a new and greater kingdom would arise, having the heavens as its throne and the earth its footstool.

THE DEATH OF ST. STEPHEN

The Conviction of the Rulers

This was the drift of the argument, but as we read it we wonder whether the rulers of the Sanhedrin could follow a line so indirect, so far-reaching. We have, however, to remember that they were trained in matters of the law, and practised in disputations of this very kind; that they were men of outstanding ability and intellect, as keen and penetrating if not as broad-minded as Gamaliel. These men saw too well the force of the argument which Stephen was presenting to them, for it was only what had already become part of their inner consciousness, what they knew because they had seen it working itself out in the events around them, what they dreaded more than death itself. Their day of grace was past. They had been forced one by one to admit the premisses, the conclusions which followed from them being all the more insupportable. The whole atmosphere of the assembly therefore gradually changed from an attitude of curiosity and cynicism to one of determined opposition and animosity.

The Swift Turn and Application of the Argument

Stephen sees by the lowering faces around him that there is not a moment to be lost, and therefore he steps aside, as it were, and makes a swift and cutting indictment. They have stopped their ears and refused to hear his reasoning, can he, by a sudden shock, dash them, as it were, to the ground, force them to awake to see their character in its true light? It is in order to do this that he sets their sin with startling swiftness and in absolute clearness before them. They are stiff-necked, they have refused both guidance and correction, they are uncircumcised in heart and ears, will they neither obey nor listen? As their fathers resisted the Holy Ghost, so do they; as their fathers persecuted the prophets because they spoke of the coming Jesus, so they have betrayed and murdered that Just One, Jesus. They have received the law by the dispensation of angels, but they have not kept it.

"The Heavens Were Opened"

Every word pierced like winged truth into the heart of his hearers and transported them with rage, so that they gnashed their teeth, and like beasts of prey were ready to spring upon him; but his spirit had passed human power, his task was done, his confession witnessed, he looked into his Master's face and saw that Master standing ready to receive His servant and to take reckoning of his persecutors; and he cried in an ecstasy of joy: "Behold, I see the heavens opened, and the Son of man standing on the right hand of God." But as the pillar of fire gave light to the Israelites and brought darkness to the Egyptians, so the Presence which brought glory to Stephen brought a foretaste of outer darkness to his persecutors, and they stopped their ears and drowned his voice in the vain hope that by doing so they might drown the voice of conscience also. With a loud cry the men, who by their calling and profession were set apart for the dignity and office of judges, dragged their prisoner forth from before their judgment-seat, and, instead of quelling the angry mob outside, joined in its uproar, and drew Stephen through the gates and cast him out of the city. There, in some vacant spot, probably near the very place where his Master had been crucified, they stoned him.

The Stoning of Stephen

According to Jewish law, each witness in turn cast a first stone upon his victim, and in order to hurl these stones more violently the witnesses took off their outer garments and laid them at a young man's feet whose name was Saul, and so "they stoned Stephen, calling upon God, and saying, Lord Jesus, receive my spirit." As the stones rained in upon him, Stephen roused himself by a last effort, and kneeling down cried "with a loud voice, Lord, lay not this sin to their charge. And when he had said this, he fell asleep." As an old writer says, "Stephen had a hard bed, but by God's mercy he fell asleep upon it." Like a tired child, with mind calmed and soothed by his Father's presence, conscious that all responsibilty had passed into that Father's hands, he fell asleep.

> "The glory which our God surrounds
> The Son of Man, th' atoning wounds,
> He sees them all, and earth's dull bounds
>   Are melting fast away."

It is as earth's dull bounds from time to time melt away that we realize the immediate presence of Jesus, a presence felt during prayer, but too often forgotten in the hurry of practical every-day life, and yet indispensable if our practical every-day life is to be all that it ought to be. Brother Lawrence tells us that he "possessed God in such tranquillity" that his time of business did not differ from his time of prayer. Dr. Arnold sought to maintain a like consciousness also by committing "eye, ear and thought to God," and praying that "as his heart beat without any thought of his, according to God's natural law, so his spiritual life might hold on its natural course even when his mind could not consciously turn to Him."

The Son of Man Standing on the Right Hand of God

The rolling back of the cloud revealed Jesus before the eyes of Stephen as the Son of Man instead of, as we might have expected, as the Son of God. Jesus is the same yesterday, to-day, and for ever. The fulness of the Godhead dwells in Him, and He brings succour to His servants in the fulness of that Almighty power, but in the form of One Who can be touched with the feeling of infirmities, yet without sin. It is joy to us to realize that our eyes will also one day see Jesus as the Son of Man, that we shall be near Him, see the glance of His love, hear Him say, in the same tone in which He spoke upon earth, "Well done, good and faithful servant."

St. Stephen saw Jesus not only as the Son of Man, but also as the Son of God, standing at the right hand of God. As St. Chrysostom beautifully puts it, Jesus had risen in order that He might succour His servant in the hour of need. We know that the eye of our Master watches us as we pass hither and thither upon our appointed tasks; but we do not always remember that in the hour of great need He rises and, as Son of Man as well as Son of God, draws near in order to see that no unnecessary pain or harm comes to His servant; and if, for the sake of the Kingdom of Righteousness, pain and harm must come, yet He is watching in order that His everlasting arm may support His servant during that hour of danger. "When thou passest through the waters, I will be with thee."

"Lord Jesus, Receive My Spirit"

There is a likeness as well as a contrast in the dying prayers of Stephen and of Jesus. Kneeling in prayer, Stephen said, "Lord Jesus, receive my spirit," that is to say, as a suppliant, he prayed Jesus of His mercy to receive him into the everlasting habitations; whereas Jesus said, "Into thy hands I commit my spirit," that is to say, by His own eternal right, of His own free will, He passed into the heavens, "the Lord strong and mighty," the "King of glory," bade "the eternal gates lift up their heads," the "everlasting doors lift themselves," because "He would come in." (Psalm xxiv. 7.)

"Lord, Lay Not This Sin to Their Charge"

In his first prayer Stephen had shown not only that he placed himself in the hands of Jesus, but also that he, together with the early Christians, believed that the spirits of the departed passed at death into the immediate presence of their Master.

His second prayer is equally memorable as showing that the disciples had learnt the spirit of forgiveness which distinguished Jesus. We see this more forcibly if we contrast such a prayer as "Lord, lay not this sin to their charge," with one of the dying prayers of the Old Testament, such as that of David (1 Kings ii.) or of the martyr Zechariah (2 Chronicles xxiv. 22). Zechariah, for instance, cries, "The Lord look upon it and require it," a prayer full of the consciousness of the presence of God and of patient dignity in suffering. But Stephen cries, "Lord, lay not this sin to their charge," a prayer equally full of dignity but showing a spirit of forgiveness also. The disciples had not only been taught but were following also the teaching which bade them when they were smitten on the one cheek to turn the other also, were praying "forgive us our trespasses, as we forgive them that trespass against us," were following the example which found its consummation in the prayer, "Father, forgive them, for they know not what they do."

THE DEATH OF ST. STEPHEN

"At a Young Man's Feet Whose Name Was Saul"

This verse comes like an anti-climax. The rage of the rulers and of the multitude has been for the moment lost in the vision of Divine glory; but this breath of hatred comes like a wintry blast across the sunshine of St. Stephen's prayer, and we ask: "What part had Saul been playing in this matter; how far had he known and been party to the deed?" If Saul had been one of the disputants in the synagogue of Cilicia who could not prevail against the arguments of Stephen, if, in consequence, he had been one of those who had accused him to the Sanhedrin, if, further, he was, as seems likely, at this time a member of the Sanhedrin itself, then he had taken no small part not only in the accusation but also in the condemnation of Stephen. There is no question that he was consenting unto his death, or, as the other reading has it, "was well pleased at his death," for it was at his directions that the first stones were cast upon Stephen. Was this the end of it all? Did Stephen die in vain, and was the increased bitterness of Saul against the Church the only answer to his life, death, and prayers? It seemed so for a time, but none know the end of thoughts, words, and deeds. There is no question that the immediate effect of Stephen's death was to make Saul even more bitter against the Church than before, and that the death of Stephen, instead of convincing him of the truth, had increased his bitterness against Christianity. But there is another side to the picture. Who can tell, despite the bitterness which for a time seemed to be the only effect upon Saul of Stephen's death, how great the influence was afterwards, not only of his words but also of his life and death? Saul is said to have sat far more truly at the feet of Stephen than at the feet of Gamaliel; and even if the witnesses laid their garments at the feet of Saul, it was Saul who caught up the mantle of Stephen, and who, when he, too, saw Jesus standing beside him, learnt the heavenly interpretation of the Old Testament, the heavenly vision of the spiritual kingdom.

The Bursting of the Bonds of Death

Saul as he stood without the city walls, not only sanctioning, but even urging on the murderers of Stephen, seemed fast bound by religious fanaticism, so fast bound that he could never be set free. In the providence of God the time came when he was set forth in the liberty wherewith Christ sets His people free, when he saw all the events of his past life, and even of that terrible day, in their true signification. A long life of service lay before him, but from time to time, in the midst of his journeyings, his imprisonment, his labour, the remembrance of that day, the remembrance of the face of Stephen, of his voice, and of his gracious words, must have sounded in his ears. At such a time how could Paul have borne it if he had not been able to recall the face of Jesus, and to hear even more clearly than the voice of Stephen His words of perfect forgiveness also?

Paul was used of God to bring thousands into the Church, to lay the foundation of the Kingdom of

Righteousness; and at the last day who can tell how many will arise and call him blessed? But, as we see from his writings, he never forgot the blood of Stephen or of the martyrs whom he had slain. He could not forget; but he could give his past sin into the hand of God and pray that it might work out for His Glory; he might let it be one of the things that lay behind, and reach forward into the things before. As he did this, he could rest in the thought that by the mercy of God even the murder of a Stephen could be overruled to the furtherance of the Kingdom of Righteousness. This mingling of the consequences of past sin with the joy of forgiveness is one of the great mysteries of our lives. Stephen died to give birth to a Paul; Paul died day by day to give birth to thousands—nay, tens of thousands—not only of his own but of succeeding generations also.

CHAPTER XVIII

ACTS VIII. 1-25

THE GOSPEL IN SAMARIA

The Great Persecution

The storm of persecution which had been gathering for years fell at last upon the Christians and forced them to flee from Jerusalem. This sudden change may have been due to three causes:

(1) Pontius Pilate having been recalled to Rome, the iron hand of Rome was for a moment loosed from the city, and the Jews found the opportunity for which they had been waiting. (2) The Sanhedrin and the multitude, having like wolves tasted blood, could no longer be restrained even by a Gamaliel. (3) A leader had at last been found. The Sadducees—who had long threatened and opposed the Christians, but, being selfish, had dreaded lest the blood of the slain should rest upon themselves and upon their children—rejoiced when Saul came forward, burning with zeal and seeing so clearly the danger which threatened the Jewish law and nation, that he was entirely regardless of any danger

to himself. What could be better than that he should hover like a hawk over the Church and, dragging out men and women, commit them to prison? There is no question that the persecution was very bitter—so bitter that it is referred to by St. Paul, both in his speeches and letters, as though the remembrance was ever with him; he himself says that he was "exceedingly mad against them"; and St. Luke says persecution became, as it were, the breath of his life. He persecuted unto the death, binding not only men but women. What could the Christians do in the face of such opposition? Stephen would not even have been buried but for the courage of devout men who had come forward, like Joseph of Arimathaea, and had taken away his body and made great lamentation over it. Jerusalem was indeed left unto them desolate; the day was darker even than at the death of Jesus, for then every man could at least go to his own house in peace, but now "they were scattered everywhere abroad."

"They Went Everywhere Preaching the Word"

But there was light even in the darkness. The Church in Jerusalem, which might have settled down like the sect of the Essenes into an experiment in Christian brotherhood and socialism, was dispersed and "went everywhere preaching the Word." The apostles remained in Jerusalem, either as a stay and support to those who could not escape, or because they were not in as much danger as the Hellenists. The first fury of the storm naturally fell upon the men who had provoked it. The

Grecians had been the advocates of a wider policy, a more spiritual interpretation of the Temple and its services, and were, therefore, more dangerous than the apostles themselves, who had been devout in their observance of the religious rites, and who were looked upon as comparatively unlearned and ignorant men.

Jews and Samaritans

After the death of Stephen, Philip went down to Samaria, for the Samaritans were nominally Jews, but practically idolaters. After the carrying away of the twelve tribes, the King of Assyria had colonized Samaria from his own country, so that it might form an outpost of the Empire. Later, hearing that judgment had fallen upon the inhabitants "because they knew not the manner of the God of the land," he sent for a priest to instruct them in the Jewish religion, and from that time forward "they feared the Lord, and served their own gods." The line of demarcation thus made became very strong between the Jews and the Samaritans; thus, for instance, no greater taunt could be given by the Jews to our Lord than "Say we not well that Thou art a Samaritan and hast a devil?" (John viii. 48.) Jesus began to break down the wall of this partition when He healed the Syro-Phoenician woman and taught the woman at the well, and Philip continued in His steps until in the very parts where Jesus had preached, he proclaimed Christ to them.

The Response Given by the Samaritans

Philip had been cast out of Jerusalem, but he was joyfully received by the people of Samaria. They might be sunk in idolatry and sin, but they had probably been affected by the wave of expectation which for a long time had been passing over the East. Men were looking for a Messiah, a great Philosopher, One Who would take of the things of God and reveal them unto men. This eagerness, whilst it prepared the way for the Gospel, prepared the way also for religious impostors, who, as we see in the case of the Seven Churches in the Book of the Revelation, led the people away from instead of to Christ. Simon Magus was a heretical leader of this description, one whose name stands out in profane as well as Biblical history as having obtained a great hold upon the people of Samaria. St. Luke says little about him, for at this time he was not as notorious as he afterwards became. In the Acts we see that he gave himself out to be some great one, a revelation of God to man. Justin, writing of his later history, says that he claimed to be immortal, the begetter of all good, the creator of angels and archangels. According to Simon's creed, men were absolutely free, for they were saved by his grace and not by works. He became more popular in Rome even than in Samaria, and a statue was erected to his honour. This was the man who confronted Philip, and who for a long time bewitched the people by his magical gifts and sorceries. Our interest in him centres in the fact that heresy for the first time touched the Church in his person. Would Philip condone the laxity of his views for the sake of gaining so powerful a man and his adherents? Would he condone his lust of gain in order that through him Samaria might be won over to Christ?

A Child of the Devil

The practice of sorcery, or contact with the powers of evil, had been condemned in the book of Leviticus as an offspring of the demoniacal practices of the Canaanites. A wizard was a man who, whilst practising chemistry and sleight of hand, had sold himself to sin and come into contact with the spirits of evil. In the time of our Lord, as well as in the Acts, there seems to have been a direct manifestation, not only of the Spirit of God, but also of the spirit of evil. It was this spirit of evil that Philip met in the person of Simon Magus and his adherents. The Samaritans soon made their choice. Simon Magus might do signs and wonders, but Philip could bring healing to soul as well as to body. They received from his lips the word of life; from his hands the touch of the God of consolation. Some years before, Jesus had told the Woman of Samaria of the water of life, and it was with this water of life that Philip was now satisfying their thirst. Simon was at first astonished, and then believed; that is to say, he decided to throw in his lot with the disciples and to give his intellectual assent to the fact that Philip possessed power greater than his own. He declared himself to be one of his followers, and continued with him, wondering at the signs and miracles which he did.

The First Deputation to an Outlying Church

The glad news that Samaria had received the word of God came to Jerusalem, and the apostles rejoiced, although it is questionable whether they themselves would have preached in Samaria. They had heard the injunction of Jesus: "Go not into the way of the Gentiles, and into the cities of Samaria enter ye not." It is true that Jesus had bidden them also, "Go and teach all nations"; but, as we see from the story of Cornelius, they had not as yet understood the command in its fulness.

They decided to send Peter and John, the two apostles who had been nearest to Jesus and most distinctly under the power of His Holy Spirit. We wonder why, when Peter came, he accepted the Samaritans so readily, and did not deem them unclean like Cornelius; but we must remember that there was a strain of Jewish blood in them, and that they were far-off adherents of the Jewish faith; they formed, as it were, a connecting link between the Israelite and the Gentile Church.

The Laying-on of Hands

Peter and John must have rejoiced at the marvellous success which had attended the preaching of Philip. If Simon Magus and his followers had so quickly given in their adhesion to the new faith, the word of God might indeed go forth conquering and to conquer. But hearing that the converts, although baptised, had not as yet received the gift of the Holy Ghost, they prayed for them and laid their hands on them.

Much question has been raised as to the exact signification of this passage. Does it mean that the Holy Spirit is given only from the hands of an apostle, or does it mean that the peculiar gift, the gift accompanied by the power of working miracles and of speaking with tongues, was given only from an apostle? The latter seems to be the more probable. Christ had said that no man could call Him Lord save by the Holy Ghost, and it is clear that many of the Samaritans had called Jesus "Lord," had understood that Jesus was their God and King, and therefore had been moved by the Holy Ghost. Again, this second gift was accompanied by signs and wonders, for we find that Simon, when he saw that "the Holy Ghost was given," offered money.

The Prayer of Simon

Simon had for the moment surrendered his allegiance to the new faith, but he had not surrendered self. Pride, avarice, and ambition still swayed and controlled his thoughts and deeds. He saw in the new religion a chance of money-making, a chance of becoming in very deed a great power, and the lust of power and gain drew out the dormant passions of his nature. He was not content to tread in the path of the other followers of Jesus. He wanted immediately to become the equal of the apostles, to be united in power with them, and he offered money, saying, "Give me also this power, that on whomsoever I lay hands he may receive the Holy Ghost." Simon is the forerunner of a long succession of self-seekers who unite themselves with religion for ambitious ends, who seek to be princes and lords over God's heritage rather than shepherds of His flock. Therefore, ever since the time of Simon, the word "simony" has been applied to all those who have been guilty of this particular sin—that is to say, to those who have trafficked and by means of money have sought to gain place and power in the Church. Simon stands as the representative not only of the open sin, but of the hidden sin also—of the hypocrisy which lurks in every Church, seeking Mammon under the form of God.

The Response of Peter

Peter made straight paths for the feet of his successors. Thus, when the question was raised as to the authority of man over the Church, he replied: "We must obey God rather than man"; so too when money was offered, and, what was more than money, the adherence not only of Simon but of his followers, he replied: "Thy money perish with thee; thou hast neither part nor lot in this matter." The Church of God makes no real advance either by favour or by money. She advances by the working of the Holy Spirit in the heart of her followers, and by the purity and obedience of their faith. It was better to lose Samaria altogether than to receive into the Church the followers of a man who sought the outpouring of the Holy Spirit in order to make himself a power among men. Peter rebukes him very sharply. He tells Simon that he has neither part nor lot in the matter. His heart is not right in the sight of God; that is to say, it is not turned upwards towards God, it is crooked downwards and inwards towards himself, and he bids him repent and pray to God, for, though baptised, he is still afar off from Him. He bids him seek if perhaps the thought of his heart may be forgiven him.

The Question of Forgiveness

Why did Peter say "if perhaps"? Does not Christ say: "Him that cometh unto Me I will in no wise cast out"? The explanation of this word "perhaps" is given in the next verse. "I perceive that thou art in the gall of bitterness and in the bond of iniquity." The doubt was not as to Christ and His forgiveness; but as to whether Simon would come to seek that forgiveness; as to whether he was not so imbued, so bound up in iniquity, that he would keep coming back to self instead of coming to Christ. And this, alas! was only too true, for, according to tradition, Simon, instead of repenting, went to Rome and became a great power, winning over many followers to his views, men who became gall and bitterness, not only to themselves, but also to the Church of Christ; Simonites who were a gall and poison running through and embittering the whole Roman Church. The very response which Simon makes to the call to repentance shows how far away, how impossible, the new teaching was to him. He says: "Pray ye to the

Lord for me that none of these things which ye have spoken come upon me"; that is to say, "that none of the calamities fall upon me." He is absolutely without conception as to what the kingdom of God may be; he is concerned only with the thought of the calamity which may fall upon himself.

Jesus Must Needs Go through Samaria

As we read of the wonderful reception of the Gospel by the Samaritans, of their ready acceptance of the Bread of Life in preference to the husks which had been given to them by Simon, we wonder whether, even at the end of these ten years, some far-off echo of the words of Jesus still lingered in Samaria, some instinct of the spirit of worship which He had taught. The Samaritans had even then been athirst for the living God, for the woman of Samaria had said to Jesus, "I know that Messias cometh which is called Christ; when He is come He will tell us all things." Jesus, in response to her request, had given her a draught of the living water, a water springing up into everlasting life, and we see here that the words of Jesus, after long years, had not returned unto Him void. One more thought comes to us as we turn away from this lesson. The clouds had settled darkly over the Church in Jerusalem, but they had gathered in love rather than in judgment. The Lord of the harvest was thrusting forth His labourers into the harvest. May it be that the darkness which is overhanging the Church of to-day is again a darkness of love rather than of judgment? May it be that the Lord of the harvest is again bidding us be more faithful to our call; is bidding us go beyond Jerusalem; forego our own privileges, our money, our Barnabas and Saul, in order that we, not only individually but as a Church, may indeed seek first the kingdom of God and His righteousness? Ought we not, in answer to this token of His, to lift up our eyes upon the fields white already to harvest, and thrust in the sickle ere it be too late?

CHAPTER XIX

ACTS VIII. 25 TO END

THE BAPTISM IN THE WILDERNESS

The Man of Ethiopia

In the midst of Philip's busy work not only in the city but also in the villages of the Samaritans, the call came to arise and go toward the South, "unto the way that goeth down from Jerusalem unto Gaza" in order that he might meet "a man of Ethiopia, an eunuch of great authority under Candace, queen of the Ethiopians." The call must have seemed as inexplicable as the reverse which had fallen upon the Church of Jerusalem through the persecution of Saul, or that which had fallen upon the Church of Samaria through the defection of Simon Magus. Why was he called away and prevented from combatting the error which had arisen on every side in order that he might go out into the desert? He could only obey the moving of the Spirit of God, and, therefore, "he arose and went."

Ethiopia was the name given to the land bounded by the Nile on the west and the Red Sea and the Arabian Gulf on the east. It is here applied probably to the country which was known as the kingdom of Meroe and was ruled over by Candace, Queen of the Ethiopians. Candace was the dynastic title of the Queens of Ethiopia, and the Queen referred to in this chapter seems to have been rich and powerful, since the eunuch had charge "of all her treasure." There is practically nothing known beyond what is here related about this Candace. The eunuch, the treasurer of her kingdom, may have been a proselyte—that is to say, may have accepted the worship of the one God—but he had not been admitted to the Temple or allowed to take part in its rites and ceremonies. He had gone up to Jerusalem expressly to worship, and whilst there must have heard of the new faith and of one Jesus Who had been crucified. There, too, he must have heard men debating about the passage in Scripture which he was reading; the Jews would explain it by saying that Isaiah referred either to the prophet himself or to some other good man, although until now they had always taught that it was a reference to the coming Messiah. The discussions which he had heard may have led him to read and ponder over this passage, or he may have been led to it by the direct inspiration of the Spirit of God; the same guidance which had brought Philip into the wilderness having drawn him to the study of the fifty-third chapter of Isaiah.

THE BAPTISM IN THE WILDERNESS

"Understandest Thou What Thou Readest?"

When Philip saw in the distance the chariot of the eunuch surrounded by the usual company of followers and fellow-travellers, and was bidden by the Spirit of God to draw near and join himself to the chariot, the purpose of his journey became manifest to him; but it became even clearer when, walking by the side of the chariot, he heard the eunuch reading aloud the familiar words of the prophet Isaiah. There was no formality on either side, for each man was in earnest; the eunuch was athirst for the living water, Philip longed to give of that water, the source of his own spiritual life. Wherever a longing for God on the part of the hearer exists side by side with a yearning on that of the preacher, languor and indifference flee away. Where life is at stake, criticism and carelessness die away. If the way of Philip as teacher was prepared by the study of the Scriptures on the part of the eunuch, so too is the way of the preacher of to-day prepared by the study on the part of the hearer not only of the Old Testament but of the New Testament also. The question of the eunuch: "How can I, except some man should guide me?" could never be asked with the same force to-day as it was then. The New Testament lights up with beauty and radiance the form dimly shadowed in Old Testament prophecy, and men see Jesus so that the way is made straight and the path prepared for the further instruction of the preacher.

"He Preached unto Him Jesus"

The eunuch had been to Jerusalem to worship, but although he had sought God in His Temple and in the Scriptures they were as yet dark and meaningless to him. He could see how both the teaching of the Temple and the Scriptures pointed towards some Great One; whether the prophet himself or One greater he did not know. But with the coming of Philip a flash of light was cast upon the dark page, and he saw the form and character of Jesus reflected in it. He saw Jesus, in the quiet dignity of His royal strength, led as a sheep to the slaughter; saw why He Who had not opened His mouth except when His silence might have been taken as an admission that He was not the Messiah. He saw Jesus, Who by His very humiliation was freed from the unjust judgment passed upon Him; Who was slain that He might leave behind Him a countless seed or generation; Jesus, Whose life had been taken from the earth that He might live for ever at the right hand of His Father in heaven.

The Baptism in the Wilderness

How long Philip continued his journey with the eunuch we do not know, but the whole plan of salvation, the mystery of the dealing of God with man, was unfolded before his eyes, and he longed to make open confession of his faith and receive the full benefit of

THE BAPTISM IN THE WILDERNESS

Christian fellowship and communion; and therefore, as they drew near to water, he asked "What doth hinder me to be baptised?" He may have thought that objection might be made to him on account of his race and personality. But Philip in his reply shows that there is no respect of persons with God. He asked: "Dost thou believe?" and the eunuch replied: "I believe that Jesus Christ is the Son of God." In the Revised Version verse 37 has been put in the margin because it is not found in some of the original texts; but, whether found in every text or not, the question and answer show what the accepted requirements of the early Christian Church were, viz. faith in Christ and Christ alone. The eunuch had found Christ as surely as St. Paul before Damascus, and therefore nothing hindered him to be baptised. Then followed that strange scene which has afforded play to the imagination of poet and painter alike. In the stillness and solitude of the desert, in the presence only of his followers, with the unknown difficulties and complications of the Eastern life awaiting him at Court, the eunuch was baptised as a servant of Christ and stood side by side with Philip in the water, a spiritual partaker of the water of life proceeding out of the Throne of God and of the Lamb.

"The Eunuch Saw Him No More"

When Jesus had been revealed to the eunuch in the Scriptures and united with him by baptism and by a living faith, Philip's errand was completed; he was caught away, and the eunuch saw him no more. The

Scriptures are silent as to the after-life of the eunuch and tell little as to that of Philip either. Each man went forth to stand in his allotted place till the fulness of his time should come. The eunuch was filled with joy, for he had found the reason of life and saw the whole vista of the hereafter opened before him. Whether his after-life and testimony were mighty for God we know not; it is sealed up until the time of the end; but one thing we do know—that he who was so earnest a seeker after truth could never forget the miraculous interposition, the angel of the Lord who had been sent to him, know also that he would be one of those who go from strength to strength until they appear before God in Zion.

Philip, who had followed the call of the spirit into the desert, was caught up by the same spirit and found at Azotus, where he preached in the surrounding cities until he came to Caesarea. He passes away from the history of the Christian Church almost as suddenly as the eunuch, except that twenty years later St. Paul and St. Luke were in Caesarea, "in the house of Philip the evangelist." It was from St. Philip that St. Luke doubtless heard the details of the work in Samaria and of the conversion of the eunuch.

"Till He Came to Caesarea"

There are strange contrasts in the life of Philip, just as there are strange contrasts in the lives of us all. He who was called to be a prominent leader, to succeed Stephen and put into practice the principles for which Stephen had died—to open the door of the Church to the Gentiles—was appointed later to stand aside and to take his place among the countless number who have given long years of their life to the gradual building-up and edifying of one particular Church of God. The character of the work which he undertook was comparatively of little moment to Philip, just as it is of comparatively little moment to any of the servants of God so long as they can hear the Master's voice, can know that it is what they are called to do. The servants of God have all alike one glorious privilege, a consciousness that they are known of Him, that their responsibility in life is assigned by Him, that they pass from place to place at His command and will. They may go down into the battle, or they may tarry by the stuff (1 Samuel xxx. 24); they may go forth conquering and to conquer, or they may stand and wait; but whatever their lot is they are the servants of the King; they are doing His will on earth as it is done in heaven; they know that

> "The soldier may not move from watchful sted,
> Nor leave his stand until his captain bed;"

they wait until

> "He that points the centonell his roome
> Doth license him depart at sound of morning droome;"

and the time is not long, for their

> "Bright radiant eyes do plainly see
> The Idea of His pure glory present still."

The Right Direction of Missionary Work

The call to leave Samaria was so clear to Philip that he had only to go forward; but the call is not always equally clear to us, and there are times when we know not whether to seek the individual soul "for whom Christ died" and for whom there is "joy in the presence of the angels of God," or to lift up our eyes to the "fields white already to harvest" and seek the evangelization of the world rather than that of the one individual soul. But light will come out of darkness, and the way clear according as we are willing to follow the leading of His will, and whilst reading all work in the light of the life of Christ to see the exquisite proportion which he kept in respect to this also. The life of Jesus seems to have been given either to the saving of the individual soul or to preparing the way for the salvation of the world, according as we read the Gospel with the one thought or with the other uppermost in our minds. Thus Jesus turned aside from the multitude to teach the woman of Samaria; turned aside, as it were, from the anguish of His soul, when the transgression of the whole world was passing over it, to the thief upon the cross. We learn a like exquisite proportion from the life of St. Paul, for St. Paul went everywhere with unfaltering aim, either to the conquest of an empire for Christ, or to the planning of a missionary tour with God-given wisdom, or to the planting of a new Church wherever he believed it would be most powerful for Christ, whilst at the same time he never forgot either the individual Church or the individual man. However hardly the strife pressed upon him, he could write to a Timothy or a Philemon, he could bear in mind and pray for the individual convert and his individual need. This lesson of the value of the individual soul is very hard for us to retain with our finite perceptions as we become interested in the onward march of the Church, the onward march of our great missionary organizations—for, owing to our limited capacity, we see through a glass darkly; we dimly outline the eternity of all around us.

Our second difficulty arises because we have to walk by faith and not by sight. We do not know the issue which may depend upon our immediate response to the direct call of God. When Philip baptised the eunuch in the wilderness, he had apparently only sought out an individual soul for Christ, but, unconsciously to himself, he had broken down a wall of partition between the Jews and the Gentiles, and had continued the work which he had begun in Samaria. Still less did he know that the effect of his reception of the eunuch would go still further, would prepare the way not only for the reception of Cornelius, but also of the Gentile world, and would encourage Peter and all who were scattered abroad to preach the Word not among the Jews and proselytes only, but among the Gentiles also. We are apt in our short sight to grieve for lives which we believe to have been sacrificed in vain. We would bid men devote their labour wherever it would be most quickly crowned with success. We need to look back and see that some of those who have led forlorn hopes, who for many years of their life have seemed to be failures not only to themselves but to others, have nevertheless founded spiritual empires for Christ. We know the long time of discouragement which Henry Martyn in India, Morrison in China, Livingstone in Africa, and Marsden in New Zealand, passed through before they conquered, as in the persons of their successors they still do conquer for Christ.

CHAPTER XX

ACTS IX. 1 AND 2
SAUL AND THE CHURCH

Saul was glad that he had made havoc of the Church at Jerusalem; he might have viewed matters differently if he had known that he had changed an ideal community of saints into a vast missionary organization. But despite his apparent success, even he himself seems to have been uneasy lest the latter state might be worse than the first, lest the men who had suffered persecution for the sake of the faith would spread that faith wherever they went, and therefore, still breathing out threatenings and slaughter, he went to the high priest and besought letters that he might bring them bound unto Jerusalem.

How marvelously for the time fortune seemed to have favoured the high priest and his party! The man whom they needed, who had the daring to incur the odium which they dreaded, had come forward—had, as they thought, extirpated Christianity in Jerusalem, and was now ready to extirpate it in Damascus also. How gladly must the high priest have given those letters!— the very giving of them was a proof that Christianity as a power was no longer dreaded in Jerusalem. How had such a man as Saul thus suddenly arisen? What country, what home had produced a character so zealous, so outstanding as his?

Saul of Tarsus

Saul was born in Tarsus, "a citizen of no mean city." The mighty Taurus mountains rose to the north, their snow-capped summits contrasting with the river Cydnus, whose blue waters, fed by the eternal snow, poured down the mountain-side and flowed thence onward to the sea. But the beauty of the mountains and of the scenery which surrounded him seems to have made little impression upon Saul; he does not, like our Lord, constantly refer to them and illustrate his teaching from them. On the contrary, he seems to have been occupied with the stream of life, with the emotions and ambitions of the men whom the same river Cydnus brought into the city. On the one side travellers kept pouring in from the southern end of the great trade and war route across Mount Taurus, through the famous pass called the Cilician Gates; on the other side sailors and travellers of all descriptions gathered into the town from the ships which, laden with produce from every distant land, kept on passing up and down the river. It was in the midst of this busy throb of life, with a nature peculiarly sensitive, peculiarly capable of understanding the characters of all around him, that the boy grew up three-sided—a Jew, a Tarsian, and a Roman.

A Jew, a Hebrew sprung from the Hebrews, a Pharisee of the strictest sect, conscious that his race possessed the oracles of God, accustomed to look beyond the present to the unseen, he thought of himself as living in the conscious presence and favour of God. He grew up surrounded by the purity of the Jewish religion, which, despite its encumbering rites and ceremonies, stood out in startling contrast to the unblushing wickedness around him.

As a Tarsian he lived in the midst of men and of affairs, the extraordinary versatility of his nature being fostered by contact with the men of varying types and nationalities around him; but still more by the influence of the wider thought and culture of the individual which was fostered in every Greek city.

Saul the Roman Citizen

But, besides being thus spiritually a Jew and intellectually a Greek, Saul was also potentially a Roman. His father had acquired the freedom of a Roman citizen, probably for some great service which either he or his family had rendered to the Roman State, but the inheritance of that citizenship affected the whole outlook of a boy as keen-witted and high-souled as Saul was. In the first place, he grew up a member of the highest aristocracy, not only in Tarsus, but having also the freedom of the land, as it were, in every city into which he came. Greater than this was the breadth of thought given by this freedom, his horizon being bounded not by the Jewish nation—although that was ever first with him—nor by the Greek thought, wide as its philosophy and teaching was, but by the mighty empire of Rome itself. Rome with its boundless possibilities would one day be the empire of the coming Messiah, a day-dream far nearer realization in afterdays when his earthly vision had been purified by the heavenly, and Rome became to him a spiritual kingdom to be conquered for another King, one Jesus.

The boy learned his trade like every other Jewish child. Along the mountain slopes of the Taurus there browsed in great abundance mountain goats, and the hair of these goats was woven into tents and coverings. This was the manual trade which was chosen for Saul, and little did the boy think as his nimble fingers twisted the hard goats' hair that one day he would ply that trade in grim earnest, and from time to time be dependent upon it for his very living.

Saul at the Feet of Gamaliel

When he was thirteen years old he went to Jerusalem and entered the school of Gamaliel, then the greatest theologian and scholar of his day. In the schools of that period great stress was laid upon argumentative learning, the boys being taught to propound problems to one another, and to argue rapidly backwards and forwards, thereby acquiring readiness of wit in understanding the general bearing of a question, as well as skill in seizing upon the chief points of an argument. When these contests were under the guidance of a man as strong and sympathetic as Gamaliel, as skilful in understanding and controlling the thoughts of all around him, as well as in supplementing the crude intelligence and reasoning of his pupils, we can see what a wonderful preparation these contests would give to a boy like Saul, and how they would prepare him for his after-life. In addition to the training which he received under Gamaliel he must, owing to his family influence, have come into contact with intellectual men of all kinds in Jerusalem. (*Cf.* Acts xxiii. 16.) This was the early training of the man who was the chosen representative of the chief rulers, the great opponent of the early Church.

The Return of Saul to Jerusalem

We do not know where Saul was or what occupied him from the time of his youth until he took the lead in the martyrdom of St. Stephen. He could not have been in Jerusalem; for if he had been, keenly interested as he was in everything which touched his religion, he must have seen and heard Jesus and have recognized Him when, like St. Stephen, he saw Him in the vision at Damascus. But, despite this, whenever he was in Jerusalem Saul must have seen and heard much about Jesus and His followers. He must, for instance, have worshipped in the synagogue in which the men of Cilicia gathered, have listened to Stephen, and in all probability taken part in the arguments against him. The immediate effect of these arguments would, however, only embitter him against Christianity; for, starting as he did from the premiss that Jesus had been powerless against the arm of the law and the curse of death, how could he look upon the account of His Resurrection as anything but an invention of the disciples? The attitude of his mind at this period can only be imperfectly gathered from the allusions which he makes to it in his later letters. From them we find that he had reached the knowledge of a double nature within himself, as well as recognizing the chasm which existed between his nature and the law of God. What had brought him to the knowledge of that nature? Partly the study of the Jewish law, partly the indirect influence of the new teaching. He had heard the arguments of the Christians, had felt the assault which they made upon his central convictions. He had seen their constancy, knew that their faith was not a matter of opinion but their very life itself. He must also have been influenced indirectly by the character of Jesus, and have known from the words of the Christians that His character corresponded to the prophecy contained in Isaiah liii.; he must have known also that despite all his efforts he could not attain to the righteousness of Christ. But on the other hand, until he received the overwhelming certainty of the Resurrection, a certainty brought about not merely by a mental vision, but also by an objective reality, he could not put the law aside, give up the national privileges of the Jews, and embrace Christianity, the far-reaching consequences of which he could apprehend far better than the Christians themselves.

SAUL AND THE CHURCH

The Problem of Judaism and Christianity

Saul therefore unhesitatingly, passionately held to the Jewish religion and persecuted the Christian Church; and the more passionately he threw himself on the side of the one religion, the more antagonistic his attitude necessarily became to the other, for the problem which lay before the Jews of that period was how to keep the Jewish life and religion pure, exposed as it was, not only to the influence of the Romans in Jerusalem, but also to the influence of Greece and Rome in the towns of the Dispersion. There was no question that Judaism had either to conquer or to be conquered. It was a life-and-death struggle between the worship of the Emperor and of the true God. Saul probably hoped that the highest intellects of Greece and Rome would be attracted by the purity of the Jewish religion, and that if they could be led to adopt the worship of God as one of their many religions its influence might pervade and raise the standard of all other religions. But if Judaism were to prevail it must stand forth as a united whole; it must not be weakened or its doctrines encumbered by the tenets of Christianity, for what Greek or Roman would accept the Jewish religion if Christianity were intermingled with it? How could a proud Roman accept the tenets and become the follower of a Galilean peasant, a Man slain by His own nation, a Man Whose followers were known to be despised and ignorant men? It was on this account that Christianity was dangerous, because it struck directly across Saul's Jewish aspirations, his chosen life-work; and it was to this life-work that in all probability he had dedicated himself, and given up marriage (1 Corinthians vii. 8), and had set his face towards eternity. The death of Stephen, the constancy of the Christians, affected him only in so far as they revealed the strength and vitality of the force opposed to him. Hence he went beyond what even his religion could have required of him, and obtained letters to Damascus, in order that the Jews who dwelt in the towns of the Dispersion and were under the same law as those of Jerusalem might, if they were "of this way," be brought "bound unto Jerusalem."

CHAPTER XXI

ACTS IX. 3-9

SAUL'S CONVERSION

The City of Damascus

The city of Damascus is the oldest city of the world. We read of it in the time of Abraham (Genesis xiv. 15). We know the love which the citizens of Damascus, such as Naaman, bore to its "golden flowing rivers," its Abana and Pharpar, "streams from Lebanon," rivers of Damascus. These streams break into countless watercourses, each watercourse fertilizing its banks so that they become "a wilderness of gardens." Above these glitter the white towers of the city, forming so dazzling a contrast to the desert around that Damascus is known as "the eye of the East." The history of the city reaches back over long years, "the burden of Damascus" being one of the notes of Jewish prophecy.

This was the town towards which Saul was hastening after a week's journey from Jerusalem, a week heavy with the anticipation of coming sorrow to the Christians in Damascus, for day by day and hour by hour they knew that their enemy was bearing down upon them. It was a week heavy also for Saul, inasmuch as it gave him a first breathing space for thought and reflection. On the one side was his determination at all costs to stamp out the hated race; on the other, his equally strong determination to uphold the Jewish religion, despite the cruelty involved by persecution, from which his naturally affectionate and warm-hearted temperament must have revolted, despite the marvellous witness of the men faithful unto death. If he had not been certain that Christianity was founded upon a delusion, and that delusion so vital a one as the question of the Resurrection, it is impossible to understand how Saul could have resisted Stephen's argument, his prayers, his peaceful falling asleep in Jesus.

"Jesus Whom Thou Persecutest"

As Saul journeyed onward a light from heaven, exceeding even the glare of the noonday sun under which he was travelling, a glory like that which Moses had seen of old in the desert, which had been with the Children of Israel in the Wilderness, and on the Mount of Transfiguration, even the glory of Jesus, surrounded him. He heard the voice of God calling him by name; heard it once again when, in answer to his startled question "Who art Thou, Lord?" the reply came "I am Jesus, Whom thou persecutest; it is hard for thee to kick against the pricks." In a moment his whole character and his past life were revealed to him in their true light. He saw himself as surely as we shall each of us one day see ourselves and our past life also when they are revealed to us in the light of God. "Ye have done it unto Me" are the words which must then sound in our ears, though now out of mercy to the infirmity of our flesh we hear only the echo of them. But whilst these words of Jesus, like a sharp sword, divided asunder, piercing even to the thoughts and intents of his heart, the love of Jesus spoke in words of tenderest mercy. The familiar proverb, "It is hard for thee to kick against the pricks"—a paradox similar to those with which Jesus was accustomed to emphasize His teaching—came with a meaning full of exquisite beauty and compassion. Whilst Saul had been persecuting Jesus, Jesus had understood every motive and every act and had been filled with compassion for him. He had seen his blindness, had felt his pain, had recognized the self-sacrifice of his mistaken zeal, and from time to time had, by a sharp pang, awakened the conscience of His servant, just as the owner of an ox may touch its shoulder with an iron goad in order to turn it into the right path.

"Arise and Go"

If Saul had been filled with trembling and astonishment at the sight of Jesus and at the revelation of his past life, he was filled with passionate love and remorse when he knew by these words that Jesus had read the inmost thoughts of his heart and had understood every step of the struggle which he had been passing through. The oil and wine of this love, of this perfect understanding, coming as it did at the moment of his lowest depth, was so marvellous, so contrary to all his previous conceptions of God and of religion, that from that instant he became the bondslave of his Lord. He had one desire, and one only—"Lord, what wilt Thou have me to do?" But it was not the outward form of Jesus, not the mere fact of His Resurrection which affected him, but the glimpses which had been revealed to him of the love and long-suffering passion of Jesus. Henceforth there could be only the pouring-out of his deeply affectionate nature, the turning from religious fanaticism to a passionate devotion towards a personal Saviour and God. He cried out as Isaiah cried out, as every man who has truly touched Jesus has cried and will cry: "Lord, what wilt Thou have me to do?" And he was answered by a miracle of self-revelation and of love, greater even, if it were possible, than that which he had experienced before. Jesus looked at Saul, and as He looked the past fled away; Jesus put it afar off, as far as the east is from the west, and Saul was a free man; and above all, Jesus, as He looked at him, saw only the future, its possibilities and its utmost. At that one glance Saul lost the burden of his sin, he gained the vision of his life, and he had at the same time a foretaste of the depth of a love which passeth knowledge, a love which alone could enable him to realize that marvellous vision of his life.

"The Men Which Journeyed with Him"

The men who journeyed with him stood speechless, hearing a voice but seeing no man. Jesus revealed

SAUL'S CONVERSION

Himself then, as ever, only to the lost; to the man who, though far off and blind, yet feeling after Him if haply he might find Him, could receive the truth of His Resurrection. The light, the sound, were present to the men who journeyed with him, but they could not interpret them, they could perceive nothing—a true picture of life and of the solitude of the soul, which, like that of Paul, must ever at its supreme moments be alone. "A stranger intermeddleth not with its joy." A true picture also of the general attitude of the world towards religion. Like the men who journeyed with him, how many know that there is something mysterious, something beyond themselves in life! but feeling dimly that this mystery lies hid in God they stand without, hearing a voice but seeing no man, hearing self, and because they hear self only, caring for naught else.

Saul rose from the earth physically shattered, blind, and trembling—a contrast to the conqueror who, at the head of his soldiers, was to have come into Damascus striking terror and destruction into the heart of every Christian who opposed him; and yet Saul of Tarsus, broken and helpless, seeking only to be alone, had found the secret of a true grandeur, far greater than any he had pictured in his dreams, far nobler even than that of his name-sake Saul when he towered head and shoulders above his fellows and brought back the victorious army from Jabesh Gilead. For Saul of Tarsus had seen that which Saul the son of Kish ever failed to see, and, having seen, had not been "disobedient to the heavenly vision."

The Miracle of Saul's Conversion

What made this mighty change? How was it that a man so determined, so entirely possessed by one overmastering passion, could as by a lightning flash change not only the purpose of his life, but even the very character of his being? How could he overcome his strongest prejudices, how sink his personality so that he was content only according as henceforth the nature and character of Christ might be manifested in and through him? To this question there can be one answer, and one answer only. Then, as now, the miracle of the transforming love of Jesus, the discovery of a personality so transcendent, a love so unfathomable that all past transgression is buried beneath its depths, effects a new creation. The trembling and astonished man sees himself no longer in the darkness of the past, but in the light of the future; he forgets the things that are behind, he reaches forward to the things that are before, he sees a new hereafter revealed to his astonished eyes, a hereafter touched with the beauty of holiness, a hereafter in which Christ becomes the centre of his life, controlling the will, heart, and thought of the servant who has surrendered himself to Him.

CHAPTER XXII

ACTS IX. 10-30

"RISE, STAND UPON THY FEET"

The Valley of the Shadow

For three days Saul lay in the valley of the shadow of humiliation, in physical and spiritual darkness, without food, as far removed from contact with the world around him as the men already dead. His nature was absorbed in one Titanic conflict within, until at last relief came; he prayed, and, praying, touched by faith the outstretched hand of Christ. Saul had surrendered wealth, rank, friendship, the freedom of the world, he had chosen Christ, and Christ only. Henceforth he was content, if need be, to be counted as the offscouring of all things, to be rejected of Christian and Pharisee alike. But Saul, though dead to the world, could not abide alone; he must bring forth fruit unto everlasting life, and therefore Christ came to him, not only in vision, but also in the person of His servant Ananias, and called him to arise and witness unto men. How grateful must have been the touch and word of Ananias; how full the token of forgiveness, coming as it did from the very lips of the man whom Saul had come to Damascus to destroy! For Ananias was at this time probably a leader in the Church at Damascus. He certainly knew Christ, and when called by Jesus responded readily, not having to say, like Saul, "Who art Thou, Lord?"

We find in this chapter three instances of men who heard the voice of Jesus and responded very differently, according as their heart was prepared to receive that call. The men who journeyed with Saul, caring nothing for the things of God, heard a voice but saw no man; Saul, having a zeal of God but not according to knowledge, heard a voice and was stricken to the ground, but found and saw Jesus; and Ananias, being a devout man, heard and communed with God as a man communes with his friend. It is true that Ananias, like Moses, hesitated to obey the voice that sent him, and before going laid the whole matter, the whole ground of his hesitation and fear, before the King; but his hesitation having been removed, he went forth at once to do his Master's bidding.

We can almost see him as he goes down the street Straight (a street still to be seen in Damascus, though no longer distinguished by the three avenues of colonnades which had formerly been the pride of the city), raises up the stricken man, confirms the heavenly vision, and restores health to soul and body alike.

The Sojourn in Arabia

We find in the Epistle to the Galatians that Saul, after having seen the heavenly vision, went immediately into Arabia. But from the reading in the Acts it seems as though he preached immediately in Damascus; whereas when we compare the two passages together we see that the "straightway" of verse 10 rather seems to refer to his preaching upon his second return to Damascus. It is difficult to see how any course except going to Arabia would have been possible to him, for the fury of the Sanhedrin and of the high priests must have known no bounds so soon as they received the almost inconceivable tidings that he, their chosen delegate, the commander of their band of soldiers, had passed over to the ranks of the enemy. He could not, therefore, either for his own sake or for that of his fellow-Christians, remain within reach of Jerusalem; but besides this, even if he had been willing to attempt to do so, he was for the time mentally and spiritually as well as physically shattered. Saul, like all other leaders for Christ, must before witnessing know the will of God, must "see that Just One and hear the words of His mouth," must in solitude and detachment of spirit "learn not of men, neither by man, but by the revelation of Jesus Christ."

It has generally been thought that Saul went into the wilderness of Mount Sinai, and there, alone, beneath the grandeur of the mountain which had once been moved by the very presence of God, spent his soul in communion with God. Under that mountain or in the surrounding wilderness he learned, like Moses and Joshua before him, what great things he must suffer, what "stripes without number, prisons more frequent, deaths oft." Scripture is silent as to the mystery of the three years spent in communion with God, but it is not silent as to the issue of that communion. From that time forward Saul deliberately faced the future, and by the power of God changed the whole current of his life. He learned by revelation the reason of the faith that was in him. He received by the same revelation that Gospel which he later declared (1 Corinthians xv. 1-3), that Gospel which stands forth with the power of God unto salvation.

And as he received it he learned to reckon that the "sufferings of this present time are not worthy to be compared with the glory which shall be revealed in us." Would that the followers of Christ to-day understood, like Saul, the meaning of the great renunciation, that alone with Christ they faced the future not only with the glow of heaven, but also with the storm and stress of the coming conflict upon it!—for the Church needs to-day, as never before, men who will be its leaders; men who are prepared through much tribulation to enter into the kingdom of God; who have stood beneath Mount Sinai, beneath the shadow of the eternal law as well as the eternal love, and have caught the hidden fire of entire consecration to God. These are the men who "seek first the kingdom of God and His righteousness," who instead of being devotees of compromise and self-preservation rather than of God, instead of going not astray because they go not at all, press forward towards the mark of the prize of their high calling in Christ Jesus.

"Jesus . . . the Son of God"

Saul, recreated anew in Christ, returned from the wilderness, and, standing in the synagogue of Damascus, preached Christ—that "He is the Son of God." This preaching marks a step forward in the progress of the early Church, for although the disciples had already recognized and preached Christ as the Son of God, yet the thought of the Messiahship had been uppermost in their minds. But Saul, in the sight of the greater, had lost all consciousness of the less. He was determined to know nothing amongst them save Jesus Christ and Him crucified, Jesus Christ the Son of God. We need not wonder that the disciples had been slow in gaining a right perspective, in losing this sense of the Messiahship in the greater sense of the Divinity of Christ; for if we look at our own spiritual life we shall see how hardly these facts which we have understood, known, and admitted, assume their right proportion, pass from subconsciousness to consciousness, attain mastery over our lives, and, attaining it, determine the character of our thoughts, words, and deeds. And what is true of the individual spiritual life is true of the spiritual life of the Church also. Truths which for a long time have lain dormant have at last, through the power of the Holy Spirit, arisen, and, having arisen and being instinct with life and power, have drawn the hearts and lives of men upward to their heights. Take, for instance, the great change which passed over the disciples as soon as Peter passed from a subconscious to a conscious perception of the truth that Jesus was the Son of God; and take the change which passed over the early Church as soon as he emphasized, in his preaching, Jesus as the Son of God. Take the change which passed over spiritual life when the Society of Friends emphasized the power of the Holy Spirit, or the change which would pass over the Church of God to-day if out of the midst of the present strife and darkness Christ were more clearly manifested as the Son of God. The Divinity of Christ was the message which Saul proclaimed in the synagogues, and in the light of that Divinity he saw the whole scheme of man's redemption and the relationship of man to God. This was the message which aroused the antagonism of the Jews so bitterly against him. They could not contradict his words, "for Saul increased the more in strength and confounded the Jews which dwelt at Damascus, proving that this is the very Christ"; but they could hinder their effect by bringing forward the contradiction of his former life. What a contrast there is between this action on the part of the Jews and that of Jesus when He met Saul on the way to Damascus! In other words, what a contrast there is between the malice and littleness of man and the greatness and love of God! God looks inward and forward; He sees the possibility, the life which in the beauty of holiness may yet be offered to Him; whereas man looks back and dwells on the deformity, the deadness, and the self-seeking of the past life. It is this littleness on the part of man which gives past sin its power, which enables it to hinder and thwart, even the men who have been set free by God and accepted in His service.

"The Jews Took Counsel to Kill Him"

Finding that they could avail nothing, the Jews took counsel to kill Saul. They recognized in him a man who would continue the work of Jesus, who would destroy the Temple and change the customs which Moses had delivered. Hence their bitter antagonism against him, so that he was forced to escape for his life. Some have thought that Saul was so much overwhelmed by the opposition of the Jews, and by the impossibility of convincing them of the truth, that he was for the time unmanned, and that an attack of the infirmity which henceforth hindered his work came upon him; but there is no authority in support of this supposition. We know only that the disciples took him by night and let him down by the wall in a basket. What a contrast does this departure of Saul, this escape in so humiliating a manner, make to the day-dream which in his imagination he must have pictured three years ago as the end of his work in the city! He had intended to leave Damascus at the head of a band of soldiers, in a kind of Roman triumph, dragging a long chain of captive men and women, demonstrating to Damascus, and through Damascus to the other towns of the Dispersion, the triumph of the Jewish religion. In later years (see 2 Corinthians ii. 32) Paul, when recounting the suffering of his past life, speaks of this midnight escape as a moment of great suffering and degradation; for his suffering of mind was, in all probability, far greater than that of body. He was rejected of men, cast away in vain. It was thus that he made his way to Jerusalem and attempted to join himself to the disciples, but they were all afraid of him. It seems very strange to us that Saul should have been shunned by the disciples. We should have thought that the whole story of his conversion and of his great renunciation would have been known in Jerusalem as it is known to us, but we forget how greatly it was to the advantage both of Christians and of Jews that the whole matter should be kept as quiet as possible. His defection was a bitter mortification to the High Priest and to the rulers; they would treat it as a result of a sudden accession of illness or madness. The Christians also would be equally afraid of speaking of it; they distrusted Saul, and even if it were true would fear lest the news of his conversion should provoke the High Priest to renewed attacks against them.

The Son of Consolation

Saul was, therefore, indeed alone in Jerusalem. As far as the Jews were concerned, he was drinking to the full the bitter cup of friendship lost for ever; as far as the Christians were concerned, the equally bitter cup of distrust and suspicion. What could he do, forsaken and dreaded by all alike? It was into this second valley of the shadow that Barnabas came on a mission as full of danger as that of Ananias, but as full of love also—Barnabas, literally "the son of a paraclete or the Holy Spirit," the one called to the side for comfort and help, so filled with the love of Christ that he could believe in the power of God to make even of Saul a new man, and, believing, could bring Saul to the apostles and proclaim the change which had passed over him. Would that we could have the same courage and tenderness also, that instead of fearing lest we might be deceived, instead of hesitating till time has shown the issue, we could take those who are seeking Christ boldly by the hand and welcome them into our midst. Had Barnabas shunned Saul, who can tell what the after-remorse of the Church might have been? Who can tell the loss to Christendom? Saul would unquestionably have gone forward and have fulfilled the mission to which he was called, but he would not have been thrown into immediate fellowship and communion with Peter; he might have founded a Church of the Gentiles apart and on different lines from that of Jerusalem. The step which had been taken by Barnabas was confirmed by all the brethren, although Peter and James seem at this time to have been the only apostles in Jerusalem. Saul was welcomed at once to the house of Peter, and abode for fifteen days in intercourse with him. How marvellous must have been the communion between these two great apostles, these two founders of the Church of Christ, these two men, each of whom had been taught by Jesus and by Jesus only.

A Life's Vision

Besides the communion with St. Peter, Saul proclaimed Jesus boldly, proclaiming even in the very synagogues in which Stephen had preached before him; he "disputed against the Grecians, but they went about to slay him." Finding, therefore, that they would not receive his words, and that he was in imminent danger of his life, the brethren besought him to go to Caesarea and proceed thence to Tarsus. But Saul, whose heart as yet yearned over Jerusalem, and who had not as yet undertaken the commission which Jesus had given to him, was cast down at the thought of this second rejection. To what purpose was the sacrifice of his life if he were thus cast out of every city? Could it be possible that it was all in vain? Thus despairing, like Hezekiah before him, he took refuge in the Temple, and pouring out his soul in prayer fell into a trance and heard Jesus saying to him: "Make haste and get thee quickly out of Jerusalem, for they will not receive the testimony concerning Me." If Saul had lost the friendship of the world, he had gained a friendship which was far greater. The voice of Jesus is now the voice that he is waiting for; he is no longer stricken down by it, but, like Ananias, casts his burden upon Him Who understands and cares for him. He tells how his past sin is letting and hindering him in the race that is set before him—how the Jews refuse to listen to a man who "imprisoned and beat in every synagogue them that believed on Jesus," and "when the blood of Stephen was shed . . . kept

"RISE, STAND UPON THY FEET"

the raiment of them that slew him." But Jesus in reply takes His servant by the hand, bids him lift up his eyes and see the life-work which He has given him, lying outstretched in all its vastness before him. "Depart, for I will send thee far hence unto the Gentiles." With these words the problem of his life is solved, and he is once again a free man. The desire of his heart, with which he set out to Damascus, will be realized in a manner different from that in which he had first conceived it. He will go forth to find men and women and to bring them bound into Jerusalem; but not to the Jerusalem below—not to the city which has despised and rejected his Master as it has despised and rejected him, but to the New City, to the Heavenly Jerusalem, the City of the Great King.

There is a vision known to Jesus of our life and of our life-work also, and He reveals it to us from time to time according as we are able to bear it. He lifts the mist, and we see His will; a change comes, the limitations and the circumstances against which we have been struggling, the pricks against which we have been kicking, and which have blocked our way, become, now that we can see them in the sunshine of God's love, the tokens to lead us to His will. Our murmurs die down; they are stilled in wonder and in love; and in the stillness our ears become attuned, and we hear the voice of Jesus saying "I will send thee far hence"; or if He so wills it, "This is the way, walk ye in it."

CHAPTER XXIII

ACTS IX. 31

THE DAYSPRING OF THE GENTILES

The Temporary Cessation of Persecution

A welcome period of rest succeeded "the great persecution against the Church which was at Jerusalem." The flame of persecution died down as suddenly as it had arisen. Saul the persecutor had himself joined the ranks of the persecuted, and the Jews were face to face with a religious war—a war in which the pride as well as the power of Rome was involved and consequently one from which there could be no release. Caligula had commanded his statue to be erected in the Temple and his worship cultivated in the city of Jerusalem, as well as in every town and Province throughout the Empire. He knew that this would be contrary to the spirit of the Jewish nation; but he was determined to bend them to his power. It was strange that the Jews, who for centuries had been left comparatively undisturbed in their worship, should have been called upon first to worship Jesus of Nazareth, and then, when they refused to do so, to fall down before the Emperor of Rome.

It is well to stop here for a moment and to consider the conflict between Caligula and the Jews, and the relative position of Jerusalem and Rome.

Jerusalem and Rome

Rome, although weakened by the corruption of her Emperors, was still by common consent the mistress of the world. Enthroned upon her seven hills, strong in herself and in every fibre of her being, she had planted her Colonies and her legions in every important centre, and they were accustomed to respond to the slightest manifestation of her will. She could ask for nothing more than unlimited power, unbroken communication by means of the great Roman roads to the remotest corners of her Empire, a common language, and a common peace. But underlying all this marvellous organization there lay a cancer of self and sin, a soul-hunger eating into the individual, provincial and national, into the very heart of the Imperial life itself. Men were weary of the old gods. They had died at the hand of Greek criticism and philosophy, and in place of them there had arisen a sullen acquiescence in a supreme fate, the last vestige of religion in the Roman world. In place of religion men attempted to stave the craving of their souls by the exaltation of pride and self, an exaltation which found its supreme expression in the action of Caligula, who proclaimed his divinity and required the whole world to subscribe to it. He knew that in one centre only would deliberate and conscientious opposition be raised to his command, and that that centre was Jerusalem.

Jerusalem, although politically subject to Rome and already riding towards her fall, still was practically, spiritually, and commercially free. She was powerful in commerce, for she lay at the heart of the great trade and war routes, and from her sea-coasts her citizens went forth far and wide and founded Colonies. The Jews were noted then, as now, not only for their activity in trade, but also for their independence of character—their commercial and religious instinct being stronger than that of any of the nations amongst whom they settled. They planted synagogues in every town, and by the purity of their worship attracted some of the noblest spirits around them, and thus began to form a link with the Gentile world stronger and more lasting than the grip of the iron-handed legions of Rome—a link of free will, and not of compulsion. There does not seem to have been any political design in the present command of Caligula, but rather a manifestation of pride aroused by the opposition of the Jews, and as his command had not been obeyed he advanced towards Jerusalem with an army to enforce his claims. The Jews made a long and determined resistance, and, aided by Herod, for a time staved off the danger; but Caligula pressed forward all the more madly until, to the relief of the world and of the Jews in particular, his career was suddenly terminated by his murder in January, A.D. 41.

It was strange that this madness of Caligula, which overhung and threatened the national life of the Jews, should for the time have been a source of protection and help to the Christians; for the Jews, instead of persecuting the Christians, were forced to concentrate all their energy upon their resistance to Caligula, and indeed found themselves for the moment almost in sympathy with the Christians, who equally detested the impiety of Caligula, and wished to maintain the worship of the One True God in the Temple, as earnestly as the Jews themselves. These two events—the conversion of Saul and the advance of Caligula—together gave the Church a period of rest, an opportunity for edification and rest.

The Relation of the Church of Jerusalem to the Churches of the Dispersion

Whilst this struggle was passing between Jerusalem and Rome, whilst the Prince of this world was calling upon Jew and Gentile alike to fall down and worship him, the attention of the leaders of the Church was drawn towards a question of graver import which was arising within the Church itself—the question of the attitude which the Church of Jerusalem ought to take, not only towards the Churches of the Dispersion which were springing up on every side, but also towards the Gentile Churches which were yet unborn. It was a time of rapid expansion. If Christianity could spread and the Christians remain united in one bond of love and spiritual understanding, who could tell whereunto this would grow? But if they were divided and torn asunder, comparatively little might be effected. Humanly speaking, the whole question turned upon the attitude of the two men who by the keenness of their spiritual apprehension and by the breadth of their outlook had the power to found the Church abroad and maintain its unity at home, and these two men were St. Peter and St. Paul. The question immediately arises, What action were they taking at this time? How far did they understand the responsibility of their position?

The Attitude of Peter and of Saul

Saul had been called to "depart far hence" to the Gentiles; but, as yet, he had not done so. During the last eight years he had remained at Tarsus occupied, like Philip in Caesarea, with the care of the Church in that one city, and had gone no further, either because he still hesitated or because he was waiting for the way to open—waiting until the Voice which had bid him go forth should bid him arise and thrust in his sharp sickle and gather in the clusters of the vine of the earth.

St. Peter was still at Jerusalem, and occupied with the care, not only of the Church in Jerusalem, but also of the outlying Churches of the Dispersion. There is little question but that at this time the future of these Churches lay very heavily upon St. Peter. He knew that Saul had been called to depart far hence to the Gentiles, for Saul had been living in the house of St. Peter at the time of the vision in the Temple; indeed he had gone up to Jerusalem for the express purpose of seeing and consulting St. Peter. He had been living in his house during the period that he was contending against the

Grecians, and whilst there, when cast down by the rejection of the Jews, had gone up to the Temple to ask what this thing might be. Every step of Saul's way— his rejection, humiliation, and vision—was therefore known to St. Peter, and must have remained with him and been pondered over by him after Saul's departure from Jerusalem. If Saul obeyed this command and preached freely among the Gentiles, and if new Gentile Churches were founded, what control would or could the Church in Jerusalem maintain over them, what would be the character of the Churches, what the means by which they could be protected from the surrounding idolatry and evil? Hitherto the Gentiles had approached God afar off or through the medium of the Jewish rites and ceremonies, and a stern line of demarcation had been maintained between Jew and Gentile. This separation had been one of necessity as well as of religious sentiment, for Moses had taught both Joshua and the Israelites that the purity of the Jewish religion would pass away for ever if once the flood-gates were opened and the corruption of the Gentile world poured in upon the Jews; hence the chasm which for centuries had existed, and which it had been the birthright of each devout Jew to widen and to deepen to the utmost of his power, hence the hesitation of St. Peter and of the Church in Jerusalem. Was this chasm to be bridged over, this stern battle-line of centuries crossed? and if so, how and why? Little wonder that year by year, as the news of the rapid increase of the Church came up to Jerusalem, St. Peter found the question one of ever-increasing difficulty. When we take all this into consideration we do not wonder that St. Luke traces step by step the events of Peter's journey to Lydda and to Joppa, shows how markedly the power of the Holy Spirit rested upon him, and how he was gradually led forward until he learned that God was no respecter of persons, and was himself ready to affirm this truth by baptising Cornelius, the representative convert of the Gentile Church.

CHAPTER XXIII (continued)

ACTS IX. 31 TO END

THE DAYSPRING OF THE GENTILES

The Healing of Aeneas

The comparative rest which had been enjoyed by the Churches throughout Judaea, Galilee, and Jerusalem gave Peter the opportunity to leave Jerusalem and visit the Churches of the surrounding districts, and it was during this visitation that he came to Lydda and healed Aeneas, who had been sick of the palsy eight years. We notice in the miracles which St. Peter performed at Lydda and at Joppa how closely he followed in the footsteps of his Master, both in his words and in his manner of healing; thus he bids the paralytic Aeneas "Arise and make his bed," just as Jesus had bidden the man sick of the palsy take up his bed and walk. He takes Dorcas by the hand and says to her *"Tabitha cumi,"* just as Jesus had taken the damsel by the hand and said to her, *"Talitha cumi."* But we note also that in all his dealings Peter speaks as man, and not as God. Thus he bids Aeneas arise in the Name of Jesus, he does not, like Jesus, bid the evil depart through his own inherent power. St. Peter had been the first to realize that Jesus was God, and he was the first to realize also the difference between his own nature and that of Christ, and to confess that all his works were begun, continued, and ended in Him, and to ascribe all power and glory to God.

What a marvellous change passed over the life of Aeneas at the words of Peter! He who for eight years had lain upon his bed powerless to help either himself or others, his life narrowed within the four walls which surrounded him, was in a moment set free, if he willed it, for service. Aeneas stands as the world-wide type of a nature paralysed by sin and self, and limited to the interests and surroundings of self. He stands also as the type of that same nature when set free by the word of God—set free in the liberty wherein Christ setteth His people free.

The Raising of Dorcas from the Dead

From Lydda Peter was summoned to Joppa. Joppa at this time was a representative Gentile town and the best seaport on the coast; but it was also the headquarters of heathenism, so that its produce was held to be ceremonially unfit for use at the sacred festivals. This was the town to which Jonah fled when he could not bring himself to believe that Nineveh should be pardoned, and had refused to undertake a mission of mercy to its inhabitants. It was to this same town

THE DAYSPRING OF THE GENTILES

that Peter came, burdened with a like difficulty—the question of free pardon to the Gentiles—a question which, instead of fleeing from, he was ready to pour out in prayer before the living God.

The immediate cause of his summons to Joppa was the distress of the Church at the death of Dorcas. Dorcas is generally supposed to have been an unmarried woman, for there is no mention made of any relatives as being among the number of those who sent for Peter or who mourned for her. If she were unmarried, her story is of particular interest, for it shows how a nature can go forth, instead of rebelling against its limitations, in sympathy and help to others. Dorcas might have thought, like many another unmarried woman, that as she had been left to care for herself she was justified in doing so with little regard to others; but in her surroundings she held her spirit free for service, and sought to relieve the wants of others. Her generosity of thought and deed has been recognized by the Church in all ages, and her name has been handed down with a fragrance as exquisite as it is rare. Dorcas died, but by the hand of Peter she arose to life again. Her life-work ended many centuries ago; but by the hand of Christian women of every country and age it has continued, and will continue; she rises from the dead and lives in those who have banded themselves together for good works and been called by her name. There is a sense in which the very faithfulness of her followers has dimmed the beauty of her character and of her work, accustoming us to associate her with those who have followed her example rather than with the women of her own day. Her life is most truly seen in contrast with the Agrippinas and Bernices of her day, just as the generosity and thoughtfulness of the Shunammite woman stands out (2 Kings iv. 8) in contrast with the heathen women of her day and generation.

Dorcas was a servant of Christ and followed in His footsteps. Like Him, she provided for the sick and needy; like Him she saw the multitude around her and was moved with compassion towards them. The grief at her death was so intense that the disciples of Joppa hoped, as it were, against hope, and in the intensity of their grief sent for Peter, desiring him to come without delay, believing and hoping that a miracle greater than any which had yet been performed by the disciples might be possible, and Dorcas be restored to life again.

The scene in the upper chamber was a very touching one, for instead of the usual clamour of professional mourners and the noise of musical instruments of all sorts the body of Dorcas was surrounded by the women lamenting and showing the touching memorials of her love which she had left behind her. How many a woman since her day would gladly on her deathbed have exchanged her jewels of gold or her social triumphs, memorials as barren as that of Absalom's pillar in the king's dale, for a memorial such as that which Dorcas day by day had unconsciously been rearing in their midst! Every man as well as every woman, whether he will or no, has perforce day by day to rear the monument of his life and works; a monument which for good or evil will live not only in the memory of that life but also in the way in which it will influence the lives and works of those who come after him; a memorial which he cannot change upon his dying bed, but which he must bear with him into the presence of his King.

Peter at once entered into and sympathized with the grief of the disciples. Following the example of his Master he put them all forth, and kneeling down and wrestling in prayer said to the body: "Tabitha, arise!" Peter's prayer was heard through the power of the Holy Spirit, and Dorcas was raised and set free once again to minister to the saints and widows of Joppa.

The Effect upon Peter and upon the Church in Joppa

The account of the restoration of Dorcas was immediately known throughout Joppa, and all men knew and recognized that the power of God was resting upon Peter, and they glorified God in him. This was of great moment, for it was from Joppa that the elders were to be taken who were to attest the visions of Cornelius and of Peter, and witness to the baptism of the Holy Spirit which would descend upon Cornelius, and they would therefore be called to confirm the action of Peter in admitting the Gentiles into the Church. It was of great moment to Peter himself also. He knew now that the hand of the Lord was evidently resting upon him, and that he might with confidence draw near and cast the burden of his care upon God. In the very fact of his entrance into the house of Simon the tanner, he showed that a change was beginning to pass upon him, that the letter of the law no longer held him, for how otherwise could he have gone to tarry with one whose trade was held in special abhorrence amongst the Jews, indeed so abhorrent that if a woman married a tanner without knowing his trade she might obtain a divorce from him?

Little did Peter think, as he entered the house of Simon the tanner, that a vision was about to pass before his eyes which would affect the whole future of Christianity and would begin to weld Christian and Gentile into one. Little did he think as he paused to rest in the midst of his busy work that in answer to his prayer a ray of glory would begin to pierce the cloud and illuminate the darkness of the Gentile world, that Jesus would draw both Jew and Gentile unto Him; would begin to see of the travail of His soul and be satisfied thereby.

CHAPTER XXIV

ACTS X. 1-33

THE CALL OF THE GENTILE WORLD

Saul, Peter, and Cornelius

The Scripture narrative turns aside quickly from the conversion of Saul to the conversion of Cornelius, and records the great change which by the grace of God passed over these two men as well as over St. Peter. Saul the persecutor becomes Paul the chosen founder of the Gentile Church; Peter, zealous in all matters of the law, the abrogater of that law to the Gentiles; and Cornelius, a Gentile of Gentiles, a member of the Christian Church. Moreover, the decisions which these three men were about to make—decisions contrary to the hereditary traditions of centuries—were destined to change the face of the world, as they changed a provincial into a worldwide worship of the one true God. Hence every detail concerning the conversion of Cornelius is carefully recorded as also the summoning of witnesses to Joppa and the confirmation of the whole movement by the Church at Jerusalem.

The Nationality and Surroundings of Cornelius

Cornelius is thought from his name to have been a member of the great Roman family of Cornelius; but whether this is so or not, he unquestionably was a man of position and standing, held in repute by Jews and Gentiles, and commanding a century of Roman soldiers in Caesarea. Caesarea was a garrison town which had been rebuilt by Herod and named after Caesar Augustus. It was noted in the surrounding districts as a centre for the worship of Rome and of the Emperor, and the image of Augustus set up in the harbour proclaimed to the world far and wide the supremacy of Rome, and demanded the devotion not only of the inhabitants of the town but also of the seafaring world who came within its harbours. It was here that Cornelius was placed in authority at the head of 100 soldiers, Italians by birth, in order that he might keep a check over the town and over the provincial soldiers stationed throughout the surrounding districts.

The Roman army was subdivided into legions, cohorts, and centuries—each century comprising one hundred men and being commanded by a centurion. These centurions were, from their nationality and calling, imbued with the spirit of Rome, and inclined, as the representatives of a conquering race, to despise those subject to them; the subject Jews on their side were as naturally inclined to hate their conquerors and to view their actions in an unfavourable light; and yet, despite themselves as it were, these centurions are

THE CALL OF THE GENTILE WORLD

always spoken of favourably by the Jewish writers of the Bible, and instance after instance is given of the way in which they were attracted towards the Jewish Faith. Thus the centurion at the Cross sees and recognizes the Divinity of Jesus even at the moment of His deepest humiliation; another loves the Jewish nation and builds them a synagogue; and a third man is well reported of by the whole nation of the Jews. It is true that the attitude of these centurions may be partly accounted for by the fact that they lived at a time when the Holy Spirit was moving over the Gentile world as well as over the Jewish world. It is true also that the Christian ideal appeals more readily, as we see in Japan at the present day, to the officer in the army than to the merchant or to the professional man. Many of the most outstanding heroes of the Christian world have been heroes also in their country's battles. It seems as though the simplicity and obedience required in the army, "I say to this man, 'Go,' and he goeth, and to another 'Come,' and he cometh, to my servant 'Do this,' and he doeth it," prepares men for the grandeur and simplicity as well as for the self-discipline of the Christian faith. So, too, the self-sacrifice which is prepared to yield life for the defence of home and country predisposes to the still higher sacrifice of yielding life for God.

A Memorial of God

Cornelius feared God with all his house, lived according to the light which he had received, and prayed and gave much alms to the people always, and so day by day his prayers and alms arose as a memorial before God, a sign that the fulness of the times was come, that the Gentile world was athirst for God. It was at the time when Peter was approaching Joppa that Cornelius, who had been fasting for four days, was praying at the ninth hour—that is to say, at one of the Jewish hours of prayer—when suddenly he received a response, not only to his prayer, but also to the half-conscious longing of the Gentile world around him. He saw in a vision evidently an angel of God coming to him and calling him by name, "Cornelius." Like all who for the first time come into the more immediate presence of God, Cornelius was stricken with fear, not because he was living in wilful rebellion before God, but because at the moment when his eyes saw the King, the Lord of Hosts, there was revealed to him, as to Isaiah, the holiness and the love of God. As Saul and Naaman were bidden to sacrifice that which was dearest to them—their national pride—so Cornelius is bidden to seek out a Jew, one of the conquered race, not even a ruler or a high priest, but a man lodging in the most despised quarter of the town, and to hear from his lips what further is required of him. Naaman turned and went away in a rage, but Cornelius sent eagerly to Joppa to find Peter, caring neither for pride nor aught else if he can find the salvation which he is seeking, the pearl of great price.

The Vision of St. Peter

As his emissaries drew nigh to Joppa, Peter went up upon the housetop to pray, about the sixth hour. If

THE CALL OF THE GENTILE WORLD

Saul had passed through a time of doubt and perplexity in the journey to Damascus, so, too, had St. Peter, as he came down to Joppa. He knew that Saul, though now labouring in Tarsus, had been bidden to go forth and preach to the Gentile world, and he knew that if that call were obeyed, Saul, with his indomitable spirit, would give an impetus to the onward march of Christianity which it would be almost impossible for human guidance to control. Whether St. Peter definitely realized the difficulty of the work before him or not, we do not know; but he certainly realized that if Paul proclaimed the Gospel far and wide in its fulness to the Gentiles, they would, they must, rebel against the limitations imposed by Jewish rites and ceremonies.

From the answer to Peter's prayer it seems evident that this formed the burden of his thoughts, and that as he went up upon the housetop and saw the busy sea before him, the harbour, with its ceaseless coming and going, the ships of various nationalities, above all, the illimitable sea, the knowledge that the Gospel was about to go forth through the highway of that sea came over him, and exhaustion of body together with exhaustion of mind took possession of him and blended with the vision which was about to be revealed to him.

The Communion of Saints

Peter, as he knelt in prayer, thought that the burden of this responsibility rested upon him alone. He did not know that Cornelius, as it were, knelt beside him and laid before God another aspect of the same matter;

still less did he know that he, together with Cornelius, carried in his prayer the longing of many nations, that, like the High Priest of the Old Testament, he bore upon his shoulders not only his own perplexity but the perplexity and doubt of the noblest of the Jews and Gentiles, and that the answer to his prayer would be given not according to his own present need, his own limited power of expression or vision, but according to the Almighty wisdom, the Almighty understanding, of God. Who can tell the depth of the riches and of the power of prayer? We, like Peter and Cornelius, do not understand the import of the matters which we bring before the King, nor do we know that whilst apparently alone we are one of a great cloud of witnesses, that our prayer, all broken and imperfect as it is, is not ours alone, but carries with it the yearnings of those for whom we are pleading, men fast bound in misery and sin, whose feet as yet have not found the outermost court, still less the presence chamber of the King. But if the true nature of prayer is thus wonderful, how still more wonderful is the attitude of God, His tender mercy towards His servants as they bend in prayer!

"What God Hath Cleansed"

Whilst Peter was thus pleading with God, a glorious sheet of light illuminated the heavens and the whole earth before him. This sheet was as it were knit at the four corners, and contained within itself four-footed beasts, creeping things, and fowls of the air; that is to say, representatives of the two great classes of clean

THE CALL OF THE GENTILE WORLD

and unclean beasts, and together with the vision came the Voice bidding him "Rise, kill and eat." Peter replied impulsively, "Not so, Lord," just as he had formerly said, "Be it far from Thee, Lord." He would not, he could not, even in a vision, break God's law. His life-long custom of obedience rose against the new command, and he replied, "I have never eaten anything that is common or unclean." It was only natural that every religious instinct within him should have risen in rebellion against this command. From a child he had known the Holy Scriptures; from a child he had been taught as part of those Scriptures to separate himself in food from the Gentile world, and by touching not the unclean thing to place himself beneath the Fatherhood of God. Some have said that the answer "I have never eaten anything that is common or unclean" is self-righteous and unreasonable, and there is a sense in which this may be true. For there is an instinct of man as well as an instinct of God, and this instinct rebels against an infringement of custom, although that custom may be nothing but the outcome of natural circumstances or of chance. Such a rebellion gradually settles into limitations of character and opportunity, but a God-given instinct which rebels against the infringement of a custom because, as in this instance, it is the upgrowth of obedience to a religious command, a religious command fraught century after century with benefit not only to the individual but to the whole nation, arises from a totally different source. This second instinct will, if placed under the guidance of God, instead of settling into a limitation, become a power mighty "to prepare the way of the Lord, to make straight the highway of our God." For we know that that which is God-given will be God-directed also, and that if the commandment be decaying and waxing old, a new commandment, having the glory of God upon it, will be manifested in such unquestioning characters that all doubt and hesitation will be taken away. Thus the vision was manifested to Peter not once but thrice. As he had thrice denied his Lord, and had thrice been forgiven, so the vision also was thrice repeated before his eyes, and, even whilst he thought upon it, confirmed by an inward voice which told him that three men sought for him. Recognizing that these three men were as certainly sent from God as the vision itself, he at once went down and admitted them, and in further token of obedience, despite the fact that they were Gentiles, received them into his house and lodged them there. Whether he ate with them or not is not recorded; but on the morrow he journeyed with them, taking with him six witnesses, chosen men of Joppa, so that the revelation of the momentous change which was about to come might be witnessed not by himself alone but by the Church also. Would that we could as rapidly translate the visions of our life into active obedience and work for God as Peter did; that we could as rapidly pass from the world of truth on the one side to the world of men upon the other; that we could translate the glory of God into the dark world around us!

THE CALL OF THE GENTILE WORLD

"I Myself Also Am a Man"

As Peter knew that the vision was from God, and had summoned witnesses to testify to it, so Cornelius also knew that the matter was from God, and had assembled his near friends and kinsmen—probably those who had been accustomed to worship at his house; for not only from his personal character, but also from his official standing, he had attracted many around him. These all waited together; and when Peter entered, Cornelius, seeing not a subject Jew but a messenger of the living God, fell at his feet and worshipped him; but Peter took him up, saying, "Stand up; I myself also am a man." St. Peter had lived too nearly in the immediate presence of Jesus upon earth, too nearly in communion with Him after He had passed away from earth, ever to forget the gulf which separated his sinful nature from the sinlessness of God. Peter knew that never for one moment should the worship instinctive and inherent in the approach of man to God be given in the approach of man to man, and he knew it the more keenly at that moment because he himself had just been standing, as it were, in the glory of Heaven, and that glory yet lingered around him as he brought Cornelius into the same light also. How strange that in the face of this record men should have offered to Peter that very worship which, in the presence of Cornelius as well as of the witnesses of the Jewish and of the Gentile Church, he had rejected as a thing abhorrent to him! Then, having raised up Cornelius in the presence of the assembled company, he stated the circumstances of the whole case, his former prejudice, his change of mind, his consequent obedience to the will of God, the intent for which he had come among them, and asks for what purpose they on their side have sent for him, and in turn from the lips of Cornelius learns that he has well done that he is come, and that in the presence of God they are all here assembled to hear the things that are commanded of God.

Many solemn gatherings have taken place at different times during the history of the world; but without doubt this was one of the most solemn amongst them. God, as it were, laid his hand upon Peter and upon Cornelius, and a solemn awe fell upon them as they realized the near presence of God. They waited in awe and silence to know what this might be, what further revelation of the Spirit would be given, what tidings of the going forth of the salvation of God, not only to themselves and to the Gentile world around them, but also to the generations yet unborn. And the same awe falls over us many centuries later as we read the words, and realize that at this moment the Gentile world was born anew to God, and Jew and Gentile were for the first time united to one another and to God.

CHAPTER XXV

ACTS X. 34 TO END; AND ACTS XI. 1-18

THE PENTECOST OF THE GENTILES

"Thou Hast Well Done That Thou Art Come"

When Peter had heard the account of Cornelius' vision he found himself face to face with one of the most momentous decisions of his life. The words, "Thou hast well done that thou art come," a first welcome from the heathen world to a missionary of the Cross, were ringing in his ears. Could he make answer to that welcome? could he open the door of faith to the Gentiles? Two alternatives lay before him. If he followed the guidance of the new light which had just broken in upon him, a light full of radiance because illuminated by the teaching of his Master, then he must go in the teeth not only of his own hereditary instincts, but of the whole Jewish nation also. He must alienate himself from his fellow-workers in Jerusalem, who, not having received a like revelation from God, would in all probability condemn so dangerous a line of action. But apart from any question as to his own feelings or the feeling of others there still remained the question as to the deed itself. How could he cast out into the sea of idolatry and gross iniquity the Church of God, which up to this time had been preserved only in so far as by the grace of God it had been separated from the Gentile world? But if he hesitated and refused to do this daring deed, an alternative even more terrible lay before him. How could he who had tasted of the water of the well of salvation deny that water to souls athirst for God? How could he deny it to the men gathered before him whose souls had been given to drink of the water of that well by God Himself? How could he who had been thrice commanded by his Master to feed His lambs, thrice bidden to call no living creature common or unclean, turn away from the Gentiles in their hour of need? How could he who had dared all and walked upon the water to come to Jesus refuse, as it were, to take the Church by the hand and bid it dare all and come to Jesus also? The words of the 34th verse imply his doubt and hesitation. There seems to have been a pause and a moment of suspense until "he opened his mouth and said." This expression is used in Scripture whenever some declaration of unusual importance is about to be made, as, for instance, when Jesus was about to proclaim the laws of the kingdom of righteousness, and the whole multitude, like the Israelites before Mount Sinai, were assembled on the mountains before him, "Jesus opened his mouth and taught them, saying."

The Gospel of the Gentiles

St. Peter's Gospel to the Jews (Acts ii. 14-37) had bidden them repent before they were summoned into the presence of Jesus, their Lord and King. His Gospel to the Gentiles bids them also repent, but emphasizes especially the thought that they will be summoned before Jesus their Judge as well as Jesus their King.

His sermon falls under three heads: the offer of salvation, the means of salvation, and the necessity of salvation. The offer of salvation is to Jew and Gentile alike. St. Peter has just seen from the history of Cornelius, as also from the foreshadowing of the prophets, that God is no respecter of persons, and that the proclamation of peace from the lips of John the Baptist and of Jesus applies to Jew and Gentile alike. The means of salvation are found in the three great facts contained in the life of our Lord: the atonement, "Whom they slew and hanged on a tree"; victory over death, "Whom God raised up"; power to remit sin, "Whom God ordained to be a Judge of quick and dead." These are the three facts which the prophets perceived afar off, which Peter and the apostles have themselves witnessed, and through these facts all who believe will receive remission of sins. The necessity for salvation is as great for Gentile as for Jew. Through salvation alone can man find peace and bridge over the chasm of sin.

"They of the Circumcision Were Astonished"

Whilst Peter was speaking the Holy Ghost fell on all who heard him, upon Gentile as before upon Jew, excepting that whereas the presence of the Spirit had been manifested by the power of speaking in unknown tongues, it was now manifested by the power of praising and magnifying God. The Jews who were present were astonished. It seemed impossible that the Gentile world should receive remission of sins only through the death and Resurrection of Jesus and belief in Him. Was this the Gospel which was to be proclaimed throughout the world? We who are accustomed to a free Gospel—so accustomed that the words proclaiming it too often fall upon dulled ears—cannot conceive what an effect it had when it was heard in its first fulness. Perhaps we can see it best when we notice how hardly it was received at the time, how hardly acted upon. Thus we read that "they of the circumcision were astonished." Then, again, we see that the truth, though perceived, was not freely followed in after years, either by the Church in Jerusalem or by Peter. A number of those who, in a moment of spiritual exaltation, had apprehended it, afterwards fell back and were known as "they of the circumcision"—that is to say, as they who could not loose the Gospel from the bands of those rites and ceremonies which had formerly held it. We see it still more markedly in Peter, who in after years, although God had put no difference between Jew and Gentile, had to be withstood by Paul at Antioch because he had again become entangled with the yoke of bondage and refused to go in to the Gentiles and eat with them.

"He That Feareth Him and Worketh Righteousness Is Accepted"

But before passing on it is well to note two points of doctrinal interest. The opening words of St. Peter's address have been wrested from their context and quoted by men who wish to escape their spiritual obligations and to prove that the heathen world will be saved, and can be left in idolatry and sin. But the question as to the ultimate position of the heathen world is not touched upon in this text; the words have nothing whatever to do with it. From all time Gentiles outside the Jewish fold, like Rahab and Ruth, have entered into communion with God, but they have entered as Jews rather than as Gentiles. What St. Peter was considering was the question as to whether God would accept a drawing near in fear and obedience in place of rites and ceremonies, and after such drawing near would receive men into fuller relationship and communion with Him. His words are the outcome of the experience he has just passed through, together with the recollection of the former teaching of his Master: "If any man will do His will he shall know of the doctrine" (John vii. 17). What he says, therefore, does not in the least touch upon the question of the position of the heathen world; it touches purely upon a question of Jewish rites and ceremonies. Nothing was further from the thoughts of St. Peter than the desire to be absolved from obeying the command of Christ to "go and teach all nations." He had himself just obeyed that command and come to Cornelius, whose previous knowledge of the one true God had not precluded the necessity for a missionary journey to him. The question as to how Christ would deal with humanity as a whole had to be left by St. Peter, as it has to be left by all, to Christ Himself. "Shall not the Judge of all the earth do right?"

The Descent of the Holy Spirit before Baptism

The second point of doctrinal interest is contained in the descent of the Holy Ghost upon Cornelius and his kinsmen before they had made a deliberate confession of faith or been received by baptism into the Church. This has given rise to much questioning and misunderstanding. What can we learn from it? In the first place, we see that as "the wind bloweth where it listeth," so the Holy Ghost is at times given independently of apostles, independently of men. We see in the second place that although the Gentiles were cleansed by the inbreathing of the Holy Spirit, yet the command of Christ as to baptism was not set aside; but Cornelius, like Saul, was baptised after he had received the token of the love of God and had been personally accepted by Christ. Therefore Christ's command to baptise all nations does not depend upon whether we have already tested that the Lord is gracious, any more than the gift of the Holy Spirit necessarily depends upon outward form or ceremony. God moves the hearts of men as He will, bestows His gifts with or without sign, and confirms the great marvel of His love by teaching that "whosoever believeth in Him shall receive remission of sins."

The Church in Jerusalem

The news of this second Pentecost reached Jerusalem; but whether it caused more joy at the thought of the marvellous door which had been opened, or hesitation as to the possible danger which might arise out of the opening of that door, is not recorded. If men are slow of heart to understand, so are they slow of heart to rejoice in that marvellous joy which is revealed in the presence of the angels of God over one sinner that repenteth.

When St. Peter came up to Jerusalem he was summoned into the presence of the Church, and charged with freeing men from the Law of Moses. Whilst we wonder at the accusation, we must remember that if Peter had been justified in hesitating before accepting Cornelius, the Church in Jerusalem was more than justified in hesitating before confirming such an action and setting aside the ordinance of God. The leaders of the Church, or of what may be called the conservative party within the Church, were well within their rights when they found fault with Peter because he had gone in to men uncircumcised and had eaten with them. How strange it seems that weighty accusations in Church matters have often been laid upon points just as trivial as this, because matters which seem trivial to those who do not understand their bearing and signification may have at stake a clear understanding of one of the vital truths of God behind them. There is a natural tendency in men to desire to be broad-minded, to sweep away immaterial things, to get rid of hair-splitting distinctions lest they should hinder union with one another and with God. It is true that there are instances, like the present, in which, owing to a change in the position of affairs, the ordinance is decaying and waxing old, and ready to vanish away. Commandments of men which are only temporary, and like crutches given to aid in time of need, should pass and must pass as soon as they become a hindrance instead of a help; but commandments which are of God—that is to say, which show an unalterable aspect of eternal truth—can never pass away, though the form may vary according to varying need. They are ageless and may not pass, for if they did they would take with them a clear understanding of the approach of God to man and of man to God. The three words "of the Son" at the time of the Arian heresy caused the division between the Eastern and Western Church, and since that day men as broad-minded as Carlyle have claimed that they should have been yielded rather than the unity of Christendom impaired by clinging to them, and yet those words contain the acknowledgment of the equality and divinity of Jesus, Son of God, with God, and we to-day can see that the acceptation of them meant life to the Western Church, the rejection the stealing of paralysis over the Eastern Church. Boundary lines are vexatious, but they separate truth from error. Men think it easier, nobler, and broader to overlook minute distinctions and to make room for others as well as themselves in the commandments of God and the commandments of men, to yield post after post, to cry "Back to Christ" rather than "Forward with Christ." The point at issue therefore, which was raised by the Church in Jerusalem, was an entirely justifiable one, and the Church was only doing its duty when it investigated the whole question and passed deliberate judgment upon it.

The Examination of St. Peter

Apart from the question raised, it seems strange that Peter, the foremost of the apostles, the leader of the early Christian Church, should have been called to account and contended with, if not practically condemned beforehand, for his conduct in this or in any matter. But from the whole tenor of the Acts we see that his position was that of a member of the Council and not a head of it, and that it was perfectly natural for the Church to call him to account, and equally natural for him to rehearse the matter to them from beginning to end.

Peter, when answering the charge laid against him, defended his conduct upon the same ground which he had taken many years before when standing before the Sanhedrin in Jerusalem; he had "to obey God rather than men." He shows the Divine intervention at each step of the way, the visions, the sending of the three men, the descent of the Holy Ghost, and lastly, the correspondence of the whole with the former teaching of our Lord. He tells how the words of Jesus, "John indeed baptised with water, but ye shall be baptised with the Holy Ghost," flashed into his mind and finally decided the whole matter; how could he withstand the living God?

The Decision of the Council

A silence fell upon the assembled Council as the past, present, and future bearing of the whole matter came before them. They waited until they too, like Peter, heard the voice of God speaking through the events—until they, too, saw that they might take part in this new joy, might fling open the gates of salvation and send the heralds of the Cross over land and sea. With a joy like that of the angels at the birth of Christ they broke forth, and with one voice glorified God, saying, "Then hath God also to the heathen granted repentance unto life."

But a short time before one man had stood alone, a sort of daysman between the Jewish and Gentile worlds, striving to interpret aright the revelation given in answer to his prayers. Now his decision had been confirmed—by the Church above, and by the Church below—and an echo of the joy in the presence of the angels above given in the song of earth below. What a contrast does this outburst of rejoicing, coming from the lips of men who have just yielded that which for centuries had been their national pride—their spiritual distinction together with their spiritual leadership—make to the spirit of the

Jewish Church as it is recorded in the Old Testament and in the New, either as we read of it before the coming of Christ in Malachi iii, or during the time of Christ when "They murmured, saying, This man receiveth sinners and eateth with them!" The age-long feeling of discontent, weariness, and insistence upon outward form and ceremony had passed away, and the Jews who had accepted Christ and had been sanctified by His Spirit were ready to cast down their earthly crowns before His feet and to rejoice because a light had broken forth to the Gentiles and gladness to such as were true of heart, because they were called to lay aside their spiritual distinction so that through their poverty men might become rich.

CHAPTER XXVI

ACTS XI. 19 TO END

THE CHURCH AT ANTIOCH

From Jerusalem to Antioch

The book of Acts falls into two divisions—the passage of the Church from Jerusalem to Antioch, and from Antioch to Rome; that is to say, the passing of the spiritual centre from the East to the world-centre of the West. The latter part of the eleventh chapter contains a brief epitome of this movement, and is very important historically as well as theologically; it is an introduction to what has been called the Acts of the Hellenists, and is written so concisely that it reads more like a brief epitome or description of a side issue than what it really is, a climax to the preceding as well as an introduction to the succeeding chapters. It covers a long period of time, some 13 years, from the persecution and death of Stephen (A.D. 32) to the famine in Jerusalem (A.D. 45), and tells the history of the last of the three great movements which were the outcome of the persecution in Jerusalem. The foundation of the Church in Samaria under the leadership of Philip, and the growth of the Church of Judaea under the supervision of Peter, contained more points of theological interest, and therefore was given at greater length and in more detail. The foundation of the Church in Antioch by unknown men was historically the more important, because it meant the turning of Christianity from East to West. From the moment of its inception we find some of the characteristics which have been the distinguishing features of the Western Church. Thus the men of Antioch from the very first held out a hand to the Gentiles, adapting the Gospel to their needs, just as the Western Church has at its best moments been distinguished for missionary zeal, and, in the main, for wisdom of missionary effort. Furthermore, as the men of Antioch determined to send relief to the Church in Jerusalem, so the Western Church has again and again given of its abundance to those who were in need.

"As Far as Antioch"

The gradual progress of the Church westward is easy to understand. The men who were scattered abroad after the persecution naturally followed the great trade routes through Caesarea and along the coast to Phoenice, whence they either sailed westward to Cyprus or followed the sea coast until they struck inland to Antioch. The Antakish of to-day shows little to remind us of the former glory of Antioch, but at the time of which we speak it was one of the three great cities of the world, Rome, Alexandria, and Antioch—Rome pre-eminent for power, Alexandria for learning, Antioch for voluptuousness and pleasure-seeking. The position and natural advantages of the city lent themselves to self-indulgence. Antioch was celebrated for its exquisite scenery, its lofty mountain ranges, the abundance of its springs, and the beautiful woods and parks by which it was surrounded. It was also architecturally beautiful, being famous not only for the vast wall—fifty feet high—which surrounded the city, going up to the mountain tops and down to the valleys beneath, but also for its streets and buildings. The long main street, like the street called Straight in Damascus, was divided into three parts and arched over on either side by colonnades and cloisters, and was bisected by another street of similar character which struck obliquely across it. But however celebrated the city might be for its beauty it was still more so for the wickedness of its inhabitants, so that Juvenal, when wishing to account for the excessive deterioration of Rome, said that the Syrian Orontes had poured into the Tiber.

Two reasons are assigned for the wickedness of the city. It had a mixed population, due to the influx of men of all nationalities, and this meant a lowering of the general standard, as each nation only too quickly learns the vices rather than the virtues of the other. The thought of a general lowering of standard, consequent upon the admixture of nationalities, bears upon the life of to-day; for if Antioch was a source of infection to the surrounding cities of the first century what kind of influence will the new world-centre, the nations gradually rising around the Pacific Ocean, have upon

THE CHURCH AT ANTIOCH

the men of future generations? The world-centre of the Atlantic Ocean has been dominated by Christianity, but the world-centre of the Pacific will be dominated by heathendom, three out of the four commanding influences, China, Japan, and India, having been as yet hardly touched by Christianity. If these nations intermingle, as intermingle they must, what will be the character of the power which they will exercise, what the light that will radiate from them, unless, indeed, Christendom awakens to its responsibility and realizes its daydream—the evangelization of the world in this generation? The question becomes all the more serious when we remember that these people, like the men of Antioch, have broken with their past and are materialists at heart, their gods and idolatry being overthrown by Western light and influence just as the deities of Antioch had been overthrown by Greek philosophy.

A second reason is found in the exceptional opportunities for pleasure-seeking which were afforded by the luxuriance of Nature, enervating the inhabitants and inclining them towards the excesses indulged in among the groves of Daphne. And yet, despite its wickedness, this was the city, this the place of all others, apparently the most impossible in itself, which was chosen to become the great missionary centre of the world! Christ, in the person of His servants, stood in the midst of these pleasure-seekers and bade them come unto Him and drink; and when some had obeyed His call and been satisfied with the pleasures of His house, even of His Holy Temple, bade them go forth and call others to Him.

"Men of Cyprus and Cyrene... Spake unto the Grecians"

But apart from the character of its inhabitants, Antioch, if it were once touched by Christianity, had exceptional advantages for becoming a great missionary centre. It was sufficiently near Jerusalem to be in constant communication with it, whilst at the same time it was sufficiently far away and strong in its Hellenistic population to be able to take a wide and generous outlook over the men of other countries. But how could a few men bring Christianity into such a town as Antioch? Would they, like the men of Phoenice and Cyprus, preach the Word to the Jews only, or would they freely impart the good tidings of liberty and rest to the weary, sin-bound throng around them? We find that, instead of separating themselves, they drew the noblest spirits of the men of Antioch towards them, either by the contrast which the purity of their lives presented to the votaries of Daphne around them, or by direct preaching, for having heard that the Church had sanctioned the preaching of Peter to Cornelius, they decided to speak to the Grecians and to preach the Lord Jesus to them. In consequence, "a great number believed and turned unto the Lord."

THE CHURCH AT ANTIOCH

The Sending Forth of Barnabas

As soon as tidings of the movement in Antioch reached the ears of the Church in Jerusalem, they responded to it by sending forth Barnabas to go as far as Antioch. In the last chapter the large-mindedness and generosity of the Church at Jerusalem had been called in question, but in the present instance we see in how wise and statesmanlike a manner they strove to keep "the form of sound words" in the Churches of the Dispersion and to send forth men "able to teach others also."

When we compare the high standard of the Churches of the first centuries with those that come after, we learn what a debt they owed to the wisdom of Saul and Barnabas, as well as to that of Peter and James, who, through the power of the Holy Ghost, guided and restrained the growing movement of the Churches. No one wiser or more capable of appreciating what was best in this new movement could have been found than Barnabas. He spoke the Greek language and belonged to the same nationality as the Hellenist founders of the Antiochene Church. Moreover, he was a good man and full of the Holy Ghost, ready to hold out the hand of fellowship to the Church of Antioch as he had formerly held out the hand of fellowship to Saul, and prepared to bring them, as he had brought Saul, into unity with their fellow-Christians. His task was a peculiarly delicate one, for the men who had preached the Word were

Hellenists, that is to say, Greek-speaking Jews, who were not under the direct rule of Jerusalem, and wished to throw open the way of salvation to the worshippers of the gate, that is to say, to the Gentiles by birth, who were even less subject to it. It is necessary from time to time to remember the clear line of distinction between the four classes spoken of in the Acts—the Jews, the Hellenists (or Greek-speaking Jews), the Gentiles (or outside worshippers of the synagogue, technically called Greeks), and the great heathen world, who knew and cared nothing either for God or Christ.

Barnabas, encouraged doubtless by what he had seen and heard from Peter, gladly welcomed these Greeks and exhorted them to cleave unto the Lord. He recognized the hand of the Lord so evidently working among them that he made no recommendation as to rites and ceremonies, not even those later enforced by the Church (Acts xv. 27), but for the moment strove only to draw them nearer to Christ.

The Call of Saul to Antioch

As Barnabas passed up and down the streets of Antioch and saw the opportunities opening out on either side of him, saw also the vast dimensions to which the work might grow, he decided to seek out Saul, who was still working in Tarsus, and at all costs to bring him to Antioch. It seems strange that although the words of Christ, "Depart, for I will send thee far hence to the Gentiles," must have been ringing in the

THE CHURCH AT ANTIOCH

ear of Saul he should have remained for eight years working quietly in Tarsus. Whether it was because, like the disciples, he was slow of heart to understand the words, or because he was waiting for the door to be opened, cannot now be known.

It is not often that men who are called to a great work voluntarily place that work in the hands of one greater than themselves. But Barnabas recognized Saul's fitness for the work just as he had recognized his sincerity when he first came to Jerusalem. His choice was as wise as it was generous, for none needed example and teaching more than the men of Antioch, newly brought out of so great iniquity. The effect of this teaching was seen in the lives of the converts, which afforded such a contrast to the general wickedness around them and attracted so much public attention that by common consent they were called Christians. The disciples would never have called themselves by a name so sacred to them as that of Christ, but the men of Antioch, who were famous for their wit, did not scruple to call them after a man whom they supposed to be either one of their gods or a priest of their gods, and added to the name Christ the Latin suffix "ian." A writer has suggested that the name Christos resembles the word Chrêstos, meaning "good fellow," and that the Christians were from the first called good fellows, or worthy folk; and, if so, the attitude of Antioch towards the Christians only expressed the attitude of pleasure-seekers generally towards the followers of Christ. They see that Christians live purely and seek the good of others; that, if called to do so, they forego ambition, triumph, riches, and pleasure, and, therefore, they despise them and think them contemptible, however willing they may be to make use of them.

It is interesting to note in passing that the name Christian, whatever its origin, grew steadily in honour, and despite the sins and frailties of those who bore it has carried with it from that day to this something of the purity and compassion of Christ. We see the drift of our own shortcomings and that of others, we do not see the greater drift of Christian life which is bearing down towards a sea of infinite love and truth.

The Great Dearth throughout All the World

It was during this period, while Saul and Barnabas were breaching throughout Antioch, that a prophet—Agabus—arose and foretold a great dearth that was coming upon all the earth. It is strange that this man Agabus stood beside St. Paul at the opening as well as at the close of his career, strange that, as it were, he loosed his feet by opening the way for him to go to Jerusalem, whence he started forth upon his missionary career, and equally strange that with his girdle he bound the same feet, thus giving the signal that his ministry was ended and that his spirit would be released at Rome to seek the more immediate presence of his Master. The errand which took him to Jerusalem was the outcome of the large-heartedness of the men of Antioch. The men of Antioch stand first in the long succession of those who have given of their substance for the love of Jesus only, just as the Israelites in the wilderness in old time were

THE CHURCH AT ANTIOCH

the first to give of their substance for the service of God.

The first Pentecost in Jerusalem had manifested its power in the spirit of love and unity which led those upon whom it fell to sell their possessions and to part with them to all men as every man had need. The second Pentecost led the men of Antioch in like manner to realize their sense of stewardship and to give of their goods for the brethren who were in need. We notice that their sense of stewardship went even further than that of the men of Jerusalem, for while the men of Jerusalem did not part with any of their leaders, the men of Antioch allowed Barnabas and Saul, the two great founders of their Church, to be separated from them in order that the relief which they sent might be as efficiently ministered as possible to the brethren in Jerusalem, and thus set an example not only of generosity but also of large-mindedness and wisdom, an example which the Western Church in its most spiritual moments has also followed.

The History of Twelve Years

The history of twelve years is contained in these twelve verses, and is outlined in so masterly a manner that the story of the Church of Antioch still seems to live before us. We see the labours of the few unknown men who sleep "none the less sweetly because there is no strife of tongues above their heads"; we see also the outstanding figures of Barnabas and Saul, and we watch the rapid growth of the Church. We see how during a few years the belief of a few men exiled for conscience' sake became the belief of a powerful Church, so powerful that it was able and willing to contribute to the need of the Mother Church in Jerusalem.

Who could outline the further acts of the Gentiles which sprang from that first effort of a few men known only to God and to the faithful? What number of verses, chapters, or books, could tell the story of the deeds reaching throughout "earth's widest bounds" and from shore to shore of "ocean's farthest coast"?

CHAPTER XXVII

ACTS XII

THE THIRD PERSECUTION OF THE CHURCH

The Outstretched Hand of Herod

The calm which had been so grateful to the Church of Jerusalem was interrupted, and the disciples exposed to the outstretched hand of Herod. The Sadducees and Pharisees had in turn persecuted the Church, but their opposition had been inevitable, and their power limited; whereas this persecution was the more terrible because of the power of the persecutor and the wantonness of his attack. The Pharisees and Sadducees might have pleaded some nobility of motive—nay, even a zeal of God, though not according to knowledge—but Herod had no justification. He sought political power for his own selfish ends, and he sought it by ministering to the animosity of the Jews. In the light of Scripture the mist which surrounds men's motives is dispelled and the actions of individuals and of the State stand outlined in all their sharpness.

In this chapter we see, side by side, Herod the persecutor and James the persecuted, and find narrated the supreme moment in their lives, that moment being the outcome of their life and character. We see clearly the true character of the struggle between Church and State, and the overruling majesty of God who may permit the sway of evil, but who intervenes according to His will, and in the stillness and majesty of His power takes vengeance on the evil-doer and sets free the Church of God.

"Ye Shall Be as Gods"

Herod the King and James the brother of John, the cousin of our Lord, stand, in the eye of the world, as far apart in life and character as possible, but both were men of keen ambition, and at the moment when their paths crossed one another received each after his own degree the height of his ambition.

The life of Herod is peculiarly a life driven forward by reckless and wild ambition. In his early days he had squandered his substance and been imprisoned for designs against the State, but Caligula, as soon as he came into power, released him and gave him, as a token of friendship, a chain of gold of the same weight as the iron chain with which he had been bound in prison. He gave him also what he really wanted,—promotion and power, making him king, the dominion of Galilee and Peraea being added to that of his grandfather's tetrarchy. Herod cared little for his Jewish dominions, preferring to carry on the ambition and intrigue connected with his court life of Rome, but at the same time he ingratiated himself both with Christians and Jews by striving to withhold Caligula from his mad determination to erect a statue of himself in Jerusalem and to require all the Jews to fall down and worship it. The sudden death of Caligula freed the Jews and changed the aspect of affairs, whilst at the same time it increased the power of Herod. As he had been largely instrumental in obtaining the accession of Claudius to the Empire, he received as a recompense the provinces of Judaea and Samaria. This turned his attention towards Judaea, and instead of continuing his intrigues at Rome he settled in Judaea and brought all his skill and unscrupulousness to play upon his subjects as he had formerly exercised them upon greater matters at Rome. He affected intense devotion to the Temple and its service, and hung up in the Temple the gold chain which had been given to him by Caligula, but the Jews distrusted him and held aloof, and it was in order to prove his good-will towards them that he "stretched forth his hand to vex certain of the Church, and having killed James the brother of John with the sword, he proceeded further to take Peter also."

"The One on the Right Hand and the Other on the Left"

When Herod put forth his hand to kill James he little thought that he was touching a man even fuller of high hope and daring than himself, but a hope and daring sanctified and purified from self, an ambition seeking first the kingdom of God and its righteousness.

It is important to distinguish carefully between James the son of Zebedee, and James the Just, the brother of our Lord, the author of the Epistle of St. James, and for many years the leading apostle in Jerusalem.

James and John, the sons of Zebedee, were men of outstanding character and personality. Jesus recognized at once the force of their character and named them Boanerges, sons of thunder—men of stormy and tempestuous zeal. Amongst the disciples James was generally recognized as the greater of the two brothers, as we see from the fact that his name is mentioned first, and that John is distinguished in his early mention in Scripture as being the brother of James. Both men rose rapidly to the first rank among the disciples, and were known as members of that inner circle of three who drew nearer to Jesus than any of the other disciples.

There were two occasions on which the fiery zeal and ambition of the brothers was especially manifested. The first was when, the Samaritans having refused to allow Jesus to pass through their coasts, James and John implored that they might call down fire from heaven to destroy them. Their spirit of vengeance was rebuked by Christ. But as that vengeance partook of a zeal of God, even though a mistaken one, it was better far than a spirit of indifference and willingness to see Jesus slighted and His cause injured without one spark of indignation. It would be better to stand in the day of judgment with the two brothers who called for flames, than with the men who stood by calmly whilst the soldiers mocked and crucified Jesus.

THE THIRD PERSECUTION OF THE CHURCH

The second occasion discloses the secret ambition of the brothers when their mother prayed that they might sit the one on the right hand and the other on the left in the kingdom of Christ. But Jesus read a deeper purpose even than ambition in their heart. He saw beneath their self-seeking and presumption the spirit of self-sacrifice and of willingness to leave all and follow Him, and by responding to it, separated the dross from the gold, cast out the self-seeking, and offered a share in His cup of martyrdom and death in place of the power which they were craving. By a sudden inspiration James recognized the higher calling and responded to it, seeking the highest fitness rather than the highest post, and being willing to cast away all if he might win Christ. This was the man whom Herod slew, this the man to whom he gave the cup of martyrdom, little knowing how willingly he who had forsaken all for Christ would forsake life also, and would pass to the place which, as a son of God, had been prepared for him.

"He Proceeded Further to Take Peter Also"

It seems strange that the death of James should be passed over in a single verse, whilst so long and detailed an account is given of the release of St. Peter; but we must remember that St. Luke, writing under the inspiration of the Holy Spirit, touched only the points which most vitally affected the character and future history of the Church. There was no question but that the loss of James was very great to the Church, but the lesson which could be learned from his death could be as fully given in a few brief words as in many; whereas the deliverance of Peter, which was full of significance in every detail, pointing not only towards the fact of the immortality of men until their work is done, but showing also the immediate presence and overruling power of God. This deliverance and its lessons were particularly full of meaning at this moment to the Church at Jerusalem as well as to Barnabas and Saul, who either then or very shortly after were in Jerusalem, before departing on their first missionary journey; and it was most probably from the lips either of Peter or of Paul, both of whom must have been greatly impressed by these events, that St. Luke received the account which he has recorded in the Acts.

Herod, "because he saw that it pleased the Jews, proceeded further to take Peter also." But even as he did so he knew enough of the story of the Christian Church and of Peter's previous imprisonment to feel uneasy over his action. He knew that in attacking Peter he was dealing with a man of mysterious and unknown power, and therefore, when he put him in prison, he imitated the Roman method of guarding prisoners, and delivered him to four quaternions of soldiers to keep him. He knew enough also of the Jewish spirit to defer killing him until after the days of unleavened bread, lest he might miss his aim by offending the religious scruples of the Pharisees. He waited, therefore, intending after Easter to bring him forth to the people. "Peter therefore was kept in prison: but prayer was made without ceasing of the Church unto God for him."

THE THIRD PERSECUTION OF THE CHURCH

Prayer Without Ceasing

On the one side we see Herod with the power of Rome behind him; on the other a band of men and women, in danger of their lives, "outstretched," as the translation more literally is, before God in prayer. What could they do before the power of Herod? The Sadducees had been restrained by fear of Pilate, and the Pharisees, if they had gone too far, might have been withheld by Rome; but Herod was supreme. Man's natural instinct of self-defence inclines him to take up weapons to defend his spiritual as well as his earthly rights; but Jesus had taught Peter, when he bade him put his sword into its sheath (Matthew xxvi. 52), where his true strength and help lay, and as the chapter proceeds we see the balance of power pass from the king upon his throne to the prisoner bound between four quaternions of soldiers. As we read, Herod and his armies fade away into the darkness of night, and a heavenly glory hovers over Peter and the little company gathered together in prayer for him.

"So He Giveth His Beloved Sleep"

Whether Herod slept in the midst of his luxury and state we know not; but Peter in his prison, between two soldiers, bound with two chains, was sleeping like a little child. His slumber was not the heavy stupor of the brute criminal—who, being but one step above the animal, neither cares nor looks beyond the satisfaction of the present moment—it was the quiet of a soldier whose work is done and who is calmly waiting for the summons of his King.

Thus waiting, he had prepared himself for rest as quietly as at any other time, until suddenly as he slept the glory of God shone around him and an angel smote him on the side, rousing him from his sleep and bidding him get up quickly.

> "The flame that in a few short years
>   Deep through the chambers of the dead
> Shall pierce and dry the fount of tears,
>   Is waving o'er his dungeon-bed.
>
> "Touch'd he upstarts—his chains unbind—
>   Through darksome vault, up massy stair,
> His dizzy, doubting footsteps wind
>   To freedom and cool moonlight air."

At the presence of the angel the chains fell from his hands; there was neither hurry nor distress, but in quiet confidence he followed the light of the vision, just as shortly before, in spiritual understanding, he had followed the light of the vision at Joppa. As he passed through the prison and city he noticed, although almost stunned by the suddenness of the transition, every object around him, saw with preternaturally sharpened sensation the iron gate which opened of itself (just as the stone had rolled away from the sepulchre), and the street which he passed through, until, when he was at last in safety, the angel departed from him, and "himself, all joy and calm." The meaning of the whole flashed upon him. He recognized his Master's hand, recognized also the power of prayer which had delivered him, and decided, despite the danger, to go to the house where that prayer was being offered up for him. In the stillness of the night, he knocked but was not heard, either because, being absorbed in prayer, they were unconscious of all around them, or hearing, were afraid lest the emissaries of Herod had once more come upon them, until at last a damsel came to hearken, named Rhoda.

The Action Taken by St. Peter

The character of Rhoda is exquisitely outlined in the New Testament in contrast to that of Herodias' daughter. Her astonishment, her joy, a joy so overwhelming that instead of admitting Peter she ran to announce his coming. All this is given in a perfectly natural manner, as also the answer which she receives, and which is typical of the attitude of mind which too often prevails amongst those who pray. We believe in the omnipotence of God, in His love, His willingness to grant our petition; we yearn to rest ourselves upon His strength; but the weakness and fearfulness of our nature turns irresistibly towards Herod and the four quaternions of soldiers. The disciples supposed that Peter, like John the Baptist, had been swiftly executed in prison, and that his spirit had stayed itself amongst them in its flight, or if not actually his spirit, yet the angel of his spirit: it was beyond their conception or belief that it was Peter himself. But Peter continued knocking, and when, though still overcome by apprehension and joy, they opened the door, his presence checked the overwhelming outburst of astonishment with which they would have greeted him. Mindful of the danger of this meeting, not only to himself but to them, and awed by the touch of God's hand which rested upon him, Peter bade them hold their peace, narrated what had passed, and gave instructions that tidings should be sent to James and to the brethren, and then immediately departed from them, whither they knew not.

The Question of the Church in Jerusalem

It is strange to see how, for the moment, the natural impulsiveness of Peter was conquered; for although he must have yearned—thus given back, as it were, from the dead—to remain for a few moments at any rate amongst those he loved, and to pour out his soul in thanksgiving to God, and although, whilst doing so, he might have thought that the angel who had delivered him could, if need were, deliver him again, yet he would not tempt the Lord his God, nor expose those who were already in danger to further peril on his account. The furtherance of the Kingdom of God transcends his thought, and his solicitude is greater for the Church than for those he loves. Peter knew how essential it was at this particular crisis that his life should be preserved; he had not lain down to sleep that evening without the knowledge that the passage across the river of death which might be swift to him would be fraught with long and lasting difficulty to those who were left behind him. At this particular crisis, when James the son of Zebedee had been killed and taken from the councils of the Church, how could Peter—he to whom the revelation of the future had so especially been given at Joppa—be spared also? Therefore, in order to relieve the anxiety of James the Just—at that time the leader of the Church in Jerusalem and of the brethren—he bids them go at once and tell James, and then without further word he departs and goes into another place.

Herod's Action Subsequent to the Release of Peter

The wrath of Herod was soon aroused, and, like Pilate before him, he saw that immediate measures must be taken if the escape of Peter were to be publicly ascribed to negligence on the part of the officials rather than to the intervention of a power greater than his own. But though Herod might slay the soldiers and deceive his subjects, he could not screen himself from the judgment which was about to fall upon him. The deliverance of Peter from prison was a last dealing of God with him—a day of visitation which, having been rejected, he was permitted to go his own way, and that way led all too surely to destruction. Being highly displeased with the men of Tyre and Sidon, but not choosing to quarrel with them on account of the heavy bribe which they had given to his chamberlain, and knowing that in any case they were completely in the power of his hand—being dependent upon his kingdom of Galilee for corn—he determined to pardon them, but at the same time to overawe them with a sense of his magnificence and power. He appointed, therefore, a public reception, and, arrayed in a garment glittering with silver, made an oration to them. The people saw his weakness, and interpreted the craving of his spirit by crying: "It is the voice of a god and not of a man." Their acclamation was as suddenly checked as raised, for Herod was seized with mortal agony; the hand which had touched Peter on the side and given him life and liberty having smitten him even unto death. The judgment which befell him was identical with that which overtook Philip II, the arch-persecutor of the Netherlands, both kings dying by that most awful of all visitations a living death—a visitation which proclaims more unmistakably than any other the inherent corruption and weakness of man and the helplessness of his mortal nature. Herod had done his utmost against James and Peter, but God had made them rich and added no sorrow with it. Herod had magnified himself, he had surpassed all his fellows in overweening ambition and pride, and had gained the summit of his ambition, but it was for one moment, and one moment only. He had made himself rich, but God spake unto him in His wrath. He gave him his own heart's desire, but He added sorrow to it.

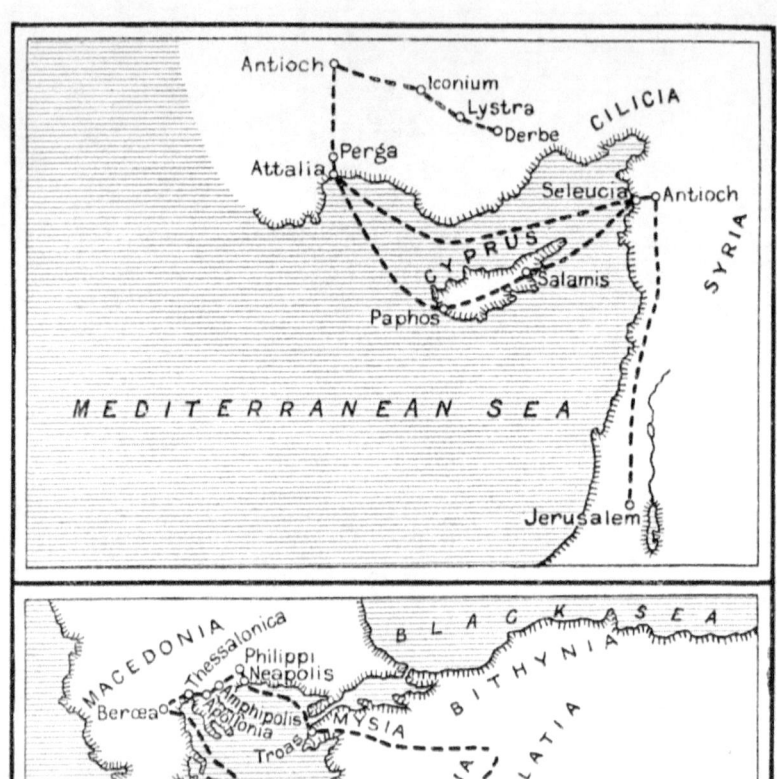

CHAPTER XXVIII

ACTS XIII. 1-13

ST. PAUL'S FIRST MISSIONARY JOURNEY

The Return of Saul to Jerusalem

Many years had passed since the night when Saul, in peril of his life, had fled from Jerusalem, and he must have rejoiced when once again his feet stood within the gates of the sacred city, even although he knew that the friends of his parents and of his own boyhood were forever alienated from him. But however widely they might be estranged, he no longer stood apart from the church of Jerusalem, and the time seemed very far away when it had been necessary for Barnabas to take him by the hand and be surety for him to the brethren.

Many years of faithful work stood between that day and this, and he was now looked upon as one of the coming leaders of the church of Antioch, a church already second in influence to none but Jerusalem. No record is left as to what took place during his visit to Jerusalem, and we may therefore conclude, either that his stay was a brief one, or that he was entirely occupied with the work which he had in hand (Acts xi. 28-30). The exigencies of the famine in Jerusalem, together with the rejoicing at the escape of Peter (Acts xii.) and the death of the persecutor, Herod, were more than sufficient to occupy the minds of the church generally. Moreover, it was hardly likely that any question of theological importance would arise in connection with the work of distribution, which would be recorded by St. Luke as being of importance to the church. The one matter which did arise and which vitally affected not only the friendship of Barnabas and Paul, but also the after course of their missionary work, was the decision made by Paul and Barnabas when they were leaving Jerusalem to take with them, as minister upon their missionary journey, John, whose surname was Mark.

"John ... Returned"

The character of Mark stands out in Scripture under two very different aspects, according as we think of him in his early days as the man who turned back at the outset of his missionary work and returned home to his mother and friends; or in later days as "established in the truth," the lion-hearted man who sustained St. Paul when others had forsaken him and fled, the man who is represented—as at St. Mark's at Venice—under the emblem of a lion, upon "the winged lion's marble piles." At the moment when Barnabas and Saul decided to take Mark, there were many circumstances which justified their choice, not only in his natural character, but also in his upbringing and surroundings. His mother was one of the leading women of the Church of Jerusalem, her house, known as the gathering-place of the early Christians, an upper room in her house having, it is generally thought, been the scene of the Last Supper and of the descent of the Holy Ghost at Pentecost. It was here also, according to tradition, that St. Mark, after the Last Supper, heavy with foreboding, hearing the uproar of the multitude and the tramping of the soldiers, was filled with alarm for the safety of Jesus, and, rising hastily, followed with the crowd until he was seized in the press, and fled, leaving his garment in their hands. If so, St. Mark was intimately connected with the whole Christian movement, and had already displayed many of the characteristics which afterwards distinguished him; and Barnabas, being his cousin, might well think that his upbringing and intimate connection with our Lord would mark him out as a man likely to be steadfast in the faith and able to help others also.

The Church at Antioch

On the return of Saul and Barnabas the Church of Antioch gathered together to consider matters of import which lay heavily upon them. Whether this gathering was due to the moving of the Holy Spirit, or whether St. Paul, after his visit to Jerusalem, felt anew the pressure of his commission to depart far hence to the Gentiles is not recorded; we only know that they drew near with prayer and fasting in order that they might discern the will of Christ. The names of the five leaders in Antioch are recorded, just as the names of the twelve apostles had been recorded at Jerusalem, and all, except Manaen, were Jews of the Dispersion; but we know nothing as to their work or character beyond the passing mention of the present chapter.

Some think from his name Niger that Simon may have came from North Africa, and that Lucius, of Cyrene, may have been influenced by his fellow countryman Simon of Cyrene who carried the cross of Jesus; but the chief interest centres in the name of Manaen, Herod's foster-brother. It seems so strange that two brothers reared together, probably sent together to Rome to be educated, should have drifted so far apart in after life, not only in circumstances but in character; that the one, by the grace of God having conquered self and passion, stood out as a leader of the church; whilst the other, enslaved by pride and passion, slew the man who would have freed him from his sin and lifted him towards God.

The Responsibility of the Church at Antioch

The church at Antioch, a church containing men like Barnabas and Saul, could not but overflow with compassion towards the world of heathendom lying around them, and seek to give light in darkness. The thought of that darkness weighed so heavily upon them, that they drew near to God, and by prayer and fasting strove to apprehend His will, until the command came to them through the Holy Ghost to separate Barnabas and Saul for the work whereunto they were called. The answer, when it came, must have been for the moment more overwhelming even than the need of the work itself. How could Paul and Barnabas, the founders and the leaders of the church of Antioch, alike be spared from it at once? How could the evil in a city like Antioch be stemmed and the converts faithfully taught if they were deprived, at one and the same time, of the sympathy and understanding of Barnabas, and the statesmanship of Paul? Further still, how could the missions which these men hoped to found be upheld if the central church itself were weakened?

But the church at Antioch had to learn, just as we have to learn, that the living dedication of its leaders to missionary work is, like the death of the martyrs, the seed of the Church. It does not seem much easier to learn this lesson of sacrifice, even in these later days; for although we owe our own Christianity to sacrifice, it takes a sore struggle and much faith to look forward, even though the harvest will be as abundant from the sacrifice of to-day as from that of old. We believe that from East to West and from North to South an evangelized world will one day arise and acknowledge the self-sacrifice of the men who, more than a century ago, founded and set in motion the great religious Societies and inspired those who came after them to carry on the work which they had begun.

The Sending Forth of the First Missionary of the Cross

If a feeling of heavy responsibility lay upon the church of Antioch, a feeling of yet greater responsibility lay upon Paul and Barnabas. The call of God was as unmistakable to them as to the church, nay, even more so, for Paul knew that it had been determined before in the councils of God. With prayer and fasting, therefore, and with renewed subjugation of body and spirit, they set forth upon their further journey and peril.

What a contrast there is between these leaders of the church of Antioch and of the church of Jerusalem, the records in the later prophets, or even at the time of Christ. We see how the spirit of God had changed the hearts of these men when we contrast their spirit of prayer and fasting with the prayer and fasting of the Pharisees, the disfigured faces, the pretended prayers, the shutting up of the kingdom of Heaven against men. But beside this contrast of the past there is in the movement at Antioch a lesson of hope for the future. We stand at a time as critical as that of the first century, and problems of missionary work press as hardly upon us now as they did upon the early church. We hear, on the one side, the cry "Come over and help us"; on the other, the call for strong men in our own country, men as urgently needed now as ever in the church of Antioch, men whose withdrawal threatens the continuance of the Church itself, surrounded as it now is by unbelief and materialism on every side.

What may we learn from the church at Antioch? Ought we not to approach God in the spirit of the men of Antioch, if not in the letter? If the problems of to-day are essentially the same as the problems of the first century, ought not the spirit in which they are solved to be identical also; ought not the pathway of ministration and fasting to be followed in order that a like response from the Holy Spirit may be given? And how is it that we find such constant exhortation to prayer in the Epistles of St. Peter, St. Paul, and St. John, whilst so little mention is made of fasting? The answer can be found in the teaching of Christ Himself. Christ warned His disciples to fast in the spirit rather than in the letter, "But thou, when thou fastest, anoint thy head, and wash thy face; that thou appear not unto men to fast, but unto thy Father which is in secret." The duty of fasting remains ever the same—that is to say, the duty of subjugating the lower nature to the higher, so that by the grace of God we may the more consciously apprehend the things of God—but the method of fasting will differ according to the country, the age, and the character of him who fasts. Although no temptations take us but such as are common to man, yet certain temptations appeal more to one character than to another. Thus, for instance, we in the Western Church may find that we are beset by temptations of a character very different from those of the Eastern Church. With a climate like ours, and living at a rate of pressure such as we do, abstention from food may bring exactly the opposite effect from that which we are seeking, may cause exhaustion fatal to self-command rather than increased attention or devotion. The Christian of to-day may find that he can more closely follow Christ, more constantly hear His voice, by abstaining from the excitement, the pleasure, the excess of emotion and passion which enter so largely into the life of the men and women of to-day, and which effectually distract the hearts and thoughts of men, than by literal fasting. Whatever the weights are which do most easily beset us, those are the weights which we must cast aside if we would the more surely run with patience the race set before us.

The First Dismissal

The departure of the good ship "Mayflower" from the shores of Plymouth has been well compared, in the smallness of its beginning, and the greatness of its after result, to the departure of this unknown ship from the harbour of Seleucia. How often from that day to this has the highway of the sea been the highway of the missionaries of the Gospel. Saul and Barnabas went forth sorrowing for the work left behind, but rejoicing for the hand of God which thus visibly rested upon them. They sailed first to Cyprus, where Barnabas, still leading the way, proclaimed to his fellow-countrymen the word of God, though still apparently only in the synagogue of the Jews. The first departure took place at Paphos, the capital of the island, at that time under the Roman Deputy, Sergius Paulus, who, like the centurions already mentioned, seems to have been "a prudent man," a man of strength and understanding.

Sergius Paulus, hearing of the preaching of Saul and Barnabas, probably concluded that they—like other scholars and learned men—were travelling from city to city of the Roman province in order to expound their theories and learning until, having gained a reputation, they were invited to attach themselves to some university or place of learning. He sent for them therefore, expecting to hear some learned disputation from them, or possibly thinking that they might be able to present before him some new aspect of truth, for he, like other Romans of the period, may have been longing for a nobler and a purer faith.

Elymas the Sorcerer

It is strange from time to time to find accounts in the Bible of the meeting of the representatives of sorcery and the representatives of pure religion. Two instincts are born in every son of man, an instinct of freedom and an instinct of slavery, a spirit of freedom yearning for the Divine and stretching out its hand towards God, and a spirit of slavery, believing in a supreme fate, working on regardless of man, whose decrees must be learned by stealth and evaded by sorcery and witchcraft. It is not strange that we should come upon these accounts in the New Testament, for the belief in this inexplicable fate, this hidden mysterious power, was at this time a prevailing force in the Roman Empire. Saul encountered it in the person of Elymas as Peter had encountered it in the person of Simon Magus (Acts viii. 18), and as Moses, at the outset of his ministry, had come in contact with it in the presence of Pharaoh and in the person of his magicians.

It is interesting to note that as Saul stands forward in the presence of the Roman Governor he takes up his position as a Roman citizen, and accepts his commission to the Gentiles and identifies himself with it. When he was working among the Jews he had taken his stand as a Hebrew of the Hebrews and been called by his Hebrew name Saul = Desire, now in the view of his life-work he is called by his Roman appellation Paul = little, and determines even more earnestly than before to cast aside every weight and to run with full strength the race set before him. The change is not a mere incident; it marks the whole-hearted acceptance of a mission.

The Struggle between the Power of Evil and the Power of Good

The address which Paul gave on this occasion is not recorded, but it must have been powerful, as we see from the resistance offered by Elymas to it, and also from the effect which it had upon the deputy, who, after seeing the miracle which confirmed the words, "believed, *being astonished at the doctrine of the Lord.*" But Elymas the sorcerer had gained far too much ascendency over Sergius Paulus to let him escape so readily from his hand, and standing forth sought with all his might to turn him from the faith. The arguments which he used consisted probably of a perverted story of the death of

Jesus. His words, like those of St. Paul; are not recorded; but partly on account of his previous ascendency over Sergius Paulus, partly by his persuasive power, he had almost succeeded in turning him away when Paul, filled with God-given power, fixed his eye upon him and, piercing to the very root of his abominable deception, exposed the iniquity of his soul not only in his own eyes but in the eyes of Sergius Paulus also, for Elymas was indeed of all men most miserable. He, a Jew, had received the knowledge of the one true God, had known the prophecies of the Old Testament, and had dared to tamper with the hidden things of God, had dared to turn his knowledge of the Divine and of prophecy into a source of deception and gain, and by mingling the Heavenly gift with the devices of his own evil imagination had not only ruined himself but had sought to ruin others also. Elymas stands as the embodiment of the lust of gain, as the man who would sacrifice the most sacred mysteries of God for the sake of personal gain and power, and hence Paul does not hesitate for an instant in his dealing with him. In unmistakable terms he exposes his connection with the spirit of evil, his deliberate warfare against God, stamps the man himself with the record of his sin, bids darkness and blackness fall not only over his spirit but over his body also, bids the gloom which he has thrown over the souls of others fall upon him also. Henceforth men will see from the judgment which has fallen upon him the character of the sin which he has committed; they will see that he who had deliberately misled others now cannot guide himself and has to go about seeking some one to lead him by the hand. Whilst Paul is speaking we cannot help wondering whether a vivid recollection of the time when a like judgment fell upon him at Damascus is very present with him, and whether that is why, in the midst of judgment, he remembers mercy, why, too, knowing the anguish which must pass over the soul of Elymas at his words, he gives a ray of hope even to him, tells him that he will be blind "for a season," thereby implying that his blindness may one day pass away, and that he, too, may be translated from darkness to light, from the power of Satan to God. Whether the effect of the judgment upon Elymas justified this hope is not recorded. His sin had been far greater than—had been, indeed, of a totally different character from—that of Saul. He had had a zeal of self; he had not had, like Saul, "a zeal of God, though not according to knowledge."

The Departure from Paphos

Whatever the ultimate fate of Elymas may have been, the law of cause and effect in regard to his actions stands as eternally true in his case as in that of all others. Sin may be pardoned and put away, but the effect of sin cannot pass away also. Elymas might one day regain his sight, but he could not undo the evil that he had done. It is true that Sergius Paulus believed and was astonished at the doctrine of the Lord; but there is no record, either here or later, in the Acts or in the Epistles, of a Church having been founded at Paphos. It seems likely that, although for the moment the victory was complete, Sergius Paulus still had a haunting recollection of the teaching of Elymas, and was not prepared, like Cornelius, to accept the new revelation in its fulness. If he had done so, surely St. Paul and his companions would have stayed in the island in order to strengthen Sergius Paulus in the faith, and from a vantage-ground like that of his Court to gain influence throughout the island, whereas, on the contrary, we find that they sailed from Paphos and came to Perga, in Pamphylia, where John departed from them.

"He That Loveth His Life Shall Lose It"

John Mark stands as the type of the man who has had the advantage of every religious privilege, who has come into contact with Christ and with His servants, but whose Christianity may still be described rather as a yielding to the force of circumstance and surroundings than as a personal and hard-won conviction; as the religion of a man who has accepted light, rather than that of one who has beaten out his own way towards it. These are the men who, like Mark, in time of temptation fall away, abandon the work they have undertaken, and cast a shadow over their fellow-labourers; and yet, as far as Mark himself was concerned, it was better for him that he should turn back than that he should continue to be a half-hearted follower; better to stand aside for a moment in order that he might return for ever; better to see himself in his true position rather than continue in a false one, better to go away grieved to his great possessions rather than endeavour to give out to others truths which were not as yet ingrained into every fibre of his being. Mark had to learn the lesson that work for God is a privilege—a privilege which, if it is cast aside, is lost—and that if a servant says "I go, sir," and goes not, another is called of God to stand in his stead.

The Departure for Cyprus

Whether the discouragement of the work at Paphos had been discouraging or not, however serious the defection of Mark, Paul and Barnabas were none the less determined to cross into the barbarous district lying between Perga and Pamphylia. The difficulty which had enervated the half-hearted Mark had braced the older disciples to renewed effort. They stepped forward the more boldly to attack the same power of superstition and scepticism which they had already unmasked at Paphos, and which they knew would meet them everywhere throughout the Roman world. If the power of God had prevailed over Elymas; if imposition and craft had been forced to yield in an outpost, as it were, like Paphos, why should not the same power prevail over the stronghold of superstition, even over Rome herself?

CHAPTER XXIX

ACTS XIII. 14 TO END

THE GOSPEL IN GALATIA

The Journey of St. Paul to Antioch

After leaving the low-lying land of Perga, Paul and Barnabas passed through the southernmost half of the Roman province of Galatia and made their way to Antioch in Pisidia. The journey was difficult and discouraging, for Paul was cast down at this time not only by the defection of John Mark, but also by an infirmity of the flesh (2 Corinthians xii. 7) which, whether it were ophthalmia or, as seems more probable, a malarial fever or epilepsy, came upon him about this time and made him contemptible not only to himself but to his followers. His illness may have been increased by the malarial climate of Perga, which, following on the nervous strain he had passed through at Paphos, decided him to seek the high land of Pisidian Antioch, the chief town between Antioch and Rome.

Antioch, now a heap of ruins, was then the military centre of the vast province of Southern Galatia, and, at the time when St. Luke was writing, at the height of its power. From the ruins which are left, and especially from the arches of its immense aqueduct, we can tell that the city must have been a place of considerable importance. The inhabitants were principally a low class of Pisidian Greek settlers, but there was also an important Roman colony and a large Jewish population, many of whom were descendants of the two thousand Jews who had been planted throughout the district by Antiochus the Great. This city into which Paul came, from his preaching, will live for ever in the record of the Acts of the Church of God, partly because it gives a typical picture of an outlying Roman colony with a large Jewish population brought into contact for the first time with the preaching of the Gospel, partly because the rejection of that Gospel confirmed St. Paul in his determination to turn towards the Gentiles. This was the city into which St. Paul came, wearied by travel and sickness, the account of which we find in the Epistle to the Galatians. It was either on the first Sabbath day or after he had been for some time teaching in the city that he came to the synagogue and sat down in it. The synagogue itself was probably similar to that of all the other synagogues of the period. There would be a raised desk for the reader, having on the right side of it the ark in which the rolls of the law were placed; the seats surrounding the building, the chief seats being appropriated for the use of the rulers of the synagogue; and the galleries screened off by lattice work, in which the women were gathered together. But although the general arrangement of this synagogue was thus similar to the synagogues of to-day, the congregation which was gathered together was peculiar to Antioch, for mingled among the Jews were many of the Greek and Roman citizens, and among the women many of the honourable women of the town. As soon as Paul and Barnabas entered the synagogue, attention was attracted to them, and the reading of the Law having been concluded, they were invited, if they had any word of exhortation for the people, to say on.

The Gospel to the Gentiles

From the moment when St. Paul stood up and beckoned with his hand he had all eyes fastened upon him, and kept their attention spellbound until the end. We do not wonder that it was so, for from the mere outline of his sermon which has come down to us we can see with what marvellous skill he caught the attention of his audience and sustained it, leading them forward, like Stephen, step by step until the iron entered into their souls and he was forced to turn his words of gracious exhortation and invitation into words of sharp warning and rebuke. He addresses his words to Jews and Gentiles: "Men of Israel, and ye that fear God." Then taking as his subject matter the words of the two lessons which had just been read and were still ringing in their ears, he follows the line of argument which they suggest. These two lessons, as all writers on this subject are agreed, were from the law, Deuteronomy i., and from the prophets, Isaiah, two chapters still coupled together even to-day in the reading of the Jewish synagogue, giving the trend to St. Paul's thought and probably suggesting the two or three unusual words which are found in his address as well as in the chapters. St. Paul speaks with winning graciousness and power, passes briefly, according to the custom of the period, over the main facts of Jewish history, bringing out the protecting love and goodness of God upon the one side, the stiff-neckedness of Israel on the other. He shows that greater than all other goodness has been the gift of leaders and kings who have protected and guided the people, and pointed towards the coming of a greater King and Leader, the incarnate God and Saviour of the people. He brings out forcibly the rejection of their Saviour, but as he does so we hear a tender note of forgiveness in his words, similar to that of his Master, "because they knew Him not, nor yet the voices of the prophets . . . they desired . . . that He should be slain." Paul knew that neither Jew nor Gentile in Antioch had had part or lot in the matter of the crucifixion and death of Jesus; therefore, having shown that the resurrection had been confirmed not only by eye-witnesses but foretold again and again by David, he passes forward to the blessings flowing from that death and resurrection, that is to say, from the death itself to the result of that death—the justification of the believer, a blessing which might be received by the men of Antioch as fully as by those of Jerusalem.

Justification by Faith

It is this forgiveness of sins, this perfect justification of the believer, which gives the note of assurance and triumph towards which Paul has been tending throughout his address, as he tended towards it in all his after teaching either by person or by letter. This word 'justified,' whenever St. Paul uses it, seems to shine forth with a radiance peculiarly its own. Technically speaking it is a law term,—a man made righteous,—one over whom neither man nor law has any claim; but when Paul uses it it signifies "an initial movement by which God puts man into a right relation with Him," thus showing forth not only righteousness but forgiveness and love also. It calls up the image of the justification which Paul himself had received on the way to Damascus; it shows a man set free through the righteousness of Christ, set free to love and work for Him. There is a ring in the words "all that believe are justified" like the clarion notes of Romans viii. 1, "there is therefore now no condemnation to them which are in Christ Jesus." But just as St. Paul reaches this point, as we wait to hear him go forward and explain, as he does in Romans viii., how through the Spirit men are freed from sin and death, he seems to stop as suddenly as Stephen and to change his voice. This sudden turn, this strange climax, is probably due to the restlessness of his hearers, for as he draws the contrast between this freedom of the Gospel and the bondage of the Law the lowering faces of his audience must have warned him, as they had warned Stephen, that he could go no further. Therefore, before it is too late, whilst he can still be heard, he bids them beware lest the judgment foretold in the time of the prophets should fall upon them also; beware lest, despising salvation, they should perish almost within the very sight of it. His address concluded, Paul descends from the desk of the reader and makes his way out of the synagogue; but as he goes many of the Jews and devout proselytes gather in groups around him, beseeching him that the same words may be spoken to them again the next Sabbath Day, and listening eagerly to the final words of exhortation which he gives them. (The account of the breaking-up of this assembly is more clearly given in the R.V. than in the A.V.) But Paul reads the faces of the Jews too well not to know that bitter opposition and persecution are already on their way towards him and towards his hearers also, and therefore both Barnabas and Paul "persuade them to continue in the grace of God," and to stand firm in that hour of trial which is about to fall upon all who believe in Antioch.

The Service of the Next Sabbath Day

Much excitement must have prevailed throughout Antioch during the ensuing week, and Paul and Barnabas would be surrounded day and night by anxious inquirers as well as by disputants until the Sabbath Day came, and the whole city, moved almost to an uproar, came together to hear the word of God. If the gathering on the Sabbath before had been strange, owing to the number of Gentiles as well as Jews who were assembled together, the gathering of the present day was stranger still, for an eager, breathless throng of Jews and Gentiles crowded every corner of the synagogue. St. Paul was invited once again to speak, and gladly accepted such an opportunity to witness for Jesus. But the Jews, who had been for some time labouring in Damascus and gathering religious proselytes around them, envied the power of Paul and Barnabas, and resented the thought that those amongst whom they had so long been labouring would be carried away by the new doctrine, and that they would have no further power over them. Therefore, filled with enmity, they contradicted everything that Paul spake, and dared even to blaspheme the name of Jesus also.

The Jews Put Away the Word of God, Judging Themselves Unworthy of Everlasting Life

Seeing that it was impossible to teach or even to argue with a multitude thus set upon evil, Paul and Barnabas waxed bold, and read aloud, as it were, to the assembled multitude the condemnation which the Jews had written upon themselves; God had numbered their kingdom and finished it. He had given it to the Gentiles. Of what avail was it for Paul and Barnabas, moved with compassion though they might be, to linger in the cities of the Dispersion as Jesus had lingered in the streets of Jerusalem. It was the Jews themselves who were turning the feet of the messengers of the Cross towards the Gentiles, who were crucifying afresh their

Lord and King. Therefore, to the Gentiles they would go, and as they went would fulfil the command of God, who had sent them to be a light to the Gentiles and for salvation unto the ends of the earth. As Paul and Barnabas made this proclamation the Gentiles rejoiced and glorified God; they rejoiced that a faith which by its purity had already attracted them, might now become theirs without a galling subjection to the customs of a subject nation; they glorified God because they knew that they were ordained to Eternal Life in place of the Jews who had deliberately cast that ordination to life away.

The Chief Men and Honourable Women Expelled Paul from the City

It is easy to understand the indignation which a judgment such as this, publicly proclaimed in the streets of Antioch and in the presence of the Gentiles, would arouse among the leading Jews. We do not wonder that henceforward the presence of Paul and Barnabas was intolerable to them and to their Rabbi. These men had obtained a hold upon the devout and honourable women as well as upon the chief men of the city, and that they would raise a ceaseless agitation in the city, until by force of active persecution they had expelled Paul and Barnabas out of their coasts. Paul may have gone forth sadly from the city of Antioch, more sadly even than from that of Paphos. In each place an exceptional opportunity of preaching the Gospel had been given, and in each place that preaching had been in vain. To what purpose the miracle, to what purpose the moving of the Spirit of God amongst the hearers of the synagogue if Paul and Barnabas were cast out and the new converts in each city left without guidance or direction. How sadly, in accordance with the will of Jesus as they had learned it from the disciples, did they shake off the dust of their feet as a witness against them, and yet if they had but known it, joy instead of sorrow might have filled their hearts, for One Mightier than they tarried with the converts of Antioch. The Spirit of God was manifested, and filled the hearts of the disciples with a joy and gladness so great that they who would otherwise have been left desolate in the midst of persecution were permitted to learn by experience the truth which Jesus had taught to His disciples, "My Word shall not return unto Me void"; "Lo, I am with you always, even unto the end of the world." Paul and Barnabas had fulfilled their commission; they went forth cast down, but not destroyed, and their work remained in measure cast down also, but not destroyed.

CHAPTER XXX

ACTS XIV

THE GOSPEL OF ST. PAUL TO THE HEATHEN

The Turning towards Iconium and Lystra

After a journey of about eighty miles, from Antioch in Pisidia, Paul and Barnabas reached Iconium, which was then, as now, a place of considerable importance, owing partly to its position in the neighbourhood of the great trade route, by means of which constant communication could be maintained with Antioch and other important cities, partly on account of the Roman roads which ran through that part of the district and afforded protection to the traders from the lawless attacks of the Pisidian mountain tribesmen.

Iconium lies on the borderland of Phrygia and occupies a prominent position in the surrounding district, somewhat like that of the city of Damascus in Syria, and is noted not only for its beautiful rivers, but also for its luxurious orchards and vegetation, whilst at the same time it is sufficiently distant from Antioch to be entirely independent of its influence.

St. Paul began his work in Iconium, as he had begun it in Antioch, by preaching in the synagogue Jesus as the Son of God, and both Jews and Gentiles gladly accepted his words; but it was not long before the antagonism of the Jews was aroused. They set at nought the tokens of Divine favour and refused to see in the signs and wonders which were wrought by the hands of Paul and Barnabas any confirmation of their words, and finally, by their sinister influence, not only counteracted all that was said, but raised such a storm of opposition against them that Paul and Barnabas became aware that they were in peril of their lives. If it had been a sudden outburst of anger it would not have been so dangerous, but in the present case they found that the rulers of the synagogue, supported alike by Jews and Gentiles, were determined to use them despitefully and stone them. Paul and Barnabas, therefore, fled from Iconium, and, leaving that district altogether, crossed to the boundaries of Lycaonia and came to Lystra, eighteen miles distant from Iconium. They were thus brought into contact with a race of semi-barbarous men who, although they had some knowledge of Greek, usually spoke a dialect of their own, and were as impetuous and superstitious as the men of mountainous districts usually are.

The glory of Lystra has passed away; its once proud fortress, the representative of Roman power, whose garrison curbed the surrounding district, is now a ruinous heap. All that can be found is a mound containing traces of some ruined buildings, and having at its feet the remains of a church with a sacred spring beside it. This mound was, some twenty-two years ago, identified as the site of the city, and this discovery was further confirmed by the finding of an inscription in honour of Augustus as well as by a coin with a Latin inscription, showing that Lystra had once been a Roman colony.

The Healing of the Lame Man

This was the city in which Paul, freed at last from the animosity of Jewish colony or synagogue, remained teaching either in street or market-place or wherever he could gather an audience round him. It was on one of these occasions, most probably on a market day, judging from the concourse which quickly gathered together, that whilst speaking he saw a lame man listening intently, his whole face lit up with a new-born faith and hope. The crowd who were pressing around him took no notice of him; his misery was so familiar and well known that they never thought of help or healing for him. But misery was never an accepted fact in the eye of Jesus or of His disciples. His heart was always moved with compassion towards those piteous beings who by their very helplessness, by their limbs deprived of throb or power of life, seem by that helplessness to protest mutely even against existence itself. But whether the crowd had forgotten him or not, the man had listened to the message of a Saviour's love and power, and, listening, betrayed his faith and longing in his eyes. Paul, with ready sympathy, perceived his faith and bade him stand upon his feet; the man, believing that God-given power would come with the God-given command, lifted himself, arose, leapt, and walked.

The effect of the miracle is emphasized by St. Luke even more than the miracle itself. When St. Peter had healed a lame man the multitude around him had lifted up their hearts to the God Whom they knew and worshipped; and so, in like manner, when Paul healed a lame man, the multitude of Lystra naturally turned towards the idols whom they also had known and worshipped. In their excitement, believing that their gods had come down to help them, they cried out in the speech of Lycaonia (forgetting for the moment the Greek in which they were accustomed to speak to strangers and had been listening to St. Paul): "The gods are come down to us in the likeness of men." Paul and Barnabas, being ignorant of the vernacular dialect and seeing only the general excitement consequent upon the miracle, neither understood what the people said nor what they alluded to, until, the excitement becoming greater, they saw a procession of oxen garlanded for sacrifice, led by the priests, slowly making their way through the crowd towards them. As they advanced the whole multitude saluted Barnabas (the more silent and dignified, and therefore, according to their belief, the greater) as Jupiter, and Paul (the more active) as Mercurius, and whilst they hailed them the priests prepared to make sacrifice and do homage to them.

The Ancient Story of Lystra

The reason for this sudden movement on the part of the people can be found in their ancient mythology. The city of Lystra was peculiarly sacred, owing to the tradition that Jupiter and Mercury had once descended in mortal form and dwelt amongst them in disguise. Little wonder, therefore, that the people, seeing the miracle, concluded that the gods had once more reappeared amongst them, and, full of excitement and joy, prepared to do sacrifice to them. But what was their amazement and distress when these so-called gods, instead of favouring their approach, rent their clothes, and running to and fro, entreated them to stay their hand, utterly refusing to receive any worship from them. Their disappointment and indignation became even greater when, not content with gesture and expostulation, they spoke, and as soon as they could obtain a hearing disclaimed not only any connection with the gods of Lystra, but dared to denounce and call in question the very existence of the gods themselves, and characterized their sacred worship as vanity. They bade them lift their eyes to the great Unknown and see the universal tokens of His presence around them, and by these and similar entreaties "scarce restrained they the people that they had not done sacrifice unto them." It is well to note carefully the whole story, the signification of the miracle of healing, and Paul's attitude towards idolaters and idolatry, as well as the way by which he lifted their thoughts to the conception of the one true God.

Effect of the Healing of the Lame Man

St. Paul, in teaching the men of Lystra, had already found that they were very far away from the knowledge of God, and therefore he gave them a sign or parable, spoke to them in a language they ought to have been able to understand, and showed them by deed as well as word that the great power of God had come amongst them, and that faith in His Name had made the lame man strong. His parable was not in vain; the men of Lystra caught a faint echo of his meaning. They, like other heathen nations, had a lingering instinct, an undefined sense, leading them to believe in gods of love as well as gods of judgment, and that these gods of love would in their love put on human flesh and come down to help them. There is something very touching in their far-away intuition, their instinctive longing for an incarnate God. But touching as this intuition might be, it was so closely mingled with error that it had to be combated at all costs, and the eyes of the men of Lystra lifted from the creature to the Creator, from idols to the one true God. If this error was broken down, there might be hope that the truth which they were dimly feeling after would be revealed to them, and that they would learn that the feet of the messengers of the incarnate God were even then within their gates, were even then telling them that the thing which they had imagined had verily and indeed come to pass, that God had come down in the likeness of men and was about to be revealed to them.

St. Paul's Address to the Men of Lystra

Intense interest centres around the declaration which Paul made to the men of Lystra owing to the precedent which it forms for missionary work of a like character. The Lystrians seem to have been entirely ignorant of truth; they had not, like the men of Athens, found out the emptiness of idolatry, but were resting in it and satisfied with it. They had not, therefore, a yearning after an unknown God, which could be appealed to, a vague aspiration after the unknown to be satisfied. Would St. Paul accept their worship, would he adapt their idolatry to the Christian faith, or would he put aside that idolatry and attempt from a new foundation to raise their thought to the one true God? He repudiated altogether any connection between himself and their own idol worship, and tried instead to lift their minds to a first conception of the one eternal God. He appealed to that which they did know and see; to the witness of Divine love which surrounded them; to the heavens above and to the earth beneath, in order that through the creation the Creator Himself might be manifest to them. He told them that that Creator had not been unmindful of them, though He had suffered them to walk in their own ways. He had given them gifts, especially that most prized of all at Lystra, the "rain from heaven," as well as "fruitful seasons," "filling their hearts with food and gladness."

THE GOSPEL OF ST. PAUL TO THE HEATHEN

"Ye Shall Be As Gods"

As St. Paul points to the vast expanse of heaven above, to the hills, to the fields so peculiarly fruitful for harvest, he insensibly draws the thoughts of his hearers away from idolatry, away from that worship of himself which they had suggested. How could he whose mind had realised the greatness of God suffer for one moment worship due to God to be transferred to himself or to any child of man? Upon his ears those words "Ye shall be as gods," which have been whispered from time immemorial into the hearts of men in order to lead them to destruction, fell in vain, for he had heard the voice of God, he had been bidden to draw near despite his weakness and to receive "power to become the son of God" (John i. 12). How could he who had tasted that the Lord was gracious, who had learned the joy of sonship, permit homage to himself or to any other being to draw men down to earth instead of lifting them up to that God Whom he himself had found and worshipped?

The Persecution of the Jews

Day by day Paul and Barnabas patiently sought by the example of their lives and by the power of their words to dispel in the minds of the men of Lystra the darkness engendered by centuries of superstition and to found a Church even in that far-off city of Lystra;

and they met with a more ready response than might have been expected, as we learn from the after-history of the Church. But their work was suddenly interrupted by certain Jews from Antioch, either men of business come to purchase the abundant produce of the city, or Jews wilfully dogging the steps of Paul and Barnabas in order that they might hinder them in their work. These men easily influenced the greater number of the people against the new teaching, for they were only too glad to oppose the disciples and avail themselves of anything which would restore to them the idolatry in which they had been brought up—an idolatry which did not, like this new teaching, make great demands upon them. Hence they readily believed anything which the Jews had to say against Paul and Barnabas, arguing that men of the same nationality must doubtless be fully informed about them. Incensed by the thought that Paul had dared to deceive them and attack their gods, in a sudden access of fury they fell upon him and stoned him, dragging him outside the city limits and leaving him there as dead. The disciples stood around him in speechless sorrow, but to their astonishment Paul at the last stood up, given back, as it were, from the dead, and returned with them to the city. The Divine power which had given vitality to the lame man had restored him also, and on the next day he was able to start out on the long journey of thirty miles to Derbe.

The Call of Timothy

The Jews had thus once again rejected the Gospel, and once again had induced the Gentiles to reject it also. But as Paul left the city, even in the midst of his rejection and humiliation there were light and hope. Through his efforts a Church which would endure hardness had been founded, which he was able to revisit from time to time with joy.

We cannot help wondering whether Paul realized that he was suffering for that Church what Stephen had suffered for the Church of Jerusalem, and whether also he knew that through that very suffering and stoning a disciple had been called who would be as faithful in carrying on his own work as he had been in carrying on the work of Stephen. Among the men of Lystra there was a youth of the name of Timothy, whose mother was a Jewess but his father a Greek. According to tradition Paul had lodged in the house of Eunice and had been interested in Timothy, and Timothy had been one of the little band who, powerless to prevent the stoning of Paul, had followed his body when it was dragged out of the city, and stood by it sorrowing for his apparent death. Whether this is so or not, there is no question but that Timothy was converted during this first visit of Paul, and that an incident like this must have had a powerful effect upon a youth brought up as he had been and with a nature as sensitive and deep as his. It is not surprising to learn, therefore, that when Paul revisited

Lystra he found Timothy well reported of by his fellow-townsmen, and so steadfast in the Faith that he decided to take him with him on his further missionary journey.

The Confirmation of the Churches of Lystra, Iconium, and Antioch

St. Paul had been cast out of Lystra, Iconium, and Antioch, but the effect of his preaching had not been cast out with him, for in each of these cities a Church had been founded and converts called out who would be steadfast to the Faith; but Paul knew well how isolated and dangerous their position was, how exposed they were to the seductions of idolatry as well as to fires of persecution similar to those which he had himself passed through, and which might be kindled against them at any time, and therefore he decided to visit them once again in order to confirm the converts and to ordain elders in each of the Churches. The meeting between Paul and the converts must have been a very touching one, for who could so truly tell them that through great tribulation they must enter into the kingdom of heaven as St. Paul, still bearing the marks of the stoning upon him? Who could so earnestly commend them to the Lord upon Whom they believed as St. Paul, who knew how near that tribulation might be and how far away they were removed from earthly support and direction? At this present moment, therefore, he commended them to the Lord upon Whom they believed, and since his continued presence would have been a source of danger to them he passed back by the way which he had come and returned to Antioch.

A period of about three years had elapsed since Paul and Barnabas had set sail from the harbour of Seleucia, a period in which they had learned something of the difficulties which lay before them, the bitterness of the Jews and the determination of their opposition. How gladly they returned to that same harbour! How gladly once again they stood in the midst of the Church of Antioch and told how great things "God had done with them, and how He had opened the door of faith unto the Gentiles. And there they abode long time with the disciples."

CHAPTER XXXI

ACTS XIV. 19 TO END

THE COUNCIL OF JERUSALEM AND THE CHURCHES OF THE GENTILES

A Retrograde Movement

St. Paul had returned to Antioch full of joy after his first missionary journey; danger and persecution had encountered him on every side, but he had abundantly proved that the preaching of the Gospel would be gladly accepted by the Gentiles, and that the "good news from a far country" would be welcomed "as cold water to a thirsty soul." As he returned he was met with joy and gladness on every side so soon as the good news was heard that "God had opened the door of faith unto the Gentiles." But although the leaders of the Church of Antioch might rejoice, he knew that it was quite possible that the Church of Jerusalem would be filled with fear rather than with rejoicing, although with united voice they had praised God when they had heard of the conversion of Cornelius, saying, "Then hath God also to the Gentiles granted repentance unto life." But this was

THE COUNCIL OF JERUSALEM

another matter, for Paul had gone several steps further than Peter. He had been brought face to face with the tragedy of the heathen world, and in the struggle to bring that tragedy to Christ he had gone fearlessly forward, taking step after step, according as opportunity and need directed, without stopping to consider as to how far his action might be sanctioned by the Church in Jerusalem. Thus he had taught justification by faith in his sermon at Antioch in Pisidia, as he had learned it of Christ, without stopping to ask or consider whether the Church of Jerusalem had as yet received that truth in its fulness. But, apart from the question as to whether they had received it or not, it would have been difficult either for Paul or for anyone to define exactly what the views of the Church were, for no decree as to the terms on which the Gentiles were to be admitted had as yet been given by Jerusalem. They doubtless held with Paul that a door of salvation had been opened to the Gentiles, but they had not as yet agreed as to how widely that door should be opened. Were the Gentiles to associate freely with the Jews and join in their love-feasts, or were they, as before, to stand outside with the God-fearing of the synagogue? This was the question which came to a crisis during Paul's brief period of rest and refreshment at Antioch, this the storm which broke so suddenly upon him. He had been baffled time and again by the deliberate opposition of the Jews themselves; but that opposition, no matter how bitter and unnecessary it might be, came in the natural course of events—it was part of the natural course of events; it had been foretold by Christ Himself, for He had said: "If they persecute Me, they will persecute you also." But the danger of the new opposition was that it came from within, and, like a kingdom divided against itself, threatened desolation unless some way of settlement could be found to it.

"False Brethren from Judaea"

Certain brethren had come down from Judaea, apparently claiming to be emissaries of the Church of Jerusalem, and had begun to teach the brethren, saying, "Except ye be circumcised after the manner of Moses ye cannot be saved."

It has been thought by Ramsay and others that the dissension spoken of in the second chapter of the Galatians took place also at this time, and further accentuated the difficulty, but this is still uncertain. It was absolutely necessary, not only for Paul but also for the Church of Antioch, to find out whether these men really represented the attitude of the whole Church at Jerusalem, or whether they were the representatives of one wing of that Church only. There was no question that although the leaders of the Church had originally confirmed the action of Peter in accepting Cornelius (Acts xi. 18), yet that they had done so under the impulse of the Holy Spirit and in opposition to their own instincts and to their preconceived ideas upon the subject. It is true they confirmed his action, but they looked upon the whole movement with hesitation, not knowing "whereunto it would grow," and desired as far as possible to keep the Gentile Church in harmony with the rites and ceremonies of the law of Moses. But

THE COUNCIL OF JERUSALEM

however easy it might be to explain the action of the Jewish Church, it was absolutely necessary to take a strong measure to change that action and to release the new-born Gentile Church from the swathing bands which they wished to throw around it. For if it were not released it would either lose vitality or it would break forth into independence and liberty, and form a Gentile Church apart from that of the Church of Jerusalem. Such a breaking apart was not a mere casting aside of the authority of the Church of Jerusalem, it was a movement heavy with misfortune to the Gentile Church itself and to the whole world also, for although the Church of Jerusalem might at times threaten the vitality of the Church, yet it ought to be capable of exercising a wise jurisdiction and guidance, and it was guidance which was especially necessary at a time like this, when new Churches were springing up on every side, and when the converts in their new-born zeal were apt to fall into error and schism of every kind. Paul knew that this question of error and schism would be the great danger of the Gentile Church, and therefore, when writing to Churches, such as the Ephesian, he set forward very clearly his ideal as to what the Church of Christ ought to be, "one Lord, one faith, one baptism" (Ephesians iv. 5), one "head, even Christ, from whom the whole body fitly joined together . . . maketh increase of the body unto the edifying of itself in love" (Ephesians iv. 16). He sought also to check the action of the false brethren and to hinder their further influence in Antioch itself. But, despite his efforts, the dissension which they sowed took root quickly and changed the feeling of joy which had been the characteristic of the Church of Antioch into one of uneasiness and doubt. Dissension and disputation began to prevail on every side, so that each man became a law unto himself. If the outlook was dark in the Church of Antioch, it was even darker elsewhere, for if the Judaisers could gain such power in a Church like Antioch, sheltered as it was by the strong influence of Paul and Barnabas, what might they not do in other more newly-founded and ignorant Churches, like that of Antioch in Pisidia, Lystra and Derbe?

The Question of Appeal to the Church of Jerusalem

The one hope of quieting the dissension lay in obtaining a doctrinal and authoritative statement from the Church in Jerusalem, giving freedom to the Gentile Churches; but two difficulties lay in the way of obtaining such a statement. In the first place, where two differing parties meet together concession must usually be made on either side if a common ground of unity is to be found, and Paul knew that he did not intend to make any concession or to change the Gospel of free salvation which he had preached to the Gentiles. The Gospel which he had preached he had received from Christ, and Christ only; and having thus received it he could not change it for any Church or council of men. If he were not prepared to yield, was he wise to carry the matter before the Council and to make his further progress more difficult by the possibility of a decision being distinctly given against him? The answer to this question came by direct revelation from

THE COUNCIL OF JERUSALEM

God. The voice which had bidden him open the way to the Gentiles bade him go up to Jerusalem and make straight the way for the Gentiles. The second difficulty lay in the character of the Council itself. Paul knew well that James, the brother of our Lord, who was at this time the head of the Church in Jerusalem, had great weight with the Council on account of the universal respect and veneration which his character inspired. He was a man of such absolute straightforwardness and uprightness that he was known by the title of James the Just, but it was this very character which might prove the greatest obstacle in the way of the Gentile Church, for James, despite his straightforwardness, had so narrow an outlook upon life that it was doubtful whether a broad and wise handling would be given to any question in a Council led by him.

St. James the Just

According to the general consensus of opinion among writers upon the Acts, St. James, the leader of the Church in Jerusalem, was the brother of our Lord and the author of the Epistle which bears his name. Very little is narrated in Scripture about him; but even from the scanty mention and allusion made to him, his character stands out in clear and distinctive outline. A veil of silence has been drawn over his early life in Nazareth, which it is not for man to draw aside, and we can only think of the quiet home and the two brothers growing up side by side with a feeling of awe and wonder—the one surrounded by the mystery of the Divine, the other, as we can see from the later impression of his character, a Hebrew of Hebrews, devout in all matters of the Law, unswerving in a strong but narrow sense of duty. It was probably this very strong but narrow sense of duty, this rigidity of character, this fixity of outlook, which held St. James from seeing the Divinity of Jesus and from believing on Him until after His resurrection. How could he who sought with all his heart to keep the Law even in its minutest detail understand that the youth who grew up beside him was the great Lawgiver—the law unto Himself? He would naturally join the number of those who sought to lay hold of Jesus and put Him under restraint because he thought He was beside Himself when He infringed the Rabbinical interpretation of the law of the Sabbath. The exquisite beauty of the patience and of the love of Christ is seen in His dealing with St. James, not only during His lifetime, but after His resurrection also; for it is specially noted that Christ appeared to James as to Saul, to the two men who had a zeal of God, but not according to knowledge—the two men who, being ignorant of God's righteousness, had gone about to establish their own righteousness, and had not submitted themselves unto Him Who was the end of the law of righteousness to everyone that believeth. No record is given as to what passed between our Lord and James at the time of His appearing. We can well believe it was too sacred to be inscribed; but if the words of Jesus to Paul were filled with Divine understanding and compassion how much more must the words of Christ to James have been filled with even greater love and understanding! for it would be far harder to bring a brother, and a man of a character like James, into the fulness of Christ, than a man of Paul's natural breadth of character. Yet James, as we can see from the issue, was as evidently born anew in Christ as Paul, and during his after-life as perfectly sought to follow Him, and he must have rejoiced that even at this eleventh hour he had seen and known Jesus; although, together with his rejoicing, there must, not only then, but ever after, have been a sense of everlasting loss when he realised what might have been his could he but have perceived the Divinity of Jesus and learned of Him during the long years at Nazareth.

The Attitude of St. James towards the Council of Jerusalem

The hardness of perception which St. James showed towards the fulness and liberty of Christ Himself helps us to understand the slowness of perception shown in a Council led by him in Jerusalem. It was only natural that the men who had been so long near Christ without recognizing Him should be equally long in recognizing the fulness of salvation and liberty brought by Christ. Thus we see that He is inclined to emphasize details and to see faith through works rather than works through faith. St. James had known, as few other men knew, the Law of Moses, had felt its power, had seen the reflection of his past life with all its failures and shortcomings; but he had been led by Christ Himself beyond that Law of Moses and into the perfect liberty of Christ. One was, as it were, the mirror reflecting his natural face in a glass; the other opened out a vista of worlds unknown—of love, and light, and hope; and yet such was the power of habit over his mind that, although he lived and walked according to that law of liberty, he yet leant towards the Law of Moses, he yet emphasized details, saw faith through works rather than works through faith. His appearance, according to tradition, harmonized with his character. We can still see the Nazarene with his austere features, his knees worn hard, like those of a camel, through being constantly bent in prayer, not only for himself but also for those around him. This was the character of the man with whom St. Paul had to deal at this juncture. We can see how easily the men, who though nominally Christians yet really Jews at heart, could by their zeal in matters of the Law commend themselves to James and obtain a prominent position and influence in his Council. But when, in addition to all this, we remember that St. James himself had remained constantly at Jerusalem, and had never been brought into actual contact with the Gentile world, we can see how hardly he would understand the swift change which had passed over the religious life of the Gentile Church by the preaching of St. Paul; and yet St. James was the one man who could help St. Paul at this juncture, and who, by the universal respect engendered by the uprightness and rigidity of his character, could turn the Council at his will. Was it possible that St. James could or would bring the whole Council of Jerusalem into liberal dealing with the Gentile Churches? We might have been inclined to answer this question in the negative had it not been for the further light thrown upon his character in his Epistle. Here we find not only the adherence to the principle which he had first imbibed, but also the wisdom that rested upon God only, that was wide, pure, and peaceable. It might be that St. James had ever before his eyes the warning of the blindness of his early life which had cost him so dearly, and which had cast away from him opportunities impossible to regain. We can almost hear an echo of his own lack in the words, "If any man lack wisdom, let him ask of God." We can almost see James bent in supplication and receiving that wisdom which he had asked for when we listen to the wise address which he gave to the Council of Jerusalem, an address which shows how liberally God had given wisdom to him in answer to his prayer.

St. Paul's Journey to Jerusalem

In order to bring the question of the Gentile Church more vividly before the Church of Jerusalem Paul decided to take with him Titus (Galatians ii. 1), one of the leading converts, so that the Jews might see in him a typical representative of the wide thought and ability of character which distinguished many of the converts in the Gentile Church.

We can imagine how grateful the companionship of Titus must have been to St. Paul upon this journey. It was a time when he peculiarly needed to have the aspect of thought not only of the leaders of the Jewish Church but also of the leaders of the Gentile Church vividly before him, and no man could have been more helpful for this purpose than Titus, for, from the mention made of him, we can see that he was a man of peculiarly strong and tactful character, one whom Paul was accustomed to lean upon, as, for instance, when he sent him to settle difficulties of an exceptionally grave character which had arisen in the Church of Corinth.

We can imagine how gladly Titus on his side would embrace the opportunity of passing through the city for ever hallowed to him with St. Paul, as well as for meeting in his company the men who had seen and walked with Jesus.

As Paul pursued his journey he passed through Phoenice and Samaria, declaring the conversion of the Gentiles and causing great joy to all the brethren; but when he came into the coasts of Judaea we notice a difference, and, instead of pausing to declare the glad tidings from place to place, he seems to have pressed forward without gathering together the men of the district or speaking to them. He probably knew that it would have been in vain, and that the Churches of Judaea were so strongly under the influence of the Church of Jerusalem that they would be out of sympathy with the new-born life of the Gentile Church.

As we close this introductory lesson to the Council in Jerusalem, and call to mind the life and character of the leader of that Council, we cannot help thinking of the practical daily lesson and warning which it contains for every one of us. As we admire the utter selflessness, the grandeur, nay, almost the majesty, of St. James, we wonder at the constraining love of Christ which could at one glance change the habits of a lifetime and turn the rigid adherent of the Law into the suppliant follower of the Cross of Christ; yet whilst we admire this change of character we can also learn a practical lesson from the failure of his early life. We, too, like James, pass through life side by side with men and women of varying types of character and thought, men and women towards whom we are irresistibly drawn or irresistibly separated, according as we are at one with them or not upon the greatest matters of life, and especially upon the matter of eternal truth, which is more than life itself. Would that, by the grace of God, our eyes, which are now holden, might be opened, so that we could see the exquisite beauty of the character of the men who journey with us, who are closest to us, in our work and in our home, but whom we do not understand, and who although familiar to us even in the smallest details of their lives, are further from us in spirit than those who accidentally cross our path. Too often the cloud of darkness which hides their character from us is not due to them, but to our own imperfect or impetuous outlook upon life. We see so clearly our own aspect of virtue or of truth; and we think that the cause of right is hindered by their lack of vision, by the narrowness or imperfection of their character. Too late, when they have passed away from us for ever, we awaken to a sense of their loss. We realise what we might have learned from them, what we might have received as well as given, and we experience the bitterness which recalls too late the beauty of character and of intellect which has passed away for ever.

CHAPTER XXXII

ACTS XV. 1-36

THE COUNCIL OF JERUSALEM

The Embassy of St. Paul to Jerusalem

St. Paul was once more about to enter Jerusalem, but not now, as in days of old, filled with ambition as a student of the law, or as a zealot of the law. His thought and hope had burst all bonds of self or race asunder, and extended over the whole future of the world and the highest ideal of that world as represented in the progress of the Gentile Church. As he entered Jerusalem he knew that a heavy responsibility rested upon him, for, unless by his intervention, the fatal policy which the Judaising party had entered upon in the council of Jerusalem could be changed, the newly founded Gentile Churches, Churches already comprising men of the highest intellectuality and spirituality, must either drift away into sects and Churches of their own or be so fatally repressed that all hope of growth or extension would be gone. St. Paul knew only too well the delicacy and difficulty of the task that lay before him; but that task had been undertaken at the bidding of the Holy Ghost, and under the guidance of the Holy Ghost he had thought out and lived out the points at issue, so that they were no longer to him matters of opinion but of absolute conviction. He who for many years had trained himself to pursue every question, as it were, back to Eternity and forward to Eternity, that is to say, he who had accustomed himself to view every question in the light of past revelation as well as in the present light of the Holy Spirit, knew that he had grasped a conception of truth clearer and greater than that of any of the men with whom he came in contact.

The object of his journey on this occasion was to bring the Church of Jerusalem into the full light of the Holy Spirit, so that guided by that Spirit they might set free the Gentile Churches and set free themselves also. But however earnestly St. Paul might desire this end, he was far too well versed in the world of men not to know that a modification of opinion so radical as this could only be effected by bringing the Jewish world into contact with the Gentile world, that is to say, by bringing apostles, like James, who had rarely if ever left Jerusalem, into contact with converts like Titus, and thus enabling them to learn and appreciate the standpoint and general outlook of the Gentile Church.

The account of this meeting between St. Paul and the leaders of the Church, James, Cephas and John, is related in the Epistle to the Galatians, and it is only by taking into consideration the interchange of thought and opinion which would take place in these meetings that we can understand the liberal views of all the great leaders as expressed in the final council of the Church. How gladly would we know all that took place in these preliminary meetings, how gladly follow the arguments by which men differing so widely from one another as James the zealot and Paul the statesman were brought together and united in thought and action. But no record remains of any discussion save one which touched a difficulty arising apparently from without rather than from within, and which, though at the first no bigger than a man's hand, threatened in very short time to overcast the future of the whole Gentile Church.

The Circumcision of Titus

This special difficulty was a question as to whether Titus, who had accompanied St. Paul to Jerusalem, must of necessity be circumcized before he come into contact with the Christians of Jerusalem (Galatians ii. 3). It was not as simple a matter as it seemed. It concerned the liberty of the Gentile Church, the liberty for which Paul was now contending in Jerusalem, and Titus as representative of that Church occupied a position of importance so great that the question of the reception which was accorded to him in Jerusalem was a matter of public and not of private signification; for Titus was known and beloved, and the Gentile Churches who were jealous of his honour would augur from the attitude of the Church towards him the attitude of the Church towards themselves also. St. Paul's distress was therefore very great when he found that instead of welcoming Titus to their midst the more narrow among the Judaisers immediately set their faces against him, and seizing upon the fact that he was uncircumcized objected to his presence among them. Their opposition was as uncalled for as it was cruel, for Titus was a Greek, and being a Greek was free from any obligation to be circumcized! But considerations of this kind were as nothing in the eyes of these "false" brethren. They were fully aware of what they were doing and were determined by insisting upon the circumcision of Titus to insist upon the circumcision of the whole Gentile Church, or failing this, upon the exclusion of the Gentile Church from fellowship with the Church of Jerusalem. Their particular mode of attack is not recorded, but in all probability they tried to exclude him from the Agape, or love feast, as well as from the general gatherings of the brethren, and justified their action by saying that although such separation might not be needful upon his account it was needful upon theirs, for it was unlawful for them to hold free intercourse with a man who was uncircumcized and a Gentile.

"To Him We Gave Place by Subjection No Not for an Hour"

St. Paul saw only too quickly the ultimate bearing of their action as well as the narrowness and meanness of their attitude towards a man who was a stranger and far nobler in intellect and character than themselves. The position was as intolerable to him as to Titus. Indeed, it is impossible for us to understand how intolerable;

we can only judge of his mortification from the fact that after the lapse of so many years St. Paul could not speak of it when writing to the Galatians without strong indignation, and becoming so agitated that his words, as he dictates them to his scribe, stumble one upon another, and became so obscure that it is difficult to catch his meaning or to learn the successive steps of the controversy and the outcome of it all. But despite the obscurity of his words we can gather some idea of the difficulty. We can see, for instance, the grave injustice which was done to Titus by the Jews in thus trying to force him to be circumcized. How could they expect a man who had tasted the full liberty of the Gospel, a man, moreover, of intellect as powerful as his, to submit to the formality and limitations of men like-minded with themselves? And even if Titus out of the fulness of his strength and magnanimity might be willing to bear with and submit to their weakness, yet on other grounds how was it possible for him to do so? He had to remember that he was the representative of the Gentile Church, and that any concession granted by him might have to be granted by the whole Gentile Church also. If Titus were circumcized, then the Gentile Church was condemned to be circumcized in his person, and the question which St. Paul had come up to debate in Jerusalem was practically yielded before the debate itself had taken place. Moreover, an unfair advantage was taken of him; Titus knew, only too well, the delicate character of the responsibility which rested upon St. Paul, and might fear if he refused to be circumcized that the Judaisers would secretly stir up the multitude of the assembly, and, by persuading them to sympathize with their imaginary grievance, raise so violent a prejudice against Paul and Titus that Paul might be unable to obtain a hearing when the whole matter was brought before the Council, and thus in another and more subtle manner all hope of a liberal settlement would be gone for ever. Would it not be wiser for St. Paul to circumcize Titus as he later circumcized Timothy, and thus by enabling Titus to mingle freely among the Jews to give them a chance of learning from him the true character and the nobility of the men who were the leaders of the Gentile Church?

How gladly would we know for certain whether St. Paul yielded to this plea of expediency, or refused in any respect to compromise his principles. The matter has given rise to much controversy and discussion, but despite one or two eminent exceptions the general consensus of opinion among scholars as well as the one most in harmony with the character and general tenor of the passage is that he stood firm and refused to allow Titus to be circumcized, that he took his courage, as it were, in his hands and refused even by implication or for one moment to yield the freedom of the Gentile Church.

The Contribution to the Church of Jerusalem

Whatever the outcome of the difficulty as to Titus may have been, there is no question whatever as to the general outcome of the consultation which took place between Paul and the leaders of the Church of

Jerusalem, for it is recorded that at the last "James, Cephas and John," "pillars of the Church," gave to Paul the right hand of fellowship (Galatians ii. 9), and agreed that whilst there should be unity of communion and doctrine, there should also be separation of leadership, that is to say, that the guidance of the Jewish Church should be committed into the hands of the leaders of the Council of Jerusalem, whilst that of the heathen world was given into the hands of Barnabas and Paul. One stipulation and one only was made—that as the Gentile world had become a partaker of the light and hope which had been jealously guarded by the Jewish Church for so many centuries and which had originally been the exclusive privilege of that Church, the Gentiles should, in return for the blessing thus derived from them, express the feeling of their indebtedness to the Church of Jerusalem by contributing to its relief, and that these newly founded Churches of the Gentiles being wealthier than the Church of Jerusalem should give of their wealth and forward it to Jerusalem by the hands of Barnabas and Paul.

Whilst St. Paul stood firm upon the question .of principle, he was willing to yield upon the question of expediency, and he therefore not only gave a ready consent, but also followed up that consent year by year with an equally ready performance, for throughout his epistles we find frequent allusions to this gift, as well as exhortations, that the Church of Jerusalem should be as liberally supported as possible.

It seems to us a strange reversal of the customary position of an older church towards a younger. We are accustomed to think of the Mother Church as tending for her daughters, and as supplying the need of the missionary outposts of the Church until those outposts are sufficiently strong enough to support themselves. But this was a position which the Church of Jerusalem never assumed towards the other churches. We have to remember that she was constantly hampered, partly by the fire of persecution, partly by the poverty which resulted from the misconception of her early days when owing to the expectation of the almost immediate return of her Lord she had permitted her members to form a community of goods, and depend upon one another, instead of labouring for themselves.

The Meeting of the Council

It is strange to turn over the minutes of the first great council and after the lapse of so many centuries consider the character of the men who took part in it, see them arise and hear them speak, men who had seen Christ, who had lived and walked with Him, who had learned from His lips the Gospel which they preached, and who knew the necessity of preserving that Gospel in its unity and purity. The meeting began, as all such meetings usually do, with much argument and disputation, the leaders at first giving a wise latitude of speech and intervening only when further discussion would have led to too great heat of argument. Then St. Peter arose, and having caught the ear of the audience spoke with decision, each word bearing the mark of indisputable truth. He takes practically the same stand as that which he had taken years before when speaking to the Sanhedrin, "we ought to obey God rather than man." He carries the whole argument back to main principles, to the work of God, to the direct action and dealing of God as manifested amongst them. He himself had been chosen by God to give the Gospel to the Gentiles, and God had witnessed to the sincerity of His Gospel and to the manner of its reception by the gift of the Holy Ghost, thus placing the Gentiles purified by faith on an equality with the Jew purified by law. Purification by faith having thus been accepted by God, why should man reimpose purification by the law? Moreover, seeing that the Jew himself had found purification by the law to be a yoke greater than he could bear, why, instead of attempting to drag down the Gentile, should he not cast away the yoke of the law and accept purification by faith also. Who could answer an argument like this? There was not a man present, not one, who had honestly tried to keep the law but found an echo in his own heart as to the impossibility of bearing the heavy yoke of that law.

In the midst of the silence which followed, each man being brought, as it were, face to face with the secret of his own heart, Paul and Barnabas rose, and, taking the same standpoint as Peter, demonstrated by actual fact, by miracle, and by wonder, the favour of God resting upon the heathen who had been brought to God by faith and faith only. Each fact, as they spoke, carried with it its own weight, until once again silence fell upon the multitude, a silence which not even the most fanatical amongst them dared to break, until at last James stood up and all men knew that from his lips the final word would be given. If James admitted the force of these arguments then the whole assembly must admit them also, for who was there in all that audience so rigid as he in the observance of the law, who so holy and venerated by Jew as well as by Christian, so venerated indeed that, according to tradition, he alone of all men had been permitted, together with the High Priest, to enter into the Holy place. If James accepted justification by faith how could any Judaiser refuse to accept it also.

The Perfect Law of Liberty

But if St. James was rigid in his adherence to the tenets of the law he was still more rigid in his adherence to the fact that every word that has come down "from the Father of lights, with whom there is no variableness, neither shadow of turning" (James i. 17), is forever true. Submitting, therefore, his will to the will of God he sought to bring the Jewish section of the Assembly, the men who, like himself, had been prepared to make everything "according to the pattern showed to them in the mount" into unison with this new thought and fuller interpretation of the law of God.

Turning the flashlight of the revelation which he had just received upon the Old Testament Scriptures also, James proclaimed the fact that he had just learned himself, namely, that this calling of the Gentiles by faith was indeed part of the immutable purpose of God. "Simeon hath declared how at the first God had visited the Gentiles to take out of them a people for His name." Amos, eight hundred years before, had declared that the fallen tabernacle, the fallen worship and glory of the Jew, would be rebuilt not by the residue of the Jews only but by the Gentiles upon whom God's name would be called. Such being the eternal purpose of God, who or what were they that they should gainsay it. All that they were called upon to do was to remove the stumbling blocks which hindered the working out of that eternal purpose. Wherefore, his sentence was that a decree should be sent to the Gentiles bidding them abstain from things offensive to the Jews, as from this time forth they would be called upon to mingle with them in one common worship. The Gentiles would readily understand the necessity for this decree. In the first place, they were accustomed to hear these particular points denounced in the law of Moses whenever they worshipped in the synagogue of the Jews; and in the second place, because they knew that these particular matters which were denounced were those which brought them into contact with idolatry and must, therefore, be contrary to the worship of the one true God.

There were two further regulations, neither of which would be irksome to them, for as they learned from Christianity the sacredness of life they would be willing to abstain from things strangled and from blood, that is to say, from meat containing blood, the blood being the life, according to the generally accepted Jewish belief; and secondly, as they grew in the knowledge of the true and living God they would understand that they must abstain from fornication and uncleanness, a sin so intermingled and identified with idol worship that it had become almost one with it; so closely intermingled that the clouded conscience of the idol worshipper had almost lost the sense of guilt.

The Decree of the Council of Jerusalem

The wisdom and moderation of James in this speech was felt by everyone, and even Paul himself probably felt that he had obtained all that he could hope for, although no authoritative decree had as yet been given, possibly because the conscience of the greater part of the assembly was not as yet prepared for it. To us at first sight the charter reads almost as if it were drawn up by Gamaliel, as though the Church had agreed to refrain from these men and let them alone lest haply they might be found to fight against God. But if we look more closely we see that it went further in deed than in word, and implied a greater sympathy and co-operation with the newly born liberty than appeared upon the surface of it. For the charter does not stand alone; in the first place, as "false" brethren had gone to Antioch, purporting to be emissaries of the Church of Jerusalem, so now two men, Judas and Silas, are sent, chosen and proved, who are to accompany Paul and Barnabas, and are to bear in their hands a letter concerning not only Antioch, Syria and Cilicia, but all the newly founded Churches, a letter which will stand after the words of explanation spoken by the emissaries themselves have passed away. In this decree the uncircumcized Gentiles are greeted as brethren by the Jews. The council altogether disallows those who have preached the doctrine of circumcision, and endorses those who have preached justification by faith; that is to say, it disallows the "false" brethren and endorses Paul and Barnabas, "men who have hazarded their lives for the Lord Jesus." In the second place, speaking not only in their own name but in that of the Holy Spirit, whose presence has been visibly manifested in their midst, they release the converts from all Jewish burdens, bidding them abstain only from open idolatry and sin, "from which if they keep themselves they will do well." Thus by the grace of God the great battle for the freedom of the Gentile Church was fought and won. It is true that the decree might have been fuller and that the contention was by no means ended, but the belief of centuries could not be changed in an hour, by any decree, or number of decrees. Men have to be led gradually according to the guidance and dictation of the Holy Spirit, and according as their conscience can follow that guidance. Nevertheless the issue of such a decree, a decree issued with the full sympathy and conviction of the Church, marks a step forward towards the liberty of the children of God, towards purity of doctrine, and towards the communion of saints.

We cannot lay aside the minutes of this first Council without feeling something of the joy which thrilled the hearts of all who were present in that great assembly, for the charter of liberty, as it was "delivered to the saints," is the charter of liberty to the saints of all ages; and apart even from the charter itself there is the further joy of learning how men who differed from one another like

James and Paul in respect of forms and ceremony were actuated by the living Spirit of Christ, and seeking for the truth were led to find that truth and thus enabled "to hold fast the form of sound words," to "avoid foolish questions," and to "exhort and convince the gainsayers."

CHAPTER XXXIII

ACTS XV. 36 TO END

THE SEVERANCE OF FRIENDSHIP

The Delivery of the Decree in Antioch

The great battle for the liberty of the Gentile Church had been fought and won. In place of the obligation to observe the whole Jewish law, the Gentile converts were exhorted to abstain from idolatry and from all the excesses connected with idolatry. In place of the doubts which the so-called brethren from Jerusalem had cast upon the teaching of Barnabas and Paul, the Church as a body, under the inspiration of the Holy Spirit, gave an unqualified expression of confidence and appreciation of their work. This was the summary and general bearing of the edict which was read in the assembled Church at Antioch and confirmed by the inspired words of Judas and Silas, ambassadors from the Church of Jerusalem. The relief was instantaneous; instead of the worry consequent upon perpetual disputation, the attention of the Church was turned to that which was of far more vital consequence, to purity of body and soul, to the struggle against the seductive power of idolatry which surrounded them on every side. It was not the Church of Antioch only which was sensible of relief, the leaders of the missionary movement, Paul and Barnabas, knew and recognized that this charter contained the freedom necessary for the evangelization not only of Asia but of Europe, and rejoiced that this charter was now within their hands. But although an intellectual or spiritual victory may be fought and won, although the delivery of a decree or charter may for a moment allay strife and mark the turning-point of a controversy, it cannot change a train of thought or uproot long-standing prejudices. The intellectual attitude of the world changes only when that attitude becomes, as it were, incarnate in the world, that is to say, when it passes from the region of pure reason into living thought and action. Martin Luther fought and won the battle of the Reformation when he required the "testimony of Scripture and clear argument for the basis of the relationship of man to God and man to man," but his victory did not immediately change the face of Europe. The spiritual advance made at Jerusalem and Antioch was followed by renewed argument and difficulty, just as the advance of a strong wave is drawn back for the moment by smaller waves which follow after it.

The Vacillation of St. Peter and Barnabas

This retrograde movement was further accentuated by the incident (Galatians ii. 4), which is generally thought, though notably not by Professor Ramsay, to have taken place at this time.

After the delivery of the decree, and during the period before Paul and Barnabas started on their missionary journey, St. Peter seems to have come to Antioch, and, according to the natural generosity of his nature, rejoiced in the new-born liberty of the Church, and mingled freely among the converts, thus witnessing not only by word but also by deed that former things had passed away, and that all things had become new. But the Church of Jerusalem, Peter and Paul being no longer present and mingling in its councils, naturally fell once again under the influence of the Judaising party, and being seized with doubt and hesitation, sent out emissaries, under the authorization of James himself, to Antioch, apparently in order that they might lay a restraining hand upon any excessive liberty which might have been the result of the edict, and might ascertain exactly what the working out and liberty of that edict might be. The effect of their influence was most disastrous, for although there is no record as to anything definite which they said or did, the mere fact of the line of separation which they created, the criticism of their deeds, rather than of their words, awakened once again the life-long beliefs and prejudices in the minds of the Jews of Antioch, and called them into activity. Thus gradually and imperceptibly an aloofness sprang up between the Jews and the Gentiles, Peter and Barnabas uniting themselves with the conservative party of thought, and by their action counteracting the charter which had been so recently delivered; and thus the danger recently averted by the Council of Jerusalem became even more threatening because less tangible than before.

The Necessity for Definite Action on the Part of St. Paul

At first sight it seems impossible that St. Peter, who had defended himself before the Council of Jerusalem for eating with Cornelius, should be the leader amongst those who were threatening the peace of the Church of Antioch by refusing in like manner to eat with them. But we have to remember that the underlying issue of the question was not the same as before. Neither Peter nor any of the disciples questioned the liberty of the Gentiles; what they did question was the liberty of the Jews to be as the Gentiles. St. Paul saw that the revival of the old controversy in another shape would involve not only a question of danger to the Church but that Peter's line of conduct would involve a question of integrity also. If he were afraid of public opinion and at one time would eat with the Gentiles and at another must eat with the Jews, then he was governed by expediency rather than by truth, and his converts were free to be governed by expediency also instead of unswerving devotion to the truth. If it were hard for a Jew to undergo a fire of criticism for eating with a Gentile it was far harder for a Gentile to undergo the still greater fire of criticism which fell upon him for abstaining from meat offered to idols. Therefore, Paul stood forth boldly and challenged Peter to his face (Galatians ii. 2), although by doing so he endangered his friendship with Barnabas, the man who had taken him by the hand and been surety for him, as also his friendship with Peter, who had accepted him when brought by Barnabas and become sponsor for his integrity. Paul, in the presence of the whole Church of Antioch, stated the doctrine of justification by faith as unequivocally as in his Epistles. "I through the law am dead to the law that I might live unto God." "I live by the faith of the Son of God." "If I build again the things which I destroyed, I make myself a transgressor" (Galatians ii. 18).

The Relation between St. Peter and St. Paul

There is something majestic and in keeping with his whole character in this action on the part of St. Paul. It would have been far easier for him to deal with the matter privately and to excuse himself by pleading that Christ had bidden the disciples tell the brother who trespassed "his fault between him and thee alone." But Paul dealt with Peter face to face and dealt with him publicly, before the assembled Church. He knew that the question was one of public rather than private principle, and that, therefore, a public avowal must be made. Had St. Paul, either through his own personal influence or through that of another, convinced Peter

THE SEVERANCE OF FRIENDSHIP

of his fault, Peter might have shown his penitence by eating once again with the Gentiles, but the precedent of his separation would have remained; whereas by this open action on the part of St. Paul not only St. Barnabas and St. Peter but the whole of the Judaising party were shown to be in the wrong, and forced to adopt a nobler and more generous line of action. The narrative breaks off abruptly at this point and does not give the response made by St. Peter or by St. Barnabas, but it must have been satisfactory as St. Paul evidently, from that time forth, considers that the whole matter is finally settled.

We cannot help wondering whether the difference here narrated affected the after-relationship between St. Peter and St. Paul. The only answer to this question can be found in the mention which St. Peter makes of St. Paul in his letter to the Churches where he speaks of our "beloved brother Paul" (2 Peter iii. 15), and bids those Churches study the letters of St. Paul even although one of those letters contains an account of the defection of St. Peter and of the open rebuke which St. Paul had ministered to him.

From this mention we gather that St. Peter remained in sympathy and fellowship with St. Paul, and that the generosity of character which had led him astray made him large-minded also. He who turned at the look of Christ and wept bitterly at the thought of his desertion turned in the same manner at the reproof of His servant and changed his course of action whilst still preserving his attitude of brotherly love.

The Contention between Paul and Barnabas

Peace having been restored to the Church of Antioch Paul suggested that he and Barnabas should visit the other Churches which they had founded in order to give them further instruction and to put them on their guard against the animosity of the Jews. This would have been carried out immediately but for a difficulty which arose as to whether Mark should accompany them as their minister or not.

We are accustomed to see Paul pass from strife to strife, from the opposition of a body of men, such as that of the elders of Jerusalem, to the opposition of individuals, such as Peter or Barnabas, until his whole life seems to be "one earnest contention for the faith once delivered unto the saints." But in all these contentions Paul shows himself so large-minded, unselfish and generous, that we cannot understand his attitude over the difficulty with Mark, a spirit of bitterness which seems out of harmony with his previous life and character, until we remember the intense anxiety he had recently passed through, which resulted in a sudden attack of illness, and also that there may have been an underlying principle at stake far greater than appears. Paul could not have forgotten that he himself would have been rejected but for Barnabas, and we can only suppose that a line of divergence had been slowly arising between the two apostles, which finally widened into a separation at the time of the difficulty with Mark. Barnabas was clearly actuated not by family

THE SEVERANCE OF FRIENDSHIP

interest but by a spirit of generosity, similar to that which had distinguished him when dealing with Saul and with the men of Antioch, when he determined to take Mark because he knew that he had repented of his lukewarmness and ought to be given an opportunity for developing the untold possibilities for good lying dormant in his character. He probably thought, and thought truly, that for one fault a man should not be outlawed for life. On the other side St. Paul, who was accustomed to cast aside every weight in order that he might the more swiftly run the race which was set before him, would not take the risk of being hindered by a man who might be daunted once again by its hardships, hardships which he probably thought would be greater than any they had yet been called upon to endure, nor was he necessarily unmindful of St. Mark himself. He may have thought that it was better for him to wait until he was worthy before being re-admitted to full confidence and work. Thus the two friends separated, never, so far as we know, to work together again, although St. Paul later expresses his appreciation of the labour of Barnabas (1 Corinthians ix. 6). Paul chose Silas and continued his work with the same integrity of purpose as before, but he lacked the sympathy and geniality of Barnabas. Barnabas went to Cyprus, taking Mark with him, but his further progress is not mentioned by St. Luke. Most probably whilst ever faithful he in like manner lacked the presence of his former companion, the statesmanship which directed his way and whose will had kept him from swerving in it.

As we turn away we cannot help asking why such a separation should have taken place and wondering exactly at whose hands it had arisen. To this question there can be no answer save in the first place that a waverer is ever the cause of strife, and in the second place, that every servant of God, even Barnabas and Paul, accomplishes his life-work in the midst of frailty and of many drawbacks. And we notice, as we read the epistles of St. Paul, his frequent warning against strife, "the servant of the Lord must not strive" (2 Timothy ii. 24). And yet from St. Paul's action we learn that it may be better to strive than to allow any appearance of evil which would darken and draw away souls from Christ, better to strive than to hinder the work of Christ by allowing those whom we believe to be lukewarm or unfitted for the work to fill important posts and thus to hinder the work of Christ.

The Ordination of Timothy

Thus Paul, who had already for the sake of the Gospel surrendered every closest earthly tie, for the sake of the more efficient preaching of that Gospel surrendered yet one more and parted from Barnabas. He had left Antioch oppressed by the separation, oppressed by the illness which for a long season now had hampered his path, but God, in the midst of his weariness, opened His hand and let rich blessing flow from it. He knew too well the struggle which His servant had passed through, knew that a stand for the right which entails the loss of friendship is far bitterer than any perils of waters or perils of robbers, and, therefore, He who had taken away gave yet more richly to His servant. Timothy, who had been but a youth when Paul was at Lystra on his first journey, was now well reported of, not only by the Church of Lystra but also by that of Iconium, and was recommended to Paul for further service. From this time forward Paul was accompanied by one who, "as a son with a father," served him faithfully until the very eve of his martyrdom. Timothy, like Paul, had been brought up in a God-fearing home and had had the priceless gift of early religious training (2 Timothy iii. 15). There are so many instances in which children seem repelled by religion rather than attracted to it that it is peculiarly grateful to remember that the great leader of the Church, as well as Timothy, who was called to succeed him, were from childhood taught the Holy Scriptures, and thus became wise unto salvation. The greatest leaders in the Church, the men who have inherited the finest type of character, are usually found among those who from their childhood up have been surrounded by the highest influences, have learned the true perspective of life, have seen the vision of eternal truth and instead of rebelling against it, instead of yielding to the inborn impulse against established order, have apprehended the truth thus put before them, and have moulded their life in accordance with it.

The Unfeigned Truth

As no mention is made of Timothy's father we may conclude that he died while the boy was still young, and that, therefore, instead of being brought up as a Greek, the Jewish ideal was constantly put before him, first in the unfeigned faith manifested in the life of his grandmother and mother, and later in the direct instruction which he received from their lips (2 Timothy i. 5). This ideal had so moulded his life and character that Paul at once found a sympathy and strength greater in him than in any other, and despite his youth and delicacy of constitution made him a partaker in the anxiety and burden of all the Churches. His name is linked in five of the Epistles with that of St. Paul, and mention is made of his faithful ministry not only to the Churches but also to St. Paul. It is in connection with Timothy that we find one of the marked illustrations of St. Paul's breadth of mind and judgment.

Paul knew and taught that circumcision was nothing, yet in the present instance, in order that Timothy might minister more efficiently to Jews as well as Greeks, he circumcized him himself and removed what might have been a cause of stumbling. Then having circumcized Timothy he ordained him for the work of the ministry and rejoiced in the special gift of the Holy Ghost, which, as we can see from after references to his ordination, was given him at that time. Thus, Paul bids him "stir up the gift of God which is in thee by the putting on of my hands," and again, "neglect not the gift that is

THE SEVERANCE OF FRIENDSHIP

in thee, which was given thee by prophecy, with the laying on of the hands of the presbytery" (1 Timothy iv. 14). What a strange thrill this echo of a far-away ordination service gives us, how readily we understand the tenderness with which Paul watched over the spirit of Timothy, how fully enter into his mother's joy at the proof that her sacrifice, what was to her "even all her living," had not been in vain, but had been accepted by her God. From that time forward her son might live the hunted life of an evangelist, but she knew that wherever he went the good hand of his God rested upon him. It is true that he would be very far away from home and friends, but he would have the friendship of the greatest men of his age, men like St. Paul and St. Luke. It is interesting to note that from this time forward St. Luke became the constant companion of St. Paul, the scenes narrated in the Acts becoming vivid with the writing of an eye-witness and the "they" changed into "we," so that St. Paul had the constant care and companionship of a physician, as well as the sympathy and affection of a son.

CHAPTER XXXIV

ACTS XVI

THE PASSING INTO MACEDONIA

"Come Over and Help Us"

When St. Paul set forth upon his second missionary journey he found himself let and hindered on every side from running the race that he had set before him. Apart from a heavy cloud of sickness, and the loss of Barnabas—a loss felt the more vividly as city after city recalled the former labour of Barnabas—his way seemed unaccountably hedged in on every side, and had it not been for the consciousness that he was being led forward and that these very lets and hindrances were pointing him whither he knew not; had it not been also for the consciousness that the Spirit of God was encompassing him on every side—a consciousness similar to that which Joshua felt when about to enter the land of Canaan—the discouragement would have been greater even than it was. But at the last the way was unexpectedly manifested to him, and he saw in

THE PASSING INTO MACEDONIA

a vision a man of Macedonia saying "Come over and help us." As we read this we see how the spiritual life of Paul has passed from strength to strength. He who had at first received visions of Christ, and then of Christ's need of him, now sees yet further visions calling him to the need of the work itself. It is the response which Paul makes to these visions, a response involving the first step towards the evangelization of the continent of Europe (although to Paul himself it seemed but the passing across from one Roman province to another), that marks the interest of the present chapter. If Paul had not responded to that cry, or had responded to it otherwise than he did, how different might the future of the world have been? How many years might have elapsed before Christianity passed over from Asia into Europe? And even if it had passed over, how different might its foundation have been had it not first been proclaimed by a man of less natural ability, one less visibly moved by the Holy Spirit? But Paul having been called was not among the number of those who draw back. He stands forever in the foremost rank of the long succession of God's elect who, following the example of their Master, have responded to the cry of his own generation, whether that cry came from the heathen world, from a slave or factory child, and responding by the power of the Holy Spirit have set free those fast bound in misery and sin. These are the men, who, from generation to generation have gradually led the world towards Christ until they passed away and let their mantle fall upon their successors who followed after them. If the world is ever to attain the future set before it by our Master, Christ, if death is ultimately to be swallowed up in victory, then the men and women of each generation must from their mother's knee, as well as from their early student days, catch a far-off glimpse of that vision of the hereafter; must, before their ears are too heavily dulled by sin and pleasure, hear the echo of the cry "Come over and help us," and hearing, respond, according as power and opportunity may open before them. They seek first and seek early the Kingdom of God and they find that Kingdom and its righteousness. To them the form of the man of Macedonia gradually becomes the form of Christ Himself. They hear in the words "Come over and help us" the undertone of the words "Feed My sheep," and "Inasmuch as ye have done it unto one of the least of these My brethren, ye have done it unto Me."

A Roman Colony

Paul and his companions pondered over the vision as also over the previous let and hindrance, over the open door before and the closed door behind, and gathered that the Lord had called them to preach the Gospel in Macedonia. They went forward, therefore, and set sail from Troas, just as Robert Morrison having been hindered from going to South Africa set sail for New York on his way to China, and Livingstone having been hindered from China set sail for the work which he alone could do in South Africa.

Paul would the more willingly accede to this call because St. Luke, who is thought to have been a native

THE PASSING INTO MACEDONIA

of Philippi, had most probably whilst he was attending him in his illness brought the condition of Macedonia before him and interested him in its needs. Hence most probably Paul and his companions, after a swift voyage across the Aegean, made their way towards Philippi instead of going to the capital town of Thessalonica; and after passing through Neapolis saw the city in its mountain slope, outspread in all its beauty of temples and dwelling-houses, with its swelling background of snow-capped mountains and the green plains below. We can form little idea of the city of Philippi as it now lies in ruins, but when Paul visited it it was at the height of its power and prosperity. Philip of Macedon had with a general's eye seen the excellence of its strategic position, and had discovered also the wealth of gold within its mines, and being determined to take advantage of both he had founded the city and called it by his name. In after years the famous battle in which Brutus and Cassius were defeated took place just outside the city walls, and Augustus, in memory of his victory, conferred special benefits upon the town, giving to the citizens the rights and privileges of Roman colonists. Philippi, therefore, became an outlying extension, as it were, of the city of Rome itself. The Philippians were free from taxation, and in every respect one with every free-born citizen who, like St. Paul, came to sojourn amongst them. These rights and privileges became the distinguishing feature of the city rather than its commercial importance, and therefore the Jews, who ever followed in the wake of commerce, were not particularly attracted to Philippi. At the time when St. Paul visited the city the Jewish population was so small that instead of a synagogue within the walls the Jews were accustomed to meet in a proseucha or meeting-place more than a mile beyond the city by the river side. These proseucha are thought by later writers to have been small and roughly-built synagogues, so carelessly put together that they were sometimes not even roofed in, and situated by the river banks that the ablutions, which formed an important part of the Jewish worship, might be the more easily performed in them. It was to this river side that Paul and his companions made their way, and entering it sat down and spoke to the women which resorted thither.

How strange it is to think that the first Christian service held upon European soil was a small prayer meeting attended practically by women only. A monument has of late years been raised in the United States to mark the spot where Sir Francis Drake's chaplain conducted the first service on the Atlantic Coast. How sacred, could we find it, would the site of this first prayer meeting upon European soil also be, and yet how insignificant a gathering it seemed to be to the worshippers themselves! Truly "the kingdom of God cometh not with observation" (St. Luke xvii. 20). How much more lasting satisfaction St. Paul might have hoped to gain from an audience like that which shortly after listened to him upon Mars Hill at Athens, and yet no Church in after years was so faithful to his teaching or a cause for so much joy to St. Paul himself as the Church of Phillippi.

THE PASSING INTO MACEDONIA

"She Worketh Willingly with Her Hands"

Whilst St. Paul was speaking it became evident that one woman of the name of Lydia was listening with more than ordinary attention. She was not a Jewess, but a native of Lydia in Thyatira, and had already been attracted to the worship of the one true God, and her heart having thus been opened "she attended unto the things which were spoken of Paul." She was either a freed woman or one of lowly origin, for such only are called after the name of the cities in which they were born. But despite her lowly origin she was a woman of wealth and standing, as well as of singularly strong and sympathetic character. She embodies the New Testament conception of a wise woman just as truly as the character outlined by Lemuel in Proverbs xxxi. contains the Old Testament conception of a wise woman. She was able in work, wise-hearted, strong, generous and far-seeing. Her baptism, together with that of her household, was the consequence of the teaching of St. Paul and was the first step forward towards the founding of an European Church. Full of gratitude for the privileges to which she had been admitted, with a delicacy and kindliness, similar to that which the Shunammite woman showed towards Elisha and Gehazi (2 Kings iv.), she entreated, nay even constrained, Paul and his companions to enter into her house and abide there, and by doing so not only gave them the support of her position and influence, but also thus identified herself fully with the new religion. Little did the inhabitants of the once proud city of

Philippi think that, as long as the world endured, the hospitality shown by this business woman of lowly birth to these travellers, together with the kindness which she subsequently showed them when they were separated from her in far-off cities, would be the most abiding and gracious memory of their city.

The Release of the Damsel Possessed with the Spirit of Divination

How long Paul continued to pass up and down the streets of Philippi and labour in them, we do not know; but his appearance and message gradually attracted the attention of a poor girl, a pythoness, inspired by the same spirit as the Pythia or priestess of Apollo, or in other words, having a gift of divination or sorcery. This poor girl followed Paul and his companions whenever she encountered them, and, repeating words which she may have heard them speaking, proclaimed that they were the servants of the most high God, and would show unto men the way of salvation. Paul, instead of being angry at the uproar which she was arousing, although he knew that it threatened the continuance of his work in Philippi, was touched with compassion for her, and, full of pity for her condition, turned and in the name of Jesus bade the evil spirit go out of her. The girl was released, but as soon as she was restored to her right mind her means of livelihood were gone, and the indignation of her masters consequently aroused. Considering the wealth which the poor girl had already drawn to them they ought to have rejoiced when they

THE PASSING INTO MACEDONIA

saw that she was calmed and restored, and that the frenzy which possessed her had gone; but on the contrary they cared nothing for the girl. Their one idea was that their hope of money was gone, and that they would take revenge upon Paul. They thus showed Paul at the very outset of his European work the character of the opposition which he would have to deal with, and they also showed the hardening effect of the lusts of gain which makes men not only in Europe but all the world over indifferent alike to the message of the most high God, and to the suffering of their fellow creatures around them. These men could not restore the frenzied spirit of the poor girl, but they could and would injure Paul in the eyes of the Governor of the city, and had lived long enough in Philippi to know the character of the charge which, in order to do so, they could best lay against him. In a Roman Colony like Philippi no offence was so criminal as one committed against the majesty of the city, and thus by implication against Rome itself, and, therefore, utterly regardless of the facts of the case, of the truth that Paul, far from making any uproar, had restored peace by calming the spirit of the damsel, they charged both him and Silas with treason against the Roman State. Whether, in the midst of the uproar which was immediately aroused, Paul and Silas attempted to make themselves heard, and to explain that they were Roman citizens or not, is not recorded, but the magistrates at the mere word of treason, without giving them any chance of appeal, and in order to show their own loyalty to the Empire, rent their clothes, and commanded that they should be beaten. These commands were carried out with fury, and the prisoners, bleeding and quivering with undressed wounds, were cast into an inner cell, probably excavated in the rock itself, and despite the torture to men in their condition, were fastened by their feet in the stocks. The gaoler was as eager as the magistrates to show his devotion to the Roman Governor, for, being in command of an important fortress, he also was probably a man of considerable rank, and, for fear of losing his position, cared not how merciless he was towards his prisoners.

The Psalms of David

But a few hours before Paul and Silas had been rejoicing in the success which God had given to their work in Philippi, now on a sudden everything was changed. Their lives were threatened, and, even if they escaped, their whole work under the Roman government was threatened also. For if the cry could be raised against them that they were working in opposition to the peace and order of the Roman Government, then they would be driven from place to place, and furthermore, if they had been condemned of uproar in one Roman city, they would be liable to a like condemnation in other Roman cities also. What hope of deliverance or of future lay before them? But Paul and Silas instead of being cast down, as we might have expected, prayed and sang praises to God. Paul from his boyhood up had been taught the Holy Scriptures; he had known the Psalms of David, and their beauty had been further illuminated by the life and teaching of Christ and of His Holy Spirit; and the words of these Psalms in all probability rose as spontaneously to his lips as they have always risen to the lips of every leader, such as Luther, Coligny, and Cromwell, in God's warfare. For in the inspired words of these Psalms men find a means of expression deeper than all other to the external emotions of joy and pain within their souls. We can almost hear the words "God is our fortress and strength" resounding through the prison walls just at the moment when the solid rock upon which it was built quivered to its very foundations, and the doors and chains built in that solid masonry were set free, the rocks separating one from another as the force of the earthquake loosened the very rocks on which the prison was built. Although Paul and Silas in the midst of the tumult and confusion might appeal in vain to their citizenship of Rome and might be unheard, no mob or force of magistrates could hinder their appeal to a higher citizenship, the citizenship of Heaven. How forcibly in years to come would the recollection of that appeal and the reply made to it be brought before the minds of the Philippians when they were reading in the Epistle sent to them by Paul, "our citizenship is in Heaven from whence also we look for the Saviour, the Lord Jesus Christ" (iii. 20).

The Philippian Gaoler

The doors of the prison having been thrown open, Paul was probably able to look towards the lightened central chamber in which, according to custom, the gaoler, having important prisoners, had lain down almost within sight and hearing of them. As he did so he saw that the keeper, having recovered from the first shock of the earthquake, supposed that the prisoners had fled and was about to kill himself, in order to escape from the torture which he knew must otherwise await him. Despite the injustice and rude treatment which he had received, Paul was moved with compassion for the gaoler, just as he had been for the poor girl, and called out with a loud voice, saying, "Do thyself no harm, we are all here." The gaoler realized, partly from the earthquake, partly from Paul's words, that he was in the presence of a mysterious and Divine power, and, falling down before Paul and Silas, entreated the aid of that power. Then as the members of the household gathered quickly together, trembling, from the different parts of the prison, Paul, with the marks of his suffering and degradation still upon him, spoke to them and taught them the first truths about God and Christ. The gaoler, whose heart had been touched alike by the character of the prisoners, by their words of love, and by the terror of what he had just passed through, cried out, "Sirs, what must I do to be saved?" words which have arisen not only to the lips of the gaoler, but to every human heart which has been brought face to face with

THE PASSING INTO MACEDONIA

death and judgment and with the Almighty power of God. The answer which Paul gave, although the gaoler in the terror of the night would probably only dimly understand its meaning, were those words of equally eternal signification which alone ever can or will satisfy the awakened heart. Making what reparation he could, the gaoler ministered to the needs of the disciples and was baptized, and so the strange night passed away, and at break of day the magistrates of the city, doubtless having been equally terrified by the earthquake and brought to a consciousness that they had also offended the God whom these men worshipped, sent the serjeants to them, saying, "Let these men go." But Paul could not take advantage of a permission grudgingly given. He had in the first place to vindicate his rights as a Roman citizen, and in the second place, to vindicate his mission and to show that as a messenger of the Most High God he was in no sense a transgressor against Roman law. Therefore he demanded that the magistrates who had thrust him uncondemned into prison should now publicly acknowledge their fault and come themselves and give him honourable release. It was absolutely essential for his after work throughout the Roman Empire that it should be known and recognized that he was under the protection of the State and had the full rights of a Roman citizen; it was essential also that it should be recognized that the Gospel which he preached, far from being hostile to law and equity, contained the noblest ideals of peace, law and equity.

Therefore, having been brought out with all due honour, Paul entered into the house of Lydia, and after a brief stay bade farewell to the Church of Philippi and departed through the Via Egnatia to Amphipolis. Although Paul had been thus forced to leave Philippi in the midst of his work, that work was already done. He had founded a Church which would be faithful to the truth and a source of future joy and satisfaction to him. He had given, moreover, by the power of the Holy Spirit, in this first European city an example of the wide sweep of Gospel blessing which would one day pass throughout the length and breadth of that great continent; the Roman official, the wealthy merchant woman, and the captive slave girl having all alike been set free and gathered into the Christian Church.

The After History of the Church of Philippi

Eleven years later, at the time when Paul was a prisoner dwelling in his own hired house in Rome (Acts xxviii. 30), bound with a chain about his waist, he wrote a letter to the Church at Philippi which throws much light upon its after character and course. The note of affectionate gratitude which had been set by Lydia when she invited the missionaries to come into her house was continued throughout the lifetime of St. Paul. The Philippians seemed to have followed his travels with sympathetic interest, to have understood his difficulties as he passed from city to city and to have been anxious to minister to him, for not only twice whilst he was in Thessalonica, but also in Corinth and in Rome, they contributed to his necessity. St. Paul seems to have accepted the gift in the spirit in which it was sent, and whilst refusing help from other Churches and labouring with his own hands, gave proof of the perfect understanding which prevailed between the Philippians and himself by his ready acceptance of their bounty (Philippians iv. 15). It is possible that Lydia, who had been the most prominent woman at the time of the founding of the Church, continued to take an active part in all Church matters, and directed the giving of these contributions with as ready a tact as when she had first invited the four travellers into her house. We do not wonder that the tone of St. Paul's letter as he writes to the Philippians is full of affection and joy, and that he seems to forget even his own imprisonment in the thought of their constancy and affection. We see another proof of the perfect understanding prevailing between him and the Philippians in the way in which he is able to speak not only of themselves and of their faith, but also of matters personal to himself with the confidence of one who knows that he is as much beloved as loving. "Rejoice in the Lord, and again I say rejoice" is the keynote of the whole Epistle. It is true that at the moment when St. Paul wrote there was a special reason for his joy. Epaphroditus, the honoured messenger of the Church of Philippi, who had been sent in order that he might personally inquire into the condition of St. Paul, and aid him in his work, had thrown himself so heartily into that work that he had fallen ill, had been sick nigh unto death, and when St. Paul wrote had just been given back, as it were, from the dead (Philippians ii. 27). Paul, therefore, rejoices all the more that he could now return to Philippi and relieve the anxiety of the Philippians not only about Epaphroditus, but, owing to his long absence, about himself also.

The Faithfulness of the Church at Philippi

But besides the faithfulness and the loving helpfulness of the Church at Philippi, Paul found a cause of rejoicing in the absence of error which was far less rife there than in the other newly founded Churches. Thus while St. Paul warns the Philippians against the influence of Judaisers as well as against men of Antinomian tendencies, we gather from his Epistle that the errors which they taught were as yet not very prevalent in Philippi. The danger, at the moment when Paul was writing, seems to have arisen from excess of zeal rather than from languor and half-heartedness. Thus whilst Paul remembers gratefully the women who were the first-fruits of the Church, and who had continued to take such an active interest in it, he finds it necessary to warn Euodias and Syntyche, probably two of the leading women, to be careful in respect to differences which seem to have arisen between them. It must have been a special joy to St. Luke, when he wrote the Acts, to record the founding of this Church, for according to tradition he was himself its first minister, and remained for at least five years amongst the men of Philippi, and it is probably due to his breadth of mind as well as large-heartedness that the truth was so well known and that the Church continued so steadfast in the faith. Little record remains beyond the mention in the Acts and in the Epistle as to the after-history of the

Church. The most important facts that are after known about it are recorded in a letter which was written by Polycarp of Smyrna some fifty years later to the Church of Philippi. According to this letter the Philippians were still full of faith and hope. But they, together with their town, from that time forward have gradually faded away from history. This story and this story alone, containing their whole-hearted acceptance, their affection and loyalty, shines out like a gem of exceeding brilliancy, not only from the obscurity of their own history, but also from amongst the darker records of the other early Christian Churches.

CHAPTER XXXV

ACTS XVII. 1-16

THE CHURCHES OF THESSALONICA AND BEREA

"If They Persecute You in One City Flee to Another"

Paul continued to pass swiftly from city to city, from Philippi to Thessalonica, and thence to Berea and Athens, although he knew that in every place, whatever its peculiar life or charm might be, one end, and one only, lay before him—his own expulsion with ignominy and reproach. But if we marvel at the way in which he literally carried out the command of Christ, "If they persecute you in one city flee to another," we marvel still more at the courage with which he bore the ever-growing burden of responsibility which lay upon him. It was hard enough to preach, knowing that it was only a matter of time before the enmity of the Jews was aroused, and he was forced to leave his work behind him; but it was even harder to leave the new converts exposed to persecution from without, and to error and schism from within, and to be able only to watch over them by messenger or epistle. If Paul had had a Luke whom he could leave behind him in every Philippi his burden would not have been so impossible, but the utmost he could do was now and again to despatch a Silas or a Timothy to their aid to watch over and to guide them. Nevertheless, Paul pressed forward on his way, despite the witness of the Holy Ghost, that in every place bonds and afflictions awaited him.

The Entry into Thessalonica

Having left Philippi, and still bearing the marks of his stripes and imprisonment upon him, Paul made his way one hundred miles along the great historic road, the Via Egnatia, passing by, with the unerring instinct of a statesman, the two smaller cities of Amphipolis and Apollonia, and coming directly to Thessalonica, the chief centre of commerce in Macedonia. Thessalonica is one of the few cities which, owing to her position as a natural metropolis, still retains some of her importance. When St. Paul visited her she was a free colony with peculiar privileges of self-government and self-organization, granted partly for her loyalty to the Roman Government, partly to mark the victory of Octavius and Antonius. As a free colony Thessalonica possessed her own constitution, was democratic, and placed under the government of a chief magistrate, being called a politarch, and chosen by the demos, or people. The use of the term politarch by St. Luke was for a long time disputed, but its accuracy of late years has been confirmed, the word having been found engraved not only upon a stone which formed part of a triumphal arch at Salonika, the modern Thessalonica, but since that time engraved upon the remains of other cities in the same district also.

As St. Paul approached Thessalonica he must have wondered at its beauty, for it was then, as now, built in the form of an amphitheatre, sloping down towards the sea and with the snow-clad heights of Olympus rising in the distance behind it. It was situated on the world's great highway of the sea as well as of the land, and was a city of great commercial importance and with a correspondingly strong Jewish element. St. Paul, as his custom was, appealed first of all to that Jewish element, going Sunday after Sunday to the synagogue and reasoning with the Jewish congregation there assembled out of the Old Testament Scriptures. We lack in the story of Thessalonica the vivid personal touches and details which are so interesting in the history of Philippi, and from this fact, as well as from the passing of the "we" into the "they," we infer that St. Luke himself was no longer with the disciples. Nevertheless some features of an interesting and distinctive character are given. Thus, St. Paul changes from the ordinary Jewish method of preaching which he had followed in Asia Minor to the Socratic method of discussion common in Macedonia. He opens and alleges, that is to say, he reasons rather than teaches, and thus adapts himself to his hearers. We notice also the prominence of women in the Churches of Thessalonica, Berea and Philippi; the influence of women then as now throughout Europe being felt. "Of the chief women not a few" believed.

And lastly, we notice that St. Paul follows the example of Christ and lays the foundation of a right interpretation of the New Dispensation upon a right understanding of the Old Testament Scriptures. From the Old Testament Scriptures he shows that the essence of all revelation lies in the life and death of Jesus, and thus convinces a great multitude of the Greeks, a few Jews, and of the chief women not a few.

"Another King, One Jesus"

A movement such as this, which threatened the supremacy of the leaders of the synagogue, necessarily aroused the enmity of the Jews. The Gentile proselytes whom they had gathered around the synagogue would be the very first to comprehend and appreciate the teaching of St. Paul, and when to these were added other Gentile converts, the balance of power in the assembly began to pass into the hands of St. Paul, and St. Paul instead of being one of their leading rabbis became the great teacher of the synagogue. The Jews at first attempted to check this movement by contradicting Paul, and arguing with him, but failing, found themselves in worse case than before, and finally determined to resort to violence. This was a far quicker method of disposing of the difficulty, for nothing was easier than to persuade the band of loafers who infested the market-place of Thessalonica, as of every Greek city, to take up their quarrel and raise an uproar. These men only too gladly followed the bidding of the Jews, and having assaulted the house of Jason, and failed to find the disciples, dragged Jason and certain of the brethren before the rulers of the city, and laid two charges against them. They claimed, in the first place, that the men who had turned the world upside down had come thither; and in the second place, that these men were dangerous to the state, as they owned allegiance to another King, one Jesus. Charges as crafty and dangerous as these had only a few weeks before been laid against Paul at Philippi; but the rulers of Philippi had not disposed of them in half so able or so far-sighted a manner as the rulers of Thessalonica; the latter recognized more evidently the maliciousness of the Jews, although for their own sakes they did not think it prudent to deal openly with them. They knew that they themselves, like the men of Philippi, were on a very delicate footing with the Roman Government; the privilege of their freedom being held on the understanding that they would maintain exceptionally good government, and show an unruffled surface of perpetual loyalty. Therefore, no matter what the religious rights of the case might have been, they stopped the uproar for ever and for aye by binding over Jason and his followers to keep the peace. It was true that the men whom they bound over were the very last men in the city who wished to break the peace, and that it was the Jews and the loafers of the market-place who should have been bound over instead of them. Nevertheless, travesty of justice though it was, it proved to be a very strong and efficient method of settling the difficulty, and had besides an appearance of justice such as neither Jew nor Christian could gainsay. The uproar was, therefore, quelled, but it is worth while noting that the charges which were brought against the disciples were like the charges brought against Christ, far truer as well as falser in their essence than the men who laid them for one moment imagined or believed. Thus, whilst it was false to say that the Christians were turning the city upside down, it was no less true that they were turning the evil of the city upside down, and that they aimed to place the evil of that city beneath the power of right, that is to say, beneath the feet of Christ Himself. Again, whilst it was false to accuse their loyalty to Caesar, for "they rendered to Caesar the things which were Caesar's," it was true to say that their highest allegiance was given to "another king, one Jesus."

The Founding of the Church at Berea

Meantime, cast out from Thessalonica, Paul and Silas set out upon their way towards Berea. The rulers had let them go without stripes or bondage, yet, at the same time, they had inflicted a bondage of a far more injurious and galling character upon them and upon their future work than any stripes inflicted by a Philippian gaoler; for whilst Paul was free to return to Philippi, the pledge taken from Jason had raised an impossible barrier against his return to Thessalonica. All that he could do was to linger in the neighbourhood of the city, and to await further developments whilst he began a similar work in Berea.

The city of Berea was in some respects more promising than that of Thessalonica, for it was in the hands of the aristocracy instead of the democracy, and the citizens were distinguished by liberality of thought and dignity of character. "These were more noble than those in Thessalonica in that they searched the Scriptures daily whether these things were so; therefore, many of them believed." The men of Thessalonica had listened when Paul opened and alleged that "Christ must needs have risen from the dead." The men of Berea searched the Scriptures, and found from them the prophecies as to the coming passion and glory of Christ, and thus learned, "that Christ must needs have risen from the dead." Their conviction, therefore, became that of the mind and reason as well as of the will, and stamped the characteristic attitude of Berea as one of nobility. There is a nobility which seeks first the Kingdom of God and His righteousness, but there is a still higher nobility which accompanies every movement of that seeking with the mind as well as with the will, which endeavours to think, as it were, the thoughts of God after Him, to know by reason as well as by fellowship and suffering. Man cannot by searching find out God, for God reveals His mystery to babes; so too intellect cannot precede character, and yet intellect added to character can, as in the case of Moses and of Paul, change the whole face of the world, can lead the thought as well as the love of men. These are the men who indeed turn the world upside down. These are the men who are called for to-day far more than in any preceding day, for the century of to-day is the century of intellect, the time when everything is called to the bar of reason, and when men dare to place themselves upon the judgment seat behind that bar of reason;

and yet at the very time when they are thus sitting in judgment the world is instinctively crying out for the men who can think further and longer, who can bring the light of Heaven to bear upon the light of earth, and who, by God's grace, can think highest thoughts upon the highest lines. These are the lineal successors of the men of Berea, the nobility of the cities and countries in which they dwell, the nobility of the Kingdom of Heaven upon earth.

The Animosity of the Jews

But at the very moment when a lasting foothold was thus being gained for Christianity in Berea, a foothold of reason rather than of emotion, the Jews of Thessalonica received tidings of what was passing, and sent messengers who, according to the literal translation, so troubled the people that the brethren with all haste sent Paul to the sea, and when his enemies thought that he was beyond their reach, turned his route and brought him with all haste to Athens. Once again, therefore, Paul found his work interrupted, and himself alone in a world of strangers. As he left Berea he did not seem to be so anxious over its future as over that of Thessalonica, for it was on account of Thessalonica that he lingered within the same district, and would, as we learn from his letters, had he been able to do so, have gone back thither once and again had not Satan hindered him (1 Thessalonians ii. 18). Whether by this expression is meant a further accession of illness or the power of the Jews still predominant in

Thessalonica, we cannot now ascertain. But whatever the hindrance may have been, the final result of the delay has proved to be a cause of strength and rejoicing to all after generations of the Church, for when Paul could not go back thither himself he sent in his stead two letters, which are as full of comfort to us to-day as they were to the Thessalonians of many centuries ago.

The First Epistle to the Thessalonians

The value of the First Epistle to the Thessalonians, as of the second, lies not so much in its doctrinal importance as in the vivid picture which it gives of the fiery trials and temptations to which a Church such as that of Thessalonica was exposed. St. Paul writes twenty years after the death of Christ, when he was at the height of his power as well as of his work, and when the tension of the first foundation of the Churches was very sharply upon him. How sharp this tension was is evident from the fulness of personality and vitality, as well as from the passionate tenderness which characterizes his words, giving them a glow of life as inspiring to the youthful Christian of to-day as to the Thessalonian Church of many centuries ago. Paul sees in the life of that Church, the possibilities not only of the work itself but also of the work which may be connected with it and which may take a tone and colour from it. The Epistle itself was written at a moment of peculiar interest. When Paul had left Berea he had bidden Silas and Timothy come to him with all speed, but when the latter came he brought only sorrowful tidings, he could only tell

Paul that the door was still closed against him, and that the Christians were suffering from persecution as well as falling into error and misconception. The suspense consequent on these tidings was so intolerable that Paul sent Timothy from Athens that he might know their estate, and determined, though it was not good for him to be alone, that Timothy must return and entreat them to stand fast in the Lord (ch. iii.) The first ray of joy came when Timothy left Thessalonica and came to Corinth bringing good tidings of their faith and charity, and that they stood fast despite the wave of "affliction and distress" which was passing over them. The relief was so intense that, as Paul expressed it, "he lived" in "that they were standing fast in the Lord." His letter is written to express his joy, and to give words of warning and exhortation. He bids them live in purity and honour, and quench not the spirit by allowing the wave of corruption from the surrounding idolatry to pass upon them also. But Paul longs to comfort as well as warn them. Timothy has told him that the Thessalonians are bewildered. They, like all other nations of the period, are being moved by a general spirit of expectation, and have gathered from the words of St. Paul a hope that the explanation of the bitter persecution which they are passing through is but a trial of their faith before Christ returns in person to avenge them and take them to Himself; but to their sorrow and surprise one after another of their brethren has fallen on sleep, and they have had to bury them without any hope of immediate resurrection. What could be the meaning of it all? Why should so glorious a hope have been given them only in order that through the gate of bitter persecution a dark cloud of death should fall upon them as upon the heathen who surround them. Paul writes to calm this restlessness and sorrow. He bids them "sorrow not concerning those that are asleep." He bids them "study to be quiet," and to work with their own hands, but even whilst they work to lift up their heads, for the day of the Lord which they long for is coming, indeed will come so suddenly that it will be like a thief in the night (ch. iv.). Then their hope having been renewed, their restlessness allayed, Paul, with the gentleness of a father towards a child, takes up, as it were, the interrupted thread of his former teaching, gives them brief exhortations or watchwords, which they can pass on from one to another, and finally closes with an exquisite prayer by means of which they may know that though absent in body he is present in spirit, and is bringing them constantly in prayer before the throne of God.

The Second Epistle to the Thessalonians

This second Epistle follows hard after the first. Paul, while still at Athens, heard that the Church of Thessalonica was torn asunder not only from without but also from within, that the persecution instead of abating had continued with unabated sharpness, and that the converts themselves had misunderstood his letter and thought that the end of the world was at hand. He therefore writes in all haste to correct their misapprehensions, and to turn away their thoughts from restless anticipation into a quiet performance of daily duty. He bids them remember that above and beyond the hosts of men who are harassing and afflicting them are the hosts of Heaven, who will one day take vengeance on their adversaries. Meantime he tells them that it is only natural that the fiery persecution through which they are passing should lead them to abandon their daily labour and to fix their heart and hope upon the expectation of the immediate return of Christ, nevertheless, they must control that restlessness, for Christ's return, according to Old Testament prophecy, as well as from the teaching of Christ Himself, will be delayed. A period of time must intervene, and the persecution now prevailing become even sharper until "that wicked" is "revealed"; and the passion of evil will not have full sway until he "who now letteth" is taken away; that is to say, until the iron hand of Rome which restrains lawlessness has lost all power of control (ch. ii.). Then for one moment Paul throws, as it were, upon the canvas of the future two vast dim shadows or forces, and portrays the final struggle between the power of good and evil, the greater power of good having called forth a correspondingly greater power of evil also. With such a forecast of the future before them, Paul bids the Thessalonians steady themselves, and as it were, bring back their thoughts to the present instead of perpetually longing for the future which cannot be. He bids them turn their attention rather to the exercise and maintenance of a wise discipline among themselves. He knows that many walk disorderly amongst them, and therefore he bids them call to mind his example and support themselves by the labour of their hands, and remember the precept which he gives them that "if any will not work neither shall he eat." Starvation, therefore, rather than communism is to be the lot of the man who is wilfully idle, for the idle, whether rich or poor, according to the general tenor of this passage, are the cancer of society. Then with renewed prayer that in the midst of conflict the God of peace might be with them, he closes the Epistle, signing it with his own hand so that it may bear the full weight of his personality and authority.

After History of the Church of Thessalonica

The outlook of the Church of Thessalonica as gathered from the last words of the Epistle was as dark as possible. Paul, no matter how he yearned over them, could not return personally to comfort and direct them; could not even send them any hope of present relief, but could only pray for them. And yet despite these gloomy forecastings the after history of that Church was full of light, for we learn that as a body they remained faithful and powerful when other Churches around them had fallen into deathly stupor or into equally deadly error. A witness of the zeal of the Thessalonians remains in the beautiful Byzantine Churches, which, although now turned into mosques, still witness to the aforetime vigour of Thessalonica. More grateful, however, to St. Paul even than this witness in stone would be the reputation which Thessalonica subsequently retained for orthodoxy throughout the Middle Ages. The epithet of "Thessalonica the Orthodox" constantly applied testifies to purity of doctrine and to the fact that the word of truth which had begun to sound out from Thessalonica even in the days of Paul continued to sound out throughout the following ages of the Church. As a wise master builder, Paul, though absent in the body yet present in spirit, had, by the grace of God, so edified the Church of Thessalonica "his glory and joy" (1 Thessalonians ii. 20) that long after he himself had passed away it continued to be the praise and glory of the Master in whose Name and for whose sake he had loved, watched, and tended over it.

CHAPTER XXXVI

ACTS XVII. 16 TO END

AT ATHENS ALONE

The Turning Aside to Athens

St. Paul, whose heart's desire from the first had been the evangelization of the Roman Empire, knew that it was of first importance that the great centres of life and commerce should be touched as quickly as possible, so that from them the word of God might sound out to other cities also. Bearing this in mind it is interesting to note the particular cities selected by St. Paul as most important for this purpose, and to trace, wherever we can, the reason for his selection of them. We can understand why he should have gone to Antioch, Pisidia, Thessalonica and Corinth, more easily than we can understand why he intended to pass by Athens, and changed from this intention only on account of his anxiety for the Church of Thessalonica. Why should not Athens have been as interesting to him as Rome? Was it not necessary for the future of the world that the mind of Greece should be laid hold upon as well as the power of Rome? The answer may have been in the condition of Athens itself. Paul may have known that, despite the attraction of her learning and literary attainment, despite also the hold which the philosophy of Athens still had over the minds of some of the greatest men throughout the Roman Empire, yet the Athenians themselves were, as a race, pre-eminently self-satisfied, and that it is not from the ranks of the self-satisfied voluptuary, either of art or of literature, that leaders are found who receive the Kingdom of God as a little child, and seek first that Kingdom and its righteousness. Whether he would or no Paul was detained in Athens whilst he waited opportunity either to write or to go to Thessalonica, and it was during this delay that he gave his celebrated address to the Areopagus, an address more closely in touch with Greek thought and learning than any of his other addresses, and distinguished not only for that learning, but also for the loftier tone of Divine yearning which characterizes and inspires it.

The Entrance of St. Paul into Athens

St. Paul, having been thrust forth from Berea as suddenly as from Thessalonica, eluded his enemies by change of route, and made his way towards Athens. He was at this time alone, for he had left St. Luke at Philippi, Timothy at Thessalonica, and Silas at Berea; and, although Timothy came to him once and again, yet owing to the difficulty in Thessalonica, Paul felt constrained to let him return immediately in order that as he could not go himself he might be his representative in that city. It was rarely, if ever, that he was thus separated for a long time from his companions. Apart from his genius for friendship, those who surrounded him were careful to leave him as little alone as possible; he was in constant danger of attack from his enemies, and liable to a sudden return of his malady. But however unwilling they might be as a general rule to leave him, on this occasion it was impossible that it should be otherwise and, therefore, Paul approached in solitude the city which must have often held its spell over him. It is improbable that a Hellenist of his ability and literary tastes, brought up in a University town like Tarsus, should not have been susceptible to the charm of the writings of Socrates, Plato and Aristotle. The time had come when he was about to visit the former haunts of these men, but it was as a lonely traveller, entirely dependent upon the work of his hands, unheeded and unknown, torn with anxiety as to the converts in Thessalonica. As such he passed from place to place and found only in the condition of the city and in the character of its inhabitants some faint echo of their words. Little did the Athenians know or understand the spirit of the man who journeyed amongst them. If they noticed him at all they must have seen a man whom they knew instinctively to be out of sympathy with their life and habits, and who interested them only in so far as they were conscious of the deep fire of enthusiasm which burned within him and which contrasted with their customary outlook upon life, which may be described generally as one of amused spectatorship rather than of active participation.

AT ATHENS ALONE

The General Attitude of St. Paul towards Athens

Paul, contrary to his wont, seems to have intended merely to wait in Athens, instead of undertaking any missionary work in the city. The reason for his apparent indifference can be found not so much in Athens itself as in the extreme importance for the moment that he should remain quietly within reach of Thessalonica. Paul knew if he began to preach that his words would take effect in Athens as in other cities, and that it would only be a question of time before interest and antagonism were aroused, and only a further question of time before persecution and death would stare him in the face. Naturally, therefore, it was a very grave question whether, without means of private intelligence or possibility of succour in case of need, he ought to expose himself to so imminent a danger. But however grave this danger might have been, and however wisely he might have reasoned when his mind was preoccupied with anxious longing for Timothy and the news which he awaited at his hands, yet after a time no consideration of prudence to self-preservation could avail to overcome the sorrowful indignation aroused within him at the sight of the city wholly given over to idolatry. Pliny tells us that in the time of Nero Athens contained over three thousand public statues, besides numberless images set upon pillars and inserted into the walls of private houses, so that, as a Roman poet once declared, "it was easier in Athens to find gods than men." Every virtue, every vice, one might almost say every emotion, was thus exalted and deified. But this deification of the passions and frailty of humanity had already begun to pall upon men. The Stoics had discovered how wide the chasm was which existed between idolatry and their highest ideals, and had bidden men, but in vain, abstain from expressing in concrete form abstract conceptions of what may be called the Divine principle. If the Stoics felt thus towards idolatry what must St. Paul have felt also? As far as the artistic, philosophical, and literary side of his nature was concerned, he doubtless found abundant satisfaction in the miracles of art and beauty which surrounded him on every side, but he would care for them only in so far as they harmonized with purity and truth. The conceptions which lent themselves towards voluptuousness and vice would jar upon his consciousness of the purity of God, and, thus jarring, would provoke his spirit within him. There is no question but that genius, wherever it is found, whether in art or literature, has power, but that power is limited over those who have breathed, as it were, the breath of Heaven; they can only rejoice in art in so far as it inclines towards, or is in harmony with, the Divine ideal of beauty and goodness. All other genius, no matter how marvellously or exquisitely expressed it may be, if it tends towards or is in harmony with sin and idolatry, cannot and will not awaken a responsive chord in the heart hallowed by the indwelling of the Holy Ghost.

AT ATHENS ALONE

How Far Had Athens Been Feeling after God?

As St. Paul visited one celebrated place after another, and came into contact with what may be called the miracles of art and beauty in the city, he could not help seeing how often this beauty and art had expressed itself in communion with idolatry and vice; and worse still, how far this conception of art had degraded the character of the Athenians themselves. It is true that the great men of Athens, such as Socrates and Zeno, had given expression to ideals so lofty that they have been said to have prepared a moral foundation in Greece and Rome for the after teaching of Christianity, an ideal of law and order, of stern duty, and of divine protection. Whether this is so or not, there is no question that during the first century these ideals were more powerful over the men of Rome than of Greece, and that the habitual attitude of the Athenians had become one of cynicism and of contemptuous curiosity. St. Paul, instead of meeting contempt with contempt, was inspired with an intense feeling of pitifulness for the chasm between thought and practice written over the whole city and over the character of the inhabitants. This pity, together with the indignation aroused by the gross idolatry and vice on every side, so stirred his spirit within him, that despite the danger to himself, he disputed day by day in the synagogue of the Jews, and in the market-place with those with whom he came in contact. The men who encountered Paul would probably be inclined to argue with him, either from the Epicurean point of view recommending prudence as a means but pleasure as the end of life, or from the Stoical point of view, seeking harmony with the law of nature and the pursuit of that law regardless of pain or pleasure, yet in practice failing to live in harmony, and following nature too often in her baser aspects. But despite this chasm between precept and practice upon the part of the Stoics, there is no question that Paul felt the attraction of their views, and assimilated into his argument whatever was noblest in their philosophy, whilst striving to raise a greater and purer ideal before them.

The Curious Interest of the Athenian Philosophers

St. Paul seems to have passed from the Jewish synagogue to the market-place or general gathering place of the Athenians. As far as the Jews were concerned his words probably had little or no effect upon them, for they must by this time have added a thin veneer of Athenian scepticism and philosophy over their outward observance of the law. But though he made no progress with the Jews he quickly aroused the curiosity of Stoic and Epicurean alike. They saw in a moment that he possessed the fire of conviction, a quality which they peculiarly lacked, and by their supercilious contempt and sarcastic curiosity showed that his words had pierced the outer surface of their affectation and indifference, expressing their contempt by calling him a "babbler," "a picker up of seeds of learning," "a worthless fellow," and their ignorance by asserting that he wished to teach them about two new gods, Jesus and Anastasis (the resurrection). They doubtless supposed that he intended to add these new gods to the thousands they already possessed, and, despite their affectation of indifference, laid their hands upon him, and brought him to the Areopagus.

Much debate has taken place as to the exact meaning of this word "Areopagus," that is to say, as to the exact character of the assembly before which Paul was summoned as well as to the exact spot where they were gathered together. For a long time men thought that the Areopagus itself was intended, that is to say, the bare rocky knoll with seats smoothed out in the rocks upon which the first politicians, orators and philosophers of Athens were accustomed to sit when they held their court upon its heights. But of late years it has been thought by some that Paul was led to the Basilica, where the Areopagus were sitting, or that his address was given in some large square beneath the shadow of the Areopagus or Mars Hill. The exact place of meeting is of little interest to us compared with the character of the assembly before which Paul was taken; that is to say, whether he was summoned before a literary assembly or before a legal tribunal, and if a tribunal, what tribunal? It seems possible that just as Sergius Paulus may have thought that Paul and Barnabas were advancing their theories with a view to becoming established as professors of learning, so the Athenian philosophers thought that Paul was in like manner advancing his views in order that he might be recognized as a lecturer or exponent of thought, and in this case they would lead him before an assembly of philosophers and learned men in order that his teaching might be tested and the attack which he was making upon the Athenian gods might be called to account. It is clear from the question put to Paul and from Paul's answer that the assembly was not a court of trial in the ordinary and legal sense of the word. The whole tenor of Paul's address points rather, as Ramsay says, to a public display in which he was intended to give a proof of his skill instead of being accepted upon his reputation only. Paul's address, therefore, was a philosophical discourse, couched in popular form and adapted not only to the learned Epicureans and Stoics, but also to the crowd of curious loiterers who had gathered to hear his words.

St. Paul Standing before the Areopagus

The assembly before which Paul was summoned was very different from any which he had hitherto addressed. Instead of being confronted by Jews bound by the national and religious pride of centuries, or barbarians such as the tribesmen of Lycaonia, these men were free thinkers in the widest sense of the term. Men "who spent their time in nothing else but either to tell or to hear some new thing." But whilst thus very far removed in thought and earnestness from Paul they were fully trained to follow his arguments and to appreciate any turn of philosophy which he might bring to bear upon them. It is evident that Paul, as his keen eye ran over the audience, felt the stimulation of speaking to intellects so highly trained and far-reaching, and yet rarely if ever did he address any audience more difficult

AT ATHENS ALONE

or under circumstances more powerfully against him. In the first place, he was a Jew, a Hellenistic Jew it is true, and versed in Greek thought and education, but still to all intents and purposes, especially in the eye of the Athenians, a Jew and, therefore, one of a commercial race, necessarily discounted in matters of philosophy. In the second place, his appearance and diction were against him. "His bodily appearance was weak, his speech contemptible," *i.e.* probably lacking in the rhetoric so much admired amongst them. The Athenians were peculiarly susceptible to personal beauty and matters of exterior detail, and could be prejudiced either for or against a speaker almost apart from the matter which he was laying before them. There is nothing more trying to the deep thinker or the enthusiast than to have to deal with the man of worldly wisdom or the contemptuous onlooker, and under one or other of these headings the Epicurean as well as the curious element of the crowd would unquestionably be found. These men were so thoroughly filled with the thought of the present life that they had put aside all feeling of need for a future; but mingled with them there was a third body of men, the Stoics, and it was to this class that Paul practically addressed himself, although they only formed a portion of the audience. But however far the outlook of St. Paul may have differed from that of his hearers, there is no question that his sympathy was strongly attracted towards them. As Christ had read into his own soul and had brushed aside all that was antagonistic and worthless in it, so Paul, filled with Divine understanding, by the Spirit of God, saw past the carelessness, the scorn, and the restlessness, and discerned an eternal groping after truth, which, owing to its equally eternal failure, had revenged itself in this attitude of contemptuous cynicism. Paul, like a great physician, sought only to lay a hand of healing upon the suffering before him, to point out the cause of the malady and to give the way of release. He did not, therefore, answer back contempt with contempt; he knew and understood the pity of it all; he saw souls far away from God, feeling after God if haply they might find Him, and longed that he might, as it were, with a live coal taken from the altar of God touch their lips with cleansing power.

The Unknown God

Under the shadow of the Parthenon, within sight of the city given wholly to idolatry, Paul, utterly alone and facing a hostile crowd, had the courage to stand and declare the one true God. With wisdom and consideration as well as with courage he opened his address with the words: "I perceive that in all things ye are too superstitious," or, according to Ramsay's translation, "I perceive that you are more than others respectful of the Divine." In answer to this very searching after God, confessed upon their own altar, he declared Him whom they were seeking, a God dwelling not in temples, no matter how multitudinous they might be, either in Athens or in other lands, neither worshipped by men's hands, but over all, Creator, Inspirer, Upholder of all. Thus far Paul only idealized the highest form of Stoicism, had breathed, as it were, the Divine into it,

AT ATHENS ALONE

but he now took a step further and declared that God had made of one blood all nations of men, and that His Providence governed and entered equally into the life of all. Theoretically, Paul still was in unison with the doctrine of the Stoics, but practically his statement militated against the pride of every Greek who listened to him, for the Greeks, despite whatever theory the Stoics might have held, in their own thought and practice divided the known world into Greek and barbarian, just as the Jew divided the known world into Jew and Gentile. In support of his words Paul quoted from one of their own poets, and as he quoted brought forward the great truth that although created of God men are the offspring of God and not part of the Divinity itself. This statement opposed the Epicurean theory as to the fortuitous happening of men upon earth, as also the Stoical theory of the close intermingling of human and divine, death being merely a reabsorption into the surrounding divine essence. Whatever the feeling of his hearers might have been they could say nothing, for just as Paul, when lifting Christ before the Jew, proved each statement from the Old Testament prophecy, as when lifting God before the Lycaonian he proved His existence by His gifts of food and gladness, so now when lifting God above man to the Athenian he quoted their own instinctive feeling according to the expression found in the lips of their own poets.

"Though He Be Not Far from Everyone of Us"

But whilst thus demonstrating the majesty of God, Paul bade men feel also the love of God as expressed in the consciousness born within each one of us of the immanence of that God, "He is not far from everyone of us." We are yearned over and known of God; so closely yearned over that not only our deeds and acts but even our thoughts are, as it were, God-haunted yet we walk in blindness, because our face is turned away from Him and we cannot see Him. Paul has come to bid men turn and see God. He had come to tell them that if their hand is outstretched towards God, according to the inscription upon the altar, so the hand of God is outstretched towards them, only they must cast aside the idolatry which had intervened and kept them apart from God. This turning is not only a joyful hope put before them, it is also a necessity, for there is a day of judgment coming, and they can meet that day of judgment only through the Saviour whose hand is outstretched towards them. This man, risen from the dead, is as far beyond any previous conception of God in love and power as the living Jesus is beyond the most exquisitely chiselled but lifeless statues which surround them.

It is this incarnation of the living God which pierces through the veil and shows what to them before had been but an abstract idea, now made manifest in flesh. But as soon as Paul reaches this point of the risen man, the Saviour, all further hope of hearing is gone; he has touched a vital point, and at that touch his Athenian hearers spring aside as instinctively as the Jews, and refuse to listen, thus stopping short the further story of the Gospel, which, without doubt, otherwise would have been given them. The Athenian might be curious enough and willing enough to listen to any interpretation or application of the words of his own poets, but he would not listen for one moment to the idea that he a Greek, an inheritor of Greek wisdom, should be judged by a Jew, a man utterly despised and looked down upon. Were all the heroes of his country, were Plato, Aristotle and Zeno also to be called in question and passed in judgment before a Jew, and not only a Jew, but a dead man, one whom Paul in his madness declared to be risen from the dead, a thing which they knew to be beyond human experience and belief? They utterly despised him, and raised a barrier of contempt more impossible to pass than any barrier of rage which had been previously raised by either Jew or Gentile, "some mocked, others said, We will hear thee again of this matter." So Paul departed, or, as the Greek is thought to imply, was forced to depart from among them.

As we read the account we may think that Paul's first intention to pass by Athens was fully justified by the issue of his preaching; there is no question that he felt cast down by his failure, for at Corinth he decided never to speak again in the same strain as at Athens, but henceforth to know nothing save Jesus Christ and Him crucified. This decision of St. Paul is of special interest at the present moment when the question as to the attitude of the missionary towards the prevailing religion of any country is one of the most living and practical topics of the day. Every man concedes that a right understanding of the religion of a people is a first requisite towards a right understanding of the character of that people; but every man will not as fully agree as to how far the Christian religion should be taught, as it were, as a thing apart and alone; or how far grafted upon the highest ideals of the existing religion.

St. Paul was the greatest and most effective missionary who ever lived. What was his experience? What his practice? As far as we can learn, St. Paul was greatly cast down by the result of his address at Athens, and the lines which he then followed (1 Corinthians ii. 2). Whether by making use of the philosophy of Athens he might have attracted those to whom Apollos specially appealed at Corinth (for Apollos probably spoke from a philosophical standpoint), yet he did not waver, but henceforward centered his preaching upon Christ and Christ only.

But despite his discouragement his labour was not in vain. Dionysius, a member of the Areopagus, and, therefore, a man of mark and learning, clave unto him and believed; also a woman named Damaris; this latter, from her name and the fact that she had been present at such a gathering, being probably of lowly birth, yet, from the mention made, like Lydia, a woman of ability and character; and together with these two converts and a few others who are unnamed also.

Thus Paul passed away from the most learned

AT ATHENS ALONE

audience that he ever addressed, and from the midst of the most learned city that he ever stayed in; and as he passed out of its gates, he seemed to leave nothing but mockery and contempt behind him; but cast down as he was, if he had been able to pierce the veil of the future, he would have been even more cast down, for he would have seen the long centuries lying outstretched before him during which the Athenians resisted the preaching of the Cross as well as the efforts of succeeding emperors to reclaim them. It is true that many legends have gathered round the name of Dionysius, the Areopagite, and it is true also that there were one or more Christian writers of mark in Athens during the succeeding centuries, but as long as the Olympic Games (393 A.D.) continued, the old spirit of Athens remained alive, and until Justinian closed the schools of philosophy (529 A.D.) paganism was alive also. It was not until the close of the fourth century that Christianity at last triumphed, and for a time side by side with these inward changes there came exterior changes also, and the monuments which had been so pitiful in the eyes of Paul as demonstrating a hopeless feeling after God, became changed into monuments of a finding of God throughout the city, and wherever an idol had formerly stood a tiny chapel took its place. A cloud of darkness overhangs the after history of the Spirit of Athens, but the general impression of the whole is one of great resistance, and that not only during the days of Paul, but also long after the preaching of the Cross remained to the Greeks foolishness. Thus Athens, supreme in its intellectual superiority, sends down throughout the succeeding ages a sorrowful answer, or echo of an answer, as it were, to the question, "Can man by searching find out God?" (Job xi. 7).

CHAPTER XXXVII

ACTS XVIII

THE BRIDGE OF THE SEA

The Passing from Athens to Corinth

The word Athens brings a far more ideal side of life before us than that of Corinth. We think of leisure and culture, of intellectual aspiration, of a striving after the unknown God, of the lofty code of the Stoics. But the word Corinth brings before us the material side of life, coupled with the sin that dares to flaunt itself even in the garb of religion, and we ask ourselves why, if so, was Athens less dear to the heart of Paul than Corinth, why did it awaken no peculiarly strong chord of sympathy in him? For it was in Corinth and not in Athens that Paul spent two years of continuous toil, and it was to Corinth that his two epistles were written and frequent expressions of love and anxiety recorded. It was to Corinth that Paul turned, and would have turned even oftener had he been able; whereas Athens was left without an epistle, without any of the touches which showed the brooding thought and care which he bestowed over other Churches. The only answer seems to lie in the character of Athens itself, in the fact that the Athenians were so stupefied by the opiate of pleasure, by a careless, self-satisfied life, that the vision of holiness passed unheeded before their eyes; whereas the Corinthians, degraded as they were (1 Corinthians vi. 9-11), did feel their degradation, did like the publican, when brought by the power of God to confess that they were sinners, shake off the stupor of immorality and sin; whereas the Athenians remained sunk under the still more deadly stupor of self-gratification. But although the Corinthians thus show that they were capable of being aroused, we cannot help wondering how St. Paul had the courage to believe that their reformation was possible, and dared to undertake the more than Herculean task of awakening spiritual life in a city so pre-occupied by business, pleasure, and vice, that it had no thought of God at all before its eyes.

There is little left to remind us of the city as it was when he saw it. The promontory still rears its colossal head two thousand feet above the level of the sea, but the rocky shelf beneath, the site of the once thriving and powerful city, is desolate, and a squalid town replaces the Corinth of the first century with its computed population of four hundred thousand inhabitants. The glory of that Corinth has passed as completely as the glory of the former Corinth which perished in the sack and fire of B.C. 146; so that the city called by nature to be "the key of the south" is as destitute of importance as of everything most prized in sculpture and art which still bears its name. It has been truly said that the treasures of Corinthian art, pillars, and statuary, can be found everywhere to-day except in Corinth.

THE BRIDGE OF THE SEA

"Limitless Opportunity, As Limitless As Lost"

Corinth as a city seemed at the time when Paul visited it to be as secure of its commercial importance as the Suez of to-day. On the one side lay the harbour of Cenchrea, courting and receiving the traffic of the East; on the other, the bay of Lechaeum, courting and receiving the traffic of the West; and between these two the Venice of the then world, uniting as by a stem the mulberry leaf-shaped peninsula of the Morea with the mainland, and receiving and exchanging a constant flow of wealth which passed from side to side of it. It is almost impossible to imagine a busier scene than the traffic-way between these two seas, swarming as it did with sailors, merchants, slaves, and burden bearers of all kinds, who passed in one continuous flow from harbour to harbour, carrying the cargo of the ships upon their shoulders, or hauling the ships themselves across the mainland from sea to sea. Who could think that the rocky passage of Cape Malea which they were trying to avoid would one day be as unfrequented and as desolate as the harbours on either side of the city, or that the shouts arising from the wild contests of the Isthmian Games would be stilled forever, and the dark pine groves from which the victors' crowns were gathered would be the sole reminder of those hard-won fights?

There is something strangely pathetic in this passing of Corinth. The exuberance and vitality of the city has exhausted itself as though the spell of the ancient curse laid upon it by Rome had hung over it until, century by century, it dwindled away, leaving only the epistles of St. Paul as the record of its spiritual life, and the seven Doric pillars as the record of a former and most beautiful epoch of its civil life.

"Working with His Hand the Thing That Is Good"

St. Paul, when he entered Corinth and felt the throb of the city, seems to have adopted a more decided line of action, differing from that which he followed elsewhere. In the first place he determined to know nothing amongst them "save Jesus Christ and Him crucified," and to oppose the atoning love and death of Jesus, in all the force of its purity and self-sacrifice, to the shameless profligacy taught of the votaries of Venus. Again, instead of preaching and teaching openly, he sought rather to awaken a quiet strength of conviction; he reasoned steadily in the synagogue with the Jews out of the Scriptures, thus avoiding notoriety and keeping himself in readiness for an opportunity to return to Thessalonica. And lastly, in order to establish for himself a name and standing as a citizen amongst the Corinthians, he determined to accept no aid from the Corinthians, but to labour with his own hands, lest in the eye of the multitude he might be associated with the pretenders and adventurers who found so ready an audience everywhere and invaded every part of the city, for the Corinthians like the Athenians were ever ready to hear and to tell of some new thing, and to throw themselves as eagerly into an intellectual as into a physical combat. Therefore, since interest thus easily aroused might easily die down, like that of the mixed multitude which followed Jesus, he decided to build upon a more lasting foundation and to work and wait. For this purpose he sought out Aquila and Priscilla, a tent-maker and his wife, probably Christians recently expelled from Rome, and abode with them, labouring at their craft, whilst Sabbath by Sabbath he reasoned in the synagogue, carrying weight not only because he spoke with the assurance of a Jew, a man well grounded in the Scriptures, but also because he was a known and accredited citizen, a man asking nothing and receiving nothing, labouring with his own hands "night and day" that he might be "chargeable to no man" (2 Corinthians xi. 9).

Aquila and His Wife Priscilla

Priscilla and Aquila had come to Corinth among the number of Christians who had been expelled from Rome by Claudius, partly because of the general hatred of the Romans against the Jews, and partly because of the storm and riot which the conflicts between the Gentiles and the Jews, as well as between the Christians and the Jews, had begun to arouse in every city, and which were peculiarly troublesome at Rome.

It is generally thought that Priscilla was of Roman origin, and of nobler family as well as quicker intelligence than her husband, for her name, a very unusual thing, is always mentioned by St. Luke before that of her husband. As St. Paul laboured side by side with Priscilla and Aquila, he had opportunity for deeper and more personal intercourse than when teaching the more mixed multitude in the synagogue, so that Priscilla and Aquila had the opportunity of becoming Christians of no ordinary type of character, and of acquiring a deep spiritual insight, such an insight as enabled them later in Ephesus to discern the limitations in the preaching of Apollos and to expound the way of God more perfectly to him, so that from a comparatively rudimentary knowledge of Christianity he became an exponent of the hidden mysteries of Christ.

Did Paul wonder why a man of his far-reaching thought and ability should be thus called day by day to give the greatest part of his time and strength to labour which could be as successfully performed by the workmen who laboured by his side? Did he whose strength was so sorely needed for Christian service, he who had the care of all the Churches, wonder why his already overtaxed and exhausted strength should be still further exhausted in daily toil? Did he, at whose lips men learned to seek Christ as at the lips of no other, wonder why, instead of preaching and teaching, he should be so confined at his daily toil that he could during the day bring the power of that truth only to bear upon a tent-maker and his wife? Do we in like manner wonder why so petty a round of daily toil is given to us, why our thought is ceaselessly interrupted, our strength frittered by endless worries, the work which we long to do compelled to wait whilst we are called aside and the iron enters into our souls even as we stand and wait? How differently might St. Paul have viewed his daily work had he known that the words spoken to Aquila and Priscilla would in their ultimate influence upon Apollos be mightier than many a word spoken in crowded market-place or synagogue; how differently might we view our daily work also if we knew the value of the opportunity given to us by God in it, and how the seed sown by the wayside might spring up more bountifully even than the seed sown of set purpose in the harvest of the hereafter. The thought of Paul's influence awakens a thrill of hope, a possibility of service, in the heart of every servant of God. We may not be able to speak or influence a crowd, but we can live and speak for Christ, and, whilst thus living and speaking, we can influence our fellow-workers, the men who stand beside us at our daily toil, who know us as we really are. In the day when the mystery of God is made manifest we shall know what the influence of the still small voice of life and lip has been, of depth of thought, and reasonable faith, and how it has prevailed even to the pulling down of the strongholds of sin. In that day also we shall know how many a man and woman, unknown to fame, how many a quiet dweller by the countryside, or patient toiler in the town, has prevailed, has changed the outlook of the worker by his side, and sent him forth to do the work which, but for let and hindrance, he would fain have done himself. It was the faith and love, together with the careful training of Lois and Eunice which trained Timothy and sent him forth to uphold the hands of Paul. It was the bearing of Paul in the workshop which indirectly reached Apollos and built up the Churches of Ephesus and Corinth.

As Paul patiently laboured at his daily work so he patiently laboured in the synagogue also, and by quiet force of reasoning prepared the way, both with Jew and Christian, for the greater and fuller witness which he was to give hereafter. As we think of this preparatory time of labour we understand the feeling of reverence and awe with which Professor Richardson discovered among the excavations at Corinth the lintel stone of the synagogue in which Paul had taught and which still bears the inscription, "The Synagogue of the Jews."

"Ye Sent Once and Again unto My Necessity"

But however patiently Paul may have laboured it must have been a matter of rejoicing to him when the limitation imposed by the necessity of earning his daily bread was taken away and free scope given, so that the words which had slowly but quietly been taking effect might be brought to fruition. The arrival of Silas and Timothy with contributions from Philippi released him from daily toil (2 Corinthians xi. 9), and together with his release there came a call from God, an obligation of spirit, nay even a constraint, to give fuller testimony and to witness that Jesus was Christ. This fuller witness Paul knew by experience must of necessity arouse opposition in the synagogue. As long as he had been willing to argue out of the Old Testament Scriptures the Jews had been equally willing to discuss and argue with him, but when he applied that reasoning and argument, when he identified the Messiah of the Old Testament with the crucified Christ, their indignation knew no bounds, and they not only opposed his words, they even dared openly to blaspheme the sacred name of Christ Himself. This blaspheming was a public act, and regarded as such not only by the Jews themselves but by all who heard them, and especially by Paul, who knew even better than they did the full bearing of their deed. For by this deed and act they, the Jews of Corinth, as deliberately and surely rejected Christ as the Jewish nation, in the person of the high priest, had already rejected Him in Jerusalem, and they too, like the Jews of Jerusalem, judged themselves unworthy of everlasting life, and rejected their election of God. As their words rang out Paul knew that he was powerless to prevent them. He had tried reason and witness and both alike had failed. One chance and one only remained; if he could possibly bring them to themselves, if he could make them see the gravity of the position which they were taking, could show them by his action what the after result of their words would be, could let them see the issue of what they were doing, something might even yet be done. He arose and, shaking his garment, said, "I am clean, from henceforth I will go unto the Gentiles." He thus explained to them their true position in the sight of God; he showed them that if the Jews of Jerusalem had blasphemed Jesus and had asked that His blood might rest upon them and upon their children, so the Jews at Corinth in blaspheming Jesus had taken a like position, and His blood in like manner rested upon them also.

How strange it seems that after so many centuries the Jews of their own free will should incur the very curse and the isolation which Cain had dreaded, that they should choose to wander with blood-guiltiness upon their head, "a blood which speaketh greater things than that of Abel." We to-day know what the penalty of that choice was, for we see the isolation, the hiding of God's face, the Jews wandering to and fro, in the midst yet alone among their fellow-men. What doom can be more terrible than this? And yet we know that the heart of Christ still yearns over the Jews, that He still weeps over Jerusalem, still bids His followers yearn over it also and look forward to the time when the Jew shall, as it were, come to himself, shall draw near instead of departing from the God of his salvation.

The House Hard By

Paul, like Pontius Pilate, testified that he was clean, but the spirit in which he testified was very far away from the spirit in which Pilate had striven to cleanse his hands. Pilate cared only to preserve himself from the consequences of a deliberate act of injustice; Paul cared nothing for any consequence to himself, but sought only to arouse the Jews to a sense of their injustice and guilt. A further confirmation of this spirit is found in the fact that he still lingered, as it were, amongst the Jews, even though he had left them, for he preached in a house hard by to the synagogue. It was dangerous for him thus to keep the Jews ever reminded of his work and influence, but he gained a full reward. The Jews recognized the sincerity and the unselfishness of his action even while they resented his words, and many still followed him and listened to him, especially

THE BRIDGE OF THE SEA

"Crispus the chief ruler of the synagogue, who believed on the Lord with all his house," and many others also. But every accession of converts meant also a further accession of danger, and Paul knew only too well that such a state of things could not last and that the smouldering indignation of the Jews would burst forth sooner or later, the only marvel being that it had not already done so. How could the Jews week by week gather in their synagogue and know that the crowds that they would fain attract were pouring into the house hard by, and that that house and not the synagogue was the centre of all the newly aroused thought and vitality. Paul knew from previous experience that he continued longer in the city only at the peril of his life; he read his condemnation too clearly in the lowering faces round him. Must he take their rising indignation as a token that his work amongst them was ended? Must he, for the sake of the still greater work lying before him, preserve his life and leave Corinth as he had left Thessalonica? It was at this crisis of doubt and hesitation that the immediate presence of God was revealed to him as it had been at every other great crisis of his life, and a marvellous shield of protection thrown over him. The will of God was manifested to him so that the city of Corinth, that city teeming with vice, the smoke of whose iniquity, as it were, ascended to heaven, became henceforth to Paul a place of hallowed ground. Had he spoken too boldly? He was to speak yet more boldly. Did he tremble at his loneliness? "I am with thee." Were the Jews ready to rend him to pieces? "No man should set on him to harm him." Was the city beyond redemption? "I have much people in this city." The Jews might turn a deaf ear to his words and the Gentiles might hurry hither and thither absorbed in their earthly pursuits, but Jesus had power to read the heart of both Jew and Gentile and to know, despite their apparent self-satisfaction and preoccupation how weary and heavy laden they were. He knew that they would hear His voice, that they would open the door and sup with Him and He with them, and, therefore, He bade His servant speak boldly; and His servant heard Him and continued "a year and six months teaching the word of God amongst them."

CHAPTER XXXVIII

ACTS XVIII

THE FURTHER HISTORY OF THE CHURCH OF CORINTH

"But Gallio Cared for None of Those Things"

The public action taken by St. Paul in leaving the synagogue and teaching in a house hard by, aroused the indignation of the Jews, and their indignation was still further augmented when Crispus, the ruler of the synagogue, seceded with all his house, and also "many of the Corinthians hearing believed, and were baptized." But, despite their anger, the Jews at the moment were in such ill odour with the Government of Rome that they dared not take open action against Paul, and this gave Paul the opportunity he so much needed for building up the Church of Corinth, the very rapid character of whose growth was in itself a source of danger. Paul regarded the Church of Corinth with peculiar affection; he had planted and watered it alone, and had received it directly from his Master; he knew, moreover, that no matter how furiously the Jews might rage together, or how determinedly they might plot against him, he must pass through the midst of them unhurt, for he had the form of the unseen but ever present God beside him. The abiding consciousness of this presence was the secret of his fearlessness, and it was the consciousness of this same presence also which all unconsciously to themselves had restrained the hand of the Jews until at last they determined, no matter at what cost, to try their chance of success and make a desperate and united effort. Gallio, famous throughout the Roman Empire for his amiability and justice, had been appointed deputy of Achaia, and the Jews thought that they would take advantage of his coming and by one mighty effort rid themselves of Paul. It is strange to think of a whole multitude plotting and banding themselves together against a man who was entirely beyond their power of injury, and, unconscious of the invisible Presence beside him, dragging him before the judgment seat of Roman law. They thought that they were taking a strong and final step, against him; they did not know that they were furthering his cause more powerfully than he could possibly have furthered it himself; still less did they think that the one result of their violence would be to cast the shield of Roman protection and law around him, so that he would issue from the court of Gallio more powerful than before. But apart from the way in which the malice of the Jews was thus turned back upon themselves, the trial scene of Paul before Gallio stands out as one of the strangest and most pathetic incidents of the book of the Acts, for it records the meeting and parting of two of the most representative men of their day, the one the embodiment of the chivalry of Rome, the other the embodiment of the chivalry of Christendom. They drew near; they almost touched one another, but, like ships in the night, they passed one another by; had they touched, had Gallio permitted Paul to speak, had Gallio learned like the centurion that Jesus was the Son of God, how mighty the issue of that meeting might have been.

"Dulcis Gallio"

It was during the last month of St. Paul's stay in Corinth that Gallio, the brother of Seneca and the nephew of Lucan, had been appointed pro-consul of Achaia. Gallio is one of the few men who have taken no part in the world's great battle scenes, have committed no thoughts to writing, and yet have lived through force of character and charm alone. He is spoken of in the writings of his day as "dulcis Gallio," "my lord Gallio"; and is portrayed as the type of the polished Roman gentleman—refined, amiable, gentle. The news of the appointment of a man so courteous and so charming filled the hearts of the Jews with hope. Why should they not try their fate with him? why not seek to persuade him to take part with them against Paul? Arguing thus, on some court day when Gallio was otherwise occupied with business, they dragged Paul into his presence and set him before the judgment seat, charging him not with treason against the Roman law, but treason against the particular religious privileges granted to them by that law. The unruly mob, thus suddenly thrusting themselves before the judgment seat of Gallio, forced him, however unwelcome their presence might be, to think out and adopt the line of action which he would follow towards all questions of religious belief in general, and Jewish disputations in particular. Gallio seems to have had but little hesitation in the matter; he probably wished to extend impartial justice to all, but at the same time to hold himself superior to all questions of this nature, and especially to avoid the quarrels of the Jews, as a race of men most repellent to him. At the same time, if a mob of Jews had come to seek punishment of some overt act of crime, for his own sake, and for that of the Roman law which he represented, he must attend to them; but nothing short of his own dignity or the dignity of the Roman Government could persuade him to intermingle himself in their broils. Their whole contention in his eyes was a mere matter of words and names, and altogether beneath contempt. He was essentially a man of the world, and from his lofty altitude as a man of the world he looked down with mingled impatience and contempt upon the struggling mass below, upon their seething passions and ambitions, and determined to rid himself of them as quickly as possible by bidding the lictors clear the court. The Greeks who had followed the disputants into the court were enchanted to see the mortification of the Jews, and took advantage of the opportunity to avenge many a longstanding grudge which they had against them by seizing Sosthenes and beating him before the judgment seat. But Gallio cared for none of those things. Why should he care? Why should he trouble himself about a petty disturbance between a crowd of Jews and Greeks any more than he would about the quarrels of the Jews amongst themselves? It would do the Jews good for once to feel the popular hatred, and would prevent them from bringing further cause of annoyance before him. Thus Gallio knew not the day of his visitation. Had he waited, had he looked into the matter, Paul might have spoken to him personally, might have opened to him the mystery of life and death, might have appealed to him with power. But Gallio was a man of exteriors, and he was swayed by exteriors. He saw in Paul nothing but a Jew and a common tent-maker; he did not see in him a citizen of the Heavenly Jerusalem, a builder of the Kingdom of Heaven upon earth. Thus despising Paul and spurning his words he turned away from him; but even in turning, despite himself, owing to his respect for Roman law and his enlightened interpretation of that law, he did Paul service, for in the very act of placing questions of this character outside the pale of Roman law he cast the shield of that law over Paul, thus guarding him from the malice of the Jews, so that he who was already invulnerable by the unseen power of God, was henceforth, in Ephesus and the surrounding cities, invulnerable by the power of man also. No matter how the Jews might resent his presence, Paul was free to remain in Corinth or to go to other cities, wherever Gallio's enlightened interpretation of the limitations of Roman law were received and known.

> *"Nemo mortalium uni tam dulcis*
> *est quam hic omnibus"*

Until recent years men had the words "Gallio cared for none of those things" so indelibly stamped upon their minds that they recognized in him nothing beyond the pure indifferentist, the man so entirely preoccupied with the things of earth that he was indifferent to the things of Heaven. But of recent years a wider and more liberal opinion has prevailed, and Gallio has now stepped forth into the light and is seen in colours brighter than even he himself might recognize. Men see in him to-day the champion of toleration, the first man far-seeing enough and bold enough to vindicate the sacredness of individual opinion and to set apart the sphere of opinion from the sphere of action. He is the champion also of impartial justice, though that justice becomes less impartial when we consider his contempt for the Jews and the fact that he suffered an act of lynch law to take place before his very judgment seat. But whether Gallio had instinctively felt rather than reasoned out the fact that justice can decide between man and man but cannot decide between man and God, there is much unquestionably to be said for this higher estimate of his character, though the very fact of that higher estimate contains something which is peculiarly sad also. For if Gallio stands as the typical man of the world, the philosopher and statesman of his day, he stands also as the type of the man who comes in contact with the greatest movements of his age but remains uninfluenced by them.

THE CHURCH OF CORINTH

The After Story of Gallio

Thus Gallio passes from the page of Scripture, leaving the judgment of his character for good or for ill to those who come after him. We may interpret that character as we will, but we cannot alter the fact that he, the learned, the high-minded courtly Roman failed to see the vision of his age; failed to see even so far as the despised Jew, Sosthenes, who was beaten before his judgment seat, and having failed went back to the pleasures of the Imperial court, to the pettiness of self-service, as uninfluenced as he came. There is little further record to be found in history save that he continued to drain the cup of self to the uttermost, until either by his own hand, or that of Nero, he came suddenly face to face with Eternity, face to face with the questions concerning which he might have learned so much, but cared to learn so little. How hardly could he have believed when he was at the height of his popularity and power that in the ages to come men would care nothing for his popularity or learning, but would wonder over the limitations rather than over the greatness of his character; that his title to immortal fame would rest not upon the political or social triumphs which he achieved at Rome, but upon the brief moment which he passed in the presence of a prisoner and the attitude which he assumed towards that prisoner; that they would see in that interview the greatest opportunity of his life, and marvel that he was unable to respond to it. Paul on his side must have gone away grieving that the Gospel which he preached could not be to Gallio the power of God unto salvation, yet rejoicing that the mantle of the Imperial protection of Rome, which Gallio had so carelessly cast across his shoulder, was now his, and that he was free to teach and to labour at his will. He stayed in Corinth for some time longer, leaving the city of his own accord, and sailing towards Syria in order that he might go thence to Jerusalem.

The First Epistle to the Corinthians

We long to learn the further fate of Corinth, and how far a Church so essentially in the world was kept from the world; and we find the answer not in the Acts but in the Epistles to the Corinthians, which are historical rather than doctrinal.

In the first Epistle, for instance, we have a vivid picture of the difficulties arising from within; in the second Epistle, of the difficulties from without; and we find that the former are those which would inevitably spring up in a Church situated in the midst of a heathen city such as that of Corinth.

St. Paul's letter is very interesting, for it shows that the best method of dealing with the troubles of the Church of Corinth, as indeed with all troubles, lies beneath the surface rather than on the surface, lies in referring back all ordinances of the Church to the spirit in which Christ himself had instituted those ordinances. The letter itself was written from Ephesus, whither Stephanas, Fortunatus, and Achaicus had come, bringing a letter from the Corinthians asking for instruction upon certain points, but omitting to mention some of the worst disorders which had sprung up in the Church. Paul takes advantage of the opening thus afforded and writes answering all questions, but at the same time touches kindly but firmly the true situation of affairs, and shows that these difficulties are the outcome of the graver disorders in the Church. These difficulties are interesting to us also, although they seem to belong to the first century rather than to the twentieth, but the method of dealing with them is as full of instruction to-day as when it was first written. St. Paul's opening words are full of sympathy and encouragement. He rejoices that the Word of God has had free course and been glorified, that they have been sheltered from persecution by the protection of Rome, and that the contrast of the light which they have received to the surrounding darkness has attracted a large number of followers and fostered the rapid growth of the Church. But that very rapid growth has been a source of danger, for the presence of the mixed multitude who have been in contact with the gross forms of sin, has engendered a lack of deep religious conviction, and a general shallowness which, added to the natural tendency of the Corinthians to excitement, has led to disorder as well as to an outbreak of party spirit, as shown in magnifying of the various leaders of the Church. Thus, those who seek simplicity say they are of Paul; those who admire eloquence, of Apollos; those who are zealots of the law, of Cephas; those who love independence, of Christ. More serious even than this has been a lack of right understanding of the things of God, as shown by the forwardness and over prominence of women; the irreverence at the love feasts; and sadder still, by the general outbreak of immorality and sin. The indictment, as we read it, is heavy, but it is written by the hand of a true physician of souls, a man full of tenderness, strength and dignity. St. Paul does not hesitate to touch the gravity of the disease, but he brings that disease, that sin and sorrow, to the mercy seat of Christ, and is careful to discriminate between his own point of view and that revealed to him in Christ. He lays a healing hand of calm upon the divisions of the Church by calling the Corinthians to a greater dignity and unity, and to one common communion in the love of Christ. He corrects the irregularities of the Holy Communion by giving the history of the institution of the Last Supper, and by showing the inner significance of that Supper. He corrects the defects of character, not by dwelling upon those defects, but by giving an ideal of Christian charity and a manifestation of that charity in faith, hope and love. He corrects the desire for vainglory, as for instance in the gift of tongues, by viewing it in the light of common-sense; overthrows the low ideal of self-glory by raising the higher ideal of stewardship before their eyes. He corrects the spirit of levity, which is inclined to mock at the resurrection of the dead, by a clear anticipation of the return of Christ.

As we read the Epistle we breathe something of the atmosphere which surrounded Christ. We see St. Paul lift all that is petty and self-seeking in the Church of Corinth into the beauty of holiness, just as Jesus lifted the questions which the Pharisees and Sadducees put before Him into the highest atmosphere of the light and love of Heaven.

The Second Epistle to the Corinthians

As we open the second Epistle to the Corinthians we pass into the inner presence chamber of St. Paul, and witness the agony of sorrow and of daily crucifixion which he passed through for the Churches. In the earlier history of the Church, divisions had arisen amongst the Christians, but they were as nothing compared to the later difficulties which had been brought into it, apparently by the same leader who had been a source of bitterness to the Church of Galatia. His method of approach was subtle and far-reaching. He attacked the person and authority of St. Paul, in order that by so doing he might attack the free salvation taught by St. Paul. Paul was distressed beyond measure. He knew that the Gospel which he taught was largely bound up with the confidence which the Corinthians had in him as teacher, and that the undermining of his authority might almost as fatally shipwreck their faith as the undermining of the Scriptures themselves. It has been thought by some that in order to undo this undermining of his teaching he visited the city, and also wrote a letter, full of scathing rebuke, calculated to arouse the Corinthians to the danger incurred by listening to this deceiver. But there is no certain record either as to this letter or visit. All we know is that at the moment when St. Paul wrote his second Epistle he had received better news, and that the relief was so great that he "lived again," just as he had lived again when he had heard of the safety of the Church of Thessalonica. But Paul knew though the danger was for the moment passed it might return, and therefore, in order to strengthen the confidence of the Corinthians, he wrote the celebrated *Apologia pro vita sua*, which is one of the most precious documents of the Church, not only because of the light which it throws upon the history of the outer and inner life of St. Paul, but also because it shows how man by the grace of God may die daily, may abandon himself so utterly to the working of the Holy Spirit that he may live, move, love and breathe in Christ. It is further precious because in this Apologia of St. Paul we catch a faint echo of what we might call the faraway Apologia of Christ Himself. From the daily struggle of His servant, we gain a far-off glimpse of the daily self-sacrifice of Him who bore not only the griefs, but also the sufferings of the whole world; or, in other words, from the love of St. Paul, as far-reaching as human limitation will allow, we seek to understand a love beyond all limitation, almighty and all-reaching. Thus the two epistles to the Corinthians are of inestimable value to the Christian as an individual as well as to the Church as a whole, and stand second only to the great Magna Charta contained in the Epistle to the Romans.

CHAPTER XXXIX

ACTS XVIII. 18 TO XIX. 13
DIANA OF THE EPHESIANS

"The Great Diana . . . and Her Magnificence"

The account of St. Paul's sojourn in Ephesus is given so discursively, and, in parts, in so much detail, that the full force of the passage does not break upon us until we see that it is the climax of St. Paul's missionary labours, and read it in connection with the history of Ephesus and the Epistle to the Ephesians. It is then that we realize that it is reading the last recorded struggle of St. Paul, as a free man, with the power of heathendom; for although in after years at Rome, like Samson, he leaned upon the pillars of the house of heathendom "with all his might," yet it was as a prisoner, a man delivered over into the hand of his enemy.

It is then, also, for the first time, that we realize how sharp that struggle was, and at what cost the victory was won. During his previous missionary journeys Paul had been in labours so abundant, in stripes above measure, in prison so frequent, in deaths oft, that the mere fact of his escape without injury to life or limb inclines us to think that the birth of the Church of Ephesus was effected by a struggle less severe than that of others. But when we compare the account in the Acts with the Epistle to the Ephesians, we see the effect of St. Paul's preaching—the Temple of Diana shaken to its foundations, the city moved, not only in its Jewish quarters, but throughout its whole population; and on the other side we catch, from the Epistle, the echo of the struggle in St. Paul's own words. We hear him say, (1 Corinthians xv. 32) that he fought with beasts at Ephesus, that the struggle was against principalities, against powers, against the rulers of the darkness of this world, against spiritual wickedness in high places (Ephesians vi. 12).

As we compare these two accounts, we realize that we are dealing with a matter weightier than appears, that we are face to face with one of the great issues of history; and we ask what made Ephesus such a headquarters of superstition and heathendom, what made the struggle harder, the overthrow more enduring than that of other cities? We turn in vain for answer to the site of Ephesus itself. The judgment foretold by the angel of the Church (Revelation ii. 5) has fallen upon her, and her very foundations are removed out of their place. The death stillness which broods over her mounds and sedge-grown harbours is unbroken until we turn to the words of St. Luke and see how, at the masterstroke of his pen, the whole city becomes instinct with life, and one of the great world centres rises before our eyes.

As St. Luke writes we see a population as swarming, a trade as active as that of Corinth, "the gate of the west, and the eye of the east." But beside the hum of traffic, we feel also the throb of living Greek thought which should have been in Athens, and we realize that the centre of Greek life has passed from the Aegean Sea into the heart of Asia Minor, and that Ephesus is another Greece, combining the wealth and luxury of the East with the peace, power, and prosperity of the West. We see also that Ephesus is standing at the zenith of her power, and enjoying to her heart's core "the peace of Rome," for she is a recognized city, a Roman centre, and the centuries of war and oppression, the bitter experience of the yoke of Persia and of Greece, have forever passed away.

The Temple of the Great Diana

But the hold which Ephesus obtained, not only over her citizens, but over the surrounding districts also, lay far deeper than either her material or her intellectual power. The forces of nature worship and of superstition were gathered together in this one city, and cast their fascination, not only over the inhabitants, but over the surrounding provinces also. From time immemorial the hills surrounding Ephesus, as well as the city itself, had been the centre of worship, but the ancient goddess of the hills, according to tradition, had been moving towards the plains, and, under the emblem of the Bee, had been gathering together in one and intermingling with herself the worship of the Grecian Artemis and of the Roman Diana. It was under the shadow of her name that the centre of the favourite religions of Greece, Rome and Asia Minor had found their home in the temple of Ephesus, the sixth wonder of the world, 425 feet long by 220 feet broad, exquisite within with her forest of arches, 60 feet high, springing up the one beside the other, and more exquisite without, her glistening pure marble lifting itself as a beacon to the nations from afar, at the entrance to the harbour. It is little wonder that the fame and the glory of Diana had spread throughout the world, and recent discoveries have shown that Demetrius was within the truth when he said that not only Asia, but the world also worshipped the magnificence of the great goddess Diana. Everything combined to heighten the temporal and spiritual power of Ephesus, for, apart from the antiquity of the nature worship of the city itself, Ephesus was now situated on the great Roman Road, and was the centre of the Roman power throughout the district, so that the organization of Rome contributed to spread the worship of Diana throughout the world, and the adherents of the goddess could be found in Rome and in every outlying province also. This was the city, this the worship sacred with the antiquity of ages, supported by numberless votaries and priests, bound up with the wealth and magnificence of Asia and of Asia Minor, into the midst of which Paul came to raise a building fitly framed, a holy temple of the Lord, of which Jesus Christ Himself would be the chief corner stone (Ephesians ii. 20).

DIANA OF THE EPHESIANS

"For He Had a Vow"

After leaving Corinth, Paul passed through Cenchrea, where he seems to have been detained by illness, and, in accordance with the custom of the Jews, to have "shorn his head in Cenchrea, for he had a vow." Much discussion has been raised as to whether this sentence applies to Paul or to Aquila, but the grammatical construction, as well as the natural rendering of the passage, points to Paul; and there is nothing strange in the fact that he should thus conform to Jewish rite and ceremony for, whilst careful to preserve the liberty of the Gentile, Paul exercised freely his own liberty of approach to God as Jew, as well as Gentile, availing himself of ancient rite or ceremony whenever he deemed it would be helpful either to himself or to others (cp. Acts xxi. 23-26).

His illness came at a time when he was peculiarly anxious to revisit the churches which he had founded, and to go up to Jerusalem, and thence, having preached the Gospel in the eastern world centre, Ephesus, to preach the Gospel in the western world centre of Rome also. It is little wonder, therefore, that his longing for a further length of days, in order that he might accomplish this purpose, inclined him to vow a vow unto God and defer not to pay it. Little wonder also that he should keep a careful remembrance and make mention (Romans xvi. 1, 2) of the succour afforded to him, in the time of distress, by Phoebe in Cenchrea. No details are given of the events which passed in Jerusalem. We only know that, having paid his vow, he passed throughout the countries of Galatia and Phrygia strengthening all the disciples, until he came at last to Ephesus.

The Gospel in Ephesus

It seems strange that a town like Ephesus should have remained comparatively untouched by the Gospel for twenty years after the resurrection of Christ, but we must remember that the disciples were few and the openings many. We must remember, also, that although "a great door and effectual" (1 Corinthians xvi. 9) was opened before Paul, it could, humanly speaking, have opened before none other, and even Paul himself seems to have been hindered by the Spirit once and again, when his steps were turning in that direction, so that he might not attempt the attack upon the stronghold of Satan until he had attained the full height and growth of his spiritual power.

Paul had preached in the synagogue once before on his way to Jerusalem, and aroused public interest, but he had not undertaken the conversion of the city until his return, when the ground had, in a measure, been broken by forerunners such as Priscilla and Aquila, who in a quiet way wrought mightily for Christ, and more especially by the influence which they exercised over Apollos.

"An Eloquent Man, and Mighty in the Scriptures"

When Priscilla and Aquila were left by St. Paul, at Ephesus, they seemed to be far removed from spiritual teaching, and their surprise, therefore, must have been very great when they found in the synagogue one so mighty and so eloquent in the Scriptures as Apollos, and heard the clear instruction which he gave, in the way of the Lord, that is to say, in the teaching of Jesus.

Few characters in the Acts of the Apostles stand out with greater interest than that of Apollos, partly from the circumstances of his life, partly from the exquisite beauty of his character. Apollos was an Alexandrian, and brought up at the fount of philosophical, critical, and theological learning. His powerful mind grasped not only the ancient and weightiest matters of the law, but it met and welcomed the newer current of thought, though the way by which those newer currents of thought came to him cannot now be ascertained. He may have passed through Jerusalem at the time when John the Baptist or Christ Himself was teaching, or if he did not meet John, he may have met one of his disciples. Apollos had a mind keenly alive to truth and a soul thirsting for the kingdom of righteousness, and the sympathetic power of his character, together with the eloquence of his words, were eagerly welcomed in Ephesus. But despite all his intellectual ability, his sympathy and his keenness of appreciation, there were two in the number of the Jews who listened to him Sabbath by Sabbath, who had learned more of the things of God even than the learned Alexandrian, for they had passed out of the twilight in which he stood into the light of day.

As Priscilla and Aquila listened to Apollos, they longed that he might be brought into the same light also, and, therefore, found means and opportunity to approach him, inviting him to accept their hospitality in order that they might expound the way of God more perfectly to him.

"To This Man Will I Look"

It is hard to know whether to admire most Priscilla and Aquila instructing Apollos privately, instead of murmuring in the synagogue against the limitations of his teaching, or Apollos learning from them the fuller revelation of God. It is to the poor in spirit that the kingdom of God is revealed, to Moses flushed with victory from the wandering sheik, Jethro; to the favoured eunuch of Candace, from the wayfarer Philip; to the learned Pharisee, Nicodemus, from the Carpenter's son, and to Apollos moving multitudes at his will, from two strangers who came to him as angels unawares.

We long to know how far this revelation of the life, death and resurrection of Jesus as well as of the Holy Spirit was poured forth from the lips of Apollos in Ephesus before he was moved to pass into Achaia. The Corinthians who were in his congregation seem peculiarly to have caught the fire of his lips and to have longed that he should go to Corinth and preach there also. Knowing the desire of the Corinthians, like that of the Athenians, to hear and to tell of new things, as well as their tendency to hero worship, we can easily understand how they rallied round him as soon as he went there, rejoicing in a freedom of speech far greater than that of Paul, so that he had been but a short time in Corinth before they appreciated the philosophical trend of his thought and began to separate themselves from their fellow Christians and call themselves by his name. Apollos soon perceived the danger of this movement, and seeking the unity of the Church rather than the founding of a Church in his own name, left Corinth and returned to Ephesus, refusing to return, lest he should further imperil the unity of the Church, despite the earnest invitation of St. Paul that he should do so. We long to know the after history of so great, so talented, and so highminded a man, but beyond a tradition that he wrote the Epistle to the Hebrews, nothing further remains. He stands for all time as the embodiment of the Christian orator and of the Christian gentlemen of the New Testament.

The Coming of Paul to Ephesus

It was shortly after Apollos had gone to Corinth that St. Paul reached Ephesus, and found himself face to face with a city whose very life and commerce were knit into as well as dependent upon idolatry; for the Greeks, who were the commercial and progressive element of the population were, through the worship of Artemis, united with the more stagnant Asiatics and circled round the temple with them, rejoicing in its splendour and immorality. Paul must have known that it was only through the power of the Holy Spirit that he could prevail against a city the very breath of whose life was idolatry, and therefore, possibly in answer to his prayer, an outpouring of the Spirit was given at the very commencement of his ministry. St. Paul was passing through the streets of Ephesus just as he had formerly passed through the streets of Athens, and as for the first time the full realization of the darkness of Ephesus came before him, he encountered certain disciples who had a knowledge of Christ but were lacking in spiritual discernment and fire. These men had followed John and had been pointed by him to a coming Christ, and Paul, after instruction given, laid his hands upon them, and the Holy Ghost descended upon them, as upon the first Christians of Jerusalem, with signs and wonders. Thus Paul found himself at once supported by a band of consecrated men who were ready to prepare the way before him either in Ephesus or in the cities of the surrounding districts.

The Aftermath of St. John's Work

More than twenty years had passed since John had been killed in prison, but, as we see in the present chapter, his work did not die with him, and the thought of the far-reaching character of his life and teaching is full of encouragement to those who, like John, may be cast down because of the shortness of their day of labour, and the sins and limitations of their character and surroundings, which, like Milton's blindness, let and hinder the work they would fain do for Jesus. None knew the sorrow limitation more keenly than John the Baptist. His lips were sealed at the time when he was longing to open them for Jesus; his feet bound when he would have gone forth, according to prophecy, preaching the Gospel of peace; his opportunities passing swiftly away, opportunities which in the beginning had been so marvellously fruitful. And beside all this, the Kingdom of God coming so slowly, even by the hand of Jesus, that to him it seemed not to be coming at all; and at the last he sent his disciples to ask, "Art thou He that should come or do we look for another?" The answer which came to him was essentially that contained in Job xxxviii.-xlii., or in the Psalm "Rest in the Lord and wait patiently for Him." The answer which comes to us is the same as that which came to Job, David, and to John, only together with that answer we can trace the working out of God's Providence, the twelve disciples prepared by John standing ready to aid Paul in his struggle at Ephesus.

The Power of the Holy Spirit

Another thought arises out of St. Paul's question, "Have ye received the Holy Ghost?" The disciples of John had repented of sin and were looking for a Saviour. They had, therefore, entered upon their Christian course, but they were following Jesus afar off, as we too often, despite our greater knowledge, follow Him. St. Paul knew that for effectual labour as well as for spiritual growth there must be living communion with the Spirit of God. Would that the same question and the same power might be given to the far-off followers of Christ to-day so that they might be led into living communion with Christ. It is the lack of living communion which is turning the present growth of Christian love and toleration into a deadly stupor, a sleeping sickness, an indifference, which is falling over all lands, until men weary themselves as little over their own souls as they weary themselves over the souls of others. And yet as certainly upon us as upon John's disciples a time of refreshing might fall which would set free hearts, lips and lives for service, just as it set free the hearts, lips and lives of the disciples of Jerusalem and of the disciples of Ephesus.

"The School of One Tyrannus"

Encouraged by this proof of Divine favour Paul entered into the synagogue and for the space of three months laboured and disputed concerning the things of the Kingdom of God. But in Ephesus, as elsewhere, divers of the Jews were hardened and spoke evil of the word, until at last they blasphemed Christ, and Paul was forced to separate himself, leaving the Jews of Ephesus as he left the Jews of Corinth. Instead of teaching in the synagogue, from this time forth he taught "in the school of one Tyrannus," a place of open instruction, where he would be no longer hampered by the antagonism of the Jews.

DIANA OF THE EPHESIANS

In Ephesus, as in all other large Greek cities, there were public gathering-places, corresponding to the Roman baths, called gymnasia, and it was to one of these halls or gathering-places, probably after the hours of instruction given by Tyrannus to his pupils, that Paul came daily and taught freely the tidings of salvation, and the Ephesians listened eagerly to his words. They probably thought at first that he was one of the many philosophers who were constantly passing through the city and demonstrating new schemes of philosophy, but they soon discovered that a teaching far nobler and a power far greater than that of any ordinary philosopher dwelt within Paul, and that within the city of Ephesus, the acknowledged centre of magic and witchcraft, there was standing amongst them one who held a mystery more marvellous than any that lurked within the dark recesses of the temple of Diana, and that although a strong man armed held Ephesus, yet in Paul a stronger had come and was about to take from him the power in which he trusted.

It is in the light of this thought that we can understand why such peculiar power was granted to Paul, and why miracles akin to those of faith-healing were permitted in Ephesus. We do not read that Paul sent material objects which had touched his person to the sick, but we read that they were taken by others, and that God honoured the faith of those who took them and permitted healing to be wrought through them. Thus in Ephesus a first beginning was made.

Paul supported himself by labouring at his own trade from daybreak until an hour before midday, and then passed to his place of public instruction; but despite his daily work and his daily teaching, he still found time to organize and to send forth missionaries, of whom the twelve disciples of John were probably the leaders, into all the surrounding cities, so that from Ephesus the word of God sounded out throughout Smyrna, Pergamos, Thyatira, Sardis, Philadelphia, and Laodicea. It is commonly agreed that it was at this time that these cities, as well as others also, came under the influence of the Gospel.

CHAPTER XL

ACTS XIX. 13 TO END

PAUL AND DEMETRIUS

The Name of Jesus

For two years Paul had laboured without ceasing day and night in Ephesus, until at the last an abundant harvest began to reward his labours and a strong Church of Jews and Gentiles grew up in the city itself, as well as in the other Churches of the surrounding province also. The work in Ephesus seems to have grown the more rapidly and with less opposition because it had been constructive rather than destructive. This was admitted even by onlookers, such as the town clerk, who in his address admitted that Paul had not openly attacked the temple of Diana nor been a "blasphemer of the goddess." But so strong a movement could not be continued without arousing imitation as well as opposition. There are always men who seek to make gain for themselves out of a new movement as well as men who resist the loss of gain which that movement causes.

The power manifested by St. Paul over evil spirits attracted peculiar attention at Ephesus, for the Ephesians, owing to their worship of Diana, were addicted to sorcery and magic of all kinds, and they might naturally suppose that Paul was exerting a sorcery akin to that of their own goddess, and would wonder whether he was a new teacher who intended to found a school of his own, or one who might in course of time be absorbed into the central worship of Diana. Amongst those who were attracted by his power, and wished to make gain out of it, were the sons of Sceva, a Jew who seems either to have been a leader in the synagogue, or having become an apostate from Judaism, a priest in the temple of Diana. There is nothing which strikes us more sadly than the self-seeking and cupidity of the Jews of this period and the way in which we find that they had abandoned themselves to sorcery. Men like Simon Magus, Elymas, and the sons of Sceva, had not only abandoned the worship of the true God, but dared to use their knowledge of the Prince of Light for the service of the prince of darkness. These were the men who looked upon the name of Jesus as a new and unknown force which might be used for their benefit, and dared to take the name of God in vain, commanding the evil spirit to come forth "in the name of Jesus whom Paul preacheth."

PAUL AND DEMETRIUS

St. Paul's Power over the Spirit of Evil

The question of evil spirits is one which constantly meets us in the Old and New Testament. In the New Testament we find that Christ had absolute power over the souls as well as the bodies of men, and that He healed the distressed in soul as freely as the distressed in body, and in measure bequeathed of the same power to His disciples also. In the present instance the sons of Sceva dared to bid the evil spirits depart in the name of Jesus, or in other words, invoked the presence and power of the Divine Saviour in order that they might cast out devils and gain a reward of money. The demoniac recognized Jesus as God, and Paul as the servant of God, but he instinctively knew that the sons of Sceva had no authority over him, and, therefore, leaping upon them he turned and rent them. The judgment which befell these men for taking the name of God in vain was as sudden as that which befell Ananias and Sapphira, and the effect produced upon the Church of Ephesus was similar to that produced upon the Church of Jerusalem. Men who had been spectators or half-hearted, were brought face to face with the reality of the new movement, and either surrendered themselves to the power of God or admitted that they had neither part nor lot in the matter. They saw that they must either abandon all contact with the power of darkness, with superstition and idolatry, or drift away like the mixed multitude who had gathered round Paul. Like Savonarola in later times, Paul bade the Ephesians decide between the world and God, and the believers in Ephesus who up to this time had kept a lingering belief and a lingering hold upon their former worship now confessed and showed their deeds, and as a proof of their renunciation brought their books of magic and of sacred incantations and burned them publicly before all the people, just as the followers of Savonarola renounced their worldliness and burned the tokens of their folly in the market-place.

The Burning in the Market-Place

Recent discoveries have shown how wide-spread the use of these magical papyri was in Ephesus, and the value set upon them. Books of any kind were valuable in those days, but none so rare and precious as books of magic and incantation; and the sacrifice which was made was very great, and was estimated at fifty thousand pieces of silver, or two thousand pounds. As we think of this strange burning in the far-off city of Ephesus we cannot help thinking of a stranger burning which many centuries later took place at St. Paul's Cross in London, and has since taken place in other European countries also, and even so late as the last century in South America, when the books of the Old and New Testament, the words of Jesus, were burned by professing Christians in the market-place of the city.

The World of the Unseen

We cannot pass away from this contact of St. Paul with evil spirits without wondering, on the one side, at those who strive unlawfully to draw aside the veil of the unseen and break the silence of God; and, on the other, at those who refuse to see aught but the material world around them and reject the instinct which teaches them that this world is not isolated or apart from surrounding influences and from the hosts of the unseen. St. Paul, as we can see from his words as well as his deeds, lived even more in the invisible than in the visible. To him the causes of evil were more real than the manifestation of evil, and the causes of good than the manifestation of good, and he bade his followers arise and play their part in the battlefield of life, and recognize, even when they cannot understand, the unseen forces, as well as the unseen issues of life.

"I Must Also See Rome"

The Ephesian Church having by this public act cast themselves adrift from all connection with the prevailing sin around them, Paul felt that his work was accomplished, and that he might carry out his heart's desire and proceed through Macedonia and Achaia to Jerusalem, and thence to the bourn towards which his steps had been slowly tending, even Rome itself. His first anxiety was to revisit the Churches, but for the moment he decided to tarry at Ephesus until Pentecost because "a great door and effectual is opened unto me and there are many adversaries." But meantime he decided to send Timothy and Erastus into Macedonia, whilst he himself stayed in Asia. The attack which he had been making upon idolatry had become so vital that it could no longer be ignored by the votaries of the temple, and his departure, in consequence, was as forced from Ephesus as from every other city, although in this instance the final touch came not from the religious hatred of the Jews but from the commercial instinct of the Ephesians themselves.

The Silversmiths of Ephesus

There was a strong link between the commercial and religious instincts of the city, the temple of Diana being practically the banking centre of the town, for in the inmost recesses of her shrine princes and merchants alike stored their treasure. Besides this close connection between religion and the capital of the country there was an equally close connection between the religion and the trade of the country, for not only did all life centre in the temple, but also an immense trade was carried on by the silversmiths and goldsmiths of all descriptions, who were engaged in the manufacture of images and shrines of Diana, which were purchased not only by the Ephesians themselves but by the pilgrims and travellers who came from every town and country.

The progress which the new faith had made under Paul is shown by the fact that although no outward attack had been made upon the temple, yet so appreciable a diminution had occurred in the sale of images to her devotees that the trade of Demetrius and his fellow craftsmen was sensibly affected, and they were compelled to take the strong step recorded in the present chapter. From the words, "at the same time there arose no small stir about that way," it is conjectured that these events took place in the month of May, the time of the annual festival in honour of Diana, at which pilgrims and travellers were gathered in immense crowds, and all the city combined to do her honour. It seems astonishing that in the midst of so vast a concourse of people the trade should have been so much diminished; but we have to remember that it was not in Ephesus alone but in all the surrounding cities that Churches had been founded, and that men had learned a new and purer faith. Calling together the guildsmen of his craft Demetrius made a skilful speech, and united them in one common hatred against Paul. Under the cloak of intense zeal for the worship of Diana and her magnificence, not only in Asia, but throughout the whole world also, he at the same time reminded them that all their wealth and trade depended upon her. Inflamed at the thought of the loss of this trade, the whole body of workmen were filled with wrath, and cried out, saying, "Great is Diana of the Ephesians." The city being already half mad with excitement and with riot, rushed towards the scene of the uproar, and having caught Gaius and Aristarchus, two of Paul's companions, dragged them at the head of the concourse into the vast theatre lying outside the city. This theatre, from the remains which have been discovered, was capable of seating about 24,000 people, and the vast mob thus gathered together in it, cried some one thing, some another, the assembly being confused, "and the more part not knowing wherefore they were come together."

The Contrast Between Paul and Demetrius

Paul's first impulse was immediately to hasten towards the theatre so that the brunt of the danger might fall upon himself instead of upon his companions, an impulse which shows the nobility of his character and his power of self-sacrifice, and contraswith the base self-seeking of Demetrius, concealed under the garb of religion. But amongst those who had either been converted to Christianity, or who at any rate thought favourably of his life and work, were certain of the most prominent men of the town, called in the A.V. "certain of the chief of Asia," but more literally translated, Asiarchs, that is to say, prominent citizens, annually chosen to finance and preside over the festivities in honour of Diana. Certain of these men were friends of Paul, and sent to him bidding him not to venture himself into the theatre.

The Action of the Jews

In the midst of this general confusion there came a sudden and strange turn in the face of affairs. The Jews, who apparently wanted to clear themselves from complicity with St. Paul, and to gain popularity by showing that they were willing to head the tumult against him, drew Alexander, one of their number (possibly "Alexander the coppersmith," 2 Timothy iv. 14), out of the multitude, and put him forward as their spokesman, so that he might disclaim on their account any connection with the Christians; but the Ephesians, when they recognized the Jewish cast in his features, refused to listen to his words, and cried out the more vehemently, "Great is Diana of the Ephesians." The excited multitude would have proceeded to further violence had not the town clerk appeared, and partly by his presence, partly by his words, brought back the assembly to their senses. His power was great, for whilst Ephesus was nominally a democracy, she was practically under the power of Rome, and the town clerk was the official empowered by Rome to gather together the ecclesia of the democracy, and to propose the edicts which were to be passed, obtaining, as a matter of course, the desired verdict. The Ephesians knew only too well that the Romans were jealous of their gatherings, and that any excitement or unruliness on their part would tend towards an abolition of their privileges, and consequently they dared not neglect his words. The address which he made was as skilfully worded towards soothing the passion of the populace as that of Demetrius had been towards exciting it. Taking for granted the authority of Diana as a matter beyond dispute, he contrasted on the one side the peaceable character and conduct of Paul and his companions, and on the other, the unruly uproar raised by Demetrius and his fellow-craftsmen, and showed them that the part which they were taking was as unnecessary as it was dangerous, for whilst a lawful assembly could at any time have been called together to look into the matter, an unlawful assembly of this description endangered the rights and privileges of the city, "and when he had spoken these words he dismissed the assembly."

The Departure of Paul from Ephesus

Paul was, therefore, once more free, once more had the protection of Rome extended to him; but though free, he knew that his presence was a source of danger to the Church and, therefore, bidding the disciples farewell, he departed immediately into Macedonia.

From this time forward Paul, wherever he might be, keenly watched over the interests of the Church of Ephesus, and on his return journey held a meeting with the elders at Miletus (ch. xx.). Four years later, when in prison, he wrote the Epistle which bears their name, and lastly, according to tradition, was set free from prison, and once again revisited Ephesus in person. The account of his meeting with the elders naturally falls under the heading of the next chapter, but his letter is best considered in immediate connection with his stay in Ephesus. Some have wondered, as there is no mention made by name of any of Paul's friends in this letter, whether it may not have been intended for the Churches of the surrounding districts as well as for Ephesus; and it may be so; but in order to gain the full force of the Epistle it is best to view it in the light and thought of those for whom it was primarily written.

PAUL AND DEMETRIUS

The Epistle to the Ephesians

Paul when he writes the letter is no longer free. He is in the power of Nero, and knows that at any moment he may have to suffer death at his hand; but the nearness of his death makes no difference to his outlook either on things present or on things to come (2 Timothy iv. 6). His thought is still bent upon the Ephesians, and he longs to raise them to the highest ideal of spiritual freedom, and as he writes the walls of his prison no longer seem to confine him. He sees the dazzling whiteness of the marble shrine of Diana rising before him in all its beauty, but foul within, with all uncleanness, and impurity, and he prays that the invisible temple of the saints of God may rise in far greater purity, both without and within, in that same city of Ephesus; and he calls upon them to remember that they are created in Christ Jesus unto good works, that they are builded together for a habitation of God in the spirit. But it is not only the visible temple of superstition and sin which rises before his eyes. He sees also the forces of evil, the power of the prince of the air, the spirit which now works so mightily amongst the votaries of Diana, and he bids the Ephesians put on the whole armour of God that they may be able to stand in the evil day, and having done all, to stand; and lastly, bids them as they make their stand recall the even greater stand that he must make against the threatening power of Rome, and pray that he may open his mouth boldly and witness at Rome also.

The Angel of the Church of Ephesus

But St. Paul's prayers, together with his fostering care of the Church of Ephesus, too soon passed away, and with it also a part of his influence, and only one more record, one last warning is recorded for them in Scripture. He whose Spirit moved among the Churches, He whose eyes were as a flame of fire, saw that whilst the Ephesians still kept the main characteristics of their Church, still could not bear evil, still guarded their purity for His Name's sake, yet they had left their first love, that love which had been so markedly shown at the farewell at Miletus, and He, therefore, bids them remember from whence they have fallen, lest He should come quickly and remove their candlestick out of his place (Revelation ii. 1-6). Words, alas! too truly fulfilled, for Ephesus is removed, her light quenched, and her buildings overthrown so that hardly a base of a pillar can be found of the once exquisite temple of Diana, hardly an outline which may signify the dimensions of her vast theatre. The river Cayster is a bog, the harbours are choked with reeds and rushes and silted up with sand, so silted that the site of the city has changed its character, and Ephesus is an inland, instead of a seafaring town. A few Turkish huts in the town of Ayasalouk, at a mile's distance from the city are the one remaining sign of humanity. Ramsay tells us that "when the wind blows across the reeds there rises to the hill tops a strange vast volume of sound of a wonderfully impressive kind." Is it not a cadence and lament of the glory of Heaven and of earth that once encompassed the city but has now passed away from it forever?

CHAPTER XLI

ACTS XX. 1-12

THE STATESMANSHIP OF ST. PAUL

A Year in Macedonia

The heat and burden of the three years' work in Ephesus is over, and Paul is turning his face towards Jerusalem, but, from this time forward, we see the change which passes over the character of his work; his step is even swifter, his face more sternly set, and he seeks a satisfactory and permanent settlement rather than a foundation of new churches, and with this intention revisits city after city. He finds the leaders in each church cast down with a consciousness of impending calamity, and his spirit, although it still wings its flight upward into the presence of his King, is bound with a like consciousness of coming calamity also. His time is short; three purposes only can be accomplished—(1) the strengthening and refreshing of the churches; (2) the placing of the churches of the Jews and of the Gentiles in the right relationship to one another; (3) the full communication of the Gospel to Rome, so that throughout the length and breadth of the Roman empire the Word of God may have free course and be glorified.

The last nine chapters of the Acts give the most striking episodes which occurred during the passage of St. Paul from Ephesus to Rome, but the first steps towards the consolidation of these churches, as well as towards the accomplishment of his purpose in Jerusalem and Rome, were taken during the year's work which is so briefly recorded in the first five verses of the twentieth chapter. St. Luke was probably in Philippi at this time, and summarized the events of which he had not been an eye-witness; but what is wanting in his words is indicated in the writings of St. Paul in the Epistle to the Galatians, the second Epistle to the Corinthians, and the Epistle to the Romans, which were all written during this period.

The Dissension in the Churches of Galatia and Corinth

A great door and effectual had been opened before Paul, not only in Ephesus but in every city which he had visited; but there were many adversaries, and pre-eminent amongst these adversaries, a leader among the proselytizing Jews, a man of unknown name but outstanding zeal and power, by whose means the newly-founded churches were torn with dissension and uncertainty.

Religious bigotry, added to hatred for Rome, found its vent in hatred against Paul for breaking down the barrier between Gentile and Jew and identifying the Gentile with the Jew, thus weakening the hand of the Jew and imperilling the temple of Jerusalem. The Jew knew full well that no working more fatal to his hopes and aspirations could take place than this founding of a common church, this opening out of spiritual privileges, this blending of Jew and Gentile into the common service of Christ. The long cherished day-dream of the Jew was the admission of the Gentile through the Jewish gate into the outer court of the Temple, and the forming of a Gentile cohort, who would rally round the Jew and be prepared to aid him in his final struggle against Rome. This was the day-dream on which the fanatical Jew had been building his hope, and this, he believed, if Paul's power were not broken, must pass away forever; and in this he had the sympathy of the Judaising party also. The Jew proper, together with the Judaisers were determined either to stay the wheels of Paul's chariot or to bring that chariot bound into Jerusalem. They were determined either to stay Paul's hand or to bring the Gentile churches into bondage to Jerusalem, and through Jerusalem into bondage to the law and to the Temple.

The Action Taken by St. Paul towards Corinthia

Paul saw the fatal tendency of their action, and the year 59 to 60 was spent in defeating his adversaries in Galatia and Corinthia as well as in writing the Epistle to the Romans and in organizing the collection for the Church of Jerusalem. The Epistle to the Galatians and the second Epistle to the Corinthians record the intense anxiety which St. Paul passed through and the imminence of the danger which threatened these two churches, the latter Epistle being especially interesting, for it seems to have been written as he moved from place to place and records the action taken according to the tidings brought to him. The situation in Corinth was finally relieved, but the church continued to be in so unsettled a condition that Paul decided to go to Corinth and remain there three months, spending himself and living toward them by the power of God (2 Corinthians xiii. 4).

Meantime he sought to fulfil the promise made to the Council of Jerusalem and sent his representatives throughout the length and breadth of Asia Minor in order that they might gather together the weekly offerings which each Christian had been bidden to lay by, so that they might be borne by the hands of seven chosen representatives to Jerusalem, and be presented as a proof of the goodwill of the Gentile Church and of their willingness to make return in material help for the spiritual wealth which they had received, as well as to acknowledge their sense of mutual obligation (2 Corinthians viii. and ix.).

The Occasion of the Writing of the Epistle to the Romans

But while St. Paul rejoiced that peace and order had been restored to the churches which, as it were, lay behind him, he knew that he must press forward to those before, until by Epistle if not by presence he reached Rome also. Rome had been his heart's desire for many years, but the malice of the Jews might intervene even at this eleventh hour and prevent his purpose, for he must visit Jerusalem before he visited Rome, and he could only enter Jerusalem at the peril of his life. Paul knew that if he fell a victim in the streets of Jerusalem, then he, the chosen apostle of the Gentiles, he to whom the churches of the Gentiles had been committed, would fail in the last and most important witness of his apostleship.

There was only too much ground for a foreboding such as this, which seems to have been ever present with him, as we learn from the vision recorded in the twenty-third chapter of the Acts, in which Christ stood beside him and answered the unspoken longing of his heart, by promising that he should "bear witness at Rome also." But until Paul reached Jerusalem this promise had not been given, and he seems to have determined that if he did not see Rome or reach it as a prisoner, he would at any rate send forth his epistle so that it might have free course throughout the length and breadth of the Roman empire, and the word which he fain would have spoken, be unhindered either by bondage or death.

The Epistle to the Romans

St. Paul's main object in writing this epistle was to place the Magna Charta of spiritual freedom, of spiritual justification and sanctification in possession of the Roman world and, through Rome, in the possession of the whole world also. The condition of the Romans at the time of the writing of St. Paul's Epistle was in one respect similar to that of the Israelites when Moses stood forth to free them from the slavery of Egypt. The Romans had, like the Israelites, sunk all too willingly beneath the slavery of sin, until their sins had become a scourge and, like the whips of the task-masters upon the shoulders of the Israelites, were beginning to arouse in them a desire for a new and pure religion.

Paul seeks to strengthen this desire by giving an all too faithful picture of their utter degradation, by showing them that they have no righteousness at all. He includes the Jews in the same condemnation (Romans iii. 9-10), and shows them the barrenness of their formalism, and that although they think they are righteous they are far away from the righteousness of God, so that the Jew cannot despise the Gentile, neither the Gentile the Jew, for both have alike fallen under sin, both can alike only be saved through the grace of God. Then having striven to arouse both Jews and Gentiles to a sense of their true position, and their isolation from God, Paul lifts before their eyes the righteousness of God, appeals to the one ideal which in the midst of their degradation still clings to them as Romans, that is to say, to their ideal of law and of the enforcement of law. He shows them while he lifts it, that however lofty that ideal may be, they can, instead of falling beneath the condemnation of its precepts, be so pardoned, so raised by the power of Christ, that henceforth there will not only be no condemnation (Romans viii. 1), but there will be no separation from the love of the great Lawgiver, even of Christ Himself (Romans viii. 35-39).

Finally, St. Paul shows how that law will work itself out in their members, how the love of Christ will awaken a love which will express itself without dissimulation, will abhor evil, will cleave to that which is good.

"I Must Also See Rome"

No letter ever has been written, or could be written, so marvellous as this, for it is nothing less than a revelation of God through the Spirit; of the coming of the Kingdom of God to the individual's soul as well as to the world, through the efficacy of the life, death and resurrection of Jesus Christ. It is a cry of victory, the triumphant outcry of one set free by God, one over whom neither approaching bondage nor death have any power.

Paul determines that if, through the malice of his enemies, he may not bear witness in his body, he will, at least, bear witness by this letter; and everywhere throughout the epistle we can see how dear that Church is to him, how he knows it and is watching over it from afar. It is true he greets it of necessity in the words and tones of a stranger, but he shows, in the closing verses, that the individual workers are known and dear to him, either from previous intercourse with them in the cities from which they have drifted into Rome, or from the record of their labours; he is following their work with an interest and a love as keen as that which yearns over the Churches which he himself has founded.

To his friends in Rome more especially, but to the whole church also, is the word of this salvation sent by the hands of Phoebe the Cenchrean (Romans xvi. 1), a word destined, next to the witness of the life and death of Christ contained in the Gospels, to be precious beyond all other to the Church and to keep in peace, not only the souls of the Romans during the approaching persecution of Nero, but the souls of those in countries far away from Rome, who have been called through much tribulation to pass into the Kingdom of God.

The Gathering at Troas

The time had now come when St. Paul must turn towards Jerusalem, but as he turned and was about to sail to Syria, he discovered that if he embarked upon the ship it would be at the peril of his life, and, therefore, he turned aside and took the longer way to Troas, being met by the delegates to Jerusalem.

From this time forth the consciousness of coming calamity hung so heavily, not only upon him, but upon the Churches that he visited, and that they so certainly believed they would see his face no more, that the gathering in each city took the form of a final charge and blessing, the planting, as it were, of a memorial cross.

St. Paul's visit to Troas is second only in interest to his visit to Miletus, partly on account of the miracle, partly on account of the record of the Christian service at which it took place. We, who are separated by twenty centuries from the time of Christ, and have only, as it were, an echo of His words and acts, and of the way in which men and women approached Him whilst He was on earth, long to know how the men who had seen Him face to face, and who had spoken to Him, approached Him after He had passed into the heavens and was no longer in the midst of them.

Whilst Christ was on earth He laid down, as it were, some first lines in regard to this manner of approach by the institution of baptism and of the Lord's supper, by teaching from His own example a reverent use of the Scriptures, and by the giving of the Lord's prayer. But when we seek for further detail, for exact form and ceremony, we find only incidental allusions, such as the one we are now studying, which tells us how the early Christians were accustomed to meet together, and how they used the various means of grace. From the account of the visit to Troas, we learn that their gatherings took place on the first day of the week, thus commemorating the resurrection of our Lord, and that they were accustomed to break bread according to the command of Christ. Probably also they were accustomed to listen to exhortation from one of their members, for on this occasion Paul preached to them, and his words being full of the thought of his approaching departure ("Ready to depart on the morrow"), and knowing that he might be addressing them for the last time, he continued his speech until midnight.

The Sacrament of the Lord's Supper

The gathering recalls our Lord's Last Supper with His disciples, the time and circumstances being in many respects identical. There was the same sense of foreboding, the same dread of coming separation and danger; the service held in the evening, either because the disciples were naturally accustomed to break bread at the hour at which Christ had broken it, or because, as was also probable, they were accustomed to assemble at the time most convenient for slaves, and for those engaged in daily labour. We wonder sometimes why there is so little mention made in the Acts of the particular forms and methods of service, and we forget that men who are face to face with sin in its most appalling forms, as well as those who are in peril of their lives, are necessarily less trammelled by form and circumstance than those who live in settled countries, and who seek to follow the traditions of their fathers.

We must remember also how immediate the return of our Lord seemed to the Christians of the first century, and how communion by communion they watched in the hope that once again, as shortly after His resurrection, He would stand in the midst and say, "Peace be unto you." Filled with the thought of that resurrection, they would long only that He would impart to them of the power of death unto sin, and of the resurrection to a life of righteousness, and would consecrate themselves body, soul, and spirit, so that Christ might dwell in their hearts by love, and being rooted and grounded in love, they might be ready to obey His every motion. They, like us, would care little for time or place, they would care only that neither form nor ceremony might intervene to draw their thought back to man and away from Christ.

The Raising of Eutychus

As many of the men as possible were gathered into the crowded upper room, and were listening in hushed silence to St. Paul's words, when a youth, named Eutychus, who had fallen asleep as Paul was long preaching, fell from the crowded upper room on the third floor into the street below. Paul descended, and embracing Eutychus, as Elisha had embraced the Shunammite's son (2 Kings iv.), restored him to life again.

Much question has been raised as to whether Eutychus had swooned or was really dead, but St. Luke noted at Lystra that Paul was not really dead when they supposed him to be so, whereas he states that Eutychus was dead. Furthermore, we have to remember that he was a physician, and he would probably descend with St. Paul, and the question as to whether Eutychus had swooned or was actually dead would be of first interest to him.

It is wise in reading Scripture to follow the natural rendering of the passage, and the natural rendering points in the direction of death. And lastly, if power were granted to Peter to work miracles and to raise Dorcas from the dead, there seems no reason why Paul should not have a like power and raise Eutychus also. It does not seem wonderful that this witness of the Divine Presence should have been granted to him, and that he should have had the joy of returning to the disciples, and of bidding them sorrow not for he was yet alive. Thus at the city of Troas, the place which Paul had more than once sought to work in, but from which he had been turned aside, a witness of Divine power was given which would remain after Paul himself had passed away, though such a miracle is not so powerful as the drawing of Divine love, for Christ Himself has taught us "that neither would they be persuaded though one rose from the dead" (St. Luke xvi. 31). It may be that the recollection of that last Communion Service, that breaking of bread in which the confine between life and death was so narrow, the boundary line so imperceptible, may have had even more lasting influence. The reality of life and death and of the hereafter must have fallen upon each heart and given a peace and hush akin to the first ray of morning light then breaking over the city, in the midst of which Paul went forth, and the men of Troas were not a little comforted.

CHAPTER XLII

ACTS XX. 13 TO END; AND XXI. 1-16

THE TURNING TOWARDS JERUSALEM

The Journey to Miletus

St. Paul had restored health and order to the Churches of Galatia and Corinth, and had also prepared the way for drawing them into more sympathetic relationship with the Church of Jerusalem. His task accomplished, he hasted, if it were possible, to be in Jerusalem at Pentecost, and that he might do so the more quickly, instead of going to the city he summoned the elders of Ephesus to meet him at Miletus, a port thirty miles distant from Ephesus, whilst he himself took the day's journey alone to Assos. It was little wonder that he wished to be alone. The foreboding of the approaching struggle at Jerusalem lay heavy upon him, as well as the anxiety over the well-being of the Churches.

A Farewell Address

There are seven recorded addresses of St. Paul in the Acts—the exposition of the Scriptures to Jews and Gentiles in the synagogue at Antioch; a philosophical dissertation to the Areopagus at Athens; a missionary appeal to the multitude at Lystra; a charge to the elders of the Church; three apologetic addresses as a prisoner to his judges. Of these seven speeches the address to the elders at Miletus is in some ways the most remarkable, because of the strong personality that runs through it, and also because it is the only recorded address of St. Paul to a body of believing Christians, delivered also at a time when he believed he was about to be parted from them forever. St. Paul had created the ideal of his age, and, through the power of the Holy Spirit and his own personality, had impelled the men of his age to follow him. His last recorded address, like his last Epistle, are peculiarly valuable, because he is speaking at a moment when he believes his life work is ended; and is scanning with prophetic eye the future of those whom he has guided, but whom he can guide no longer.

The Gathering at Miletus

The elders who were gathered together at Miletus were Jews and Gentiles, learned and unlearned, but alike accustomed to keen Ephesian life, and now united by one common sorrow. Paul stands in the midst of them bearing about in his body the marks of his suffering for the Lord Jesus (Galatians vi. 17), filled with a like sorrow, but with a light of consecration in his eyes. St. Luke seems also to be standing in the midst, and to listen with such sorrowful tension that he gives the outline of the words almost as they were spoken, or the record which he took of them at the time of their utterance.

The Question of Egotism

The self-sacrifice, devotion and love of St. Paul thrills through every word he utters, and his audience are drawn very near to him by the personal reference which he makes. At first sight we might wonder why such a personal strain mingled with his words, but we have to remember that he is speaking to a particular audience and in view of the temptation to which that audience will be exposed. The Church of Ephesus is not a Church resting upon the witness of generations, but a newly founded Church resting upon the witness of one man, Paul himself. The Judaising party which has brought desolation upon the Churches of Corinth and Galatia will, all too surely, bring the same upon Ephesus also, and the means which they will take will be the subversion of the character of St. Paul, in order that they may subvert the character of the truth which he taught. St. Paul meets this danger by a spoken *Apologia pro vita sua*, just as he had met it in other Churches by a similar apology in writing. He knew only too well, in the face of his own impending imprisonment and death, that his character must stand forth in unclouded sunshine before them if his teaching were to stand in like unclouded character also. This would be his first reason, but there was a second reason also.

The Impress of Personality

St. Paul is about to pass over the leadership of the Church of Ephesus, as well as of the surrounding Churches to the men assembled before him, and he wants to teach them the lesson which he himself has learned, that is to say, the indissoluble connection between the personal character of the teacher and his teaching. The Divine character and life of our Lord enforced the Divine character of His words. The absence of self-seeking, and the self-sacrifice of St. Paul enforced the influence of his words, and called upon the Ephesian elders in like manner to enforce the purity of their teaching by the purity of their lives. His words, therefore, are as far removed from egoism, self-glorification, or self-justification, as the east from the west. He gives of himself, that his word may be given with a power which can never be taken from it.

A Comparison between St. Paul and Samuel

As Paul stands before the elders of Miletus he recalls, by his action and words, the recollection of Samuel when he stood before the elders of Israel upon a like occasion. Both men are being called to stand aside from their work, not like Moses and Joshua through old age, but through the power of their enemies. They are forced to leave their work at the moment when it is approaching its consummation, when their presence is needed for it. Samuel has created the Israelitish nation by welding together a number of tribes who, but for him, would have been a prey to surrounding marauders and the first use which the nation makes of the organization and vigour which he has thrown into it, is to turn against the man who has been their saviour. Paul found the Jew fettered by the law, and the Gentile by sin; he placed before them the liberty of Christ and sought to found a spiritual Kingdom; but the Jews will not hear, and, if they cannot kill him, will send him as a prisoner to Rome. Both Samuel and Paul, when thus rejected, in their parting charge bid men know that they have sought not theirs but them, and that their one desire and prayer for Israel is that it may be saved.

The Foundation of St. Paul's Teaching and the Spirit of His Teaching

St. Paul is addressing the episcopi, or elders of the Church of Ephesus, and he holds up before them the ideal that he has followed, in order that they may follow it also. He tells them how he has agonized for souls, how he has not shunned to declare the whole truth; how he has not only taught the assembly, but has sought the individual soul from house to house, as the Good Shepherd His sheep upon the mountain. His work is over, and the shadow of the Cross is falling upon him as it fell upon His Master, but he heeds neither the depth of the shadow nor the premonition of approaching pain and separation in the thought of the shadow of spiritual death which may fall over those assembled before him, or over those committed to their care. In the first place he emphasizes the indifference to personal pain or pleasure which marks the founders of the Kingdom of God, and calls upon them to exercise a like indifference also. In the second place, he points out the essence of Christianity,—repentance towards God and faith towards our Lord Jesus Christ. Repentance, the turning from a past course as he turned at the word of Jesus; faith, the touching of the outstretched hand of Jesus which inspired him with love and service. Thirdly, he reminds them of the weight of their responsibility. They are over-seers of souls, and each soul is of such immortal value, that it can only be redeemed by the Blood, that is to say, the imparting of life through the death of Christ Himself. Lastly, he warns them of the need of vigilance, great beyond their knowing, for after his departing grievous wolves will enter in among them, persecutors who care nothing if they can destroy the Church of God; a prophecy too surely fulfilled in the after-history of Ephesus, when Ephesus became notorious not only for persecution in the city itself, but also as a highway for sufferers on their way to Rome, so that Ephesus was called the highway of those who were on their way to die for God. Further, he sees the foes from within who will arise speaking perverse things, and drawing away disciples after them, a prophecy again too surely fulfilled, although, as we learn from the words of the Angel in the Revelation, the Ephesians were faithful to

St. Paul's warning, and could not bear those who were evil, and tried those who said they were apostles and were not, and hated the deeds of the Nicolaitanes. Paul knows when this danger arises he will be no longer there to avert it, and, therefore, he passes the Church of Ephesus, as it were, by a conscious act directly into the hand of God, and prays not only that they may be delivered from danger, but that they may be raised as a spiritual building to His eternal glory. Then lifting his toil-worn hands, he bids them know that those hands are unstained by either just or unjust gain, and bear the mark of daily labour for his own necessities and the necessities of others, and bids them remember that such labour is in accordance with the words of the Lord Jesus, "It is more blessed to give than to receive."

The last object a dying man sees is said to be photographed upon the retina of his eye, and the last sight of those we love remains when other impressions have passed away. What a keynote to service, not only to the elders of Ephesus but to us also, is that last vision of St. Paul's uplifted hands.

"It Is More Blessed To Give Than To Receive"

These last words, as it were, float back to us from afar and give the keynote of Christ's ministry and of the example which He set before His followers. At the opening of His ministry He bade them "Give, hoping for nothing again," and He taught the meaning of those words by giving of Himself and His love and taking in return the weight of the sin, pain and weariness of the world, until it lay like a vast, impenetrable cloud upon Him. "Not as the world giveth, give I unto you" (St. John xiv. 27), not with an underlying strain of getting, but of spending and being spent.

St. Paul's Departure

With the words of Christ upon his lips, Paul turned to leave them, and the love and the pain which had been expressing itself in his words and had awakened an equal response in the hearts of those who heard him, found relief where alone at such a time it can be found—in prayer, and after prayer they all wept sore and fell on his neck and kissed him.

Their grief was probably intensified by the fact that they had never, until this moment, fully realized the beauty of his character which had been so closely intermingled with their daily life, that it had never, until he addressed them, been manifested in its full unselfishness before them. After one last embrace, they followed him to the ship and, as we may well imagine, watched that ship until it receded forever from their sight. We can understand why, in after years, when seeking to reawaken a glow of love in the Church of Ephesus, the angel of the Church (Revelation ii. 4) should remind them of their "first love."

The Journey to Caesarea

Leaving Miletus, Paul and his companions made a favourable journey to the Island of Coos, and thence to Rhodes, celebrated for the huge Colossus which at that time commanded the harbour, but is now a ruin, and thence by way of Plataea to Tyre, where, as the ship had to wait seven days to unlade her burden, Paul sought out the disciples and tarried with them.

From time to time we come upon the account of Churches such as this, which have been brought together and taught by some servant of Christ, whose name is not recorded. The Church of Tyre was clearly living under the influence of the Holy Spirit, for they also felt the shadow of approaching calamity and besought Paul that he should not go up to Jerusalem, but at the last, finding they could not prevail, they brought him to the ship, and, like the elders at Miletus, knelt in prayer before they parted from him.

This scene naturally lacks something of the pathos of the farewell of the Ephesians, amongst whom Paul had laboured so long, but it has its own attraction in the picture of the children kneeling on the sea-shore, and showing that even in the first century children were brought up in the fear of the Lord and admitted into Christian fellowship and worship. After a day spent with the brethren at Ptolemais, Paul came to Caesarea, to the house of Philip the evangelist, one of the seven deacons who had been associated with Stephen (ch. vi. 5), and who, after his ministry in Samaria (ch. viii. 5) and special mission to the eunuch (ch. viii. 29), had taken charge for twenty years of the Church in Caesarea.

Philip the Evangelist

There is something that is almost pathetic in this meeting between Philip and Paul. Philip had at first taken so prominent a part that it seemed as if he were to be the missionary to the Gentiles, but he had been called to stand aside and to work apparently unnoticed and alone in the town of Caesarea, whilst Paul, who had been the chief instigator in the murder of Stephen, had been called to be the apostle of the Gentile Church.

We cannot tell why Philip was thus set aside. Why, for instance, though he was living in Caesarea, was it to Peter and not to Philip that Cornelius was sent? There is nothing in the words of St. Luke that indicates the thought of anything save true and faithful service. The fact that Philip's four daughters were following in his steps points in the same direction also, for a household united in the service of God shows faithfulness on the part of the leaders of that household, and nobility of spirit in the younger members who follow in their steps and are capable of appreciating the beauty of the example set before them. If Philip's life were comparatively uneventful, it was filled with joy in his own home; and if Philip's words seemed to be stayed in Caesarea, yet they were being sent forth not only from the lips of men of all nationalities who came to Caesarea and who might bear away the truth with them, but also through the writing of St. Luke, for it is probable that it was from Philip, during these seven days, that St. Luke gathered much of the information as to the early Church which from his pen has gone forth wherever the Gospel has been made known.

The Last Appeal

Paul found both Philip and the Church of Caesarea filled with the thought of impending calamity, not only to Paul but to the whole Gentile Church if evil befell him at Jerusalem, and Philip's four daughters, who were dedicated to Christian work, prophesied, as also did Agabus, who came down from Judaea to meet Paul at the close of his active ministry, just as he had met him at the beginning, and by a token, similar to that which the prophet Jeremiah had used, took Paul's girdle and bound with it his own hands and feet, prophesying, through the Holy Ghost, that Paul should be thus bound at Jerusalem and delivered into the hands of the Gentiles. This prayer, like the echo of a funeral knell, overwhelmed the remaining courage of all present, and St. Luke and his companions, as well as the Church of Caesarea, made a last appeal to Paul, beseeching him not to go up to Jerusalem. For a moment it seemed as if Paul must yield before this last and most bitter drop in his cup of temptation, but he knew that he must go to Jerusalem, even although, as we can tell from his words, it was likely that he would die there and his mission to Rome be unfulfilled. The strain and the grief were so great that they were almost beyond his power of resistance, and he prayed those who surrounded him to accede to the will of God instead of weakening him in his struggle, to strengthen him so that he might carry out that will. Finding that his face was set towards Jerusalem they ceased, saying, "The will of the Lord be done." Then gathering together that which they were carrying (their carriages) they set forth, accompanied especially by one Mnason, an early disciple, with whom Paul would lodge in Jerusalem.

The words "an early disciple" bring vividly to our mind the lapse of time since the day of Pentecost. It is hard to realize as we follow the swift footsteps of St. Paul that twenty years have elapsed since the day of Pentecost, and that the number of disciples who either then or in the days of our Lord had become his followers, were marked out as noted men among the converts of the newer generation.

St. Paul's Determination To Go to Jerusalem

As St. Paul passed forth on his way to Jerusalem, despite the warning and entreaties of his friends, it is worth stopping to think of the light which his determination throws upon one of the hardest problems of our Christian life. It is easy enough to go forward when the path is clear, but it is hard indeed when those who live very near to Christ tell us that the call of duty lies in one direction, whilst we feel that the will of God is pointing us in another. There are times when we are only too ready, like the disobedient prophet (1 Kings xiii.), to make excuse from the words of another for the turning aside from the sterner path of duty. But there are other times when we know not what to do, when the path of duty, which is hard enough anyhow, is rendered infinitely harder because, at the time of treading it, those who might have thrown light upon our path are darkening it with their counsels, and we have to tread it alone. We can then only pray to God to make clear His way before our eyes so that we may follow the guiding of His Spirit, and fulfil our life-work, even though that life-work may lead us to Jerusalem.

CHAPTER XLIII

ACTS XXI. 17 TO END AND XXII

THE APPEAL TO THE MULTITUDE

The Attitude of Jerusalem

As St. Paul stands within Jerusalem, and makes his last appeal, we see the approaching climax of Jewish history and hear the note of impending doom and persecution. Christ had given a like note of doom twenty-seven years ago with the result that He had been condemned, acquitted and delivered to be crucified. Paul would be condemned and acquitted also, but delivered from the hands outstretched to slay him, and then Jerusalem, who had cast out her kings and prophets, would be herself cast out, and her kingdom given to others; but that final overthrow is found not in the present history, but in the stones of her city, of which not one is left standing upon another. The silence of Scripture falls as soon as this last visit of St. Paul is ended, and she has finally invited her fate. It was the nearness of her overthrow that pressed Paul in the spirit, he knew not fully why, to go up to Jerusalem, and it was a like leading of God also which impelled him to bring the Jewish converts into harmony with the Gentiles before they fled from the approaching storm, and were scattered among the Churches of the Dispersion.

St. Paul's Reception in Jerusalem

As soon as Paul arrived in Jerusalem, the brethren received him gladly, and he "declared particularly" to James and to the elders the things which God had wrought among the Gentiles by his ministry. He had much to tell that was painful. The history of the Churches of Galatia, Corinth and Ephesus was in large measure a history of the error introduced through the action of the Judaising party and the measures he had been forced to take to meet it.

He knew that the men who had done this evil claimed that they were emissaries of James and of the elders, and, therefore, if their statement were even partially true, that they had been countenanced by some of the very men now listening to him. Would they resent his words, or, conscious of the cruelty of their action, would they seek to make amends for it?

The Seven Days of Purification

His heart must have thrilled with joy when he heard the song of thanksgiving to God; but he knew that he

THE APPEAL TO THE MULTITUDE

must not neglect the warning of the elders as to the enemies which surrounded him on every side, for it was only too true that reports similar to those which had worked so much ill in Corinth and Galatia had worked ill in Jerusalem also, and had misrepresented his teaching and influence, saying that he encouraged the Jewish Christians to neglect the circumcision of their children, and to despise forms and ceremonies.

This rumour had received such general credence that it had aroused much bitterness, for such teaching meant a neglect of religious observances, and a weakening of the national spirit, as well as a loss of offerings to the temple. The elders entreated Paul to rebut these charges, and change the tide of popular feeling as quickly as possible, and suggested that the best way of doing so was to show his loyalty to the Temple by purifying himself, and taking upon himself the charge of four Christians, who were waiting for purification, but could not pay the necessary offerings. These offerings (Numbers vi. 13 to 18) were beyond the reach of the poor, and the richer Jews, as a mark of piety, were accustomed to make an offering for them also. Thus Agrippa I. had made himself responsible for the vows of several Nazarites.

The Outbreak against Paul

It is impossible at this distance of time to judge whether the elders themselves had been affected by the rumour, or how far they were wise in their advice as to the best way of meeting it. The appearance of

Paul in the Temple naturally aroused attention, and ended disastrously, for he was taken prisoner; but his imprisonment may have been his best means of safety; and further, when taken prisoner he was able to prove his loyalty to the God of his fathers, and to the Temple, by showing that he had been taken in the act of purifying himself, and had proved his influence over others in like manner, by showing that he had been accompanied by poorer brethren, who were performing at his cost a like rite of purification. He went day by day to the Temple, "until that an offering should be offered for every one."

Paul knew, none better, the dangerous temper of the Jews. They might tolerate the Christians as long as they were peaceable and adhered scrupulously to Jewish custom, but they were hardly likely to extend a similar toleration to Paul and to his followers.

The Freedom of the Churches

What could the Jews say? They could not question the loyalty of Paul nor of the Gentiles, for the Gentiles were standing in their midst, bearing in their hands a collection which testified their loyalty to the Church of Jerusalem. They could not question Paul, for God had testified to his working. They could not discourage the Church, for with their own lips they had decreed with a full council that neither James nor any of the elders should "trouble those which from among the Gentiles have turned unto God." Therefore, though they feared that Christianity might be made so easily acceptable

THE APPEAL TO THE MULTITUDE

that it would become a mere religion of popularity (just as we fear to-day lest a State religion should be established before Japan and China are ready for it, like the State religion in the days of Constantine), they cast their faith upon God, and sought only means whereby Paul could disarm his enemies, and proclaim his loyalty to God and to the Temple.

But as each day passed his danger increased, for the Jews began to gather more thickly in Jerusalem, and with the tread of their approaching footsteps came their murmurings also, showing that they were all united, no matter from what city they came, in one common grievance against Paul, whom they had ejected from their synagogues, but who had drawn away with him a large number of their Jewish and of Gentile adherents. Their fury knew no bounds when they saw him quietly passing up and down the streets with Trophimus, the Ephesian, and making his way into the Temple. They knew that he had set the Gentiles free in their various cities from the observances of the synagogue, and they now believed that he was daring to set the Temple free also to them.

Rushing together, in one of those sudden outbursts of excitement to which the gatherings of the Jews in Jerusalem were at this time peculiarly liable, they gave the national outcry, "Men of Israel, help," and crying out that Paul was a leader of sedition against the nation, the law, and the Temple, declared that he had brought Greeks into the Temple, and polluted even the Holy Place.

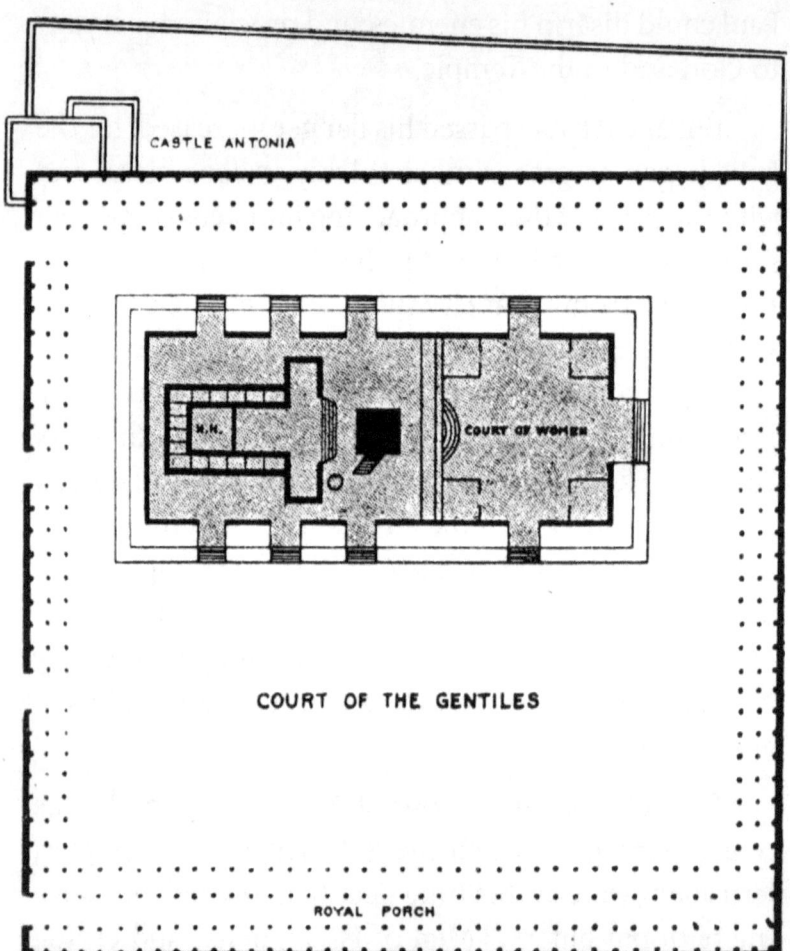

THE APPEAL TO THE MULTITUDE

The Pollution of the Temple

The Jews knew in a moment what this outcry meant. The outer court of the Temple was common to men of all nationalities, but the inner court was separated by a middle wall, and had inscriptions placed upon it forbidding any man of alien race, under penalty of death, to pass the balustrade which protected the inner from the outer court of the Temple.

The charge was an entirely false one, for Paul had never entered into the Temple except with the Nazarites, who were performing the vows; but the general attitude of toleration which he had shown towards the Gentiles, and the fact that he had not used his influence to further the political aims of the Jews, gave an element of truth to the outcry sufficient to inflame the credulity of the people, and to incite them to any deed of violence against him.

Rushing forward as one body, they seized Paul within the inner court of the Temple and, dragging him forth, only waited until the gates of the inner court were shut, lest it should be polluted with his blood, before they fell in violence upon him. How strange it seems that men should be so blinded with fanatical zeal that they should think more of the question of the pollution of the stones of the Temple than of the suffering of the helpless victim in their hands!

The Chief Captain of the Band

But the moment's pause, whilst the gates of the Temple were being shut, gave the opportunity which saved Paul's life, for the noise of the uproar had ascended to the tower of Antonia, and the band of soldiers, who, at a time of national gathering, were kept in relays, stationed under arms in order that they might be ready for any emergency, rushed down into the outer court, and by their presence so startled the multitude that they "left beating of Paul."

The maintenance of order in the Temple was usually entrusted to a band of Levites who were under an official, nominated by the High Priest, and called the Captain of the Temple (cp. St. John xviii. 3 and St. Luke xxii. 52), but whenever there was a great gathering of the Jews, the authority of the Captain of the Temple was for the time superseded by a band of Roman soldiers who were kept under guard in the outer cloister, as such a multitude quickly got beyond the control of the Levites. It was fortunate, indeed, for St. Paul that the discipline of the Temple was at this time under the control of Lysias, the chief captain of this band of Roman soldiers, and not under the command of the Captain of the Temple, Anamus, the nephew of the High Priest, who would have been bitter in his resentment against him.

Hearing the disturbance, Lysias was on the alert to intervene, for he wished to capture the Egyptian who, some five years before, had made an uproar and led "out into the wilderness four thousand men that were murderers," and he thought he was about to secure this very dangerous ringleader. Therefore as the Jews, startled at the onrush of the Roman soldiers, fell back astonished, he seized Paul and bade the soldiers bind him with two chains, whilst he endeavoured to find out from the Jews who Paul was and what he had done. But the Jews, seeing that their prey was about to be delivered out of their hands, broke forth into yet wilder fury, crying some one thing and some another, until their violence became so great that the soldiers had to lift Paul aloft and bear him by main force into the shelter of the castle.

"Suffer Me To Speak unto the People"

It was at this moment when Paul had been hunted down by his fellow-countrymen, who like wolves were thirsting for his blood, that Paul, instead of being filled with resentment against them for their wanton cruelty, and leaving them to their fate, sought means to stay their rage, and to make one last appeal before he was parted from them for ever. Forgetting his own personal danger, and filled with the spirit of pity and self-sacrifice, akin to that in which Christ had prayed "Father forgive them for they know not what they do," he turned to the Chief Captain, and requested that he might speak to them. Lysias saw at a glance that Paul was no ordinary prisoner, and gathering from his Greek words that he could not be the Egyptian whom he sought, he accepted his statement that he was a citizen of Cilicia, and acceded to his request that he might speak unto the people.

It seems strange that Lysias should have been thus willing, but he, doubtless, thought that Paul would speak in Greek, and that from his words he would be able to gain a clue to the cause of the uproar, and it is also possible that he was for the moment carried away by the personality of St. Paul, for, in moments of extreme peril, character transcends all else, and Lysias, without exactly knowing why, may have given Paul leave to speak, hoping that he would say something that would appease the raging mob, and restore peace and order to the Temple.

St. Paul's Address in the Temple

Thus on the eve of the last day that he ever spent in Jerusalem, at a moment's notice, torn and aching in every limb, opportunity was given to Paul to carry out his heart's desire and to appeal to his own people of Jerusalem. His appeal was the more remarkable because it was made, not to the Jews of Jerusalem only, but to the Jews of every nationality who were gathered together, as thick as autumn leaves upon the ground, within the inner court of the Temple. Nowhere else, either in sacred or in secular history, has so wonderful an address been given under such strange circumstances, or to so unpropitious an audience. Paul a prisoner, bound between two soldiers, his form emaciated and scarred, and surrounded by the glittering lances of the soldiers, looked down upon the raging faces of the Jews assembled from every quarter under Heaven, who gnashed upon him with their teeth, whilst he made his last appeal to them. To their astonishment, instead of being moved with anger at the treatment he had received, his opening words were full of understanding and compassion, and astonished at his words and the Hebrew in which he spoke, their passion lulled as suddenly as it had arisen. They must have wishtd also to know more of him, for it was more than twenty years since he had gone in and out of the synagogues of Jerusalem and stood amongst the leaders of the people. The younger generation knew him only as a Hellenist, and one so closely connected with the Greek cities that they were as much astonished when they heard him speak in Hebrew as the Chief Captain had been when he heard him speak in Greek. Thus carried away, partly by interest and partly by his irresistible argument, Paul found opportunity to appeal to them.

"I Persecuted This Way"

Paul, as he spoke, stepped down, as it were, into the midst of his audience, showed them that he was a "Hebrew of the Hebrews," brought up at the feet of Gamaliel, jealous toward God beyond any now standing in the Temple court before him, for what they had done by an impulse of indignation he had done of set purpose; nay, he had gone further, for he had attacked in Damascus, as he had attacked in Jerusalem, until he was cast down and blinded by a light from Heaven.

In the glory of that light he had seen Jesus and heard His words also. It was no mere trance or vision, for Ananias, a man as well versed in the law as any standing before him, had seen Jesus also and been sent by Him to confirm those words and to give a sign, similar to the signs which, throughout the long course of Jewish history, they had again and again received from the God of their fathers. He had opened Paul's eyes, as Paul was to open the eyes of Jews and Gentiles also. He had turned the world of darkness for Paul into a world of light, as Paul would turn the world of spiritual darkness into light, and bade him arise and be baptized. So far the multitude had listened patiently, but Paul is now about to touch the living issue, the question of his own commission to the Gentiles, and in that commission the freedom of the Gentiles to worship God. He showed that his will had been to witness to the Jews but that they would not hear him, and he was kneeling in the Temple, pleading that the Jews might listen to him when Jesus appeared and he heard Him say, "Depart: for I will send thee far hence unto the Gentiles." But as he reaches this point the Jews are face to face with the declared will of God as Paul had been face to face with it. They know that he is speaking the truth, and that they must choose between their national pride and the revelation of God. The choice which has been put to them again and again in the life-time of Jesus, both in the synagogues of the Jews and in the synagogues of the Dispersion, wherever Paul or his companions have spoken, is placed once more before them. They make their choice and cry out, "Away with such a fellow from the earth, for it is not fit that he should live." As they speak we catch the echo of the words, "Crucify him, crucify him." Thus far the Chief Captain had permitted Paul to speak, but the uproar had now become so violent, the Jews tearing off their clothes and throwing the dust of the Temple court where they would fain have hurled stones could they have found them, that Lysias commanded Paul to be brought into the castle, and as soon as he had got him into a place of safety, bade the soldiers strip him and examine him by scourging, so that he might find out the cause of the excitement, for he had not been able to understand a word of the Aramaic in which Paul had spoken.

"I Was Free Born"

Therefore, Paul was dragged within the castle and, whilst still quivering with excitement, was stripped of his clothing, and bound with thongs, in the hope that in the midst of his agony between the lashes of the soldiers, he might give forth the innermost truth of the matter. But Paul, amidst the very voices of the Jews upraised against him, seems to have heard, as it were, the voice of Jesus saying, "Make haste, and get thee quickly out of Jerusalem: for they will not receive thy testimony concerning me," and recognizing anew the necessity that his life should be preserved in order that he might witness at Rome, he determined to cross in Jerusalem the same boundary line which he had previously crossed in Philippi and to declare himself a Roman citizen. Therefore, turning to the centurion who stood by whilst the soldiers bound him with thongs, he said, "Is it lawful for you to scourge a man that is a Roman, and *uncondemned?*" In a moment the centurion perceived the dangerous step he was taking, and went to the Chief Captain and said, "Take heed what thou doest, for this man is a Roman." Lysias knew that none would dare to make appeal to Roman citizenship if he could not substantiate his claim, and that he had rendered himself liable to Rome by touching the person of a Roman citizen, and therefore astonished, and wondering who this Jew might be and what the cause of this strange agitation, he loosed Paul and enquired how he had obtained his freedom, marvelling, since he had himself bought his privilege with immense wealth, how a prisoner like Paul could have acquired it also. But Paul's claim to the citizenship is higher than that of Lysias, it is a matter of noble birth, a citizenship without beginning or end. Therefore he was the more afraid and determined to give Paul a lawful trial and to require the Jews to make good their case against him.

"A Citizen of No Mean City"

Paul might be stoned, scourged, torn asunder, but beneath every trial which befell him he carried with him an ever-sustaining consciousness of citizenship; he was a citizen of Tarsus, with all its boyhood's association; a citizen of Rome, with its nobility and privilege; a citizen of Heaven, whence he looked for the Saviour, the Lord Jesus; and it was this latter citizenship which gave to him, as it gives to each of us his fellow-citizens, the secret spring of life and love, the dignity of the man who lives in the presence of his King. How grandly does St. Paul's self-sacrifice and nobility of bearing contrast with the fanaticism of the Jews, with the uproar more unbridled even than the heathen uproar of Ephesus.

As we place Paul and his fellow-countrymen side by side, we see how necessary it was that a great change should pass over his nation, that the discipline of centuries should be brought to bear upon them if they were ever to attain to the privilege to which they were originally called, a privilege like that of Paul of being the spiritual leaders of their day and generation. We see not as yet that day fulfilled, we look only for its appearing.

CHAPTER XLIV

ACTS XXIII

THE LAST APPEAL TO THE SANHEDRIN

The Chief Captain, Lysias

From time to time a Roman official passes across the scene of St. Paul's history and brings with him a feeling of relief as he allays the passions of the multitude and introduces, for the moment at any rate, the sense of Roman law and order. Amongst these Roman officials there is none who intervenes at a more critical moment, or towards whom we are more drawn than the Chief Captain, Lysias, and we do not wonder that he was chosen by the Roman Government for the difficult task of controlling the Jews in the Temple during the Feast of Pentecost. He is calm, resourceful and generous; he manages to effect the rescue of St. Paul despite the violence of the Jews, and seeks to obtain from the meeting of the Sanhedrin a reasonable understanding of the matter. It is true he gave a hasty order for the scourging of St. Paul, but he did it at a time of great disturbance, when it seemed necessary to learn as quickly as possible the cause of the disturbance; and it is true also that he passes lightly, to say the least of it, over his error in his letter to Felix. Lysias had learnt nothing from St. Paul's address to the multitude, for it had been delivered in Aramaic and was unintelligible to him, but he could see that Paul was touching a live question, one which roused the fanaticism of the Jews and stirred them to their lowest depths. He could see also that the Jews hated him personally as much as they hated the cause which he had in hand; and yet Paul was a man of no ordinary type, but a Roman citizen, with a dignity and self-command which placed him beyond the range of the ordinary political leader. In order, therefore, that he might know the certainty of the matter whereof they accused him, Lysias freed Paul from the soldiers, to whom he was chained, and brought him down to the hall of judgment. This hall would not be the Gazith in which Stephen had spoken, but a place of meeting outside the Temple limits in which he would have the opportunity to speak to the Sanhedrin and yet be under the protection of the Roman soldiers, so that he could be rescued in case of uproar.

The Animosity of the Sanhedrin

It is far easier for us than it was for Lysias to trace the cause of the disturbance, and to understand the virulence of the Jews, for we know the history of their ambitious designs during the preceding thirty years, as well as during the events which issued in the overthrow of A.D. 70. They saw in Paul the man who was thwarting their political and religious power, by drawing away from their synagogues numberless Jewish and Gentile adherents, and uniting them in a distinct and separate body, which they were determined to disintegrate and overthrow. Paul was unquestionably the great power of God in these new Churches, and they hoped if he were taken away that they might separate them, the one from the other, and thus give the Judaising party the opportunity to draw them back into union with the reactionary party of the Church of Jerusalem, and thence even into union with the Temple itself.

The Condition of the Church of Jerusalem

There may have been sufficient tendency in the Church of Jerusalem at this period to justify such a hope on the part of the Sanhedrin, for if we look carefully at the history of the period, even whilst making full allowance for the fact that St. Luke was writing a history of St. Paul rather than that of the whole Jewish Church, we can see how far many of the Christians of Jerusalem had drifted, and how comparatively lifeless they had become. Jerusalem, which ought to have been the active and spiritualizing centre of the Church, had sent out no great leader during these later years, the fruits of whose labours have come down to posterity either by the memory of the Churches which he founded, or the letters which he wrote. If the Jews were not sending out new leaders, why were they not giving active support to St. Paul in his missionary labours, instead of increasing his burden by being themselves in large measure dependent upon the contributions of the Gentile Churches? It is true that whenever St. Paul came to Jerusalem they were willing to gather together and listen to the account of the deeds which God had wrought by his hand, and would rejoice and glorify God, but even in their rejoicing we notice a lack of warmth and wholeheartedness of word as well as action.

St. Paul before the Sanhedrin

St. Paul is set free for the moment from the Roman soldiers, and stands "earnestly beholding" the men who are to be his judges. There may have been amongst them one or two aged men who some thirty years ago had been of the number hastily gathered together in the palace of the high priest, and who had sought witness against Jesus to put Him to death. More certainly Paul sees some who were once his fellow-students in the halls of Gamaliel, and sat beside him during the trial of Stephen, but who had been separated from him for many years; and he sees the Sadducees under their leader, Ananias, gathered in a body against him. Can it be that these seventy-one elders, men chosen for learning and weight of character, leaders in religious law and order, are seeking blood and blood only, and in reality as wild and ungovernable in their resentment as the multitude in the Temple?

The Declaration of the Sanhedrin

But if Paul, like Stephen, cannot find justice, is it not possible that a witness might be found, a man who would arise and take his place as he had taken the place of Stephen? It is true that his address in the Temple had failed, but who could appeal to men in the midst of a seething multitude? Is there not a better chance now when they are sitting calmly by and comparatively open to reason? Upon one point, however, he is determined, he will not stand before the Sanhedrin as a criminal, nor allow, even by implication, that he has lost the position he once held as a member of the Sanhedrin, and a true son of Israel, and, therefore, he addresses them as "men and brethren," and declares that he has lived in all good conscience before God until this day.

The Action of Ananias

The words have scarcely passed his lips when Ananias, the high priest, he upon whom it is incumbent to preserve the dignity and order of the assembly, commands those who stand by to smite him on the mouth, thus repudiating his claim to innocence, and insulting him as wantonly as his Master had been insulted before him. Paul feels this insult the more bitterly because it is a command given by the high priest, and directed against a Roman citizen standing under the protection of the Roman bar. It seems impossible that a High Priest, even such an one as Ananias, should have dared to give a command so contrary to decency or order, and we cannot wonder if St. Paul felt like a man hunted and in peril of his life, who must use his utmost alertness to confound and set his enemies at variance, in order to save himself alive. There was much in his position and in his experience of the last twenty-four hours which might have justified such a position. Paul had passed through a very grievous strain, he had been beaten by the multitude, and snatched from death by the Roman soldiers; he had, moreover, whilst still bleeding and torn, nerved himself, and delivered a marvellous address. After an interval of one night, and one night only, he stood face to face with a tribunal composed in part of his old companions and friends, and these men, instead of treating him courteously and granting him a hearing, permitted him to be insulted in their midst. But there is a nobler interpretation of St. Paul's actions, and one more in accord with his character and with his willingness to die daily for his people. We have also to remember that St. Luke may only have given an abstract of the meeting and recorded the most salient words, but even if these words were all that were spoken, we can see that Paul proclaimed in unequivocal terms to Pharisee and to Sadducee that he was as far removed from the position of the Sadducees as possible, that he was not a despiser of the law or a denier of the spiritual, but that he believed, like the Pharisee, in the resurrection of the dead.

St. Paul's Retort to Ananias

Then turning to Ananias he denounced in scathing words the action he had taken. How dared he—a whited wall, fair without, but foul within, he whose iniquity and extortion had driven the Jewish nation and the poorer priests to such an extremity that it had excited the wrath even of the Government of Rome—he who was set to judge Paul according to the law, how dared he break that law and lower its dignity by commanding him to be smitten contrary to that law? The underlying meaning of his words must have been recognized by all who heard him, but despite the depths to which Ananias had degraded the high priesthood, there still remained a lingering respect for the office, if not for the person, of the high priest; and, therefore, they who stood by said, "Revilest thou God's high priest?" Paul officially withdrew his words, that is to say, admitted that he should not have spoken against Ananias as a high priest, but will not admit that he should not have spoken against him personally. Much question has arisen in the first place as to exactly what St. Paul meant, and in the second place, as to how far he was justified in his retort; and further still, as to the exact truthfulness of the way in which he withdrew that retort. There is no question but that ample provocation had been given, but a Christian has to govern his conduct, not according to the amount of provocation, but according to a Christ-like bearing of the provocation, and there is no question that his conduct fell far short of the patience and conduct of Christ, who, when smitten, said, "If I have done evil, bear witness of the evil: but if well, why smitest thou me?" (John xviii. 23).

"I Wist Not That He Was the High Priest"

But apart from any question of Christ-like bearing or excitement that Paul may have been labouring under, there remains the question of truthfulness, and we ask how Paul could possibly not have known that Ananias was the high priest? It has been thought that he may not have recognized him because he was not wearing his robes upon this occasion, and was not sitting in the place of authority, for the Roman Tribune who had summoned the meeting of necessity presided over it, and the high priest would attend without his robes as an ordinary member of the Sanhedrin, or Paul may have been short-sighted, and did not recognize him; but Paul "earnestly scanned" the faces of the council, and it is by no means certain that he was short-sighted. Another suggestion is that when he said "I did not know," he used the word "know" in the sense in which Christ said "I know you not," "I never knew you." A last explanation harmonizes better with his evident intention to antagonize the Sadducees and rouse the Pharisees on his behalf, and according to this he implies that he was not aware that Ananias was high priest at this time, and skilfully alludes to the fact that Ananias had been deposed for crime and had reassumed his office without the sanction of Rome, and therefore was not technically the high priest. If he had been the high priest Paul would not have spoken ill of the ruler of his people.

St. Paul's Appeal to the Pharisees

As soon as St. Paul had spoken, or after a further address, which is not recorded, the assembly fell into confusion and Paul cried out, "Men and brethren, I am a Pharisee, the son of a Pharisee: of the hope and resurrection of the dead I am called in question." Some think that St. Paul intended to divide the assembly, still further ranging himself on the side of the Pharisees; others think, which is more probable, that he made the statement because he was determined whilst he had the opportunity to state his true position before the one body of men who were alone capable of understanding and appreciating his meaning.

His words were literally true; he had been born a Pharisee and had consistently held all that was best in their belief, but he had also shaken off rites and formulas and brought the hope of the Pharisee to its full fruition and power through his belief in the risen Jesus, the Messiah for whom they still, alas! were only seeking. Some think he was not justified, even so, in making a statement which would increase the hostility of the Sadducees, and say that Paul himself admitted before Felix that these words contained the only claim that could be made against him. But Christ had promised His disciples that when they were brought before kings and rulers for His sake, they would speak,

THE LAST APPEAL TO THE SANHEDRIN

not in their own strength, but in that of the Holy Ghost. Furthermore, Paul, when he stated his position, stated the literal truth, and one which, however he worded it, must arouse the indignation of the Sadducees. His appeal was successful, he obtained an acquittal from the lips of the only men in the Sanhedrin who represented the spiritual side of the nation, the men amongst whom true religion still lingered; for the Pharisees and the Scribes, who belonged to the party of the Pharisees, immediately banded themselves together and defended Paul almost on the same lines that Gamaliel defended Peter, saying, that if an angel had spoken to him they ought not to fight against God, and finally pronounced his acquittal, saying, "We find no fault in this man."

A great dissension "immediately arose" between the Pharisees and Sadducees, for they hated one another more bitterly than they hated Christianity, and they turned upon one another instead of turning upon Paul. But the Chief Captain, who must have been filled with contempt as he watched the raging tumult of what should have been a learned court of justice, gave immediate orders to separate them, and fearing "lest Paul should have been pulled in pieces of them" commanded the soldiers to go down and take him by force and bring him into the castle.

"The Night Following"

Paul was rescued, and for the moment sheltered from his persecutors; but he was a prisoner, exhausted and alone, and out of reach either of his own friends or of the Christians of Jerusalem. In addition to his loneliness there was the despondency consequent upon the failure of his appeal to the Jews, and an agony of spirit lest in any respect he had spoken unadvisedly with his lips and shunned to declare the whole counsel of God. He sank into utter dejection of spirit, and in the midst of his dejection he lifted up his eyes and saw Jesus standing beside him and heard Him speak and answer all the pain and longing of his heart. Jesus told him that he had not failed, for he was to witness at Rome as he had witnessed at Jerusalem; and as He spoke Paul knew that Jesus had pierced beneath the imperfection which might have mingled with his witness, had understood his heart's desire, and would allow the Jews to have no power over him until he had witnessed at Rome; knew also "that Christ had need of him." In the light of that love Paul stayed his soul in peace, caring nothing, so that he might finish his course with joy and receive the crown of righteousness which the Lord, the righteous judge, would give him at that day (2 Timothy iv. 8).

The message of good cheer to Paul is a message of good cheer to us also, for according as we strive for the Kingdom of God and His righteousness we are cast down at the failure and imperfection of our witness, and inclined to fall into dejection of spirit at the thought of the word which we might have spoken, or the deed which we might have done had we lived nearer to Christ, had we worked more directly, under the influence of His Spirit. Jesus stood beside St. Paul, and beholding, pardoned him and read his heart's desire; Jesus stands beside us also and knows our heart's longing. He gives us also that which He granted to Paul, fuller opportunity of service according to the service rendered.

The Conspiracy of the Jews

But whilst Paul, thus imprisoned in the castle of Antonia, stayed his soul in peace, the Jews in the Temple courts below were transported with a rage that knew no bounds, and spent the night in consultation as to how they might outwit the Roman authority and slay Paul. They knew the time was short, for if Paul were taken out of Jerusalem he would be taken out of their power also; and, therefore, at daybreak, a band of forty made a conspiracy together, and bound themselves under an oath that they would neither eat nor drink until they had killed Paul. Deeds of assassination of this nature were, alas! too frequent amongst the Jews at this period, and a band of robbers, called Sicarii, bearing concealed daggers, were accustomed to mingle with the crowd, not only in the streets of Jerusalem, but even in the Temple, in order to assassinate their own enemies or the enemies of those who had hired them.

At daybreak the conspirators came to the chief priests and elders, as Judas had come before them, and divulged the plot which they had made. They asked the chief priests to make request to Lysias that Paul might be brought down to them once again in order that further inquiry might be made concerning him. The plan was plausible enough, and Lysias, knowing how the former assembly had been interrupted, might readily have granted their request had not their design been frustrated through the action of Paul's nephew, who became aware of the plot, and found means of access into the castle and told Paul.

The Defeat of the Intrigue

We cannot help stopping to note the goodwill and daring of Paul's nephew, as well as to wonder at the influential position which he must have held in order to have obtained intelligence of the plot from the Jews, and right of entrance from the Romans to so important a prisoner as Paul. It is also interesting to note from the fact that he rendered this help to St. Paul, that St. Paul's relatives at this eleventh hour must have been reconciled to him, and have entered into friendly relationship with him.

St. Paul was doubtless touched by the affection shown him by the young man, but he saw at once the peril in which he stood, and summoned a centurion and bade him take the youth to the Chief Captain. Lysias and his subordinates seem by this time to have been fully aware of the importance of their prisoner, and anxious to atone for their offence in binding and preparing to scourge him; for we see that the centurion makes immediate opportunity for the lad to speak to Lysias, and Lysias takes him by the hand and draws him aside so that he may speak privately to him. In words of earnest supplication the youth unfolds the matter, and entreats Lysias to be on his guard, and resist the solicitations of the Jews, but Lysias recognizes as

THE LAST APPEAL TO THE SANHEDRIN

instantly the gravity of the situation as St. Paul, for the events of the last twenty-four hours, apart from the words of St. Paul's nephew, have shown him that the Jews are on the brink of a very dangerous riot, and that there is no time to be lost. Therefore, telling the lad to observe the utmost caution lest he should draw attention to the action of the Roman soldiers, Lysias lets him go, and summoning two centurions, orders a band of two hundred soldiers, accompanied by two hundred spearmen and seventy horses, together with a relay of horses for Paul, to be ready at the third hour of the night so that they may bear him with all haste to Felix, the Governor, at his headquarters in Caesarea. At the same time he writes a letter acquitting Paul, and placing Felix on his guard against the Jews, and commands the company of horsemen and spearmen to take him as far as Antipatris, and forward him next morning as soon as he is in comparative safety to Caesarea, and there deliver Paul, together with the epistle, to the Governor. Thus Paul made his final departure from Jerusalem, and was delivered over to Felix, who, when he had read the letter and found that Paul came from the province of Cilicia, said, "I will hear thee when thy accusers are also come," and commanded him to be kept in Herod's judgment hall.

CHAPTER XLV

ACTS XXIV AND XXV. 1-13

THE INVESTIGATION BEFORE THE ROMAN GOVERNOR, FELIX

The Policy of the Jews

The uproar at Jerusalem seems as unpremeditated as that of Ephesus, but it has a more deep-seated malice behind it. Demetrius and his companions intend to lay violent hands upon Paul, but are satisfied as soon as they know that he is gone out of the city, whereas the Jews are thirsting for the blood of Paul, and their rage knows no bounds when they find that he has escaped out of their hands and passed under the protection of Rome. They made their mistake when they attacked Paul in the Temple, instead of in the street, for the uproar in the Temple provoked the immediate intervention of Lysias and the rescue of Paul. The only resource left is either to secure his condemnation or to find means of assassinating him. According to Roman law a prisoner had to be tried within three days of his arrest, but owing to the circumstances of the case an interval of five days was allowed in order that his accusers might have the opportunity to come from Jerusalem to Caesarea. Felix had been governor of the Jews eight and a half years, and from his past knowledge he caught the temper of the Jewish people and saw that a case of no common importance had passed into his hands. This conviction was strengthened when at the trial a professional advocate, Tertullus, was appointed to lay the case against Paul, and Ananias the high priest descended with the elders, although the Jews held that it was contrary to the dignity of a high priest to take such a journey, so contrary that from this circumstance alone Calvin held that Paul must have been in the right when he insinuated that Ananias was not legally the high priest.

The Oration of Tertullus

Tertullus opens his oration with what is technically called a Captatio Benevolentiae, that is to say, with an address skilfully worded to gain the good-will of the governor; but in this particular instance especially skilful, because at one and the same time it complimented Felix upon his good deed in the recent suppression of the brigands and ignored the disgraceful action he had taken in aiding and abetting the Sicarii, professional robbers who had assassinated Jonathan, the high priest, and whose outrages had become so prevalent that Felix would not have retained his power over the country generally but for his influence at Rome.

Tertullus indicted the prisoner upon the three following accusations: (i) Treason against the Roman Government; (ii) Treason against the Jewish religion; and (iii) Profanation of the Temple. He declared that Paul had been arrested on these three charges, and would have been tried by the Jews had not Lysias come with violence and taken him away to Caesarea. The Jews vehemently endorsed the statement of Tertullus; but Felix knew that a totally different complexion might be given to the affair, and that in all probability the statement of Lysias was far nearer the truth when he wrote that Paul would have been "killed of the Jews" had not he rescued him and delivered him out of their hands and despatched him to Caesarea. Therefore Felix, as soon as Tertullus had concluded, called upon Paul to speak in his own defence.

St. Paul's Defence

St. Paul opened his address by words more skilful and truthful even than those of Tertullus. He bespoke the goodwill of Felix by alluding to his unusually long tenure of office in Caesarea—his tenure having exceeded three times the length of that of any of his predecessors—and consequent exceptional knowledge of the Jews and Jewish law. He denied altogether the first charge of treason against the Roman Government, by proving that he had been in Jerusalem only twelve days, and during that period had neither taught nor entered into contention with any man; he had lived purely as a private citizen, and he challenged the Jews to prove anything to the contrary against him. On the second charge, of being a ringleader of the Nazarenes, and, therefore, a traitor against the Jewish religion, he replied that the Nazarenes were the truest worshippers of the God of his fathers, for they believed in the law and the prophets, and the resurrection of the dead, tenets as strongly held by the Jews as by the Nazarenes, and in this faith, confessedly the purest amongst the Jews, he exercised himself to have a conscience void of offence towards God and towards man.

As to the third charge, the profanation of the Temple, he denies it as absolutely as either of the former, and asks how a man who had come to bring alms and offerings, and who was in the very act of carrying out a vow of purification, could have come up at the same time with a deliberate intention of profaning the Temple? He defies his accusers to prove that he had made any disturbance whilst carrying out his vow, or had been accompanied with multitude or tumult. One charge of disturbance only could possibly be laid against him, that he had cried, touching the "resurrection of the dead I am called in question by you this day." This last appeal, as Paul well knew, could bring condemnation neither upon himself nor upon his fellow-Christians. The question of the resurrection was an outstanding matter of dispute between the Sadducees and the Pharisees, and formed part of the integral dissensions of the nation, whereas if he had been condemned of treason against the Roman government or the Jewish religion, it might have been fatal to him and to his fellow-Christians, for owing to this disturbance the Jewish Christians might have been outlawed and declared alien to Israel.

The Judgment of Felix

Felix saw at a glance the futility of the charges as well as the innocence of St. Paul. He had not been governor of the Jews for eight years without gaining some "knowledge of the way," and he had married a Jewess, Drusilla, a Herod, who, as after history shows, had curiosity as well as interest in matters that concerned the worship of the Jews. Had Felix been a true representative of the justice of the Roman law, he would have set Paul at liberty, and bade the Jews abstain from further molestation of him; but Felix had been guilty of too many crimes against the Jewish nation as a body to dare to do this, and he was afraid to go any further in provoking their indignation against him. He recognized the innocence of St. Paul, but he saw the danger to himself of opposing leaders as powerful and representative as these men, and therefore he decided to take refuge under the subterfuge of requiring further witness from Lysias, and, pronouncing the word "amplius," promised as soon as Lysias came to give the fullest investigation to the matter. Lysias, however, did not come, and Felix made such amends as was possible to Paul and was at the same time compatible with his own interest also. He commanded that Paul should be kept a prisoner, but bade the centurion who had charge of him let his acquaintance come to him and minister to him.

"His Wife Drusilla, Which Was a Jewess"

If the record of Scripture ended here we might have thought that Felix had dealt more favourably with Paul than might have been expected, either from his record in secular history, or from the outline of his character left to us by Tacitus, who represents him as wielding the power of a tyrant with the heart of a slave; but the next few verses give a further light upon his character, and show his love of money as well as his deliberate stifling of conscience.

Felix was at this time living with Drusilla, his so-called wife, but in reality the wife of Azizus. She was a daughter of the Herod who had slain James, and would have slain Peter also, and history tells us that she was singularly beautiful even for a Herod, and only about eighteen years old; but young as she was she had already learned to sweep aside duty whenever it stood in the path of ambition or pleasure. Both she and her family had for four generations been connected with the most stirring events in Jewish and in Christian history, and had probably for a long time desired to see Paul, as her grandfather, Herod, had desired to see Jesus also. Therefore, as soon as Drusilla came to Caesarea and heard that Paul was in bonds, she caught eagerly at the opportunity of seeing him, and hearing his words.

Paul "Reasoned of Righteousness, Temperance and Judgment to Come"

It was now St. Paul's turn to stand in the presence of a man and his illegal wife and either condone their sin in the hope of obtaining freedom, or witness, as John the Baptist had witnessed before Herod and Herodias. Paul might have justified himself in speaking on broad general lines instead of trying to bring home to Felix and Drusilla their true position before God, for they had not asked, much less wished for, a personal application of Christianity. They had sent for Paul that he might speak "concerning the faith in Christ," that he might give them an outline of the life, death, and resurrection of Christ; and if Paul had done as they desired, had spoken of His loving-kindness, His deeds of mercy and healing, it would have been to Felix and Drusilla as a pleasant dream, a music of the Heavenly sphere. How often does a preacher of to-day tell a story of love and mercy, and call upon his hearers to uplift themselves to a like love and mercy also, and omit the sterner reasoning of righteousness, temperance and judgment to come, such as may open out to them the plague of their own hearts, and awaken a true and lasting desire for love and mercy. The temptation to omit the weightier matters of the law could never be greater to the preacher of to-day than it was to Paul in Caesarea, for Paul had only to soothe and flatter Felix as David soothed Saul, and he might perchance have gone forth a freed man, with a renewed life before him.

But Paul, despite his knowledge of the fate which had befallen John the Baptist for a like faithfulness, moved with compassion towards Felix and Drusilla, opened his mouth boldly and made known to them the things of the Kingdom of God.

"Felix Trembled"

Paul's words are not recorded, but the nobility and simplicity of his character was evident from the very beginning to the governor and his wife. They knew that he was risking life and liberty that he might redeem them from evil; but the thought of his self-sacrifice was forgotten in the intensity of his words. They saw one by one the thoughts of their hearts rise in dark and ever darker outline before the judgment-seat of God—their intrigues at the Court of Rome, their deeds of self-seeking, murder and adultery, until Felix trembled as he experienced a first consciousness of the torment of the hereafter. It is not recorded that a like consciousness was awakened in the heart of Drusilla. She was a woman, but young as she might be, she had already sealed up the fountains of her gentleness, honour and chastity, had destroyed all that was noblest within her soul, and rendered herself by her shallowness incapable of being moved by the approach of a servant of God, even such a servant as St. Paul. "There is a tide in the affairs of men," but there is none in the affairs of a Jezebel, a Herodias or a Drusilla. Drusilla had denied her faith when she allowed the sorcerer Simon (possibly Simon Magus), to entice her from her husband Azizus; she denied her faith again when she joined the court of Felix, and she continued to deny it until she perished with her child in the eruption of Vesuvius, A.D. 79.

"A More Convenient Season"

It is thought that it was Drusilla who saw and feared the consequences of the awakened conscience of Felix, and suggested the impulse which made him shake himself free from the sense of impending evil and say, "Go thy way for this time, when I have a convenient season I will call for thee." The convenient season did come, and he called for Paul again and again; but the season of awakening did not return. "He that being often reproved hardeneth his neck, shall suddenly be destroyed and that without remedy" (Proverbs xxix. 1). His house, which, for the moment, stood empty, swept and garnished, was entered into by other spirits more wicked than himself, which dwelt there, so that his last state was worse than the first (St. Matthew xii. 44).

"Felix . . . Left Paul Bound"

Paul, therefore, was kept in prison, but he learned the way of escape open before him; he saw that Felix hoped that money would be given him, and that this was the real reason why "He sent for him the oftener, and communed with him." Felix had doubtless heard of the great contribution which Paul had taken to Jerusalem, and thought that the converts who had at

THE INVESTIGATION BEFORE FELIX

Paul's bidding been willing to contribute for the poor of Jerusalem, would contribute still more largely to set free the man they loved. He did not know the character of Paul, for if Paul had refused to receive the righteous wages of his labour, when working for the Churches, how much more would he refuse to receive unrighteous wages for a tyrant like Felix.

Two years spent their weary way, until Felix, becoming more daring in sin, abetted the soldiers in an attack upon the Jews, and the sacking of their houses. Such iniquity passed even the endurance of the Jews, despite their dread of Rome, and an uproar broke out in Caesarea, and Felix was summoned to Rome to answer for his misdeeds; and therefore Felix, having now only too good cause for desiring to show the Jews a pleasure, left Paul bound.

The Imprisonment in Caesarea

Paul might well ask himself to what purpose he had spoken so faithfully during the past two years since, as far as man could see, he had lost everything and gained nothing. Felix and Drusilla had gone away, and Festus would be naturally anxious upon his appointment in Judaea to conciliate as far as possible the Sanhedrin and their followers in order that he might be the better able to keep the peace in Judaea, which was looked upon as one of the most difficult of the Roman provinces. But Festus was shrewd enough to see at a glance that Felix had not removed Paul, and kept him in Caesarea for two years without some good reason, and, therefore, he preferred, at first at any rate, to walk warily in the footsteps of his predecessor. He probably distrusted the priests, and thought it wiser to keep a Roman citizen in his own hands until that citizen would take upon himself the responsibility of having his case tried at Jerusalem. He promised, therefore, to take the matter in hand immediately upon his arrival in Caesarea, and invited the Jews to come and plead their cause before him. He must have seen the importance of the case, for he stayed only ten days in Jerusalem, and ordered that the trial should take place immediately upon his arrival in Caesarea. The Jews instead of having a professional advocate themselves made many and stormy charges against him, but Paul denied each charge and declared his innocence.

The Offer of a Trial at Jerusalem

Thereupon Festus found himself in a strait betwixt two. He had either to discharge Paul and displease the Jews, or to attempt to judge him upon technicalities of the Jewish law, about which he knew nothing and cared nothing. The only way out of the dilemma was to force Paul's hand, and persuade him to agree to a trial at Jerusalem, thus pleasing the Jews, and making Paul take the responsibility of the trial. His case fell fairly enough under their jurisdiction, if he would agree to it, and his blood, if mischief befell him by the way, would be required at his own hands or at the hands of the Jews, and not at the hands of Festus. But if Festus had grasped the difficulty of the situation, Paul had grasped

THE INVESTIGATION BEFORE FELIX

it also. He knew that his life was at stake, and that it was hopeless to expect or wait for justice from Caesarea. If Felix, who had been convinced of his innocence, and knew Jewish law, strove only to obtain a bribe from him; if Festus, who had a fair reputation, and approached the question from an outsider's point of view, sought only to ingratiate himself with the Jews, there was nothing but imprisonment before him in Caesarea, and nothing but death in Jerusalem, and, therefore, he took a final step and appealed to Caesar, all hope of approaching Rome as a free man having gone for ever.

"Caesarem Appello"

The one hope of escape lay in this appeal to Rome; but if Paul took this last arrow out of his quiver he crossed the boundary line and, as far as the Jews were concerned, proclaimed his apostasy from the Jewish nation, and arraigned them at the bar of Roman law. But in reality it was not Paul who was arraigning the nation, but the Jews, who were forcing him to take this step; for it was they who caused the first intervention by their uproar in the Temple; it was they again, who, by their scheme of assassination, caused the removal to Caesarea; and it was they who, at the eleventh hour, by their continued accusations, were bringing about the removal to Rome. There was, therefore, no recourse but for Paul to proclaim his innocence and say, "To the Jews have I done no wrong, as thou very well knowest," and to refuse to go to Jerusalem, saying, that if he had committed anything worthy of death he was willing to die, but if not he would not be delivered into their hands. "I appeal unto Caesar."

"Unto Caesar Shalt Thou Go"

The moment Paul uttered these words the whole scene changed, for neither the Jews nor Festus had any further power over him. Amidst all the corruption of Roman law and justice, the rights of the Roman citizen and the power of appeal had been jealously guarded by the emperors on account of the power which it put into their hands; for, with the utterance of these words a Roman citizen obtained immediate right of entry into the presence of his emperor, and right of judgment from that emperor's lips alone. Festus immediately arose from his judgment-seat and withdrew, in order that he might confer with his council. He had driven his prisoner further than he had intended, and had exposed himself almost on the first day of his jurisdiction in Judaea to a refusal to abide by his degree, and an appeal which passed him by and carried the matter to the emperor. But whether he were piqued or not at the result of his time serving-policy he had no recourse save to reply, "Hast thou appealed unto Caesar? unto Caesar shalt thou go."

The privilege of every Christian, as of every Roman citizen, is his court of appeal, which stands ever open to him, so that he passes as he will into the presence of his King, and lays the matter in order before him. This is a privilege which permits of no intervention from any fellow creature; a privilege which neither angel, principality, nor power can take from him, a freedom of the courts of Heaven, a freedom bought by the life and death of Jesus.

CHAPTER XLVI

ACTS XXV. 13 TO END AND XXVI

THE LAST OF THE KINGS

The Indictment of St. Paul

When Festus took up the reins of Government in Judaea, he found the nation on the verge of an outbreak, and we cannot wonder if, like Pilate before him, he strained a point of justice to propitiate the Jews. His attempt failed, for Paul refused to be transferred into their hands, and appealed to Caesar, thus placing Festus in worse case than before. It was a reflection upon his Government that a prisoner, the very first day he held his court, should appeal past his judgment to that of Caesar; but, having appealed, it only remained for Festus to state the case in the way most likely to commend it to Rome. But here a difficulty arose—how could he draw up an indictment upon technicalities of a religious law about which he knew nothing; how declare a case against a man who ought to have been acquitted, and whose offences, even if truly charged against him, lay altogether outside the pale of Roman law?

In the midst of his perplexity an unexpected opening arose for a better understanding of the case. Agrippa II came down to Caesarea, accompanied by his sister Bernice, to congratulate Festus upon his accession to the procuratorship of Judaea, and, according to custom, join in the congratulatory festivities; and Festus, shortly after his arrival, laid the circumstances of the case fairly enough before him, and showed him how he had withheld Paul from the Jews until he knew that his offence was clearly within the compass of Jewish law. He told him further that having found that the whole matter turned upon questions and technicalities of law of which he was ignorant, he had requested Paul to go to Jerusalem, and be tried by experts of his own nation; but Paul had refused to be handed over to the Jews, and had appealed unto Caesar.

The Dynasty of the Herods

As Festus speaks to Agrippa we see, for the last time, a king, or shadow of a king, pass across the page of Jewish history, and affect a pomp of which the reality has passed away. It seems a far cry from "Saul who slew his thousands, and David his ten thousands" (1 Samuel xxix. 5), from "Solomon in all his glory" (St. Matthew vi. 29), to Agrippa, King of Northern Palestine, whose authority consisted chiefly in the oversight of the Temple and the appointment of the High Priests; and yet Agrippa was a man who in some respects might have held his own during any period of Jewish history, for he belonged to a race as renowned as any in Israel for splendour as for daring.

The Herods seemed destined one after another to come into contact with Christ, or with the greatest of his followers, at a vital point in their own history and in the history of Christianity. The great-grandfather of Agrippa, Herod the Great, had assisted the Romans in the capture of Jerusalem, B.C. 37, and had massacred the Innocents in his determination to sweep aside every possible claimant to his throne. His grandfather, Herod, had slain John the Baptist, and had examined Christ before his judgment-seat; but Christ had read his intention as clearly as on the earlier occasion when he sent for Him, and answered him never a word, but left him; and he went down to posterity branded with the name of "Fox" (Luke ix. 32). His father, Agrippa I, the Herod of the Acts, had slain James and stretched out his hand to take Peter also, but had been smitten down in the midst of his pomp in the same city of Caesarea (chap. xii.). Agrippa himself is the one Herod in whom it almost seems as if there might have been some good thing found toward the Lord God of Israel, for Paul, instead of refusing to speak to him, as Christ refused to speak to Herod, unfolded the mystery of the Kingdom of Heaven; but the revelation, although at one time very near, in its long issue passed by and left him as untouched as any of his predecessors; and yet as we read the story we can understand the charm which enabled the Herods, despite their self-seeking and unscrupulousness, to maintain their ascendency on the one side with the court of Rome, and on the other among the Jewish people, the Jews detesting the Herods, and yet relying upon them in every time of trouble.

The Scene of the Trial

Agrippa, like Drusilla, had for a long time been desirous (lit. wishing to hear) Paul, and, accompanied by his sister Bernice, he descended with great pomp into the palace hall. The trial was held in the "place of hearing," instead of the hall of justice, because Paul, having appealed to Caesar, could not appear in any court or be tried by any king except Caesar or his representative. Did Agrippa, as he made his way through the assembled multitude, remember how his father, eighteen years before, had made a like way in even greater pomp, and taken his place upon his throne in Caesarea? Did he recall the judgment which, for his innumerable crimes and above all for his impiety, descended upon him? Festus, as he presented Paul to Agrippa, confessed that nothing worthy of death had been found in him, but that the Jews were crying out that he ought not to live. Paul is to speak in order that his case may be fully known; but a decision as to life or death cannot be given, as, owing to his appeal, his case has passed into the hand of Augustus, *i.e.* Caesar. Paul's address on this occasion is considered the greatest of all that he delivered. He speaks neither as Jew nor as Roman, but as a citizen of the world; his appeal is world wide, and he views the struggle between Christ and the world as the struggle between the King of Light and darkness. He stands apart, as it were, as Malachi stood over the city of Jerusalem five hundred years before, and viewed the day coming that would burn as an oven. Paul at the close of the New Dispensation, as Malachi at the close of the Old, strove to turn men's eyes to the Sun of Righteousness, to the new King that would arise with healing in His wings (Malachi iv. 1-2).

The Address of St. Paul

Agrippa, by the courtesy of Festus, had been given the control of the assembly, but with a like courtesy he passed it back, as it were, into the hands of Festus, and tells Paul that he is permitted (of Festus) to speak for himself. Paul, as he stands up and speaks, has the assembly in his power; he stretches forth his hand and draws all men unto him. He opens his address by words as skilful and as true as those by which he had opened his address to Felix. Agrippa, like all the other Herods, had affected great interest in the Temple, and in everything connected with it, and was probably more qualified than any other official of the Roman court for hearing his appeal. Moreover, Agrippa, although anxious to propitiate the Jews, had shown that he was capable of being independent of them, as, for instance, at the present time, when, despite their remonstrances, he had continued to build the wall which overlooked the Temple. Paul, therefore, thinks himself happy to answer before Agrippa, and contrasts vividly the stern upbringing of his youth in law and ceremony in the strictest sect of his religion with the spiritual freedom which he now enjoys as a Christian, and which he claims is the legitimate outcome of that upbringing, for he has found the realization of the hope towards which the twelve tribes night and day have been stretching forth their hands; that is to say, he has found the risen from the dead, the Messiah.

The Question of the Resurrection

The resurrection of the Messiah had been as incredible to him as it is to his hearers, so incredible that he persecuted to the death not only in Jerusalem, but in other cities until arrested by the risen Christ, who in the glory of the resurrection light appeared to him and spoke in tones of mingled pity and rebuke, bidding him arise from a life of dead works, and go forth and call upon all men to arise also. The witness he is called upon to give is the witness that they are to give also. They are to open their eyes and see the glory of the resurrection light, to turn from the king of darkness to the King of Light, to receive forgiveness for deeds of darkness and go forth to deeds of light. He had gone forth in obedience to the call throughout Damascus and Jerusalem and all the coast of Judaea, as also among the Gentiles, and had called all men to turn to God and do works meet for repentance. But whilst the Gentiles had heard his words, the Jews had sought only to kill him; but Paul in the power of the risen Christ still witnesses amongst them, testifying that, according to their own prophecy, Christ must suffer and rise from the dead and bring light and liberty to Jews and Gentiles. As he speaks he seems to be transported with the glory of that light, and Festus, who has been following a line of argument as unknown to him as to Gallio, and who like Gallio has a contempt for everything which he cannot understand, sees the light of Heaven shining in Paul's face, and cries out with a loud voice, "Paul, thou art beside thyself; much learning doth make thee mad."

Paul's Application of His Argument to Festus

The words jarred Paul as cruelly as the words of the materialist ever jar the spiritually minded. It was nothing that he was called mad, his Master had been called mad before him (Mark iii. 21); and he had used the same expression when speaking of himself, "whether we be beside ourselves, it is to God" (2 Corinthians v. 13); what he did care for was his utter failure to awaken the spiritual understanding of Festus. He knew immediately that it was useless to make any further appeal. All he could do was to show by his reply his own truth and soberness as well as the truth and soberness of the subject of which he had been speaking, and he therefore answered, "I am not mad, most noble Festus, but speak forth the words of soberness and truth." Then whilst all were wondering at the quiet strength and moderation of his answer he turned to Agrippa, and reading, as it were, the inmost thoughts of his heart, convicted him of a knowledge of the truth of the life, death, and resurrection of Jesus, a life lived openly, and a death died openly, in Jerusalem, the spiritual centre of the world, and in accordance with the light of prophecy; and he called upon Agrippa to arise and avow his belief in that prophecy, "King Agrippa, believest thou the prophets? I know that thou believest."

"Thou Persuadest Me To Be a Christian."

Paul had come to very close quarters with Agrippa, as but a few months before he had come to very close quarters with Felix and Drusilla, and it took all Agrippa's courtliness and skill to turn his appeal aside. He was unquestionably moved by the personality of Paul and by the words which he had spoken, but he was not prepared to avow his belief in the face of the assembled Jews, and of the Roman courtiers and soldiers. Like Felix, he had habitually placed self-interest before truth and honour, and, like Felix, he cast the presentation of truth away, and made a half-ironical, half-courteous reply, "With but a few words, thou wouldst persuade me to be a Christian," thus committing himself neither the one way nor the other. Paul knew as surely in the case of Agrippa as he had known in that of Felix that the opportunity once gone by had passed forever, and, therefore, since it was useless to plead with him any longer, in a few well chosen words, he prayed that not only Agrippa, but all who heard him that day, might be not only almost but altogether such as he was, that is to say, witnesses for the King of Kings, "except these bonds." But whilst he prayed he feared that they would go forth from that assembly resembling him in one respect and one respect only, *i.e.* that of bondage; for whilst he was fast bound a prisoner to Nero, they were still faster bound, bound hand and foot to the power of darkness, given over to eternal death. At the last he lifted his chain-bound hand as a symbol of warning to Agrippa and to Jerusalem, just as he had lifted his toil-worn hand as an inspiration of self-sacrifice to the elders in Miletus, and none of those present before him could hear his tone of infinite love and pity, could see that chained hand without being moved more than they liked to confess. The assembly rose, and Agrippa and Festus, having gone aside, agreed together as to the innocence of Paul, but passed over the impression made by his words, and said, "This man might have been set at liberty, if he had not appealed unto Caesar."

CHAPTER XLVII

ACTS XXVII

THE SHIPWRECK

The Centurion, Julius

Nothing further could be gained by keeping Paul in Caesarea and, therefore, Festus decided to despatch him to Rome, under the charge of Julius, a centurion of Augustus' band. The Roman Government, in addition to the ordinary military system, had a body of provincial troops who travelled backwards and forwards, superintending the transport of the corn supply and convoying state prisoners to and from Rome. This particular band was called Augustus' band, a title of honour, and was under the charge of a centurion of the name of Julius, whose bearing, generosity and kindness to Paul gives us another example of the type of men who formed the strength of the Roman Empire, and helped to preserve it from decay.

Julius had several other prisoners under his charge at the same time, but their names are not given; they were probably condemned prisoners being taken to the arena of Rome to make a Roman holiday. Paul was accompanied by Luke and Aristarchus, a fellow prisoner and physician, unless Ramsay is right in his conjecture that to obtain the right of sailing they went with him as his slaves. Paul must have been glad enough to exchange the confinement of his prison in Caesarea for an onward step towards life and liberty, although he had experience enough to know the discomfort and danger which almost necessarily accompanied a sea voyage of that period. The two or three stories of travel by sea and allusions to the sea in the Bible show that the Jews were not a seafaring people and had none of the salt breeze of adventure and daring which invigorates maritime life and history among the Saxons.

The Coasts of Tyre and Sidon

After one day's sailing the vessel stopped at Sidon to take on cargo or to land passengers, and Julius, according to the courtesy and consideration which characterized all his dealings with St. Paul, "gave him liberty to go unto his friends to refresh himself." What a welcome change his short sojourn in Sidon must have been after his long imprisonment, and how great the joy of taking part once again in a Christian service.

We know nothing of the Church of Sidon save that Paul probably ministered to it when passing through the coasts of Phoenice and Samaria. It is most probable that it had been founded at an early date by those who had been scattered abroad after the martyrdom of Stephen, but the first movement towards it may in a sense be said to have been given by Christ Himself when He healed the daughter of the woman of Sidon and His footsteps passed to and fro throughout the coasts of Tyre and Sidon.

The short breathing space came to an end all too soon, and Paul had hardly re-embarked before a contrary wind set in, making it necessary to sail along the north-east coast of Cyprus instead of attempting the more direct eastern course, but despite the delay they arrived in safety at Myra, where there was an excellent harbour, and had the good fortune to find an Alexandrian corn ship (possibly driven into the harbour by the same contrary wind which they had encountered), upon which Julius embarked together with his prisoners.

The Ship of Adramyttium

Rome was dependent upon Egypt for her corn supply as England is upon Canada, and the transport of corn was looked upon as an important part of the imperial service, the arrival of a corn ship being so welcome that its arrival was eagerly hailed by the watchers in Puteoli, and it was permitted to come into the harbour with unfurled sail.

The Imperial Government had beneath their charge a seething mass of idle paupers, indeed, it has been estimated that two-thirds of the population of Rome, that is to say, two hundred thousand men received gratuitous provision from the State; and if this were the case we can understand the straits to which the Government would be reduced if these ships were lost or delayed, and how difficult it would be for them, if any accident occurred, to appease the tumultuous citizens.

The question of the corn trade explains the size and the importance of the ship in which Paul sailed. We can see that it was large, for it contained two hundred and seventy-six passengers as well as a lading of cargo, and must have been a welcome change after the smaller vessel, but Paul soon found that there would be little benefit or comfort connected with the journey, for almost immediately contrary winds prevailed, and it was only with the greatest difficulty and by sailing slowly that they were able to make their way to Cnidus, a dividing point between the western and eastern coast of Asia Minor. Cnidus had two excellent harbours, but they seem to have made no stay there, either because, owing to the contrary winds, they were not able to make the harbour, or because they still hoped to make the direct journey to Rome. The wind, however, was still so contrary that they did not dare to face the open sea, but turned southward and sailed under the lee of Crete along the southern coast until they came to a place called the Fair Havens, a small bay which still bears the same name.

The Debate as to Winter Quarters

Having reached Fair Havens they decided it was impossible to continue the immediate journey to Rome,

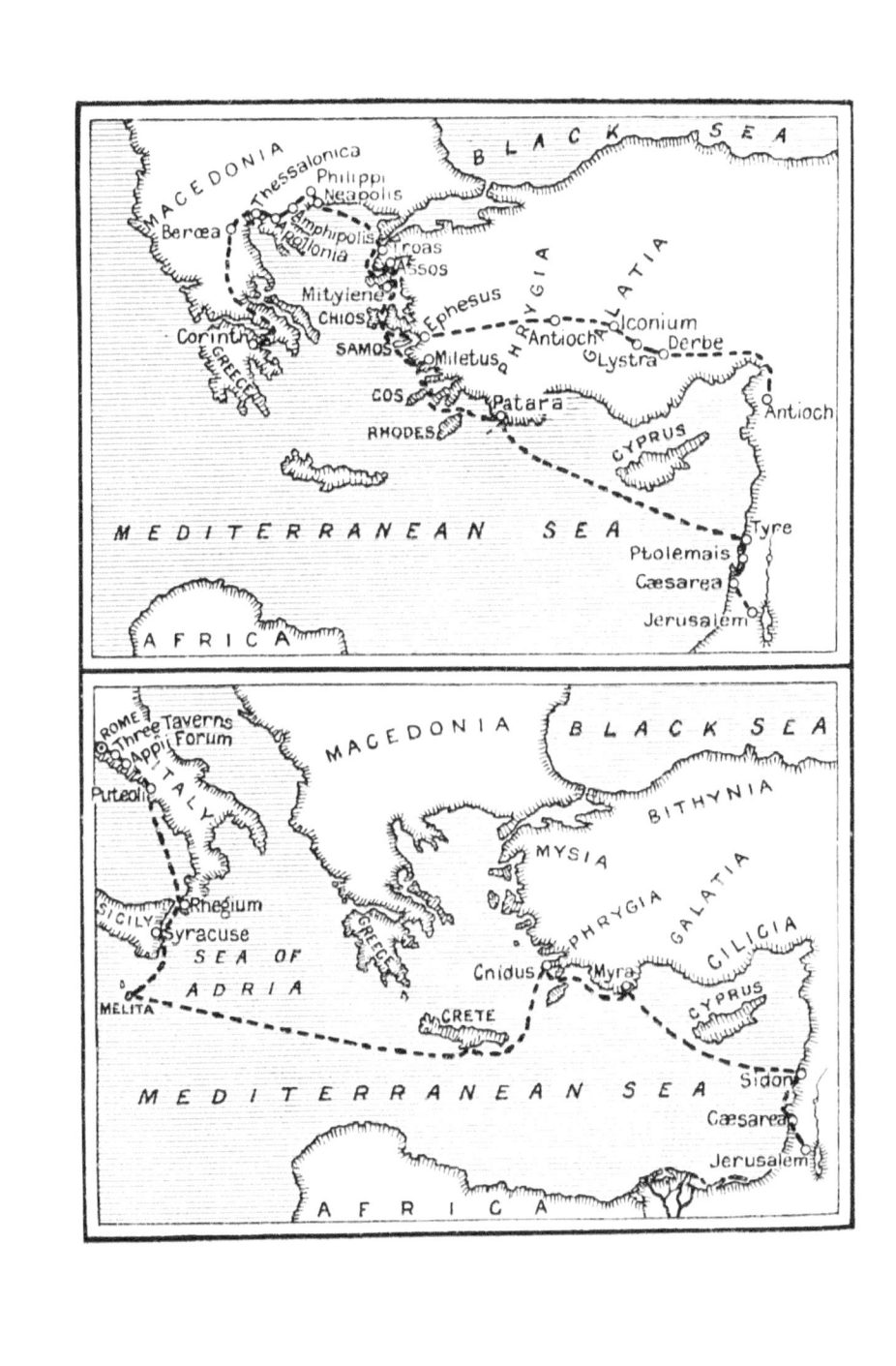

and the question arose as to whether they should winter in the harbour of Fair Havens or make one more effort to reach Phoenice. Phoenice had the better harbour, being sheltered on all sides, and had the name of being "the only secure harbour from all winds on the south coast of Crete," whereas Fair Havens was protected only from the north and north-west winds. It had, moreover, the further advantage of being within reach of a city, whereas Fair Havens presented a desolate reach of coast on either side. The matter was not decided as now by the captain of the vessel, in whose hand all authority lies, but by a gathering of three or four of the leading men in the vessel, and amongst these Paul was included. It seems strange that a prisoner should have been present at such a gathering, but from the first Paul had been treated with unusual respect, and Julius seems to have had a personal affection for him. It is possible that Julius had been present at the assembly in Caesarea and had listened to his speech before Agrippa, for we read that "the chief captains and principal men of the city were present at it," and the words which failed in lasting influence over Agrippa may have more powerfully influenced Julius. But apart from any question as to Paul's character or standing, his opinion would be of value as a man of ability who had been a constant traveller at sea. His advice was entirely opposed to that of the other counsellors; he urged them to remain at Fair Havens, and warned them that disaster to the lading of the ship and to life would follow if they attempted to go further now that the season was so far advanced and the winds so determinedly contrary. "Nevertheless, the centurion believed the master and the owner of the ship more than those things which were spoken by Paul," and as it was a short distance to Phoenice and the haven so much safer and more commodious, they decided that it was worth while to incur some trouble and risk in order to reach it, and therefore the moment a "south wind blew softly," thinking they had obtained their chance they loosed thence and sailed as closely as they could beneath the shelter of the mountainous shore.

The Euraquilo

They would have attained their purpose, had not a hurricane called the Euraquilo, from the north-east, caught the ship so that they were powerless, and had to let her drift by day and by night until they came beneath the shelter of the Island of Clauda.

By this time they were fully alive to the danger they were in, and made all preparations, as far as they could, to meet it by calling all hands together, Luke and Aristarchus probably among them ("we"), and proceeded with great difficulty to haul up the boat into the ship. The boat was probably a large one, as we see later on that the sailors had hoped to escape in her, and she was also full of water. The sailors next cast a cable round the framework of the ship, and fearing that they should be driven upon the African sandbanks which made that part of the Mediterranean so dangerous, they lowered the mainsail as far as possible and turned the ship to the wind, and strove to keep her under control by every means in their power.

But as the ship continued to be exceedingly tossed to and fro with the tempest, and quivered throughout her timbers, they decided to still further lessen the strain on the mainsail by casting out the cargo, and next day sacrificed the ship's fittings and equipment, the passengers being so panic-stricken that they joined in throwing overboard everything that was not absolutely necessary.

Paul's Address to the Crew

But whilst the vessel was thus driven at the mercy of the wind, and neither sun nor stars appeared to guide their course, and the men became too dispirited to attempt to prepare or eat the food, and only cast despairing glances at the clouds above and the yet darker waves below, Paul, at the last, after long prayer and fasting, stood forth and bade them be of good cheer. It was a strange message to give to men in immediate expectation of death, worn with hunger and toil, men who had been drifting sunless by day and starless by night, and who had probably reached a point at which life itself seemed but of little value, if only the struggle could be over. But Paul, strong in the force of his words and of his own personality, assumed from this time forth the real command of the ship and of all that was in her. He reminded them that if they had listened to him they would not have gained this harm or loss, and he says this not to cast their failings in their teeth, or still further to depress them, but because he knows that it is necessary for their safety that they should heed his words, and tells them that "there shall be no loss of life but of the ship." He tells them that he has seen a vision, that his King has stood beside him in the midst of the darkness, and has told him that the lives of all that are in the ship have been granted to him in answer to his prayer.

What a thrill of wonder and of joy must have passed through them as they heard his words. A lightning flash of hope illuminated their dark horizon and inspired them with courage for the coming days and nights of sorrow.

"Whose I Am and Whom I Serve"

There is something unspeakably grand in the picture of Paul as he stands out like a beacon light in the midst of the dark horizon, and gives a token that even though the storm and the winds may mount up to Heaven and go down again to the deeps below, yet they are still under the command of God, and that though their souls may be melted because of trouble, still if they cry unto the Lord He will bring them out of their distress (Psalm cvii. 28). At first sight we wonder how they believed his words, for although Paul had wrestled in prayer and prevailed with God, he had not shown that he could control the violence of the tempest nor prevent the infinite suffering and anxiety. He could not, like Jesus on the Sea of Galilee, control the forces of Nature and rebuke the sea and winds, and bring a great calm. But though Paul could not do this, he could appeal to his known conduct, character, and bearing, which had taught them something of the character of God, for he had served his God as continually on the ship as Daniel had served Him at the Court of Babylon (Daniel ix.). The rough ship's crew by their obedience to his words yielded their unconscious testimony to the power of his God speaking through him. A man's words tell according to his character and his past life. The force of his life is the outcome of his hourly and daily thought, feeling and purpose, just as the force of his life is the outcome of his hourly and daily thought expressed in words and acts; these together summed up the personality of Paul, and by that personality he commanded the confidence and revived the despairing spirits of the assembled crew. It was the power of prayer and of a close walk with God which inspired confidence and life and hope to all within the ship.

The Attempt of the Sailors

Until the fourteenth night they were driven up and down in the Adriatic Sea (a name then applied to the whole expanse of water between Crete and Sicily), until, by the sound of the breaking wave, they fancied they were nearing land, and by a steady taking of the soundings found that they were drawing nearer and nearer until, at the last, fearing that they would be dashed upon the rocks, they cast four anchors out of the stern (instead of as usually out of the bow), in order to keep the bow turned towards the land, so that at the first moment of daybreak they might drive the ship upon the beach. Then with an intensity of longing, such as only

THE SHIPWRECK

those can appreciate who have been day after day and night after night in a like peril, "they wished for the day." But under cover of that darkness a peril greater even than that of shipwreck was approaching both Julius and his company, for the sailors in the midst of the darkness determined to make a desperate attempt to gain the land, and gathered together under colour of casting an anchor out of the ship, but in reality in order to let down the boat into the sea. It might not be possible to row in such a surf, and Paul knew that it was only by the united labour of every hand on board that the ship could be saved. The incessant toil of keeping the water down in the ship would have been impossible but for the sailors, as also would the running of the ship aground in the morning, and, therefore, he told the centurion "except these abide in the ship, ye cannot be saved." We notice that St. Paul here says "ye" and not "we." He knew that his life was immortal until he had witnessed at Rome. The soldiers instantly clave their way through the midst of the sailors, and, drawing the daggers which they always wore upon their person, cut the ropes and let the boat fall. It must have seemed like cutting adrift a last hope, but it was only through absolute obedience to the will of God that they could be saved, and therefore, as soon as they returned from the baffled sailors, Paul called the whole ship's company together for a further act of obedience. The day was beginning to break, and Paul, passing up and down the ship, besought them to take food in order that they might have strength to meet the coming shipwreck. When they were gathered together, he stood in the midst, and took bread, and brake it, giving thanks to God in the presence of all, and when he had broken the bread he began to eat. The example of his words and of his acts was contagious, and they, too, began to be of good cheer, and to eat also. It was a strange sight, two hundred and seventy-six rough soldiers and sailors, sin-hardened criminals, idolaters, who before they came on board knew not God, standing with bowed head in outward reverence, and believing His word, despite its apparent impossibility. A stranger thanksgiving to God and a stranger meal cannot be found anywhere recorded in history. The vision of Paul in the face of instant shipwreck, giving thanks to God before he ate, recalls the still more beautiful vision of Jesus giving thanks upon the hillside, and ought to rise before us when, through cowardice or carelessness, we are inclined to pass over our acknowledgment to God of His bounty, and eat, forgetting to thank Him "who opens His hand and fills us and all things living with gladness."

Thus Paul, by his presence in the ship, by his life and conduct, and by his prayer, saved the lives of all who were with him, and brought them into outward obedience and reverence to God. What a contrast does he present to the story of Jonah in a corresponding picture of a shipwreck in the Old Testament. Jonah is unwilling to carry a message of salvation, and is reproved even by idolaters for his unmindfulness of his God, and these idolaters sacrifice to God, not because he is among them, but because his presence has been removed from them.

The Shipwreck

Having eaten all that was necessary, they threw the rest of the food overboard, and as the light became clearer, finding themselves upon an unknown shore, determined to drive the ship as far as they could upon the beach before it was smashed to pieces in the storm. "But the ship chanced on a rock between two seas," and being held fast in the clay, the forepart was immoveable, whilst the stern was broken by the violence of the waves. It was at this moment, expecting that the ship would part asunder beneath them, that the soldiers, lest any of the prisoners might be drowned in the onbreaking waves, determined to kill them, knowing that unless they could produce each prisoner alive in Rome their lives would be forfeit in their place. It shows how lost men can be to every feeling of gratitude and humanity when in utmost peril of their lives; but the centurion, though the lives of the prisoners would equally be required at his hand, knew that they owed all to Paul, and decided to risk his life for Paul's, and, therefore, staying the soldiers from their purpose, he bade all who could swim cast themselves overboard, whilst the rest, some on planks and some on broken pieces of the ship, escaped safe to land; and thus Paul having cried unto God in trouble was brought out of his distress. Then "were they glad because they were at rest, and so He brought them unto the haven where they would be" (Psalms cvii. 30).

CHAPTER XLVIII

ACTS XXVIII

ROME

The Island of Melita

Among the names of the islands of the Mediterranean Sea there is none which calls up in our mind a more vivid picture of gaiety and splendour than the Island of Malta, whether we think of it as occupied by the Knights of St. John or by the Imperial garrisons of to-day; but an interest far greater than either gaiety or splendour is connected with one corner of the island, the Bay of St. Paul, upon which St. Paul and his companions were cast in the midst of a blinding rain, and which ever since that day has been named after him.

At the time when St. Paul was cast upon its shore the island was probably only thinly settled by Phoenician settlers, called barbarians (*i.e.* non-Greek speaking), who had at first come from Carthage, but had then passed under the dominion of Rome. The presence of the poisonous snake leads us to infer that the island was as yet only half cultivated and thickly wooded, but the inhabitants were a kindly race, and instead of seeking to enrich themselves from the remains of the ship, like the wreckers in many a Christian country, they lit a fire, and strove to make amends for the inclemency of the weather; and never was kindness and hospitality more acceptable, for Paul and his companions were drenched not only by the violence of the waves, but by the yet colder rain which poured in pitiless torrents upon them.

"A Man Who Hath Escaped the Sea"

St. Paul takes the lead on land, as he had taken it at sea, and rouses his companions, despite their exhausted state, to gather sticks and prepare material for a fire. The heat of the flames called forth a poisonous snake that had been gathered unwittingly amongst the sticks, and now came and fastened itself on Paul's hand. The barbarous people, who had gathered in crowds around the shipwrecked mariners, seeing the viper fasten itself on his chain-marked hand, and concluding, according to the belief of Orientals, that misfortune is an immediate consequence of sin, cried out that he was a murderer who had escaped the sea, but whom "vengeance suffereth not to live." At the first moment St. Paul may have shuddered when he felt the animal fasten itself upon him, knew that he was shipwrecked, poisoned and alone, and knew also from the mutterings of the group that their suspicions were aroused against him; but his apparent calamity was one no longer when he saw that it was a means of giving him command over the inhabitants of the island as the storm had given him a command over the company at sea, for their countenance gradually began to change when they saw that instead of falling down dead the poison had no effect upon him, and cried out that he was a god. A parting promise given by Christ to His disciples was thus fulfilled, "They shall take up serpents and it shall not hurt them," and with a swift turn, like the men of Lystra, the people of Melita accepted the miracle as a token of Divine favour, and treated Paul and his companions with renewed courtesy and kindness.

"They Shall Lay Hands on the Sick and They Shall Recover"

It is difficult to know how St. Paul's exhausted frame could have stood the exposure to the rain after the exhaustion of the shipwreck, had not Publius, the chief man of the island, and probably the representative of the Roman Government, received him together with other of his companions and lodged him three days courteously. Paul found opportunity to make ample amends for his courtesy, for Publius' father lay sick of a fever and of a bloody flux, probably dysentery, and Paul entering in laid his hands upon him and healed him. This brought him once again into prominence, and further healing having been performed at his hand, and possibly at the hand of Luke also, the inhabitants "honoured them" with many honours.

St. Luke passes briefly forward without telling us whether St. Paul began a missionary work here as elsewhere, or founded a Christian Church in the island. Christian monograms and inscriptions have been found which are said to date back to the second century, and there are many traditions lingering about the island—the cave, for instance, in which Paul lodged being still shown—but there is nothing which we can certainly accept save that St. Paul, for a short period of three months, lived and worked in what is now an outpost of the British Empire, and that the power of God manifestly rested upon him.

The Voyage to Rome

News of the marvellous gift of healing quickly spread throughout the island, but, with the first breath of spring, Julius and his companions embarked upon a ship of Alexandria, which had wintered in the island and was about to sail for Italy. After a three days' voyage they reached Syracuse and at last came within sight of Puteoli. As Paul sailed towards Puteoli, one of the two great harbours for Rome, and saw the sunny vine-clad summit of Vesuvius, how little he thought that a fire of destruction was smouldering which, within a few years, would burst forth over the magnificent and luxurious cities of Pompeii and Herculaneum, lying at its base, a figure of the smouldering fire of persecution which would one day burst forth and overwhelm the Christians from the hands of Nero.

THE ACTS OF THE APOSTLES

Rome in the Early Days of Nero

The city of Rome, and the Emperor Nero himself, might at this period of their history be very aptly compared, in more ways than one, to a smouldering volcano. Seneca and the prefect Burrus were, with difficulty, maintaining their ascendency over Nero, and through Nero over the Empire, and men liked to believe that the nobility which characterized the first public addresses, as well as the early administration of law and order, under the new Emperor, had their fountain in his character as well as in the known wisdom and justice of his two great officers. And never were wisdom and justice more needed than at this epoch, for the heart of Rome was becoming more and more corrupt, although order and justice were still maintained in the outlying arteries of the Empire. The ideal of the Roman citizen was wealth, in order that through wealth he might indulge his love of ostentatious display, and satisfy the animal instincts of his nature. A carnival of human and animal blood upon the arena and a carnival of immorality upon the stage best satisfied the debased craving of the people.

Religion and Slavery

Two cancers lay at the root of Roman society—the debased state of religion, and slavery. Religion had sunk until it was a mere superstition, or even lower than a superstition, and the Romans looked upon the gods as powers who menaced their happiness but who might if entreated become the aiders and abetters of their crime, might even help them in the carrying out of a successful murder or theft.

The slaves, at this time, numbered half the population, and seemed destined from the very hopelessness of their condition to feed all that was most base in the passion of the populace. The slave was reckless of life, for his own life lay at the will of his master; he was unwilling to work, for his master reaped the harvest of his toil; he had a low moral standard, for his master was his god, and he sought, by fostering his whims and spoiling the children placed under his charge, to gain his own way and reap advantage for himself.

Such is the dark record which is left of Rome; but there must have been a brighter side also, a healthy class of men from whom centurions, such as we read of in the Acts, were recruited, men who had a standard of courtesy, law and order, though they might not always live up to it. It was towards this Rome that Paul was now making his way and asking himself what he might expect from it.

The Roman Jews and Christians

In Puteoli, as in Sidon, Paul, by the courtesy of Julius, was permitted to tarry with the Christians instead of remaining with the other prisoners. If he had rejoiced to meet the brethren in Sidon, how much more must he have rejoiced to meet the Christians in Puteoli, now that the perils of his journey were over and he was at last within sight of Rome. But his seven days of rest and refreshment too quickly passed away, and when he left the Christians he fell again into a heavy dejection of spirit, and we cannot wonder at it, for if the past had been one long succession of storm and tempest, the future lay shrouded in even darker clouds before him. If he looked at the Emperor, who was to be his judge, he saw a youth brutalized by the murder of his mother, who was rebelling against the greatest men of his age, and was falling beneath the sway of his wife, Poppaea, a Jewish proselyte, who would almost of necessity use her influence against Paul. If he looked to the Jews he saw a colony whose name was legion, and who were so wealthy and powerful that they excited the perpetual jealousy of the citizens and forced their way into every position and grade of society. They had already declared themselves against the Christians, and had raised so many riots in the city that Claudius had expelled them from it; but at the first opportunity they had returned and would hotly resent Paul's appeal to Caesar, as it would bring questions of their law and custom before the judgment seat of Caesar. If he looked to the Christians, he saw men divided amongst themselves, for the Judaising element was as present in Rome as in every other Gentile Church and was distinctly hostile to Paul. And besides the common feeling of hostility there was the danger which Paul's coming of necessity meant to every Christian in Rome, for, if the decision in his trial were given against him, the government would almost certainly adopt a hostile attitude towards the Christians generally. These considerations naturally affected the Church as a whole, but they did not affect the Christians in particular, for Paul had many and powerful friends among them. The edict of Claudius, which expelled the Christians and seemed so fatal at the time, had in reality been fraught with lasting benefit, for it had brought the exiles into contact with the Christians of other Churches, and many, like Aquila and Priscilla, had already passed under the influence and teaching of Paul.

"He Thanked God and Took Courage"

In the midst of his despondency, hope and help came at Appii Forum, about forty miles from Rome, where he was met by a group of brethren who had taken the long journey in order to encourage him, and about ten miles further forward, at the Three Taverns (or three places of merchandise), by another band of thirty, whom when Paul saw "he thanked God and took courage."

Thus at the last Paul came within sight of Rome, the restless, crowded metropolis of the world, containing within its twelve miles of area a million and a half of inhabitants, who swarmed on every side amidst its narrow, ill-built streets, but still Rome, the mistress of the world, the city of stately palaces and temples.

When Paul at last caught sight of Rome he must have longed to shake himself free from his chain, and to go hither and thither in the streets, to address the synagogues of the Jews and visit the Christians in their homes and meeting places, and begin a conquest of Christ similar to that which he had achieved in so many other cities. But even if he could, despite his chain, impart some spiritual gift to Rome, how could he, unless he was free, attain the goal of his journey and go forward into Spain? How often, during the past, must he have pictured his entry into Rome, as many years ago he had pictured his entry into Damascus. As one and another of his friends drifted back to the Imperial city he had looked forward to the day when he would take his place among them, and his heart thrill with pleasure at meeting them. But now at the last he entered Rome as he entered Damascus, led by a chain, as then by a hand, and under a cloud, not only as regarded the Romans but his fellow-countrymen also.

A Prisoner of the Lord

As soon as Paul reached Rome the task of the centurion Julius was ended; and he delivered Paul to the Prefect Burrus, telling him, doubtless, of the favourable letter which had been sent by Festus, but had been lost in the shipwreck, and giving his own impression of the prisoner also. Paul's imprisonment was made as light as possible, and he was permitted to dwell in his own house, where Aristarchus and Luke, as well as other of his Christian friends, continued to minister to him. It is true that he was still bound by a chain to a Roman soldier, but the very limitation of that chain, however galling it may have been, gave opportunity also for the teaching of the Gospel, for soldier after soldier of the Roman guard was brought within reach of his words and character, and listened whilst he expounded to Jew and Gentile the things of the Kingdom of God. The effect of this teaching upon the soldiers, and through the soldiers upon the men in the Roman army with whom they came into contact, and even possibly upon the countries in which they afterwards were stationed, cannot now be estimated. Paul never called himself a prisoner of the Roman Government but of the Lord, and his patient endurance and the way in which he looked upon his bonds must have aroused the wonder of all the soldiers with whom he came in contact.

The Summoning of the Jews

Paul had been only three days in Rome when, as he could not go to the synagogue, he summoned the leaders of the Jews to his own house to meet him. As we hear him send for these men we marvel at his long patience towards his nation, like that of his Master over Jerusalem, for Paul was then suffering from the malice of the Jews; it was they who had cast him into prison and who had rejected the Word of God again and again, until we cannot understand why they were not rejected of Paul also. But Rome was rapidly becoming the temporal centre of the Jews, just as Jerusalem was their spiritual centre, and Paul gathered them together so that he might rectify any misconception they might have as to his mission and make an appeal to them. He told them, as he had told the Sanhedrin, that he had committed nothing against his people, or the customs of his nation, that he had been acquitted by Rome, but through continued persecution of the Jews had at last been forced to appeal to Caesar. He had done this, not that he had aught to accuse his nation of, but that he might save his life; and he declared to them, as he had declared in Jerusalem, that it was not against Israel but for the hope of Israel that he was bound with this chain.

The Reply of the Jewish Leaders

The Jews replied in terms as cautious as diplomatic; they stated that they had not received letters out of Judaea (which was exceedingly probable, as Paul himself had only just managed, with the greatest difficulty, to reach Rome, and it was not likely that letters containing accounts of the distant disturbances in Jerusalem had preceded him); and in the second place, that they had not received evil reports about him (and it is possible that the Jews had sent no further report, as they expected to deal with him themselves in Jerusalem). They then expressed their readiness to hear anything which Paul might have to say about the sect of the Christians, of which they knew nothing, save that it was everywhere spoken against. This last statement is less probable, for the Jews had been expelled by Claudius on account of the riots which they had raised against the Christians; but the Jews may have intended in as courteous a manner as possible, whilst stating their prejudice against Christianity, to show that since Paul was no ordinary man, and considered by the Roman Government to be a prisoner of more than usual consequence, they were willing to hear what he might have to say to them about it.

The Last Appeal to the Jews

Paul expounded and testified with marvellous weight and authority the things of the Kingdom of God, but with the same result as in every other city, "Some believed the things that were spoken and some believed not," and at last, as the shades of evening began to fall, he pronounced in solemn words the final judgment which they had drawn down upon themselves, words which Jesus Himself had used when foretelling the overthrow of the Jews, words of prophecy spoken centuries before under the inspiration of the Holy Spirit by the prophet Isaiah. Isaiah had foreseen, even in his day, that the habitual refusal of the Jewish people to put into action the truth which they had received must deaden their power of understanding the will of God as well as of obeying it; and now the time had come when, having hardened their hearts like Pharaoh, the salvation of God would turn from them to the Gentiles. Little did the Jews think as they listened to these words of doom that the page of the long chapter of appeal to their nation was at last turned, and that their children's children would have to meet the judgment which they had drawn down upon them. St. Paul quoted the words of Isaiah, clearly spoken under the inspiration of the Holy Spirit, as Christ had quoted them also, and the Jews departed, having great reasoning among themselves, a proof that a more than unusual impression had been made upon them, and that in their inmost heart they could not but admit the reasoning of Paul.

Two Whole Years

For two whole years of imprisonment Paul remained in his hired house receiving all who came to him. We can see the group of friends who gathered round him to receive his directions and cheer him in his long imprisonment. We see Aristarchus (Colossians iv. 10-11) still his fellow-prisoner; Mark, after his long estrangement, once more with him, having joined him either in Caesarea or in Rome; Priscilla and Aquila, Tychicus and Timothy, the runaway slave Onesimus, together with Luke and other of his followers. These men seem from time to time to have been sent on various missions, coming backwards and forwards to St. Paul, and, through the favour of the Roman Government, being permitted to make their headquarters in his house.

Here the record suddenly ends, and the account of the trial, as also of the after story, can only be gathered from the later Epistles of St. Paul. It seems strange that the teaching of a few men in Rome, from time to time gathered in the room of that hired house, should be the goal towards which Paul had been tending and which had filled so large a place in his hopes and aspirations; but we have to remember that it is the apparently weak things of the world which confound the things that are mighty. It is the life and death of a Peasant of Galilee, who never went beyond the boundary line of His own coast, which changed the whole aspect of human life; and it is a prisoner who, though subjected to the perpetual companionship of a soldier, and unable to make a movement without his consent, directs the band of missionaries and writes epistles which have translated the life and death of Jesus into the hope and inspiration of the world.

CHAPTER XLIX

LATER EPISTLES OF ST. PAUL

"No Man Forbidding"

The days are beginning to lighten and the long four years' captivity to come to a close as St. Luke lays down his pen and closes his writing of the Acts. There is a note of hopefulness in his last words, in the freedom of access given to St. Paul, "No man forbidding," and in his own expectation, "I know that I shall abide and continue" (Philemon i. 25), "prepare me also a lodging; for I trust . . . I shall be given unto you" (Philemon 22). It is evident that the Prefect to whom Paul has been entrusted, is taking a favourable view of the case, and that as soon as the letters of indictment from Caesarea have come, the trial will be held, and Paul once more permitted to go upon his way, but until then Paul remains imprisoned and occupies himself with the work in Rome, and with the care of all the Churches. He watches keenly their progress, and sends letters, until the time comes when he can be amongst them again. He seems to have been very anxious as to the state of the Churches of Ephesus and Colosse, and to have followed up his letters by going to them in person as soon as he was released from prison. These Epistles, together with the Epistle to the Philippians, show an ever deepening spiritual experience, and are the words of a man who pauses on the threshold of the last stage of his journey, and views it already with a light of the hereafter upon it.

The Epistle to the Colossians

Standing on the great highway between Ephesus and the Euphrates were three ancient Phrygian cities, Laodicea, Colosse, and Hierapolis, now ruined, but then trading and banking centres, "knots on the road system," growing rapidly under the Roman peace, and famous for the manufacture of a glossy, black texture, the secret of which has passed away together with those who made it.

The site of Hierapolis still attracts the eye by its "immense frozen cascade" or stalactite cliffs which rear themselves above the surrounding landscape, and witness to the springs of mineral water which made the city so famous as a health resort. Laodicea is as deserted and uninhabited as Colosse, but from the letter to Colosse, and the message of the angel to Laodicea (Revelation iii.), we can tell that these cities were powerful and wealthy in their day, and exercised a strong influence over the surrounding country.

The Church of Colosse had been founded by Epaphras, a disciple of St. Paul, but after a time, owing to the spread of error, Epaphras found it necesssary to make the long journey from Asia Minor to Rome in order that he might seek advice from Paul and learn how to deal with this new philosophy.

St. Paul speaks of the heresy as a growth of "philosophy and vain deceit" which leads to "a show of wisdom in will-worship and humility and punishing of the body." What the exact tenets were we cannot say; they have left as little trace behind them as the once stately streets and buildings which were the habitation of those who held them; and we may ask why, if we care little or nothing for a city and a people who have passed away, should we concern ourselves with a heresy, or a letter condemning that heresy, which in like manner has passed away also? The answer is that although the form of error has passed, error itself in its essentials lives eternally, and will live until men have themselves ceased to live and move and have their being. It is because St. Paul's letter bears upon some of the great essentials of Christianity that it touches the Christian of to-day as it touched the Christian of Colosse. Christ in the person of His servant Paul calls for the allegiance of the heart to-day as He called for it in the letter to Colosse, and as He called for it in the message to Laodicea (Revelation iii. 20), "My son, give me thine heart"; but the men of Colosse, like the men of to-day, were ready to offer everything except the heart, to give words and deeds, the outward form and punishing of the body. But outward form and worship cannot satisfy the heart which asks for love. Paul had at the first given will-worship, but he had been united to Jesus by a living faith, that is to say, he had seen

Jesus and yielded his heart's affection, together with his heart's service, to Him. Paul knew that the men of Colosse would never yield true life service until they too saw Jesus and yielded their true heart's service also; and, therefore, in his Epistle he leads them beneath the shadow of the Cross, bids them stand at the foot of that Cross and look up at the handwriting of the ordinances which was against them, and see them nailed to the Cross; bids them look down at the principalities and powers of evil which had triumphed over them, but are now vanquished and lying at the foot of the Cross; bids them see Jesus pass through the gate of death, see Him risen also, so that they too through death may rise to newness of life, and being risen set their affection on things above, breathe the pure atmosphere of Heaven and hate the taint and breath of sin.

The Epistle to Philemon

The Epistle to Philemon is practically an appendix to the Epistle to the Colossians. Paul writes to a Christian gentleman of Colosse, the father of Archippus, afterwards bishop of Laodicea, and entreats his goodwill for a runaway slave who has become a Christian and repented of his evil deeds.

But if it is comparatively easy to see that the Epistle to the Colossians has a practical bearing on the spiritual life of to-day, it is not as easy to see a like hearing in the Epistle to Philemon, when we remember that the letter touches difficulties which arose between a master and his slave many centuries ago, and that the old world slavery has passed away like this old world quarrel also; but if we look carefully at the letter to Philemon we find that it has more than a passing value, for it contains in small compass matter which is unique and suggestive and bears upon the practical conduct of the life of to-day in as much as it deals with three ever present problems—the conduct of a master towards his servant; of a gentleman towards his fellow gentleman; and of a reformer towards a great social evil.

I. The spirit of forgiveness and brotherly affection.—Onesimus, according to the letter of the law and the age which he lived in, deserved to be tortured, if not to die. He had been a member of a Christian household, had robbed his master and fled to Rome, where, after hiding amongst the scum of the population, he had in some way been brought under the influence of St. Paul and made willing to return and endure the vengeance of his master. Paul writes to Philemon apparently fearing lest he should deal harshly with his servant and pleading that he will see in Onesimus one who has been accepted and is a member of the brotherhood of Christ, "above a servant," a brother beloved, and asks that he will accept him as such. Paul admits the theft and admits the duty of restitution; but here he stops the letter he is dictating and takes the pen out of his scribe's hand so that he may write his own note of hand upon it. "I Paul have written it with my own hand, I will repay it," thus giving Philemon a legal claim and pleading that when such claim has been satisfied Philemon will forgive the trespass as he himself has been forgiven of God.

II. The spirit of honour.—Paul is in bonds and greatly needs the ministration of Onesimus, but he will not accept any furthur service from him unless the service of Onesimus is freely granted to him by Philemon himself. The tone of the letter shows that Paul knows that Philemon would only too gladly have permitted Onesimus at such a juncture to remain with him, but being a man of honour and chivalrous he cannot take a liberty of any kind, and, therefore, despite the weariness of his imprisonment, prefers to wait until Onesimus has taken the long journey into the heart of Asia Minor and back again to Rome.

III. The attitude of a reformer towards a great social leader.—Paul, from his childhood up, must have been brought into contact with slavery, but never so closely or in so intensified a form as in Rome, owing to the condition of the Roman slave and the fact that the slaves formed an unusually large proportion of the Christian community of Rome. As he worked among them his sympathy must have gone out very constantly to them, for they were often far better educated and accomplished than their masters, and as Christians had a totally different standard of right and wrong from that of their masters, and we ask, How did Paul deal with this whole question of slavery; did he not arbitrarily call upon the masters to emancipate the slaves or incite the slaves to rise against their masters? We see from time to time that he sends a special message in his epistles to the masters of slaves and to the slaves themselves, and places before master and slave alike an ideal of Christian love and Christian principle, so that the two classes may gradually come into such a relationship with one another that enfranchisement will, as in Onesimus' case, be the only rational outcome of the position. Slavery, as far as civilized nations are concerned, in its crudest form, is or ought to be a thing of the past; but slavery in its other forms, in the demons of intemperance, lust or greed of money, is present with us. One of the most cheering aspects of the present century is the determination shown by the rising generation to grapple with these demons instead of accepting their existence in the form of oppression as one of the necessary evils of society. There is no question but that the difficulty has to be met; but the difficulty is how far it can be met by arbitrary force and will, how far by permeating oppressor and oppressed with a Christian ideal of purity and love. And it is here that the Epistle to Philemon is of value as it shows the influence of Christianity in drawing master and slave together in one common brotherhood of love and gives some guiding light as to one way, at any rate, in which St. Paul might deal with one of the issues of to-day.

The Epistle to Timothy

When St. Paul writes this letter he is at last free and beginning to lay his hand upon the Western Empire. Clement, St. Paul's own disciple (Philemon iv. 3), tells us that he went as far as "the extremity of the west," and we can trace his footsteps in the allusions contained in what are known as the pastoral letters, the First and

LATER EPISTLES OF ST. PAUL

Second Epistles to Timothy and the Epistle to Titus.

As soon as he was released, he seems to have gone with Timothy and Luke to Ephesus (Philemon i.), and thence to Spain (Romans xv. 34-38), but after he had left Ephesus for the second time, the condition of the Church weighed so heavily upon him that he wrote a letter to Timothy, whom he had placed in charge, not only over the Church of Ephesus, but over the surrounding churches whose names are so well known to us from the Book of the Revelation. Timothy had been very dear to Paul ever since the day when he had been converted at Lystra, and upon his second visit Paul had heard so good a report of him that he had taken him as his minister and companion. Timothy was a man of peculiarly refined and sensitive temperament, and Paul had that kinship of the love of God towards him which, as men advance towards the Kingdom of God, becomes deeper than the kinship of blood. But although his companionship was especially grateful to St. Paul, he was obliged to part with him from time to time whenever, as on the present occasion, it was necessary that a man of purity and strength should be sent to organize a church or to deal with it at a particular crisis. It was at a time of crisis that Paul wrote to Timothy, knowing that, in addition to the ordinary difficulties connected with a church like that of Ephesus, he would have to meet the growing power of gnosticism, that is to say, of a dangerous mingling of speculative philosophy and Jewish fable. Such a leadership would have taxed even the power of a Paul. It was peculiarly difficult to Timothy, for being by birth half Greek and half Hebrew, he was naturally plastic and yielding in disposition. But Paul never sent forth a disciple without following him in spirit and in prayer, and the present epistle shows how thoroughly he understood the character of Timothy and especially the way in which the difficulties he must meet would react upon his character. He entreats him to fight the good fight of faith, to war a good warfare, and defines clearly the right relation not only of the Church to the State, and also of the various members of the Church to each other, bishop, deacon, elder and widow, and bids him keep them in their own sphere, and keep himself in his own sphere also. He knows that Timothy is young for such a task as this, but the time is approaching when Paul himself will be called away, and Timothy will have to meet responsibility greater even than this, and therefore it is necessary that he should at once assume the responsibility foreign to his nature, lead where he would sooner follow, and struggle against the overpowering consciousness that the heresies which are springing up in the churches will break with overwhelming force upon him when once the lion-hearted Paul has passed away. He bids him meet the present and prepare for the future, not by disputation, "profane and vain babblings and oppositions of science, falsely so called," but by attention to reading, exhortation, and doctrine, so that by meditating upon these things he may keep sound doctrine, and in doing so save himself and others also.

The Epistle to Titus

Timothy and Titus were the strongest and nearest of all the youthful disciples of St. Paul. Timothy being the more sensitive and affectionate, while Titus was the abler and stronger. But whilst Paul relied upon Titus in dealing with the difficulties which arose amongst the Churches, he turns to Timothy, who has been called Melancthon, with a note of yearning affection which runs more steadily through the Epistles to Timothy than through the Epistle to Titus, although both Epistles deal practically with the same subject and are written about the same time.

Titus had been with St. Paul at Jerusalem at the time of the great council, and had travelled with him after he was released from prison until they came to Crete, and Paul, whose interest had probably been aroused in the Cretans during the time when the ship was touching at Fair Havens, visited Crete and left Titus to continue the work which he had begun. The Cretes and Arabians were amongst those who had been present at the Day of Pentecost, so that there may have been before Paul's visit to the island some knowledge of Christianity, but probably of a low type, for we find that St. Paul had to spend his time chiefly in organizing the Church and endeavouring to give a higher tone of morality and spirituality to it.

Titus remained in Crete, as Timothy remained in Ephesus, and St. Paul brooded over the thought of his work and character with the affectionate interest which characterized him. Titus was strong, but Paul, as well as other contemporary writers of the period, knew that the Cretans were a peculiarly low type of men, avaricious, quarrelsome, and intemperate, and, therefore, he sends a letter full of detailed instructions, containing what may be called the first principles of the morality of Christianity, which, although written for the use of the unruly and difficult Cretans, contains throughout a note of highest aspiration. Thus the Cretans are told to "deny ungodliness and worldly lust," and "to look for that blessed hope and the appearing of the great God and our Saviour Jesus Christ." These letters to Timothy and Titus form what may be called the pastoral charters of Church order and discipline and contain definite instruction for the use of the student in the Theological college of to-day, which is far more direct, incisive and far-reaching than any other teaching that can be put into his hand.

As we read the Epistles we see that Paul in giving his parting charge to the two men who so soon were to fill his place is giving, though he does not know it, a charge through the Holy Ghost to the long succession of witnesses of Christ of all nationalities and throughout all succeeding ages, a standard of life and conduct which will continue until the great Shepherd and Bishop of their souls returns to call His servants to render account to Him of that which has been committed to their charge.

CHAPTER L

THE LAST IMPRISONMENT OF ST. PAUL

The Changed Attitude of Rome

We trace St. Paul's footsteps from Ephesus, where Alexander, the coppersmith, did him much evil, to Miletus where Trophimus is left sick, and from Corinth where Erastus remains, to Troas where he lodges in the house of Carpus (2 Timothy iv. 13-14). Here the trace ceases, for it was probably either at Troas or at Nicopolis that he was arrested and given over as a leader of a sect which was suddenly thought to be threatening Rome and must be stamped out at all costs. This sudden change of attitude upon the part of Rome was due to general consternation at the result of the fire which, though now held to have been the work of Nero himself, at the time, owing to his insinuations, was charged upon the Christians; and it is generally thought that Paul, as a leading Christian, was brought to Rome to answer for the part he might have taken in instigating the work of destruction. This last journey to Rome is one of the most pathetic episodes, either in sacred or secular history. Paul was apparently arrested whilst travelling with Timothy and forcibly parted from him, leaving him in an agony of grief (2 Timothy i. 4), for Timothy knew only too well that he was being parted from him for ever.

The Second Epistle to Timothy

It is strange to stand within the walls of the Mamertine prison and to think that the man who strove, at greater cost and sacrifice than any other of his day and generation, to introduce the spirit of law and order, was chained up within those walls, as a menace to the peace and prosperity of the kingdom of Rome; but it is sadder and stranger still to stand upon the stone of the Pauline Basilica and to think that, according to tradition, Paul stood there before Nero, was called to question by a youth so brutalized in lust and crime that he is said to have exhausted the list of all known evil; but the servant is not above his master, and as Christ stood before Pilate, so Paul stood before Nero, and listened whilst he tried to fasten the responsibility of his disgrace and crime upon him, although Paul had been far away from Rome at the time of the conflagration. We cannot tell exactly what the character of the charge was, but we can tell that the shadow of impending evil hung so heavily upon him that he was utterly alone when the time came for pleading his cause, for there was not one who dared to accompany him before the judgment seat of Nero. This sense of loneliness would weigh very heavily upon a man of as affectionate and

THE LAST IMPRISONMENT OF ST. PAUL

sensitive a nature as St. Paul, and however bravely he might confront the splendour and majesty of Rome and the power of the world, as it were, arrayed against him, his heart must have been very heavy within him, until on a sudden the scene changed and Paul became conscious that he was no longer alone, and that the responsibility of pleading his case and witnessing for the Gospel of Christ no longer rested upon him, but had passed into the hand of One who stood beside him, that is to say, even into the hand of the King of Kings. "At my first answer no man stood with me; notwithstanding the Lord stood with me and strengthened me."

How marvellous must the pleading of that day have been, how marvellous the inspiration of the advocacy of Jesus! The words themselves have passed away, but we know that the mystery of Christianity was fully declared, and Paul was, for the moment at any rate, delivered out of the mouth of the lion (Nero) (2 Timothy iv. 17). But though delivered and led back to prison Paul's instinct warned him that the time was short, and that if he were ever to see Timothy again he must bid him hasten, without delay, and, therefore, he writes a second epistle to Timothy, and turns with the longing of a dying man to the one most closely connected with his life-work and with his affection; but he writes fully in case, even if he were to come with all speed, he might be too late to receive his last will and testament.

This explains the alternate glow of passionate yearning for the future steadfastness of Timothy, on the one hand, and the flashes of joyful anticipation on the other, which fill the heart of the warrior, as he thinks of the moment when he may lay down the shield, which he has never lowered, at the feet of his Lord.

Paul's Blessing upon Timothy

As Moses gave a parting charge to Joshua, so Paul delivers a parting charge to Timothy also. He, himself, is standing where the weariness of the desert track is passing into the joy of the streets of the New Jerusalem, but as he looks back upon his weariness, upon the extremity of suffering he has passed through, he does not shrink from calling upon the man whom he loves, and bidding him follow also. He tells Timothy that he is to look upon persecution as a test of faithful following (a prophecy too truly fulfilled in his subsequent martyrdom), and bids him if he will find strength to seek it in the study of the Holy Scriptures, given by the inspiration of God and first placed in his hands by his mother.

He bids him still more urgently bring the books, and "especially the parchments," and then with one last triumphant cry, one last prayer for Timothy, he ceases, and the lips of Paul are sealed to us for ever. Only a few days, and Paul is condemned and led out on the Ostian way to be beheaded. Little recks the gay court of Rome, little reck the passers-by, amongst whom, accompanied by a band of soldiers, he threads his way, that the greatest of the Romans is about to pass from the gate of the Eternal City into the gate of the City without foundations, Eternal in the Heavens. One flash of the executioner's axe, and Paul is with the Master who, in his darkest hours, has ever been with him. As he left the Mamertine prison and passed along the Ostian way, he believed that his life-work was ended; he little knew that that life-work contained within itself the Spirit of the living God which would quicken the souls of men throughout succeeding ages. He saw a harvest of his own day, city after city taken for Christ, and watchmen planted who would in their turn take other cities also; he saw a battle won for the liberty of the Church, and charters left in his epistles to protect that liberty. He did not see the aftermath of the greater harvest than that of his day, the harvest which will never be reckoned until the Lord of the harvest Himself comes to take account of the labourers of His harvest.

"St. Paul without the Walls"

Ever since Paul died men have vied with one another in reverencing his words and acts, and in tracing his footsteps over land and sea. They gather year by year within the catacombs wherein his body was first laid, and beneath the Basilica upon the Ostian way where it now rests; but the secret of Paul's life is not revealed in the traces of his earthly footsteps; it is found in his following of the spiritual footsteps of his Master, in the truth inscribed over the altar of the Basilica, "To me to live is Christ, and to die is gain."

www.ingramcontent.com/pod-product-compliance
Lightning Source LLC
Chambersburg PA
CBHW030236170426
43202CB00007B/26